RACE AND ETHNICITY IN AMERICA

ISSN 2334-542X

RACE AND ETHNICITY IN AMERICA

Erin Brown

INFORMATION PLUS® REFERENCE SERIES
Formerly Published by Information Plus, Wylie, Texas

GALE
A Cengage Company

Farmington Hills, Mich • San Francisco • New York • Waterville, Maine
Meriden, Conn • Mason, Ohio • Chicago

Race and Ethnicity in America

Erin Brown

Kepos Media, Inc.: Steven Long and Janice Jorgensen, Series Editors

Project Editor: Laura Avery

Rights Acquisition and Management:
    Ashley M. Maynard, Carissa Poweleit

Composition: Evi Abou-El-Seoud,
    Mary Beth Trimper

Manufacturing: Rita Wimberley

Product Design: Kristin Julien

Cover photograph: © Monkey Business Images/Shutterstock.com.

Gale
27500 Drake Rd.
Farmington Hills, MI 48331-3535

ISBN-13: 978-0-7876-5103-9 (set)
ISBN-13: 978-1-5730-2702-1

ISSN 2334-542X

This title is also available as an e-book.
ISBN-13: 978-1-4103-3271-4 (set)
Contact your Gale sales representative for ordering information.

TABLE OF CONTENTS

PREFACE vii

CHAPTER 1
Who Are Minorities?. 1

Hispanic, African American, Asian American, and Native American populations make up a growing percentage of the United States. Data from the U.S. Census Bureau are analyzed to discuss minority groups in terms of classification, origin, age, geographic distribution, immigration, and other characteristics.

CHAPTER 2
Family Life and Living Arrangements. 15

The role and makeup of families, particularly minority families, have been undergoing great change. This chapter focuses on family structure, marital status (including a section on interracial marriages), teen pregnancy, the living arrangements of minority children, and homeownership.

CHAPTER 3
Education 29

The educational attainment and performance of minority groups differs significantly from that of the white population. This chapter looks at educational risk factors, reading and math scores, and high school dropout rates, as well as minorities in college, including the debate over affirmative action in admissions.

CHAPTER 4
Minorities in the Labor Force 57

Minorities have long been an important part of the U.S. labor force. This chapter surveys minority labor force participation past, present, and future, as well as the different types of jobs and careers that are held by minorities. Minority-owned businesses are also discussed.

CHAPTER 5
Money, Income, and Poverty Status 77

Racial and ethnic backgrounds play a big role in the economic status of Americans. Within this chapter, income and poverty are examined by demographic characteristics.

CHAPTER 6
Health 87

Some minority groups are healthier than the white majority, while others fare worse. This chapter highlights differences in pregnancy, fertility, and health problems that are particularly common among certain minorities, as well as health-harming and health-promoting differences in behaviors in minority populations.

CHAPTER 7
Crime 123

Minorities are more likely than whites to be the victims of crime, and the volume of crime that is allegedly perpetrated by some minority groups, as well as their representation in prisons and jails, is disproportionately large. This chapter reports on minority crime statistics.

CHAPTER 8
Political Participation 143

The political participation of minority groups plays a critical role in correcting imbalances in the way they are treated in U.S. society. This chapter explores several issues, including the number of minority voters who are registered and who vote, minorities elected to public office, and the racial ramifications of redistricting and voter identification laws.

IMPORTANT NAMES AND ADDRESSES 155

RESOURCES 157

INDEX 159

PREFACE

Race and Ethnicity in America is part of the *Information Plus Reference Series*. The purpose of each volume of the series is to present the latest facts on a topic of pressing concern in modern American life. These topics include the most controversial and studied social issues of the 21st century: abortion, animal rights, capital punishment, care for the elderly, crime, death, the environment, health care, immigration, social welfare, world poverty, youth, and many more. Although this series is written especially for high school and undergraduate students, it is an excellent resource for anyone in need of factual information on current affairs.

By presenting the facts, it is the intention of Gale, a Cengage Company, to provide its readers with everything they need to reach an informed opinion on current issues. To that end, there is a particular emphasis in this series on the presentation of scientific studies, surveys, and statistics. These data are generally presented in the form of tables, charts, and other graphics placed within the text of each book. Every graphic is directly referred to and carefully explained in the text. The source of each graphic is presented within the graphic itself. The data used in these graphics are drawn from the most reputable and reliable sources, such as from the various branches of the U.S. government and from private organizations and associations. Every effort has been made to secure the most recent information available. Readers should bear in mind that many major studies take years to conduct and that additional years often pass before the data from these studies are made available to the public. Therefore, in many cases the most recent information available in 2017 is dated from 2014 or 2015. Older statistics are sometimes presented as well, if they are landmark studies or of particular interest and no more-recent information exists.

Although statistics are a major focus of the *Information Plus Reference Series*, they are by no means its only content. Each book also presents the widely held positions and important ideas that shape how the book's subject is discussed in the United States. These positions are explained in detail and, where possible, in the words of their proponents. Some of the other material to be found in these books includes historical background, descriptions of major events related to the subject, relevant laws and court cases, and examples of how these issues play out in American life. Some books also feature primary documents or have pro and con debate sections that provide the words and opinions of prominent Americans on both sides of a controversial topic. All material is presented in an evenhanded and unbiased manner; readers will never be encouraged to accept one view of an issue over another.

HOW TO USE THIS BOOK

Race and ethnicity have acted as some of the most divisive factors in U.S. history. Many people, from all racial and ethnic backgrounds, have struggled, sometimes at great peril to themselves, to provide equality for all people in the United States. Nevertheless, it is an undeniable fact that African Americans, Hispanics, Native Americans, Asian Americans, and other minority groups have a different experience living in the United States than do whites. This book reports on and examines the differences between minority groups and white Americans across the economic, political, and social spectrums.

Race and Ethnicity in America consists of eight chapters and three appendixes. Each chapter is devoted to a particular aspect of minorities. For a summary of the information that is covered in each chapter, please see the synopses that are provided in the Table of Contents. Chapters generally begin with an overview of the basic facts and background information on the chapter's topic, then proceed to examine subtopics of particular interest. For example, Chapter 5: Money, Income, and Poverty Status begins by surveying income differences among minority groups, examining some of the factors that contribute to disparities in economic well-being. The chapter proceeds to discuss how poverty affects different racial and ethnic groups and the prevalence of poverty among minority children living in various types of households. Next, it outlines the main government means-tested assistance programs that are designed to help those in poverty, including Temporary Assistance to Needy Families, the Supplemental Nutrition Assistance Program, and Supplemental Security Income. The chapter considers the rates at which different minority groups access these programs and the factors that limit the programs' efficacy at lifting people out of poverty. It concludes by discussing the uncertain future of federal assistance programs, in light of the significant funding cuts proposed by President Donald Trump during his first year in office. Readers can find their way through a chapter by looking for the section and subsection headings, which are clearly set off from the text. They can also refer to the book's extensive Index if they already know what they are looking for.

Statistical Information

The tables and figures featured throughout *Race and Ethnicity in America* will be of particular use to readers in learning about this issue. These tables and figures represent an extensive collection of the most recent and important statistics on minorities, as well as related issues—for example, graphics cover the number of different minority people living in the United States overall and in specific regions, their media household and per capita income as compared with whites, the rates at which they are the victims of various crimes, and the health problems that disproportionately afflict certain minority groups. Gale, a Cengage Company, believes that making this information available to readers is the most important way to fulfill the goal of this book: to help readers understand the issues and controversies surrounding minorities and reach their own conclusions about them.

Each table or figure has a unique identifier appearing above it, for ease of identification and reference. Titles for the tables and figures explain their purpose. At the end of each table or figure, the original source of the data is provided.

To help readers understand these often complicated statistics, all tables and figures are explained in the text. References in the text direct readers to the relevant statistics. Furthermore, the contents of all tables and figures are fully indexed. Please see the opening section of the Index at the back of this volume for a description of how to find tables and figures within it.

Appendixes

Besides the main body text and images, *Race and Ethnicity in America* has three appendixes. The first is the Important Names and Addresses directory. Here, readers will find contact information for a number of government and private organizations that can provide further information on aspects of minorities. The second appendix is the Resources section, which can also assist readers in conducting their own research. In this section, the author and editors of *Race and Ethnicity in America* describe some of the sources that were most useful during the compilation of this book. The final appendix is the detailed Index. It has been greatly expanded from previous editions and should make it even easier to find specific topics in this book.

COMMENTS AND SUGGESTIONS

The editors of the *Information Plus Reference Series* welcome your feedback on *Race and Ethnicity in America*. Please direct all correspondence to:

Editors
Information Plus Reference Series
27500 Drake Rd.
Farmington Hills, MI 48331-3535

CHAPTER 1
WHO ARE MINORITIES?

In broad terms, a minority is defined as a group of people who, based on various ethnic, racial, and other characteristics, account for less than half of the total population of a particular country or geographic region. Throughout U.S. history, minorities have played an important role in shaping the diverse and multifaceted character of the nation's cultural identity. Unfortunately, minority status is also typically accompanied by various forms of discrimination, both social and economic. In his landmark essay "The Problem of Minority Groups," which was published in the 1945 anthology *The Science of Man in the World Crisis* (Ralph Linton, ed.), the sociologist Louis Wirth (1897–1952) defines a minority as "a group of people who, because of their physical or cultural characteristics, are singled out from the others in the society in which they live for differential and unequal treatment, and who therefore regard themselves as objects of collective discrimination." For this reason, Wirth argues, "minority status carries with it the exclusion from full participation in society."

Since the publication of Wirth's essay, the question of what precisely constitutes a minority has remained a subject of debate. In *Study on the Rights of Persons Belonging to Ethnic, Religious and Linguistic Minorities* (1979, http://undocs.org/E/CN.4/Sub.2/384/Rev.1), Francesco Capotorti, a special rapporteur with the United Nations (UN) Subcommission on Prevention of Discrimination and Protection of Minorities, asserts that the concept of a minority varies according to the nation or culture:

> Despite the many references to minorities to be found in international legal instruments of all kinds (multilateral conventions, bilateral treaties and resolutions of international organizations), there is no generally accepted definition of the term "minority." The preparation of a definition capable of being universally accepted has always proved a task of such difficulty and complexity that neither the experts in this field nor the organs of the international agencies have been able to accomplish it to date. The reason for this is the number of different aspects to be considered. Should the concept of a minority be based on the numerical ratio of the "minority" group to the population as a whole or is this quantitative aspect secondary or even unimportant? Is it necessary to limit the concept by introducing the idea of a minimum size? Should only objective criteria be taken into account or should it be assumed that "subjective" factors also have a part to play? Does the origin of the minorities matter for the purposes of a definition? Should we understand by minorities groups of nationals only, excluding groups of foreigners?

Later in the report, Capotorti offers a "limited" definition of a minority, one rooted in the clause devoted to the protection of minorities in the UN's International Covenant on Civil and Political Rights of 1966: "In that precise context, the term 'minority' may be taken to refer to: A group numerically inferior to the rest of the population of a State, in a non-dominant position, whose members—being nationals of the State—possess ethnic, religious or linguistic characteristics differing from those of the rest of the population and show, if only implicitly, a sense of solidarity, directed towards preserving their culture, traditions, religion or language."

The UN reaffirms Capotorti's definition in *Minority Rights: International Standards and Guidance for Implementation* (2010, http://www.ohchr.org/Documents/Publications/MinorityRights_en.pdf), stressing the idea that being in a "non-dominant position" is an essential aspect of minority status. "In most instances a minority group will be a numerical minority," the UN notes, "but in others a numerical majority may also find itself in a minority-like or non-dominant position, such as Blacks under the apartheid regime in South Africa. In some situations, a group which constitutes a majority in a State as a whole may be in a non-dominant position within a particular region of the State in question."

MINORITIES ARE A GROWING PERCENTAGE OF THE NATION

The U.S. Census Bureau reports that in the 2010 census the U.S. population totaled 308.7 million people. (See Table 1.1.) Of that number, 196.8 million (63.7%) people identified themselves as non-Hispanic white alone, down from 69.1% in the 2000 census. The other 36.3% were members of one or more minority racial or ethnic groups. The Census Bureau presents a similar picture in *2015 American Community Survey* (2016, https://factfinder2.census.gov/bkmk/table/1.0/en/ACS/15_1YR/DP05/0100000US). According to this report, in 2015, 197.5 million (61.4%) of the nation's estimated 321.4 million people, identified as non-Hispanic white. (See Table 1.2.)

Minority populations in the United States are growing faster than is the non-Hispanic white population. The Census Bureau projects that between 2015 and 2020 the non-Hispanic white population will grow by only 0.53%, whereas the non-Hispanic African American population will grow by 4.55%, the Asian American population will grow by 13.41%, and the Hispanic population will grow by 11.98%. (See Table 1.3.)

CHANGING RACIAL AND ETHNIC ORIGIN CLASSIFICATIONS

The U.S. government uses race and ethnic origin data to make decisions, among other things, about funding and making laws. For example, federal programs use the race information to monitor and ensure that the civil rights of African Americans and other minority groups are not being violated, and states use the data to ensure compliance with political redistricting requirements.

For the 1980 and 1990 censuses the Census Bureau divided the U.S. population into the four racial categories that were identified by the Office of Management and Budget—White, Black, Native American/Alaskan Native, and Asian/Pacific Islander—and added the category "Some Other Race." Katherine K. Wallman explains in "Data on Race and Ethnicity: Revising the Federal Standard" (*American Statistician*, vol. 52, no. 1, 1998) that these standards came under attack because many Americans believed they did not accurately reflect the diversity of the nation's population. Between 1993 and 1995 the Census Bureau conducted hearings and invited public comment about adding new choices to the categories that had been used during the 1990 census. Among the Census Bureau's findings were that Arab Americans were unhappy with their official designation as "white, non-European." This group included people from the Middle East, Turkey, and North Africa. In addition, many indigenous Hawaiians wanted to be recategorized from Pacific Islander to Native American, reflecting historical accuracy and giving them access to greater government benefits.

Some Hispanics wanted the Census Bureau to identify them as a race and not as an ethnic origin, and to replace the word *Hispanic* with *Latino*. They asserted that *Hispanic* recalled the colonization of Latin America by

TABLE 1.1

Population by Hispanic origin and by race, 2000 and 2010

Hispanic or Latino origin and race	2000 Number	2000 Percentage of total population	2010 Number	2010 Percentage of total population	Change, 2000 to 2010 Number	Change, 2000 to 2010 Percent
Hispanic or Latino origin or race						
Total population	281,421,906	100.0	308,745,538	100.0	27,323,632	9.7
Hispanic or Latino	35,305,818	12.5	50,477,594	16.3	15,171,776	43.0
Not Hispanic or Latino	246,116,088	87.5	258,267,944	83.7	12,151,856	4.9
White alone	194,552,774	69.1	196,817,552	63.7	2,264,778	1.2
Race						
Total population	281,421,906	100.0	308,745,538	100.0	27,323,632	9.7
One race	274,595,678	97.6	299,736,465	97.1	25,140,787	9.2
White	211,460,626	75.1	223,553,265	72.4	12,092,639	5.7
Black or African American	34,658,190	12.3	38,929,319	12.6	4,271,129	12.3
American Indian and Alaska Native	2,475,956	0.9	2,932,248	0.9	456,292	18.4
Asian	10,242,998	3.6	14,674,252	4.8	4,431,254	43.3
Native Hawaiian and other Pacific Islander	398,835	0.1	540,013	0.2	141,178	35.4
Some other race	15,359,073	5.5	19,107,368	6.2	3,748,295	24.4
Two or more races*	6,826,228	2.4	9,009,073	2.9	2,182,845	32.0

*In Census 2000, an error in data processing resulted in an overstatement of the two or more races population by about 1 million people (about 15 percent) nationally, which almost entirely affected race combinations involving some other race. Therefore, data users should assess observed changes in the two or more races population and race combinations involving some other race between Census 2000 and the 2010 Census with caution. Changes in specific race combinations not involving some other race, such as white and black or African American or white and Asian, generally should be more comparable.

SOURCE: Karen R. Humes, Nicholas A. Jones, and Robert R. Ramirez, "Table 1. Population by Hispanic or Latino Origin and by Race for the United States: 2000 and 2010," in *Overview of Race and Hispanic Origin: 2010*, U.S. Census Bureau, March 2011, http://www.census.gov/prod/cen2010/briefs/c2010br-02.pdf (accessed September 2, 2017)

TABLE 1.2

Population estimates, by race and Hispanic origin, 2015

Subject	United States	
	Estimate	Percent
Race		
Total population	321,418,821	321,418,821
One race	311,437,291	96.9%
Two or more races	9,981,530	3.1%
One race	**311,437,291**	**96.9%**
White	234,940,100	73.1%
Black or African American	40,695,277	12.7%
American Indian and Alaska Native	2,597,249	0.8%
Cherokee tribal grouping	284,858	0.1%
Chippewa tribal grouping	115,280	0.0%
Navajo tribal grouping	323,757	0.1%
Sioux tribal grouping	117,019	0.0%
Asian	17,273,777	5.4%
Asian Indian	3,699,957	1.2%
Chinese	4,133,674	1.3%
Filipino	2,848,148	0.9%
Japanese	757,468	0.2%
Korean	1,460,483	0.5%
Vietnamese	1,738,848	0.5%
Other Asian	2,635,199	0.8%
Native Hawaiian and other Pacific Islander	554,946	0.2%
Native Hawaiian	176,482	0.1%
Guamanian or Chamorro	78,522	0.0%
Samoan	120,019	0.0%
Other Pacific Islander	179,923	0.1%
Some other race	15,375,942	4.8%
Two or more races	9,981,530	3.1%
White and Black or African American	2,654,878	0.8%
White and American Indian and Alaska Native	1,911,158	0.6%
White and Asian	2,038,169	0.6%
Black or African American and American Indian and Alaska Native	305,975	0.1%
Race alone or in combination with one or more other races		
Total population	**321,418,821**	**321,418,821**
White	243,479,179	75.8%
Black or African American	44,655,257	13.9%
American Indian and Alaska Native	5,431,402	1.7%
Asian	20,416,808	6.4%
Native Hawaiian and other Pacific Islander	1,314,433	0.4%
Some other race	17,051,509	5.3%
Hispanic or Latino and race		
Total population	**321,418,821**	**321,418,821**
Hispanic or Latino (of any race)	56,496,122	17.6%
Mexican	35,797,080	11.1%
Puerto Rican	5,372,759	1.7%
Cuban	2,106,501	0.7%
Other Hispanic or Latino	13,219,782	4.1%
Not Hispanic or Latino	264,922,699	82.4%
White alone	197,534,496	61.5%
Black or African American alone	39,597,600	12.3%
American Indian and Alaska Native alone	2,069,645	0.6%
Asian alone	17,081,093	5.3%
Native Hawaiian and other Pacific Islander alone	502,876	0.2%
Some other race alone	699,309	0.2%
Two or more races	7,437,680	2.3%
Two races including Some other race	279,052	0.1%
Two races excluding Some other race, and Three or more races	7,158,628	2.2%

Spain and Portugal and argued that the term was as offensive as the term *Negro* was for African Americans. However, when Hispanics were surveyed, the results showed they preferred to be identified by their families' country of origin, such as Puerto Rican, Colombian, Cuban, or sometimes just American.

TABLE 1.2

Population estimates, by race and Hispanic origin, 2015 [CONTINUED]

Notes:
Data are based on a sample and are subject to sampling variability. The degree of uncertainty for an estimate arising from sampling variability is represented through the use of a margin of error. The value shown here is the 90 percent margin of error. The margin of error can be interpreted roughly as providing a 90 percent probability that the interval defined by the estimate minus the margin of error and the estimate plus the margin of error (the lower and upper confidence bounds) contains the true value. In addition to sampling variability, the ACS estimates are subject to nonsampling error (for a discussion of nonsampling variability, see Accuracy of the Data). The effect of nonsampling error is not represented in these tables. Estimates of urban and rural population, housing units, and characteristics reflect boundaries of urban areas defined based on Census 2010 data. As a result, data for urban and rural areas from the ACS do not necessarily reflect the results of ongoing urbanization.

SOURCE: Adapted from "DP05. ACS Demographic and Housing Estimates," in *2015 American Community Survey*, U.S. Census Bureau, 2016, https://factfinder2.census.gov/bkmk/table/1.0/en/ACS/15_1YR/DP05/0100000US (accessed September 2, 2017)

A number of African Americans wanted the Census Bureau to retire the term *Black*. However, there was some difference of opinion. For example, people from the Caribbean preferred to be labeled by their families' country of origin, such as Jamaican American or Haitian American. Africans who were not American also found the term *African American* inaccurate. Although the term has become more prominent in spoken English in recent years, lack of agreement and the length of the term have been significant factors in preventing its adoption by the government.

Furthermore, as ethnic identity becomes more complex because of immigration and interracial marriages and births, a growing number of people object to any categories that are based on race. It is no longer unusual to find Americans whose backgrounds include two or more races.

The 2000 Census

Conforming to revised standards that were issued by the Office of Management and Budget, the 2000 census recategorized the races into White, Black/African American/Negro, American Indian/Alaskan Native, Native Hawaiian/Other Pacific Islander, and Asian. The Census Bureau also added a sixth category: Some Other Race. In addition, the bureau included two ethnic categories: Hispanic/Latino and Not Hispanic/Not Latino. To provide an accurate count of multiracial Americans, the 2000 census allowed Americans to select more than one race. Write-in spaces allowed Native Americans to record their tribal affiliation, and individuals of Hispanic origin could write in a national affiliation other than the major groups of Mexican, Cuban, and Puerto Rican.

In "Impact of Census' Race Data Debated" (USA Today.com, March 12, 2001), Martin Kasindorf and Haya El Nasser explain that many Americans thought that the official recognition of multiracial Americans would profoundly change how Americans think about race in the long term. Some believed that racial lines

TABLE 1.3

Projected change in population size by race and Hispanic origin, 2015–60

[Percentage]

Hispanic origin and race[a]	(Percent change in resident population as of July 1.)								
	2015–2020	2020–2025	2025–2030	2030–2035	2035–2040	2040–2045	2045–2050	2050–2055	2055–2060
Total population	**4.09**	**3.84**	**3.47**	**3.04**	**2.67**	**2.41**	**2.29**	**2.28**	**2.30**
One race	3.75	3.48	3.09	2.64	2.23	1.94	1.80	1.76	1.76
White	2.81	2.53	2.15	1.69	1.27	0.98	0.85	0.83	0.87
Black	5.03	4.79	4.37	3.92	3.57	3.35	3.25	3.23	3.24
AIAN	5.93	5.48	4.91	4.28	3.66	3.11	2.64	2.31	2.05
Asian	13.29	12.13	10.99	9.91	8.93	8.09	7.38	6.77	6.21
NHPI	8.07	7.47	6.63	5.81	5.17	4.59	4.01	3.52	3.13
Two or more races	16.76	15.83	14.92	14.04	13.33	12.73	12.19	11.65	11.13
Race alone or in combination:[b]									
White	3.24	2.99	2.65	2.23	1.87	1.63	1.54	1.56	1.64
Black	6.34	6.17	5.84	5.46	5.20	5.07	5.04	5.06	5.10
AIAN	6.86	6.43	5.87	5.24	4.67	4.20	3.84	3.58	3.37
Asian	13.86	12.74	11.64	10.61	9.70	8.91	8.25	7.68	7.15
NHPI	9.77	9.37	8.75	8.12	7.62	7.22	6.85	6.54	6.30
Not Hispanic	**2.40**	**2.19**	**1.82**	**1.37**	**0.98**	**0.75**	**0.70**	**0.78**	**0.91**
One race	2.04	1.80	1.40	0.90	0.47	0.19	0.10	0.14	0.25
White	0.53	0.23	−0.23	−0.80	−1.32	−1.68	−1.82	−1.79	−1.68
Black	4.55	4.35	3.95	3.49	3.14	2.94	2.88	2.90	2.95
AIAN	3.09	2.77	2.25	1.62	1.01	0.51	0.17	−0.02	−0.13
Asian	13.41	12.22	11.06	9.96	8.97	8.11	7.40	6.79	6.23
NHPI	8.34	7.76	6.91	6.04	5.35	4.78	4.29	3.91	3.59
Two or more races	16.46	15.60	14.67	13.76	13.05	12.48	11.97	11.45	10.91
Race alone or in combination:[b]									
White	1.01	0.78	0.37	−0.12	−0.56	−0.82	−0.88	−0.76	−0.58
Black	5.72	5.59	5.26	4.88	4.62	4.50	4.50	4.56	4.63
AIAN	4.51	4.23	3.73	3.11	2.57	2.20	2.00	1.93	1.87
Asian	13.89	12.73	11.60	10.54	9.60	8.78	8.11	7.53	6.98
NHPI	9.52	9.08	8.40	7.69	7.14	6.72	6.38	6.09	5.82
Hispanic	**11.98**	**10.84**	**9.97**	**9.14**	**8.38**	**7.66**	**7.00**	**6.44**	**5.96**
One race	11.80	10.65	9.77	8.93	8.15	7.42	6.75	6.18	5.68
White	11.88	10.73	9.84	8.98	8.20	7.46	6.78	6.21	5.71
Black	12.04	10.82	9.90	9.15	8.52	7.88	7.23	6.66	6.19
AIAN	10.02	9.12	8.28	7.45	6.65	5.88	5.15	4.56	4.08
Asian	9.72	9.09	8.54	8.08	7.70	7.23	6.61	6.09	5.80
NHPI	7.32	6.66	5.84	5.18	4.66	4.04	3.17	2.35	1.75
Two or more races	17.96	16.72	15.87	15.10	14.39	13.67	12.98	12.41	11.96
Race alone or in combination:[b]									
White	12.08	10.93	10.05	9.21	8.44	7.71	7.05	6.49	6.01
Black	14.10	12.87	12.03	11.36	10.79	10.22	9.64	9.15	8.77
AIAN	11.09	10.15	9.32	8.50	7.71	6.95	6.25	5.68	5.20
Asian	13.27	12.80	12.42	12.08	11.74	11.29	10.77	10.37	10.15
NHPI	10.56	10.27	9.83	9.44	9.09	8.70	8.22	7.84	7.68

[a]Abbreviations: Black = black or African American; AIAN = American Indian and Alaska Native; NHPI = Native Hawaiian and other Pacific Islander.
[b]'In combination' means in combination with one or more other races. The sum of the five race groups adds to more than the total change because individuals may report more than one race.
[c]Rounds to zero.
Note: Hispanic origin is considered an ethnicity, not a race. Hispanics may be of any race.

SOURCE: Adapted from "Table 12. Projected Change in Population Size by Hispanic Origin and Race for the United States: 2015 to 2060," in *2014 National Population Projections Tables*, U.S. Census Bureau, Population Division, December 2014, https://www2.census.gov/programs-surveys/popproj/tables/2014/2014-summary-tables/np2014-t12.xls (accessed September 2, 2017)

would blur until racial differences no longer became so important in American life. Others took a more pessimistic view, arguing that because African Americans marry outside their racial categories less than other minorities, the difference between an "expanded majority" of whites and the African American minority group would harden even further.

The 2010 Census

For the 2010 census, the U.S. government announced the inclusion of even more specific racial categories. The Population Reference Bureau notes in "The 2010 Census Questionnaire: Seven Questions for Everyone" (April 2009, http://www.prb.org/Articles/2009/questionnaire.aspx) that there were 15 racial categories: White; Black, African American, or Negro; American Indian or Alaskan Native; Asian Indian; Japanese; Native Hawaiian; Chinese; Korean; Guamanian or Chamorro; Filipino; Vietnamese; Samoan; other Asian; other Pacific Islander; and "Some Other Race." The 2010 census also considered Hispanic origin separately from race, with Hispanics able to identify with any race. The census also allowed respondents to choose more than one race.

Stephanie Sy reports in "2010 Census Offends Some Americans with Handling of Race" (ABCNews.com, April 1, 2010) that despite its attempt to be more inclusive, the Census Bureau still came under criticism for its handling of racial and ethnic categories during the 2010 census. For example, the Census Bureau included "Negro" on the 2010 form, a historically offensive term. In addition, it did not include a way for Arabs to mark either their race or ethnicity, and mixed-race people were forced to choose "other."

A more in-depth discussion of the major race and ethnic groups follows.

HISPANICS AND LATINOS

Hispanic is a broad term that is used to describe a varied ethnic group of individuals who trace their cultural heritage to Spain or to Spanish-speaking countries in Latin America. The term can also refer to people whose Spanish ancestors were residents of the southwestern region of the United States that was formerly under Spanish or Mexican control. Although some Americans with origins in Latin America have asked the Census Bureau to refer to them as Latinos, for the purposes of this book the term *Hispanic* will be used to refer to all minority populations of Hispanic or Latino descent.

The Census Bureau indicates that in 2015 there were 56.5 million Hispanics living in the United States. (See Table 1.4.) Of these, 34.7 million, or 61.4%, were born in the United States. Of the approximately 19.5 million foreign-born Hispanics in the United States in 2015, roughly 6.7 million (34.5) had attained U.S. citizenship. (See Table 1.5.)

Immigration and high birth rates are two major reasons for the large growth of the Hispanic population. In *Estimates of the Unauthorized Immigrant Population Residing in the United States: January 2012* (2013, https://www.dhs.gov/sites/default/files/publications/Unauthorized%20Immigrant%20Population%20Estimates

TABLE 1.4

Hispanic origin population, by birth status, 2015

	United States Estimate
Total	**56,496,122**
Born in state of residence	28,113,280
Born in other state in the United States	6,577,020
Native; born outside the United States	2,306,425
Foreign born	19,499,397

SOURCE: Adapted from "B06004I. Place of Birth (Hispanic or Latino) in the United States. Universe: Hispanic or Latino Population in the United States," in *2015 American Community Survey 1-Year Estimates*, U.S. Census Bureau, 2016, https://factfinder.census.gov/faces/tableservices/jsf/pages/productview.xhtml?pid=ACS_15_1YR_B06004I&prodType=table (accessed September 2, 2017)

TABLE 1.5

Hispanic origin population, by citizenship and birth status, age, and sex, 2015

	United States Estimate
Total:	56,496,122
Male:	28,526,183
Under 18 years:	9,237,366
Native	8,697,994
Foreign born:	539,372
Naturalized U.S. citizen	86,412
Not a U.S. citizen	452,960
18 years and over:	19,288,817
Native	9,892,130
Foreign born:	9,396,687
Naturalized U.S. citizen	3,045,980
Not a U.S. citizen	6,350,707
Female:	27,969,939
Under 18 years:	8,875,829
Native	8,369,822
Foreign born:	506,007
Naturalized U.S. citizen	83,994
Not a U.S. citizen	422,013
18 years and over:	19,094,110
Native	10,036,779
Foreign born:	9,057,331
Naturalized U.S. citizen	3,505,391
Not a U.S. citizen	5,551,940

SOURCE: Adapted from "B05003I. Sex by Age by Nativity and Citizenship Status (Hispanic or Latino). Universe: People Who Are Hispanic or Latino," in *2015 American Community Survey 1-Year Estimates*, U.S. Census Bureau, 2016, https://factfinder.census.gov/faces/tableservices/jsf/pages/productview.xhtml?pid=ACS_15_1YR_B05003I&prodType=table (accessed September 2, 2017)

%20in%20the%20US%20January%202012_0.pdf), Bryan Baker and Nancy Rytina of the U.S. Department of Homeland Security (DHS) estimate that as of January 2012 approximately 11.4 million unauthorized immigrants lived in the United States. This figure represented a decline from 11.8 million in 2007, a trend driven largely by high U.S. unemployment, an improving economy in Mexico, and stepped-up U.S. border patrols and enforcement. Jeffrey S. Passel and D'Vera Cohn of the Pew Research Center offer slightly different estimates in *Overall Number of Unauthorized Immigrants Holds Steady since 2009* (September 20, 2016, http://assets.pewresearch.org/wp-content/uploads/sites/7/2016/09/31170303/PH_2016.09.20_Unauthorized_FINAL.pdf). According to Passel and Cohn, the number of unauthorized immigrants living in the United States peaked at 12.2 million in 2007, before gradually falling to 11.2 million in 2012 and 11.1 million in 2014.

Hispanic Origins

Hispanic Americans trace their origins to a number of countries. As Table 1.6 shows, of the 56.5 million Hispanics living in the United States in 2015, 35.8 million (63.4%) were of Mexican heritage. Nearly 5.4 million (9.5%) were of Puerto Rican heritage, 5.2 million (9.2%) were of Central American heritage, 3.4 million (6%) were of South American heritage, 2.1 million (3.7%) were of

TABLE 1.6

Hispanic origin population by type, 2015

	United States	
	Estimate	Margin of error
Total:	321,418,821	*****
Not Hispanic or Latino	264,922,699	+/−8,415
Hispanic or Latino:	56,496,122	+/−8,415
Mexican	35,797,080	+/−91,689
Puerto Rican	5,372,759	+/−57,569
Cuban	2,106,501	+/−30,210
Dominican (Dominican Republic)	1,873,097	+/−45,443
Central American:	5,210,908	+/−73,868
Costa Rican	156,084	+/−8,883
Guatemalan	1,377,500	+/−36,629
Honduran	851,501	+/−36,243
Nicaraguan	416,768	+/−19,074
Panamanian	200,265	+/−9,825
Salvadoran	2,171,894	+/−43,875
Other Central American	36,896	+/−6,902
South American:	3,403,619	+/−50,942
Argentinean	266,306	+/−13,306
Bolivian	119,115	+/−11,536
Chilean	145,540	+/−10,404
Colombian	1,081,838	+/−29,738
Ecuadorian	712,084	+/−26,788
Paraguayan	18,352	+/−3,052
Peruvian	646,395	+/−23,294
Uruguayan	59,645	+/−7,158
Venezuelan	321,609	+/−15,953
Other South American	32,735	+/−5,187
Other Hispanic or Latino:	2,732,158	+/−45,920
Spaniard	781,859	+/−25,387
Spanish	489,014	+/−18,239
Spanish American	14,956	+/−2,348
All other Hispanic or Latino	1,446,329	+/−29,872

Note: An '*****' entry in the margin of error column indicates that the estimate is controlled. A statistical test for sampling variability is not appropriate.

SOURCE: Adapted from "B03001. Hispanic or Latino Origin by Specific Origin. Universe: Total Population," in *2015 American Community Survey 1-Year Estimates*," U.S. Census Bureau, 2016, https://factfinder.census.gov/faces/tableservices/jsf/pages/productview.xhtml?pid=ACS_15_1YR_B03001&prodType=table (accessed September 2, 2017)

Cuban descent, and 1.9 million (3.3%) traced their heritage to the Dominican Republic.

Geographic Distribution

Hispanics are unevenly distributed throughout the United States. The Census Bureau describes in "Hispanic Heritage Month 2017" (October 17, 2017, https://www.census.gov/content/dam/Census/newsroom/facts-for-features/2017/cb17-ff17.pdf) that in July 2016, 54.4% of the total Hispanic population in the United States lived in California, Texas, and Florida. Of these three states, California had the largest Hispanic population, with 15.3 million, 4.9 million of whom lived in Los Angeles County. Overall, nine states reported have a Hispanic population of 1 million or more in July 2016.

Mexican Americans

Many Hispanic Americans are descendants of the Spanish and Mexican people who lived in the West and Southwest when these regions were controlled by Spain

(starting in the 1500s) and Mexico (after Mexico gained its independence from Spain in 1821). In some cases their forebears were absorbed into the United States when Texas revolted, broke away from Mexico, became a republic, and then finally joined the United States during the 1840s. The Mexican-American War (1846–1848) added Arizona, California, Colorado, New Mexico, Utah, and territories north of the Rio Grande to the United States with the signing of the Treaty of Guadalupe Hidalgo in 1848. As a result, Hispanics living in these areas at the time became Americans. Other Mexican Americans immigrated to the United States more recently.

The Mexican-origin population, which more than doubled during the last two decades of the 20th century, continues to grow in the 21st century. According to the Census Bureau, 35.8 million people (11.1% of the U.S. population) were of Mexican origin in 2015. (See Table 1.6.) In *U.S. Lawful Permanent Residents: 2015* (March 2017, https://www.dhs.gov/sites/default/files/publications/Lawful_Permanent_Residents_2015.pdf), Ryan Baugh and Katherine Witsman of the DHS report that by far the largest number of legal immigrants to the United States come from Mexico. In 2015, 158,619 Mexicans legally immigrated to the United States, accounting for 15.1% of the nation's more than 1 million legal immigrants that year. The next-largest source of legal immigrants was China, which accounted for 74,558 (7.1%) of all legal immigrants to the United States.

Puerto Ricans

The situation of Puerto Ricans is unique in American society. The Caribbean island of Puerto Rico, formerly a Spanish colony, became a U.S. commonwealth after it was ceded to the United States by the Treaty of Paris in 1898, which ended the Spanish-American War (1898). In 1917 the Revised Organic Act (Jones Act) granted the island a bill of rights and its own legislature. It also conferred U.S. citizenship on all Puerto Ricans.

Ruth Glasser explains in "Tobacco Valley: Puerto Rican Farm Workers in Connecticut" (*Hog River Journal*, vol. 1, no. 1, 2002) that following World War II (1939–1945) an industrialization program was launched in Puerto Rico. Although the program benefited many, it also sharply reduced the number of agricultural jobs on the island, driving many rural residents to the cities. Combined with a high birth rate, this led to unemployment, overcrowding, and poverty. These conditions led many Puerto Ricans to move to the mainland United States, particularly New York City. Since 1993, when President Bill Clinton (1946–) eliminated tax exemptions for manufacturing firms in Puerto Rico, industries have moved away from the island in search of cheaper labor, further compounding the economic problems of Puerto Rico and encouraging emigration. According to Virginia E. Sánchez Korrol, in *From Colonia to Community: The*

History of Puerto Ricans in New York City (1994), in 1940 fewer than 70,000 Puerto Ricans lived in the contiguous United States. The Census Bureau notes that by 2015, 5.4 million Puerto Ricans called the mainland United States home. (See Table 1.6.) Partly because of the ease with which Puerto Ricans can travel in the United States, many move freely back and forth between the United States and Puerto Rico.

In "A Puerto Rican Rebirth in El Barrio; After Exodus, Gentrification Changes Face of East Harlem" (NYTimes.com, December 10, 2002), Joseph Berger explains that most of the first Puerto Ricans who arrived in the United States settled in New York City in the Manhattan neighborhood of East Harlem, which came to be known as El Barrio (the neighborhood). Eventually, Puerto Rican immigrants moved in greater numbers to other boroughs of the city and into New Jersey.

Gustavo López and Eileen Patten of the Pew Research Center indicate in *Hispanics of Puerto Rican Origin in the United States, 2013* (September 15, 2015, http://assets.pewresearch.org/wp-content/uploads/sites/7/2015/09/2015-09-15_puerto-rico-fact-sheet.pdf) that 3.6 million Hispanics of Puerto Rican origin lived in Puerto Rico in 2013. Meanwhile, 5.1 million lived within the 50 U.S. states or the District of Columbia. More than half (51%) of these lived in the Northeast, with more than one-fifth (21%) in New York State alone.

Cuban Americans

According to the Pew Hispanic Center, in the fact sheet *Cubans in the United States* (August 25, 2006, http://assets.pewresearch.org/wp-content/uploads/sites/7/2011/10/23.pdf), many Cubans fled Cuba during the early 1960s after the Fulgencio Batista (1901–1973) regime was overthrown by Fidel Castro (1926–2016). Cuban immigrants tended to settle in Miami, Florida, and in the surrounding Dade County. Most of these political refugees were older, middle class, and educated. A second phase of Cuban immigration took place from about 1965 to 1974, legally bringing middle- and working-class Cubans to the United States through Cuban and U.S. government programs. In "Mariel Boatlift" (May 7, 2011, https://www.globalsecurity.org/military/ops/mariel-boatlift.htm), John Pike reports that 125,000 people seeking refuge from Castro's government fled Cuba in 1980 in what became known as the Mariel Boatlift, named after the town in Cuba from which they sailed. Because most of these new immigrants were from less wealthy and less educated backgrounds than their predecessors, and some were actually criminals or people who were mentally ill, many had difficulty fitting into the existing Cuban communities in the United States.

Mireya Navarro reports in "Last of Refugees from Cuba in '94 Flight Now Enter U.S." (NYTimes.com, February 1, 1996) that in 1994 more than 29,000 Cubans tried to enter the United States after fleeing a severe economic crisis in their own country. Most attempted the trip by boats and rafts but were intercepted by the U.S. Coast Guard and taken back to Cuba, where they were detained at Guantánamo Bay, a U.S. naval base on the island. By January 1996 most detainees had been allowed to enter the United States, and the detention camps were closed. The Pew Hispanic Center notes that under current U.S. policy, Cubans who are able to reach the United States are allowed to stay, whereas those who are intercepted at sea are returned to Cuba.

In *Hispanics of Cuban Origin in the United States, 2013* (September 15, 2015, http://assets.pewresearch.org/wp-content/uploads/sites/7/2015/09/2015-09-15_cuba-fact-sheet.pdf), López reveals that Cubans have the highest level of educational attainment and are the most economically successful of the various Hispanic ethnic groups in the United States. According to López, 25% of Cubans aged 25 years and older had a bachelor's degree in 2013, compared with 14% of Hispanics overall. The median annual per capita earnings for Cubans ($25,000) was also higher than the median annual earnings for all Hispanics ($21,900).

AFRICAN AMERICANS

In 1619 the first Africans arrived in colonial North America. Subsequently, their numbers increased rapidly to fill the growing demand for slave labor in the new land. The first slaves were brought in by way of the West Indies, but as demand increased, they were soon brought directly to the English colonies on the mainland in North America. Most were delivered to the South and worked on plantations.

The vast majority of African Americans in the United States were kept as slaves until the Civil War (1861–1865). According to the 1860 census (https://www2.census.gov/prod2/decennial/documents/1860a-02.pdf), the states that made up the Confederacy in the South at the outbreak of hostilities had a slave population of 3.5 million, compared with a white population of nearly 5.5 million. In 1863 President Abraham Lincoln (1809–1865) issued the Emancipation Proclamation, which freed slaves in the Confederate states, although those states did not recognize the legality of the proclamation. In 1865 the 13th Amendment to the U.S. Constitution abolished slavery throughout the United States. In 1868 the 14th Amendment afforded former slaves and other African Americans equal protection under the law, and in 1870 the 15th Amendment granted them the right to vote. The present population of African Americans in the United States includes not only those who have descended from former slaves but also those who have since emigrated from Africa, the West Indies, and Central and South America.

According to the Census Bureau, in 2015, 39.6 million people who identified their race as non-Hispanic African American alone lived in the United States. (See Table 1.2.) Due to the rigid politics of race in the United States, even individuals whose background includes a mixture of African American and other races tend to identify as African American. In 2015 African Americans made up 12.3% of the population.

Geographic Distribution

Few African Americans migrated from the southern farms and plantations that had been their homes during the first decades after the abolition of slavery. As a result, at the beginning of the 20th century a large majority of African Americans still lived in the South. However, when World War I (1914–1918) interrupted the flow of migrant labor from Europe, large numbers of African Americans migrated from the rural South to northern industrial cities to take advantage of new work opportunities there. Compared with the oppressive system of segregation in the South, economic and social conditions were better in the North for many African Americans, thereby encouraging a continuous flow of migrants. According to the article "North by South: The African American Great Migration" (August 28, 2005, http://northbysouth.kenyon.edu/), between 1900 and 1960, 4.8 million African Americans left the South and settled in northern cities such as Chicago, Illinois; Detroit, Michigan; Cleveland, Ohio; Pittsburgh, Pennsylvania; and New York City. The African American migrations following World War I and World War II are among the largest voluntary internal migrations in U.S. history.

Most African Americans moved to the Northeast and Midwest, although after 1940 significant numbers also moved West. The traditional migration from the South to the North dwindled dramatically during the 1970s. In fact, after 1975, largely due to the favorable economic conditions that were developing in the booming Sunbelt cities, African Americans started migrating in droves to the South. As Table 1.7 shows, in 2016 all six states whose populations were estimated to be more than 25% African American were in the South: Mississippi (37.2%), Louisiana (32.3%), Georgia (30.9%), Maryland (30%), South Carolina (28.2%), and Alabama (26.3%). At the same time, in 2016 more than half (51.6%) of the residents of the District of Columbia were African American.

ASIAN AMERICANS

Asian American is a catchall term that did not gain currency until the late 1960s and early 1970s. It was not until 1980 that the Census Bureau created the "Asian and Pacific Islander" category, a departure from the previous practice of counting several Asian groups separately. Although seemingly a geographic description, "Asian and Pacific Islander" contains racial overtones, given that natives of Australia and New Zealand are not included, nor are whites born in the Asian region of Russia. In 2015 roughly 17.1 million people identified their race and ethnicity as non-Hispanic Asian American alone, making up 5.3% of the U.S. population. (See Table 1.2.) People who identified as exclusively non-Hispanic Native Hawaiian and Other Pacific Islander had a population of 502,876, making up 0.2% of the total U.S. population.

Historical Immigration

In "Chinese Immigration" (2017, http://www.loc.gov/teachers/classroommaterials/presentationsandactivities/presentations/immigration/chinese.html), the Library of Congress explains that the first major immigration of people from Asia to the United States involved the Chinese. From the time of the California gold rush of 1849 until the early 1880s, it is estimated that as many as 250,000 Chinese immigrated to the United States, with the vast majority coming from the Pearl River delta of Guangdong Province.

After the Civil War, when most African Americans were able to gain citizenship with the adoption of the 14th Amendment in 1868, an exception was carved out for Asian immigrants. They were designated "aliens ineligible to citizenship." The Chinese Exclusion Act of 1882 then stopped the entry of Chinese into the country altogether, except for a few merchants and students. Laws regulating Chinese immigration to the United States did not change until World War II, when China became an ally. President Franklin D. Roosevelt (1882–1945) persuaded Congress to repeal the Chinese Exclusion Act in 1943.

People of other nationalities that make up the Asian American category also began immigrating to the United States before World War II. The Japanese first came to the United States in significant numbers during the 1890s, although many laborers had previously settled in Hawaii. Like the Chinese, the Japanese mostly lived in the western United States. There was some call for a "Japanese Exclusion Act," but because Japan was an emerging Pacific power, such legislation was never passed. Overall, Japanese immigrants fared better than their Chinese counterparts and soon outpaced them in population. However, the Library of Congress notes in "Japanese Immigration" (2017, http://www.loc.gov/teachers/classroommaterials/presentationsandactivities/presentations/immigration/japanese.html) that when Japan and the United States went to war in 1941, more than 100,000 Americans of Japanese descent, including many who were native-born U.S. citizens, were removed from their homes and confined in detention camps. By 1945 approximately 125,000 people of Japanese descent had been sent to these camps. It is noteworthy that although the United States was also at

TABLE 1.7

Population, by race and state, 2016

| Geography | Total | Race alone | | | | | Two or more races |
		White	Black or African American	American Indian and Alaska Native	Asian	Native Hawaiian and other Pacific Islander	
United States	308,745,538	241,937,061	40,250,635	3,739,506	15,159,516	674,625	6,984,195
Alabama	4,779,736	3,362,877	1,259,224	32,903	55,240	5,208	64,284
Alaska	710,231	483,873	24,441	106,268	38,882	7,662	49,105
Arizona	6,392,017	5,418,483	280,905	335,278	188,456	16,112	152,783
Arkansas	2,915,918	2,342,403	454,021	26,134	37,537	6,685	49,138
California	37,253,956	27,636,403	2,486,549	622,107	5,038,123	181,431	1,289,343
Colorado	5,029,196	4,450,623	214,919	78,144	144,819	8,420	132,271
Connecticut	3,574,097	2,950,820	392,131	16,734	140,516	3,491	70,405
Delaware	897,934	645,770	196,281	5,929	29,342	690	19,922
District of Columbia	601,723	251,265	310,379	3,264	21,705	770	14,340
Florida	18,801,310	14,808,867	3,078,067	89,119	474,199	18,790	332,268
Georgia	9,687,653	6,144,931	2,993,927	48,599	323,459	10,454	166,283
Hawaii	1,360,301	349,051	22,473	4,960	531,633	138,292	313,892
Idaho	1,567,582	1,476,097	10,950	25,782	20,034	2,786	31,933
Illinois	12,830,632	10,030,587	1,903,458	73,846	604,399	7,436	210,906
Indiana	6,483,802	5,638,833	603,797	24,487	105,535	3,532	107,618
Iowa	3,046,355	2,839,615	91,695	13,563	54,232	2,419	44,831
Kansas	2,853,118	2,501,057	173,298	33,044	69,628	2,864	73,227
Kentucky	4,339,367	3,864,193	342,804	12,105	50,177	3,199	66,889
Louisiana	4,533,372	2,902,875	1,462,969	33,037	71,829	2,588	60,074
Maine	1,328,361	1,269,764	16,269	8,771	13,783	377	19,397
Maryland	5,773,552	3,541,379	1,731,513	30,885	326,655	5,391	137,729
Massachusetts	6,547,629	5,524,937	504,365	29,944	359,673	5,971	122,739
Michigan	9,883,640	7,949,497	1,416,067	68,396	243,062	3,442	203,176
Minnesota	5,303,925	4,623,461	280,949	67,325	217,792	2,958	111,440
Mississippi	2,967,297	1,789,391	1,103,101	16,837	26,477	1,700	29,791
Missouri	5,988,927	5,038,407	700,178	30,595	100,213	7,178	112,356
Montana	989,415	891,529	4,215	63,495	6,379	734	23,063
Nebraska	1,826,341	1,649,264	85,971	23,418	33,322	2,061	32,305
Nevada	2,700,551	2,106,494	231,224	42,965	203,478	19,307	97,083
New Hampshire	1,316,470	1,248,321	16,365	3,530	28,933	532	18,789
New Jersey	8,791,894	6,546,498	1,282,005	49,907	746,212	7,731	159,541
New Mexico	2,059,179	1,720,992	49,006	208,890	31,253	3,132	45,906
New York	19,378,102	13,901,661	3,378,047	183,046	1,481,555	24,000	409,793
North Carolina	9,535,483	6,898,296	2,088,362	147,566	215,952	10,309	174,998
North Dakota	672,591	609,136	8,248	36,948	7,032	334	10,893
Ohio	11,536,504	9,664,524	1,426,861	29,674	196,693	5,336	213,416
Oklahoma	3,751,351	2,851,510	284,332	335,664	67,126	5,354	207,365
Oregon	3,831,074	3,403,252	74,414	66,784	145,009	14,649	126,966
Pennsylvania	12,702,379	10,663,774	1,431,826	39,735	358,195	7,115	201,734
Rhode Island	1,052,567	910,253	75,073	9,173	31,768	1,602	24,698
South Carolina	4,625,364	3,164,143	1,302,865	24,665	61,247	3,957	68,487
South Dakota	814,180	706,690	10,533	72,782	7,775	517	15,883
Tennessee	6,346,105	5,056,311	1,068,010	26,256	93,897	5,426	96,205
Texas	25,145,561	20,389,793	3,070,440	251,209	1,000,473	31,242	402,404
Utah	2,763,885	2,547,329	33,864	40,729	57,800	26,049	58,114
Vermont	625,741	598,592	6,456	2,308	8,069	175	10,141
Virginia	8,001,024	5,725,432	1,579,414	41,525	449,149	8,201	197,303
Washington	6,724,540	5,535,262	252,333	122,649	491,685	43,505	279,106
West Virginia	1,852,994	1,746,513	63,885	3,975	12,637	485	25,499
Wisconsin	5,686,986	5,036,923	367,021	60,100	131,828	2,505	88,609
Wyoming	563,626	529,110	5,135	14,457	4,649	521	9,754

Notes: The estimates are based on the 2010 Census and reflect changes to the April 1, 2010 population due to the Count Question Resolution program and geographic program revisions. Hispanic origin is considered an ethnicity, not a race. Hispanics may be of any race. Responses of "some other race" from the 2010 Census are modified. This results in differences between the population for specific race categories shown for the 2010 Census population in this table versus those in the original 2010 Census data. The 6,222 people in Bedford city, Virginia, which was an independent city as of the 2010 Census, are not included in the April 1, 2010 Census enumerated population presented in the county estimates. In July 2013, the legal status of Bedford changed from a city to a town and it became dependent within (or part of) Bedford County, Virginia. This population of Bedford town is now included in the April 1, 2010 estimates base and all July 1 estimates for Bedford County. Because it is no longer an independent city, Bedford town is not listed in this table. As a result, the sum of the April 1, 2010 census values for Virginia counties and independent cities does not equal the 2010 Census count for Virginia, and the sum of April 1, 2010 census values for all counties and independent cities in the United States does not equal the 2010 Census count for the United States.

SOURCE: Adapted from "PEPSR6H. Annual Estimates of the Resident Population by Sex, Race, and Hispanic Origin for the United States, States, and Counties: April 1, 2010 to July 1, 2016," in *2016 American Community Survey*, U.S. Census Bureau, 2017, https://factfinder.census.gov/faces/tableservices/jsf/pages/productview.xhtml?pid=PEP_2016_PEPSR6H&prodType=table (accessed September 2, 2017)

war with Germany and Italy, citizens of German and Italian descent or birth were not subject to incarceration due to their heritage.

Before World War II Filipinos, Asian Indians, and Koreans represented a small share of the Asian American population. In *Historical Census Statistics on Population*

Totals by Race, 1790 to 1990, and by Hispanic Origin, 1970 to 1990, for the United States, Regions, Divisions, and States (September 2002, https://www.census.gov/content/dam/Census/library/working-papers/2002/demo/POP-twps0056.pdf), Campbell Gibson and Kay Jung of the Census Bureau indicate that in 1940 there were 254,918 Asian Americans living in the United States; 126,947 were Japanese, 77,504 were Chinese, and 45,563 were Filipino. Asian Indians totaled 2,405, and Koreans numbered even fewer, at 1,711. As was the case with Puerto Ricans, Filipinos began immigrating to the United States in the years following the Spanish-American War, when their country was annexed by the United States and eventually granted commonwealth status. Designated "American nationals," Filipinos held a unique position: They were not eligible for citizenship, but they also could not be prevented from entering the United States. Many Filipinos immigrated during the 1920s looking for work, but the Great Depression (1929–1939) stemmed this flow. The Philippines became independent in 1946.

Asian Indians had come to the United States in small numbers, generally settling in New York City and other eastern ports, but it was not until the early years of the 20th century that they began immigrating to the West Coast, generally entering through western Canada. Koreans came to the United States from Hawaii, where several thousand had immigrated between 1903 and 1905. Both Asian Indians and Koreans lost their eligibility to enter the United States following the Immigration Act of 1917, which accounted for their small populations before World War II. Once the Chinese Exclusion Act was repealed, however, the door was also open for Filipinos and Asian Indians to gain entry to the United States as well as to earn citizenship during the postwar years. The Korean War (1950–1953) led to a long-term U.S. military presence in Korea, resulting in a number of Korean-born wives of military personnel relocating to the United States. In addition, many Korean-born children were adopted and brought to the United States. A larger influx of Korean families immigrated during the mid-1960s.

Sharp Rise in Immigration

Asian immigration during the 1980s can be divided into two so-called streams. The first stream came from Asian countries that already had large populations in the United States (such as China, the Philippines, and South Korea). These immigrants, many of whom were highly educated, came primarily for family reunification and through employment provisions of the immigration laws. The second stream consisted primarily of immigrants and refugees from the war-torn countries of Southeast Asia (Cambodia, Laos, and Vietnam). They were admitted under U.S. policies that supported political refugees after the Vietnam War (1954–1975), as well as those escaping

unstable economic and political conditions in neighboring countries. The Office of Refugee Resettlement notes in *Annual ORR Reports to Congress—1999* (1999, https://www.acf.hhs.gov/sites/default/files/orr/annual_orr_report_to_congress_1999.pdf) that between fiscal years 1975 and 1999, 1.3 million refugees from Southeast Asia arrived in the United States.

According to Baugh and Witsman, China was the top country of origin for Asian immigrants in 2015. In that year 74,558 immigrants from China made their way to the United States. India was second, with 64,116 immigrants. The Philippines was third with 56,478 immigrants, followed by Vietnam (30,832), Pakistan (18,057), and South Korea (17,138).

Geographic Distribution

The Census Bureau reports in "Annual Estimates of the Resident Population by Sex, Race Alone or in Combination, and Hispanic Origin for the United States, States, and Counties: April 1, 2010, to July 1, 2016" (June 2017, https://factfinder.census.gov/faces/tableservices/jsf/pages/productview.xhtml?src=bkmk) that in 2016 more than 5.7 million Asian Americans lived in California, 32.3% of the total Asian American population of 17.7 million. New York had the second-highest number of Asian American residents, with 1.6 million, followed by Texas with 1.1 million. Hawaii had the highest proportion of Asian American residents relative to the overall population in 2016. That year, 785,488 (43.8%) of 1.8 million Hawaiians were of Asian American descent.

NATIVE AMERICANS AND ALASKAN NATIVES

Most archaeologists agree that the people known as Native Americans and Alaskan Natives arrived in North America from northeast Asia at least 30,000 years ago during the last of the Ice Age glaciations (coverings of large areas of the earth with ice). At that time the two continents were connected by a land bridge over what is currently the Bering Strait. However, some archaeologists dispute this theory by citing evidence that indicates that migrants may have actually arrived many thousands of years earlier, perhaps by boat. For example, the article "New Evidence Puts Man in North America 50,000 Years Ago" (ScienceDaily.com, November 18, 2004) notes that artifacts have been discovered along the Savannah River in Allendale County, South Carolina, that date back to at least 50,000 years ago. The article indicates that "the findings are significant because they suggest that humans inhabited North America well before the last ice age more than 20,000 years ago, a potentially explosive revelation in American archaeology." Colin Barras indicates in "First Americans May Have Been Neanderthals 130,000 Years Ago" (NewScientist.com, April 26, 2017) that remains found in San Diego County, California, during the 1990s suggested that groups of

Neanderthals might have arrived in North America as early as 130,000 years ago. According to Barras, this discovery has led some scientists to conclude that *Homo sapiens* might have also populated the continent far earlier than generally believed.

Migrants who settled on the northern coast of Alaska and the Yukon River valley, which were free of ice barriers, became known as Eskimos and Aleuts. Those who ventured farther south followed the eastern slope of the Rocky Mountains and continued along the mountainous spine of North America into South America. They eventually moved east throughout the central plains and eastern highlands of both continents and were later erroneously named Indians by exploring Spaniards. The misnomer is attributed to Christopher Columbus (1451–1506), who, on landing in the Bahamas in 1492, thought he had reached the islands off the eastern region of Asia, called the Indies. He therefore greeted the inhabitants as "Indians." In the 21st century many descendants of the original settlers prefer to be called Native Americans.

In 2015, 2.1 million people who identified their background as non-Hispanic Native American or Alaskan Native alone lived in the United States, making up approximately 0.6% of the population. (See Table 1.2.) When those who combined Hispanic ethnicity with a Native American or Alaskan Native heritage are included, the total rises to 2.6 million (0.8%). In addition, the Census Bureau reports in "American Indian and Alaska Native Heritage Month: November 2017" (October 6, 2017, https://www.census.gov/content/dam/Census/newsroom/facts-for-features/2017/cb17-ff20.pdf) that in 2016 roughly 6.7 million Americans reported their heritage as Native American or Alaskan Native, either alone or in combination with one or more other races.

Geographic Distribution

In "Annual Estimates of the Resident Population by Sex, Race Alone or in Combination, and Hispanic Origin for the United States, States, and Counties: April 1, 2010, to July 1, 2016," the Census Bureau indicates that in 2016 California had the largest number of Native Americans and Alaskan Natives. That year, more than 1 million of the state's residents reported being Native American or Alaskan Native, either alone or in combination with one or more races. Other states with substantial Native American and Alaskan Native populations in 2016 included Oklahoma (499,270), Texas (398,481), Arizona (394,196). According to the Census Bureau, in "American Indian and Alaska Native Heritage Month: November 2017," a total of 21 states had Native American and Alaskan Native populations of 100,000 or more in 2016. The state with the highest proportion of Native Americans and Alaskan Natives was Alaska, where nearly one in five (19.9%) identified with one or both of these groups. Other states with high percentages of Native Americans and Alaskan Natives in 2016 included Oklahoma (13.7%), New Mexico (11.9%), South Dakota (10.4%), and Montana (8.4%).

Many Native Americans and Alaskan Natives live on or near reservations and are members of groupings called tribes. The Census Bureau states in "American Indian and Alaska Native Heritage Month: November 2017" that in 2016 there were 326 federally recognized Native American reservations and 567 federally recognized tribes.

RELATIONS BETWEEN WHITES AND MINORITY GROUPS

In *Americans' Views of Black-White Relations Deteriorate* (August 6, 2015, http://www.gallup.com/poll/184484/americans-views-black-white-relations-deteriorate.aspx), Jeffrey M. Jones of Gallup, Inc., reports on race relations in the United States between 1963 and 2015. As Figure 1.1 shows, the number of respondents who believed that whites and African Americans could eventually resolve the problem of race relations in the United States declined between the civil rights era of the 1960s and the mid-1990s, before gradually rising again between 1996 and 2015.

This trend notwithstanding, many African Americans continued to express dissatisfaction with the way they were treated in the United States. In 2007, only 30% of African Americans reported being either very or somewhat satisfied with the current treatment of African Americans in the United States. (See Figure 1.2.) African Americans' satisfaction with their treatment improved significantly between 2008 and 2013, a period that nearly coincided with the first five years of Barack Obama's (1961–) presidency. Jones reports in *U.S. Blacks Less Satisfied with Way Blacks Are Treated* (August 26, 2013, http://www.gallup.com/poll/164129/blacks-less-satisfied-blacks-treated.aspx) that African American dissatisfaction rose abruptly in 2013, after George Zimmerman (1983–) was acquitted in the fatal shooting of the African American teenager Trayvon Martin (1995–2012), an incident that sparked nationwide outrage over Florida's controversial "stand-your-ground" gun law. After the verdict the percentage of African Americans who believed that the government should play a "major role" in improving the lives of minorities in the United States also rose sharply, from 54% in 2013 to 64% in 2016. (See Figure 1.3.) Meanwhile, the percentage of African Americans who were either very or somewhat satisfied with the treatment of African Americans in the United States plummeted, from 47% in 2013 to 33% in 2015. (See Figure 1.2.) In the midst of these tensions, fewer than half (47%) of Americans believed that relations between whites and African Americans were good in 2015, down from 70% in 2013. (See Table 1.8.)

FIGURE 1.1

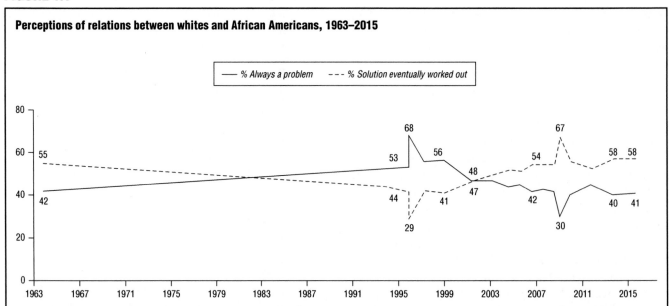

Perceptions of relations between whites and African Americans, 1963–2015

SOURCE: Jeffrey M. Jones, "Do you think that relations between blacks and whites will always be a problem for the United States, or that a solution will eventually be worked out?" in *Americans' Views of Black-White Relations Deteriorate*, Gallup, Inc., August 6, 2015, http://www.gallup.com/poll/184484/americans-views-black-white-relations-deteriorate.aspx (accessed September 3, 2017). Copyright © 2017. Republished with permission of Gallup, Inc.; permission conveyed through Copyright Clearance Center, Inc.

FIGURE 1.2

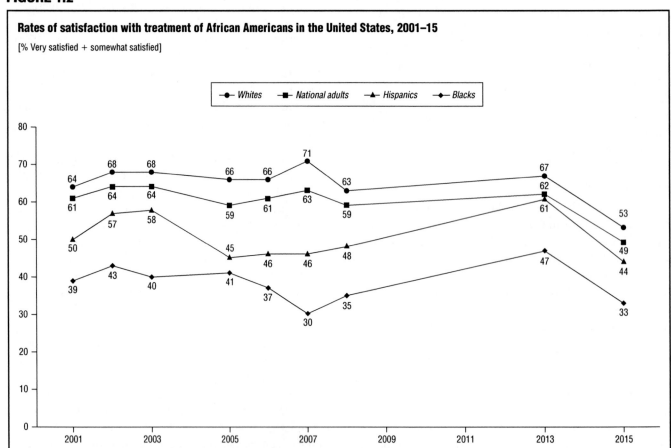

Rates of satisfaction with treatment of African Americans in the United States, 2001–15

SOURCE: Jeffrey M. Jones, "Satisfied with the Way Blacks Are Treated in U.S. Society," in *Americans' Satisfaction with Way Blacks Treated Tumbles*, Gallup, Inc., August 4, 2015, http://www.gallup.com/poll/184466/americans-satisfaction-blacks-treated-tumbles.aspx (accessed September 3, 2017). Copyright © 2017. Republished with permission of Gallup, Inc.; permission conveyed through Copyright Clearance Center, Inc.

FIGURE 1.3

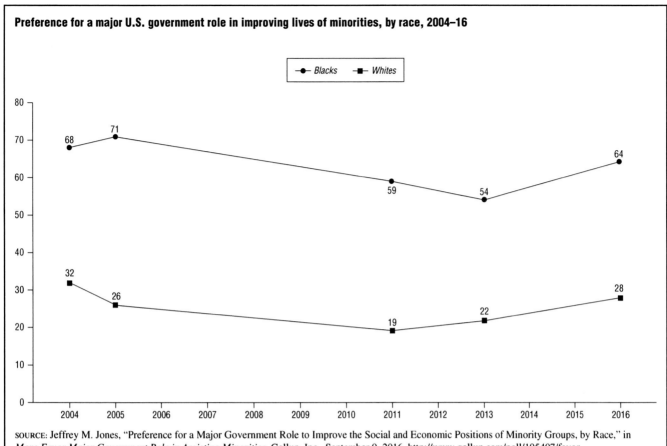

Preference for a major U.S. government role in improving lives of minorities, by race, 2004–16

SOURCE: Jeffrey M. Jones, "Preference for a Major Government Role to Improve the Social and Economic Positions of Minority Groups, by Race," in *More Favor Major Government Role in Assisting Minorities*, Gallup, Inc., September 9, 2016, http://www.gallup.com/poll/195407/favor-major-government-role-assisting-minorities.aspx (accessed September 3, 2017). Copyright © 2017. Republished with permission of Gallup, Inc.; permission conveyed through Copyright Clearance Center, Inc.

TABLE 1.8

Perceptions of relations between various races in the United States, by racial group, 2013–15

	2013	2015	Change
	%	%	pct. pts.
Whites/Blacks	70	47	−23
Whites/Asians	87	86	−1
Whites/Hispanics	70	69	−1
Blacks/Hispanics	60	60	0

SOURCE: Jeffrey M. Jones, "Rating of Intergroup Relations as Somewhat/ Very Good," in *Americans' Views of Black-White Relations Deteriorate*, Gallup, Inc., August 6, 2015, http://www.gallup.com/poll/184484/americans-views-black-white-relations-deteriorate.aspx (accessed September 3, 2017). Copyright © 2017. Republished with permission of Gallup, Inc.; permission conveyed through Copyright Clearance Center, Inc.

CHAPTER 2
FAMILY LIFE AND LIVING ARRANGEMENTS

The family has historically been regarded as the cornerstone of society in the United States. For many years, particularly when the nation was primarily an agricultural society, extended families (multiple generations living in the same household) were common. As the culture became more urban and mobile, nuclear families (two parents and their children) became the American norm.

Nevertheless, the makeup of families and their role in society have been undergoing a massive change. Shifts in economics, employment, moral values, and social conditions have led to an increasing number of single men and women living alone, cohabitations without marriage, and single-parent families. A growing number of children, including minority children, are being raised by one parent or by neither parent, as in the case of children being raised by grandparents or foster parents. How these changes affect minorities in the United States can be best understood through a detailed look at minority families.

MARITAL STATUS

The U.S. Census Bureau reports in *Current Population Survey, March and Annual Social and Economic Supplements* (November 2016, https://www.census.gov/programs-surveys/cps.html) that 52.1% of all Americans aged 15 years and older were married in 2016. African Americans were the least likely to be married (34.4%), while Asian Americans were the most likely (62.2%). Hispanics (48.9%) and whites (54.7%) fell between these two groups.

Interracial and Interethnic Marriage

Laws that prohibited interracial marriage were on the books in many states until 1967. In that year the U.S. Supreme Court unanimously decided in *Loving v. Virginia* (388 U.S. 1) that prohibitions against interracial marriage were unconstitutional. Nevertheless, interracial marriages were rare even into the 1970s. After 1980 interracial marriages became much more common. The

Census Bureau (2012, ftp://ftp.census.gov/library/publications/2011/compendia/statab/131ed/tables/12s0060.pdf) indicates that the number of interracial married couples nearly quadrupled between 1980 and 2010. For example, in 1980 there were 167,000 African American–white interracial married couples; by 2010 there were 558,000 such couples. In 1980 there were 450,000 married couples with one white spouse and one spouse of a race other than white or African American (such as Native American or Asian American); in 2010 more than 1.7 million married couples fit this description. The number of married couples in which one member was Hispanic and the other was not Hispanic grew from 891,000 in 1980 to 2.3 million in 2010. Although the number of interracial and interethnic married couples is rising, the vast majority of married couples continue to be made up of two spouses of the same race and ethnicity. The Census Bureau reports in "Household and Families: 2010 Census Brief" (April 24, 2012, http://www.census.gov/population/www/cen2010/briefs/tables/appendix.pdf) that by 2010 there were a total of 5.4 million interracial and interethnic couples in the United States. This was up from just over 4 million in 2000, but these couples represented only 9.5% of all married couple households in the United States in 2010.

Considerable progress has been made in the public acceptance of interracial marriage. According to Frank Newport of Gallup, Inc., in *In U.S., 87% Approve of Black-White Marriage, vs. 4% in 1958* (July 25, 2013, http://www.gallup.com/poll/163697/approve-marriage-blacks-whites.aspx), in 1959 only 4% of Americans approved of interracial marriage between African Americans and whites. (See Figure 2.1.) This percentage grew steadily over the next several decades, and by 1995 nearly half (48%) of Americans approved of marriages between whites and African Americans. As Figure 2.1 shows, public approval of interracial marriage rose even more dramatically over the next two decades, reaching 87% by 2013.

FIGURE 2.1

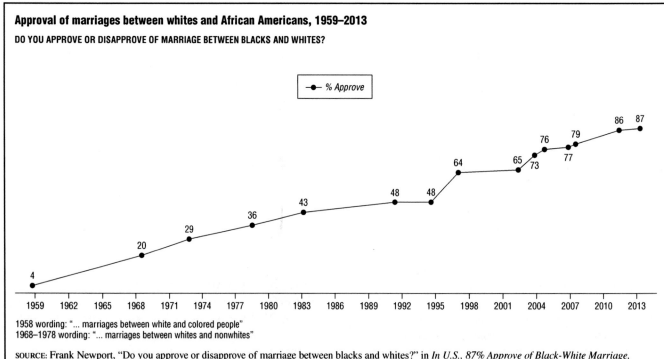

Approval of marriages between whites and African Americans, 1959–2013

DO YOU APPROVE OR DISAPPROVE OF MARRIAGE BETWEEN BLACKS AND WHITES?

1958 wording: "... marriages between white and colored people"
1968–1978 wording: "... marriages between whites and nonwhites"

SOURCE: Frank Newport, "Do you approve or disapprove of marriage between blacks and whites?" in *In U.S., 87% Approve of Black-White Marriage, vs. 4% in 1958*, Gallup, Inc. July 25, 2013, http://www.gallup.com/poll/163697/approve-marriage-blacks-whites.aspx (accessed September 3, 2017). Copyright © 2017. Republished with permission of Gallup, Inc.; permission conveyed through Copyright Clearance Center, Inc.

Divorce

The Census Bureau reports in *Current Population Survey, March and Annual Social and Economic Supplements* that 25.5 million adults aged 15 years and older were divorced and unmarried in 2016. This was 9.9% of all people in that age group. However, the number of people who had ever been divorced is higher, because this figure does not include people who divorced and subsequently remarried. Overall, 11.1% of African Americans and 10.2% of whites were divorced and unmarried, whereas lower proportions of Hispanics (7.7%) and Asian Americans (3.6%) were divorced and unmarried.

Death of a Spouse

According to the Census Bureau, in *Current Population Survey, March and Annual Social and Economic Supplements*, 14.9 million (5.8%) people aged 15 years and older in the United States were widowed (and had not remarried) in 2016. Across all racial and ethnic groups, more women than men were widowed because of the shorter average life span of men, the tendency of wives to be younger than their husbands, and the greater likelihood that men will remarry. Asian American and Hispanic individuals were less likely to be widowed than African American and white individuals. Hispanics were the least likely to be widowed, with just over 1 million (4.9%) widowed women and 317,000 (1.5%) widowed men. Among Asian Americans, 492,000 (6.2%) women were widowed, compared with only 96,000 (1.4%) men.

Whites had the highest percentages of widows, both male and female; 9.3 million (9%) white women were widowed, compared with 2.9 million (2.9%) white men. The rates for African Americans were nearly as high, with 1.4 million (7.9%) widowed African American women in 2013 and 415,000 (2.8%) widowed African American men.

Never Married

In *Current Population Survey, March and Annual Social and Economic Supplements*, the Census Bureau indicates that in 2016, 32.2% of all Americans 15 years and older had never been married. A higher percentage (49%) of African Americans had never been married than any of the other groups discussed in the report. Whites were the least likely (29.1%) to have never been married. Hispanics (40.2%) and Asian Americans (30.3%) fell between these two groups.

PREGNANCY
Unwed Mothers

Over the generations, a major change in American attitudes has removed much of the social stigma from unwed motherhood. Unmarried women of all ages are having children openly and with a regularity that was unheard of just a few generations ago. Joyce A. Martin et al. of the Centers for Disease Control and Prevention indicate in "Births: Final Data for 2015" (*National Vital Statistics Reports*, vol. 66, no. 1, January 5, 2017) that in 2015 more than 1.6 million babies were born to single

TABLE 2.1

Births and birth rates to unmarried women, by age, race, and Hispanic origin of mother, 2015

[Population estimated as of July 1]

Measure and age of mother	All races[a]	White		Black		American Indian or Alaska Native[b]	Asian or Pacific Islander[b]	Hispanic[c]
		Total[b]	Non-Hispanic	Total[b]	Non-Hispanic			
Number								
All ages	1,601,527	1,077,618	621,314	448,531	415,554	29,130	46,248	489,358
Under 15	2,489	1,501	578	898	845	53	37	979
15–19	204,043	143,134	77,222	53,130	48,739	4,417	3,362	70,813
15	7,497	4,962	2,101	2,250	2,076	167	118	3,062
16	17,791	12,260	5,575	4,854	4,464	415	262	7,119
17	33,259	23,416	11,537	8,540	7,737	791	512	12,778
18	57,032	40,449	22,015	14,425	13,261	1,201	957	19,751
19	88,464	62,047	35,994	23,061	21,201	1,843	1,513	28,103
20–24	560,639	372,317	224,094	166,405	155,047	10,258	11,659	160,158
25–29	435,339	289,467	171,977	124,527	115,662	7,868	13,477	126,195
30–34	252,397	170,365	94,806	67,187	61,977	4,270	10,575	80,447
35–39	116,670	79,928	41,812	29,448	26,962	1,873	5,421	40,283
40 and over	29,950	20,906	10,825	6,936	6,322	391	1,717	10,483
Rate per 1,000 unmarried women in specified group								
15–44[d]	43.4	40.4	31.6	59.6	—	—	20.4	67.4
15–19	20.2	18.8	13.9	31.5	—	—	5.5	31.6
15–17	9.6	8.8	5.7	15.4	—	—	2.5	16.6
18–19	36.5	34.3	26.3	55.8	—	—	9.7	55.7
20–24	59.7	54.6	43.3	94.2	—	—	17.9	87.9
25–29	66.9	63.3	48.8	91.9	—	—	28.8	109.1
30–34	60.3	59.8	44.4	63.9	—	—	47.3	101.4
35–39	34.1	34.8	24.8	32.6	—	—	33.6	60.3
40–44[e]	9.0	8.2	6.8	9.1	—	—	11.2	18.1
Percent of births to unmarried women								
All ages	40.3	35.8	29.2	70.1	70.6	65.8	16.4	53.0
Under 15	99.6	99.3	99.3	100.0	100.0	100.0	100.0	99.3
15–19	88.8	86.3	85.0	97.1	97.4	93.2	78.2	88.1
15	98.8	98.4	98.4	99.8	99.9	99.4	95.9	98.5
16	96.5	95.5	95.2	99.4	99.5	98.8	92.3	95.8
17	94.6	93.2	92.9	99.0	99.2	96.1	88.0	93.7
18	89.8	87.4	86.6	97.5	97.9	93.3	82.2	88.8
19	84.2	81.0	80.0	95.3	95.9	90.3	70.6	82.8
20–24	65.9	60.0	56.1	87.6	88.3	76.2	44.5	67.8
25–29	37.8	32.7	26.8	69.1	69.7	61.3	18.4	49.3
30–34	23.1	20.0	14.7	51.4	51.7	50.2	10.0	38.4
35–39	22.1	20.0	14.4	44.3	44.3	49.0	9.4	36.0
40 and over	24.8	23.7	18.1	40.3	39.9	44.5	11.9	36.6

— Data not available.
[a]Includes origin not stated.
[b]Race and Hispanic origin are reported separately on birth certificates. Race categories are consistent with 1977 Office of Management and Budget standards. Data for persons of Hispanic origin are included in the data for each race group according to the mother's reported race. Forty-nine states and the District of Columbia reported multiple-race data for 2015 that were bridged to single-race categories for comparability with other states.
[c]Includes all persons of Hispanic origin of any race.
[d]Birth rates computed by relating total births to unmarried mothers, regardless of age of mother, to unmarried women aged 15–44.
[e]Birth rates computed by relating births to unmarried women aged 40 and over to unmarried women aged 40–44.
Notes: For 49 states, the District of Columbia, and New York City, marital status is reported in the birth registration process; for New York, mother's marital status is inferred.
Rates cannot be computed for unmarried non-Hispanic black women or for American Indian or Alaska Native women because the neccessary populations are not available.

SOURCE: Joyce A. Martin et al., "Table 15. Births and Birth Rates for Unmarried Women, by Age and Race and Hispanic Origin of Mother: United States, 2015," in "Births: Final Data for 2015," *National Vital Statistics Reports*, vol. 66, no. 1, January 5, 2017, https://www.cdc.gov/nchs/data/nvsr/nvsr66/nvsr66_01.pdf (accessed September 3, 2017)

mothers; 40.3% of all births were to unmarried mothers in that year. (See Table 2.1.)

Teenage Mothers

Births to teenagers are of particular concern because they can have negative consequences for both the children and the mothers involved. As Figure 2.2 shows, the birth rate for teens began a gradual decline during the early 1990s, a trend that continued through 2005. Birth rates among teen mothers experienced a slight rise between 2005 and 2007, before falling steadily through 2015.

Table 2.2 shows birth rates for teenage mothers in 2014 and 2015, by age group and race and ethnicity. Among girls between the ages of 15 and 17 years, Asians or Pacific Islanders saw the largest decrease in birth rates between 2014 and 2015, with an 18% decline over that

FIGURE 2.2

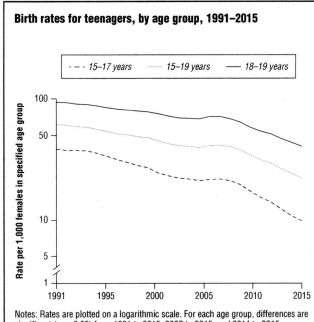

Birth rates for teenagers, by age group, 1991–2015

Notes: Rates are plotted on a logarithmic scale. For each age group, differences are significant ($p < 0.05$) from 1991 to 2015, 2007 to 2015, and 2014 to 2015.

SOURCE: Brady E. Hamilton and T. J. Mathews, "Figure 1. Birth Rates for Females Aged 15–19, by Age Group: United States, 1991–2015," in "Continued Declines in Teen Births in the United States, 2015," *NCHS Data Brief*, no. 259, Centers for Disease Control and Prevention, National Center for Health Statistics, September 2016, http://www.cdc.gov/nchs/data/databriefs/db259.pdf (accessed September 3, 2017)

span. Overall, births among young girls between the ages of 10 and 14 years fell 33% across all racial and ethnic groups between 2014 and 2015.

Pregnancy and Health

Table 2.3 and Table 2.4 report various health characteristics of mothers and their babies in 2015, by race and ethnicity of the mother. As Table 2.3 shows, more than one out of 10 (11.1%) pregnant Asians or Pacific Islanders suffered from diabetes in 2015, compared with 6.5% of pregnant women of all races. At 15.8%, African American women were the most likely to give birth to babies born with a low (less than 5 pounds, 8 ounces [2,500 g]) or very low (less than 3 pounds, 5 ounces [1,500 g]) birth weight. African American women were also the most likely to give birth to babies born prematurely (13.2%), followed by Native Americans or Alaskan Natives (10.5%). Among mothers of Hispanic origin, Puerto Ricans (11%) were the most likely to give birth to babies born prematurely. (See Table 2.4.)

MINORITY FAMILY STRUCTURE
Married-Couple Families

The Census Bureau defines a family as two or more people living together who are related by birth, marriage, or adoption. However, a household can be family or nonfamily and is simply all people who occupy a housing unit. In 2016 married couples accounted for 71.8% of households consisting of some form of family group—such as a married couple, or a combination of at least one adult and one child. (See Table 2.5.) Asian Americans (82%) had the highest percentage of family households with married couples, followed by non-Hispanic whites (79.2%), Hispanics (61.2%), and African Americans (43.6%). Of the roughly 15.1 million Hispanic households in the United States in 2015, slightly fewer than half (7.2 million, or 47.8%) were married-couple families. (See Table 2.6.) As Table 2.5 shows, Asian American married couples were the most likely (40.5%) to have children under the age of 18 years living in their household, followed by Hispanic married couples (34.5%).

Single-Parent Households

In 2016 there were 13.9 million single-parent families in the United States, meaning that a single parent had primary responsibility for maintaining a household that contained one or more children under the age of 25 years. (See Table 2.7.) Nearly 11.5 million (82.5%) of these families were maintained by a single mother. More than nine out of 10 (91.5%) African American single-parent homes were maintained by a single mother that year. By comparison, single mothers headed up 85.1% of single-parent Hispanic households, 79.6% of single-parent Asian American households, and 77% of single-parent non-Hispanic white households. Although they represent a definite minority of single-parent families, single fathers clearly play an important role in raising children in the United States. As Table 2.7 shows, there were 2.4 million single-father households in 2016.

Figure 2.3 shows the living arrangements of children in the United States in 2016, by race and Hispanic origin. A much greater percentage of African American children (53%) were living in such households than were children from any other racial or ethnic group. Asian American children (29%) were also more likely than average to be living in a single-parent household.

Multigenerational Households

As Table 2.8 shows, of the 80.5 million family households in the United States in 2012, 3.7 million, or 4.6%, were multigenerational. Among Hispanic families, 970,000 (8.4%) out of 11.6 million family households were multigenerational, the highest proportion among all racial and ethnic groups surveyed. African American families had nearly the same proportion of multigenerational households, with 799,000 (8.3%) out of 9.6 million family households categorized as multigenerational. Hispanic family households were also the most likely to include a foreign-born family member, with 684,000 (5.9%) out of 11.6 million Hispanic families including a member who was born outside the country.

TABLE 2.2

Birth rates for women aged 10–19, by age, race, and Hispanic origin, selected years 1991–2015

[Rates per 1,000 women in specified age and race and Hispanic-origin group. Population estimated as of July 1]

Age and race and Hispanic origin of mother	Year				Percent change		
	2015	2014	2007	1991[a]	2014–2015	2007–2015	1991–2015
10–14 years							
All races and origins[b]	0.2	0.3	0.6	1.4	−33	−67	−86
Non-Hispanic white[c]	0.1	0.1	0.2	0.5	†	−50	−80
Non-Hispanic black[c]	0.6	0.6	1.4	4.9	†	−57	−88
American Indian or Alaska Native total[c, d]	0.3	0.3	0.7	1.6	†	−57	−81
Asian or Pacific Islander total[c, d]	0.1	0.1	0.2	0.8	†	−50	−88
Hispanic[e]	0.4	0.4	1.2	2.4	†	−67	−83
15–19 years							
All races and origins[b]	22.3	24.2	41.5	61.8	−8	−46	−64
Non-Hispanic white[c]	16.0	17.3	27.2	43.4	−8	−41	−63
Non-Hispanic black[c]	31.8	34.9	62.0	118.2	−9	−49	−73
American Indian or Alaska Native total[c, d]	25.7	27.3	49.3	84.1	−6	−48	−69
Asian or Pacific Islander total[c, d]	6.9	7.7	14.8	27.3	−10	−53	−75
Hispanic[e]	34.9	38.0	75.3	104.6	−8	−54	−67
15–17 years							
All races and origins[b]	9.9	10.9	21.7	38.6	−9	−54	−74
Non-Hispanic white[c]	6.0	6.7	11.9	23.6	−10	−50	−75
Non-Hispanic black[c]	15.3	16.6	34.6	86.1	−8	−56	−82
American Indian or Alaska Native total[c, d]	12.7	13.2	26.1	51.9	†	−51	−76
Asian or Pacific Islander total[c, d]	2.7	3.3	7.4	16.3	−18	−64	−83
Hispanic[e]	17.4	19.3	44.4	69.2	−10	−61	−75
18–19 years							
All races and origins[b]	40.7	43.8	71.7	94	−7	−43	−57
Non-Hispanic white[c]	30.6	32.9	50.4	70.6	−7	−39	−57
Non-Hispanic black[c]	56.7	61.5	105.2	162.2	−8	−46	−65
American Indian or Alaska Native total[c, d]	45.8	48.6	86.3	134.2	−6	−47	−66
Asian or Pacific Islander total[c, d]	12.8	13.9	24.9	42.2	−8	−48	−70
Hispanic[e]	61.9	66.1	124.7	155.5	−6	−50	−60

[†]Difference not statistically significant at $p = 0.05$.
[a]Excludes data for New Hampshire, which did not report Hispanic origin.
[b]Includes births to race and Hispanic-origin groups not shown separately, such as white Hispanic and black Hispanic women, and births with origin not stated.
[c]Race and Hispanic origin are reported separately on birth certificates. Persons of Hispanic origin may be of any race. Race categories are consistent with the 1977 Office of Management and Budget (OMB) standards. Forty-nine states and the District of Columbia reported multiple-race data in 2015 that were bridged to the single-race categories of the 1977 OMB standards for comparability with other states. Multiple-race reporting areas vary for 2007, 2014, and 2015.
[d]Includes persons of Hispanic and non-Hispanic origin and origin not stated, according to the mother's reported race.
[e]Includes all persons of Hispanic origin of any race.
Note: Comparisons are made with 2007 and 1991 because these years represent recent and longer-term highs in teenage birth rates.

SOURCE: Joyce A. Martin et al., "Table A. Birth Rates for Women Aged 10–19, by Age and Race and Hispanic Origin of Mother: United States, 1991, 2007, 2014, and 2015," in "Births: Final Data for 2015," *National Vital Statistics Reports*, vol. 66, no. 1, January 5, 2017, https://www.cdc.gov/nchs/data/nvsr/nvsr66/nvsr66_01.pdf (accessed September 3, 2017)

Same-Sex Households

During the early part of the 21st century, same-sex households began gaining widespread acceptance in the United States. Table 2.9 offers a breakdown of same-sex households in 2015, by racial, ethnic, and other demographic characteristics. Of 858,896 same-sex households, 83% consisted of two white individuals, 7.8% consisted of two African American individuals, and 3.1% consisted of two Asian American individuals. Nearly one out of 10 (9.7%) female same-sex couples were African American. Overall, 15.1% of all same-sex couples were interracial in 2015.

Living Arrangements of Children

Changes in the marital circumstances of adults naturally affect the living arrangements of children. High divorce rates, an increased delay in first marriages, and more out-of-wedlock births have resulted in fewer children living with two parents. In 2016, 50.7 million (68.7%) children under the age of 18 years were living with two parents (not necessarily both birth parents), meaning that more than three out of 10 (31.3%) children were living with either a single parent or no parents. (See Table 2.10.) African American children have been particularly affected by these changes; only 38.7% of African American children lived with two parents in 2016, compared with 67.2% of Hispanic children, 76.5% of non-Hispanic white children, and 88.6% of Asian American children.

AFRICAN AMERICAN CHILDREN. In 2016, 4.3 million (38.7%) African American children under the age of 18 years lived with two parents, whereas 5.7 million (51.5%) lived with their mother only. (See Table 2.10.) A higher proportion of African American children lived with neither parent (648,000, or 5.8%) than lived with their father

TABLE 2.3

Selected health characteristics of mother and infant at birth, by race, 2015

Characteristic	All races	White	Black	American Indian or Alaska Native	Asian or Pacific Islander
			Percent		
Mother					
Diabetes during pregnancy	6.5	6.2	5.8	9.9	11.1
Weight gain of less than 11 lbs	9.1	8.3	13.1	13.1	7.1
Weight gain of more than 40 lbs	21.0	21.6	21.4	22.2	14.3
Induction of labor	23.8	24.5	22.9	24.2	18.5
CNM delivery[a]	8.5	8.7	7.4	17.8	7.2
Cesarean delivery	32.0	31.3	35.3	28.3	33.0
Infant					
Gestational age:					
Preterm[b]	9.6	9.0	13.2	10.5	8.6
Early preterm[c]	2.8	2.4	4.7	2.8	2.2
Late preterm[d]	6.9	6.6	8.4	7.7	6.4
Birthweight:					
Very low birthweight[e]	1.4	1.1	2.8	1.3	1.1
Low birthweight[f]	8.1	7.0	13.0	7.5	8.4
4,000 grams or more	8.0	9.0	4.6	10.1	4.8
Twin birth[g]	33.5	32.8	38.7	25.1	29.9
Triplet or higher-order birth[h]	103.6	107.1	101.7	38.4	81.4

[a]Births delivered by certified nurse midwives (CNMs).
[b]Born before 37 completed weeks of gestation based on the obstetric estimate.
[c]Born before 34 completed weeks of gestation based on the obstetric estimate.
[d]Born between 34 and 36 completed weeks of gestation based on the obstetric estimate.
[e]Less than 1,500 grams.
[f]Less than 2,500 grams.
[g]Live births in twin deliveries per 1,000 live births.
[h]Live births in triplet and other higher-order multiple deliveries per 100,000 live births.
Notes: Race and Hispanic origin are reported separately on birth certificates. Race categories are consistent with 1977 Office of Management and Budget standards. Forty-nine states and the District of Columbia reported multiple-race data for 2015 that were bridged to single-race categories for comparability with other states. In this table, all women, including Hispanic women, are classified only according to their race.

SOURCE: Joyce A. Martin et al., "Table 18. Selected Medical and Health Characteristics of Births, by Race of Mother: United States, 2015," in "Births: Final Data for 2015," *National Vital Statistics Reports*, vol. 66, no. 1, January 5, 2017, https://www.cdc.gov/nchs/data/nvsr/nvsr66/nvsr66_01.pdf (accessed September 3, 2017)

only (439,000, or 4%). The Census Bureau reports in "Living Arrangements of Black Children under 18 Years Old: 1960 to 2005" (September 21, 2006, https://www.census.gov/population/socdemo/hh-fam/ch3.pdf) that in 1970 the proportions of African American children who lived with one parent (31.8%) or two parents (58.4%) were virtually the reverse of their living arrangements in 2016.

HISPANIC CHILDREN. In 2016 a lower proportion of Hispanic children (5.3 million, or 29.1%) than African American children were living with one parent, but this proportion was still higher than the proportion of non-Hispanic white children who lived with one parent (7.7 million, or 20.4%). (See Table 2.10.) More than 4.6 million (25.3%) Hispanic children lived with a single mother and 700,000 (3.8%) lived with a single father. This proportion was considerably higher than among non-Hispanic whites—6 million (15.9%) non-Hispanic white children lived with a single mother and 1.7 million (4.4%) lived with a single father—but well below the proportion of African American children living with a single parent. Approximately 673,000 (3.7%) Hispanic children lived with neither parent. Some of these children likely lived with other relatives, such as grandparents, or with foster parents.

ASIAN AMERICAN CHILDREN. The Asian American family is typically a close-knit unit, and members are traditionally respectful of the authority of the elder members of the family. However, as the younger generation becomes more assimilated into American culture, the unchallenged role of elders may not remain as strong. Even so, family tradition and honor are still held in high regard. In 2016 only 346,000 (9.2%) Asian American children were living with one parent, a proportion lower than that of non-Hispanic whites. (See Table 2.10.) About 279,000 (7.4%) Asian American children lived with a single mother and 67,000 (1.8%) lived with a single father. Approximately 81,000 (2.2%) lived with neither parent.

FOSTER CARE. Sometimes, when a child's parents are unable or unwilling to care for him or her, another relative may step in to informally assume responsibility for the child. In other cases the government assumes legal responsibility for the child, which generally leads to the child being placed in foster care. Foster care is provided through a network of federal, state, and local governmental agencies. Therefore, details of the foster care system vary from one location to another within the United States, but broadly speaking its purpose is to provide

TABLE 2.4

Selected health characteristics of mother and infant at birth, by Hispanic origin of mother, 2015

Characteristic	All origins[a]	Hispanic Total	Mexican	Puerto Rican	Cuban	Central and South American	Other and unknown Hispanic	Non-Hispanic Total[b]	White	Black
					Percent					
Mother										
Diabetes during pregnancy	6.5	7.1	7.7	6.8	5.3	6.4	6.1	6.3	5.8	5.7
Weight gain of less than 11 lbs	9.1	10.5	11.1	9.8	6.1	9.9	9.9	8.6	7.5	13.3
Weight gain of more than 40 lbs	21.0	16.5	15.3	22.2	25.2	14.8	18.6	22.5	23.7	21.5
Induction of labor	23.8	19.3	18.8	21.7	18.9	18.0	21.3	25.3	26.8	23.0
CNM delivery[c]	8.5	8.1	7.6	10.5	5.0	10.0	7.2	8.6	9.0	7.2
Cesarean delivery	32.0	31.7	30.4	34.2	47.4	31.5	33.2	32.1	31.1	35.5
Infant										
Gestational age:										
Preterm[d]	9.6	9.1	8.9	11.0	9.3	8.7	9.6	9.8	8.9	13.4
Early preterm[e]	2.8	2.5	2.4	3.5	2.8	2.3	2.8	2.8	2.3	4.8
Late preterm[f]	6.9	6.6	6.5	7.5	6.5	6.4	6.8	6.9	6.5	8.6
Birthweight:										
Very low birthweight[g]	1.4	1.2	1.1	1.7	1.4	1.1	1.4	1.4	1.1	2.9
Low birthweight[h]	8.1	7.2	6.8	9.4	7.2	6.7	8.1	8.3	6.9	13.3
4,000 grams or more	8.0	7.1	7.4	6.2	7.8	6.8	6.3	8.3	9.7	4.5
Twin birth[i]	33.5	24.5	23.0	31.9	31.6	24.0	25.9	36.0	36.1	39.4
Triplet or higher-order birth[j]	103.6	66.1	59.7	67.6	94.8	78.0	73.8	114.4	122.8	104.4

[a]Includes origin not stated.
[b]Includes races other than white and black.
[c]Births delivered by certified nurse midwives (CNMs).
[d]Born before 37 completed weeks of gestation based on the obstetric estimate.
[e]Born before 34 completed weeks of gestation based on the obstetric estimate.
[f]Born between 34 and 36 completed weeks of gestation based on the obstetric estimate.
[g]Less than 1,500 grams.
[h]Less than 2,500 grams.
[i]Live births in twin deliveries per 1,000 live births.
[j]Live births in triplet and other higher-order multiple deliveries per 100,000 live births.
Notes: Race and Hispanic origin are reported separately on birth certificates. Race categories are consistent with 1977 Office of Management and Budget standards. Forty-nine states and the District of Columbia reported multiple-race data for 2015 that were bridged to single-race categories for comparability with other states. Persons of Hispanic origin may be of any race. In this table, Hispanic women are classified only by place of orgin; non-Hispanic women are classified by race.

SOURCE: Joyce A. Martin et al., "Table 19. Selected Medical or Health Characteristics of Births, by Hispanic Origin of Mother and by Race for Mothers of Non-Hispanic Origin: United States, 2015," in "Births: Final Data for 2015," *National Vital Statistics Reports*, vol. 66, no. 1, January 5, 2017, https://www.cdc.gov/nchs/data/nvsr/nvsr66/nvsr66_01.pdf (accessed September 3, 2017)

temporary care for children who cannot live with their parents until permanent living and care arrangements can be made for them, such as reunification with their parents or adoption.

The U.S. Department of Health and Human Services reports various statistics about foster care in *AFCARS Report* (June 2016, https://www.acf.hhs.gov/sites/default/files/cb/afcarsreport23.pdf). The report shows that as of September 30, 2015, there were 427,910 children in foster care. Most (75%) children in the system were living in the home of one or more adults who were not their parents (a foster home). This included 30% who were living in the home of a relative. The mean (average) time children in the system had been in foster care was 20.4 months. Many children in foster care are ultimately reunited with their parents, including 51% of those who left the system in fiscal year (FY) 2015.

African American children make up a disproportionate share of the children living in foster care. As shown in Table 2.10, 15.1% of all U.S. children were African

American in 2016. The *AFCARS Report* indicates that there were 103,376 African American children in foster care, 24% of the total. By contrast, whereas 51.5% of all children were non-Hispanic white in 2016, they were only 43% of all children in foster care in FY 2015. Hispanic children, who were 24.7% of the total population of children in 2016, accounted for 21% of the foster care population in FY 2015. These proportions were roughly the same as the percentages of white, African American, and Hispanic children who entered foster care during FY 2015.

HOMEOWNERSHIP

Owning one's home has traditionally been the American dream. However, for many Americans, especially minorities, purchasing a home can be difficult or impossible. The Census Bureau's Housing Vacancy Survey calculates homeownership rates by race and ethnicity of householder (the rate is computed by dividing the number of owner households by the total number of households).

TABLE 2.5

Types of family groups, by race and Hispanic origin, 2016

[Numbers in thousands, except for percentages]

	Total	White alone	White alone, non-Hispanic	Black alone	Asian alone	All other single races and combinations	Hispanic (any race)
				Race of family reference person			
Total	87,209	68,702	55,800	10,626	5,192	2,688	14,383
Number							
Married couples	62,628	52,249	44,185	4,618	4,258	1,504	8,796
With children under 18	24,638	19,899	15,398	1,877	2,103	758	4,964
Without children under 18	37,990	32,349	28,787	2,740	2,155	746	3,831
Unmarried parent couple[a]	1,824	1,373	824	282	56	112	611
Mother only with child(ren) under 18[b]	9,781	6,019	4,090	3,007	217	537	2,321
Father only with child(ren) under 18[b]	2,033	1,588	1,203	301	56	88	423
Householder and other relative(s)[c]	10,942	7,472	5,497	2,419	605	446	2,232
Grandparent householder with grandchild(ren) under 18	1,214	794	552	315	35	70	274
Householder with adult child(ren)	5,959	4,215	3,340	1,329	205	210	982
Householder with young adult child age 18–24	2,350	1,631	1,230	544	82	93	451
Householder with parent	2,750	1,820	1,094	513	290	127	819
Percent	100.0	100.0	100.0	100.0	100.0	100.0	100.0
Married couples	71.8	76.1	79.2	43.6	82.0	56.0	61.2
With children under 18	28.3	29.0	27.6	17.7	40.5	28.2	34.5
Without children under 18	43.6	47.1	51.6	25.8	41.5	27.8	26.6
Unmarried parent couple[a]	2.1	2.0	1.5	2.7	1.1	4.2	4.2
Mother only with child(ren) under 18[b]	11.2	8.8	7.3	28.3	4.2	20.0	16.1
Father only with child(ren) under 18[b]	2.3	2.3	2.2	2.8	1.1	3.3	2.9
Householder and other relative(s)[c]	12.5	10.9	9.9	22.8	11.7	16.6	15.5
Grandparent householder with grandchild(ren) under 18	1.4	1.2	1.0	3.0	0.7	2.6	1.9
Householder with adult child(ren)	6.8	6.1	6.0	12.5	3.9	7.8	6.8
Householder with young adult child age 18–24	2.7	2.4	2.2	5.1	1.6	3.5	3.1
Householder with parent	3.2	2.6	2.0	4.8	5.6	4.7	5.7

Dash ("—") represents or rounds to zero.
[a]These couples have at least one joint never married child under 18.
[b]Parent may have a cohabiting partner, but none of their children are also identified as the child of their cohabiting partner.
[c]Sub-categories of "householder and other relative" are not mutually exclusive.

SOURCE: "Table FG10. Family Groups: 2016," in *America's Families and Living Arrangements: 2016*, U.S. Census Bureau, April 6, 2017, https://www2.census .gov/programs-surveys/demo/tables/families/2016/cps-2016/tabfg10-all.xls (accessed September 3, 2017)

TABLE 2.6

Hispanic origin households, by household type, 2015

	United States Estimate
Total:	**15,062,452**
Family households:	11,498,898
Married-couple family	7,200,213
Other family:	4,298,685
Male householder, no wife present	1,316,071
Female householder, no husband present	2,982,614
Nonfamily households:	3,563,554
Householder living alone	2,658,900
Householder not living alone	904,654

SOURCE: Adapted from "B11001I. Household Type (Including Living Alone) (Hispanic or Latino). Universe: Households with a Householder Who Is Hispanic or Latino," in *2015 American Community Survey*, U.S. Census Bureau, 2016, https://factfinder.census.gov/faces/tableservices/jsf/pages/ productview.xhtml?pid=ACS_15_1YR_B11001I&prodType=table (accessed September 3, 2017)

In 2016, 63.4% of all U.S. householders owned their home. (See Table 2.11.) The homeownership rate for non-Hispanic white householders, 71.9%, was much higher than that for any other racial or ethnic group covered in the survey. Asian or Native Hawaiian/ Pacific Islander householders had a homeownership rate of 55.4%, for Native American or Alaskan Native householders it was 47.6%, for Hispanic householders it was 46%, and for African American householders it was 41.6%.

Subprime Mortgage Crisis

Although the proportion of minority homeownership was low in 2016 when compared with non-Hispanic white homeownership, these numbers actually reflect significant growth in the purchase of homes by minorities. Homeownership rates rose for all groups between 1994 and 2004, but for many minority groups they rose faster than among non-Hispanic whites. (See Table 2.11.) A number of factors were responsible for the growth of minority homeownership during the 1990s. The administration of President Bill Clinton (1946–) provided more lending opportunities for minorities by revitalizing the Federal Housing Administration and improving enforcement of the Community Reinvestment Act, which was passed by Congress in 1977 to encourage banks and other lending institutions to invest in the communities in which they operate. Furthermore, the U.S. Department of Housing and Urban Development pressured the Federal National

TABLE 2.7

One-parent households, by race, and sex, 2016

[Numbers in thousands, except for percentages]

		Race of household reference person				
	Total	White alone	White alone, non-Hispanic	Black alone	Asian alone	Hispanic (any race)
Total	**125,819**	**99,313**	**84,445**	**16,539**	**6,328**	**16,667**
Number						
Mother, no partner present	11,461	7,170	5,220	3,500	296	2,305
With children under 25[a]	8,682	5,219	3,638	2,847	204	1,898
With children under 18[b]	7,020	4,156	2,852	2,379	138	1,576
Father, no partner present	2,425	1,918	1,555	327	76	404
With children under 25[a]	1,719	1,372	1,088	227	46	308
With children under 18[b]	1,204	949	753	167	32	216
Percent						
Mother, no partner present	9.1	7.2	6.2	21.2	4.7	13.8
With children under 25[a]	6.9	5.3	4.3	17.2	3.2	11.4
With children under 18[b]	5.6	4.2	3.4	14.4	2.2	9.5
Father, no partner present	1.9	1.9	1.8	2.0	1.2	2.4
With children under 25[a]	1.4	1.4	1.3	1.4	0.7	1.8
With children under 18[b]	1.0	1.0	0.9	1.0	0.5	1.3

[a]These couples or parents have at least one biological, step, or adopted child under 25.
[b]These couples or parents have at least one biological, step, or adopted never-married child under 18.
Note: This table uses the householder's person weight to describe characteristics of people living in households. As a result, estimates of the number of households do not match estimates of housing units from the Housing Vacancy Survey (HVS). The HVS is weighted to housing units, rather than the population, in order to more accurately estimate the number of occupied and vacant housing units.

SOURCE: Adapted from "Table H3. Households by Race and Hispanic Origin of Household Reference Person and Detailed Type: 2016," in *America's Families and Living Arrangements: 2016*, U.S. Census Bureau, April 6, 2017, https://www2.census.gov/programs-surveys/demo/tables/families/2016/cps-2016/tabh3.xls (accessed September 3, 2017)

FIGURE 2.3

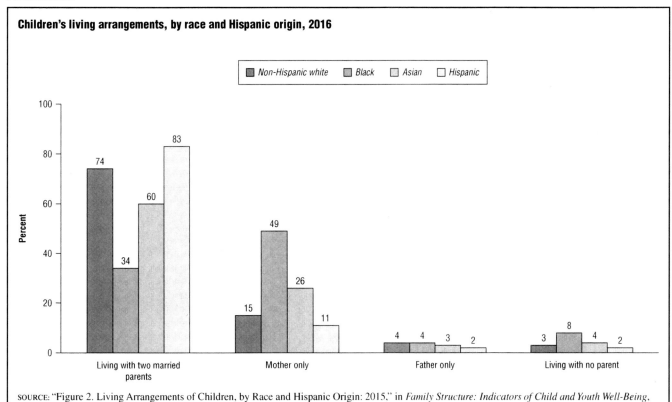

Children's living arrangements, by race and Hispanic origin, 2016

SOURCE: "Figure 2. Living Arrangements of Children, by Race and Hispanic Origin: 2015," in *Family Structure: Indicators of Child and Youth Well-Being*, Child Trends DataBank, December 2015, https://www.childtrends.org/wp-content/uploads/2015/12/59_Family_Structure.pdf (accessed September 3, 2017)

Mortgage Association (Fannie Mae) and the Federal Home Loan Mortgage Corporation (Freddie Mac) to initiate programs to help minority and low-income borrowers in securing mortgages. Fannie Mae is a private company that

TABLE 2.8

Multigenerational households, by race and Hispanic origin, 2012

[Numbers in thousands]

Characteristic	Total all family households	Total multigenerational households	Race of family reference person				
			White alone	White alone, non-Hispanic	Black alone	Asian alone	Hispanic (any race)
Total all family households	80,506	3,726	64,614	54,146	9,651	4,149	11,585
Total multigenerational households	3,726	3,726	2,533	1,638	799	262	970
Percent multigenerational households	4.6	100.0	3.9	3.0	8.3	6.3	8.4
Number	**80,506**	**3,726**	**2,533**	**1,638**	**799**	**262**	**970**
Type of multigenerational household[a]							
Householder with child and grandchild	2,390	2,390	1,690	1,187	544	91	539
Householder with child and parent	1,274	1,274	798	425	245	164	412
Householder with grandchild and parent or four-generation household	62	62	44	25	9	6	19
Presence of foreign-born persons in household							
No foreign-born persons	63,829	2,519	1,716	1,463	671	30	286
Householder is foreign-born	3,010	105	81	18	18	4	68
Other person beside householder is foreign-born	13,667	1,102	736	157	109	228	616
Poverty status							
Below 100 percent of poverty	9,486	694	414	206	209	40	229
100 to 199 percent of poverty	6,572	514	362	196	100	20	183
200 percent of poverty and above	64,448	2,518	1,756	1,236	489	202	558
Presence of children under 18[b]							
No children under 18	45,522	2,252	1,591	1,157	493	105	458
At least one child under 18	34,984	1,474	942	481	306	157	512
At least one child under 15	30,413	1,222	776	372	244	138	448
At least one child under 12	25,596	990	621	299	199	115	360
At least one child under 6	15,342	581	366	161	110	68	228
At least one child under 3	8,606	296	192	79	58	27	126
At least one child under 1	2,802	106	75	25	17	7	54
Percent	**100.0**	**100.0**	**100.0**	**100.0**	**100.0**	**100.0**	**100.0**
Type of multigenerational household[a]							
Householder with child and grandchild	3.0	64.1	66.7	72.5	68.1	34.7	55.6
Householder with child and parent	1.6	34.2	31.5	25.9	30.7	62.6	42.5
Householder with grandchild and parent or four-generation household	0.1	1.7	1.7	1.5	1.1	2.3	2.0
Presence of foreign-born persons in household							
No foreign-born persons	79.3	67.6	67.7	89.3	84.0	11.5	29.5
Householder is foreign-born	3.7	2.8	3.2	1.1	2.3	1.5	7.0
Other person beside householder is foreign-born	17.0	29.6	29.1	9.6	13.6	87.0	63.5
Poverty status							
Below 100 percent of poverty	11.8	18.6	16.3	12.6	26.2	15.3	23.6
100 to 199 percent of poverty	8.2	13.8	14.3	12.0	12.5	7.6	18.9
200 percent of poverty and above	80.1	67.6	69.3	75.5	61.2	77.1	57.5
Presence of children under 18[b]							
No children under 18	56.5	60.4	62.8	70.6	61.7	40.1	47.2
At least one child under 18	43.5	39.6	37.2	29.4	38.3	59.9	52.8
At least one child under 15	37.8	32.8	30.6	22.7	30.5	52.7	46.2
At least one child under 12	31.8	26.6	24.5	18.3	24.9	43.9	37.1
At least one child under 6	19.1	15.6	14.4	9.8	13.8	26.0	23.5
At least one child under 3	10.7	7.9	7.6	4.8	7.3	10.3	13.0
At least one child under 1	3.5	2.8	3.0	1.5	2.1	2.7	5.6

[a]For total all family households, categories do not add to total or 100 percent, as there is no category for nonmultigenerational households.
[b]Excludes ever-married children under 18 years, as well as householders.

SOURCE: Jonathan Vespa, Jamie M. Lewis, and Rose M. Kreider, "Table 2. Multigenerational Households by Race and Hispanic Origin of Reference Person: CPS 2012," in *America's Families and Living Arrangements: 2012*, U.S. Census Bureau, August 2013, https://www.census.gov/prod/2013pubs/p20-570.pdf (accessed September 3, 2017)

was created by Congress in 1938 to improve the housing industry during the Great Depression. Its smaller counterpart, Freddie Mac, is a shareholder-owned company created by Congress in 1970 to support homeownership. Both Fannie Mae and Freddie Mac buy mortgages, package them into bonds backed by the government, and sell them to investors, thereby freeing up money for additional mortgage lending. Besides these efforts,

minority homeownership was also helped by a strong economy and a robust stock market during the 1990s and by low mortgage rates during the first few years of the first decade of the 21st century.

President George W. Bush (1946–) also made minority homeownership a priority of his administration. During his tenure, several initiatives were launched to help

TABLE 2.9

Same-sex couples, by differences in race, Hispanic origin, and age, 2015

Household characteristics	Married opposite-sex couples	Unmarried opposite-sex couples	Total same-sex couples	Total male-male couples	Total female-female couples
	Percent	Percent	Percent	Percent	Percent
Total households (number)	56,290,438	6,914,218	858,896	412,001	446,895
Age of householder					
15 to 24 years	1.2	11.7	4.0	3.0	4.9
25 to 34 years	13.1	35.2	17.8	15.5	19.9
35 to 44 years	19.9	21.3	19.3	18.6	19.9
45 to 54 years	22.0	15.8	25.3	27.0	23.7
55 to 64 years	21.2	10.1	19.0	20.4	17.7
65 years and over	22.5	5.9	14.6	15.4	13.9
Average age of householder (years)	52.0	39.2	48.2	49.4	47.2
Average age of spouse/partner (years)	51.3	38.4	46.3	46.8	45.9
Race of householder					
White	81.8	76.2	83.0	84.7	81.4
Black or African American	6.9	11.4	7.8	5.8	9.7
American Indian or Alaska Native	0.5	1.1	0.7	0.4	0.9
Asian	5.7	2.4	3.1	3.6	2.5
Native Hawaiian or Pacific Islander	0.1	0.2	0.3	0.3	0.3
Some other race	3.3	5.8	2.6	2.6	2.6
Two or more races	1.6	2.9	2.6	2.6	2.6
Percent of couples interracial	7.0	13.5	15.1	17.8	12.6
Hispanic origin of householder					
Hispanic or Latino origin (of any race)	12.7	19.1	11.4	11.6	11.2
White alone, not Hispanic or Latino	72.9	64.0	75.0	76.5	73.7
Educational attainment					
Householder has at least a bachelor's degree	38.8	25.2	48.2	51.5	45.1
Both partners with at least a bachelor's degree	24.2	13.1	30.1	30.8	29.4
Employment status[a]					
Householder employed	67.2	78.5	74.5	74.6	74.4
Both partners employed	48.0	60.4	59.5	59.3	59.6
Children in the household					
Children in the household[b]	39.4	40.2	17.2	9.7	24.1
Own children in the household	39.3	37.1	16.0	9.2	22.2
Household income					
Less than $35,000	14.3	25.5	14.1	10.7	17.2
$35,000 to $49,999	11.2	15.7	10.4	8.6	12.0
$50,000 to $74,999	19.1	22.1	17.3	16.8	17.9
$75,000 to $99,999	16.1	14.6	15.4	14.6	16.1
$100,000 or more	39.3	22.0	42.8	49.3	36.8
Median Household Income (dollars)[c]	82,293	58,879	87,300	98,486	79,494
Home tenure					
Own	79.0	41.8	66.2	68.1	64.4
Rent	21.0	58.2	33.8	31.9	35.6

[a]Employed or in the armed forces.
[b]Includes own children and nonrelatives of the householder under 18 years.
[c]In previous years this table displayed estimates of mean household income.

SOURCE: Adapted from "Table 1. Household Characteristics of Opposite-Sex and Same-Sex Couple Households: ACS 2015," in *Families and Living Arrangements*, U.S. Census Bureau, 2016, https://www2.census.gov/programs-surveys/demo/tables/same-sex/time-series/ssc-house-characteristics/ssex-tables-2015.xlsx (accessed September 4, 2017)

minority and low-income Americans buy homes. Arguing that many Americans could afford a monthly mortgage payment but lacked the funds for a down payment, Bush signed in 2003 the American Dream Downpayment Assistance Act, authorizing $200 million per year in down payment assistance to at least 40,000 low-income families.

However, expanding mortgages to low- and moderate-income borrowers at high interest rates, combined with an increase in the prevalence of high-risk home loans—called the subprime market—ultimately destabilized the American economy. By 2007 an increasing number of borrowers were unable to meet their mortgage payments and home foreclosures skyrocketed. Home prices declined, and securities backed by subprime mortgages, which were widely owned by financial firms, lost their value. A precipitous decline in the capital available to banks began, leading to a worldwide credit crisis and plunging the United States into a deep recession. Due to the mounting crisis, homeownership rates began declining among some groups as early as 2005. By 2007 rates

TABLE 2.10

Living arrangements of children and marital status of parents, by age, race, and Hispanic origin, 2016

[Numbers in thousands]

	Total	Living with both parents		Living with mother only					Living with father only					Living with neither parent
		Married to each other	Not married to each other	Married spouse absent	Widowed	Divorced	Separated	Never married	Married spouse absent	Widowed	Divorced	Separated	Never married	No parent present
All children	73,745	47,724	2,955	878	606	5,131	2,389	8,219	160	174	1,164	366	1,142	2,836
Age of child														
Under 1 year	3,877	2,520	441	20	4	61	72	546	1	2	6	11	92	101
1–2 years	8,067	5,222	605	93	26	212	202	1,205	11	2	30	28	168	263
3–5 years	11,887	7,708	612	120	42	528	359	1,644	22	8	106	64	216	457
6–8 years	12,410	7,947	517	162	64	783	425	1,569	29	24	158	85	193	455
9–11 years	12,401	8,123	353	151	102	1,015	436	1,260	28	30	212	64	174	453
12–14 years	12,322	8,173	226	151	129	1,099	458	1,075	32	43	251	67	166	452
15–17 years	12,780	8,031	202	180	239	1,432	437	919	37	65	401	47	133	656
Race														
White alone	53,628	37,819	2,035	494	424	3,766	1,546	3,501	114	140	959	285	776	1,769
Black alone	11,101	3,785	509	269	115	907	637	3,794	25	15	121	43	235	648
Asian alone	3,758	3,248	83	52	34	84	38	71	14	13	12	5	23	81
All remaining single races and all race combinations	5,258	2,872	328	64	33	374	168	854	8	7	72	34	109	338
Race														
Hispanic*	18,231	10,990	1,262	269	114	993	961	2,269	57	40	189	90	324	673
White alone, Non-Hispanic	37,951	28,063	956	275	334	2,945	704	1,783	58	102	825	198	501	1,207
All remaining single races and all race combinations, non-hispanic	17,563	8,672	737	334	158	1,193	725	4,167	45	32	150	77	317	956

*Hispanics may be of any race.

Note: Excludes children in group quarters, and those who are a family reference person or spouse.

SOURCE: Adapted from "Table C3. Living Arrangements of Children under 18 Years and Marital Status of Parents, by Age, Sex, Race, and Hispanic Origin and Selected Characteristics of the Child for All Children: 2016," in *America's Families and Living Arrangements: 2016*, U.S. Census Bureau, April 6, 2017, https://www2.census.gov/programs-surveys/demo/tables/families/2016/cps-2016/tabc3-all.xls (accessed September 3, 2017)

TABLE 2.11

Homeownership rates by race and Hispanic origin of householder, 1994–2016

	1994	1995	1996[a]	1997	1998	1999	2000	2001	2002	2002[c]	2003	2004
U.S. total	**64.0**	**64.7**	**65.4**	**65.7**	**66.3**	**66.8**	**67.4**	**67.8**	**67.9**	**67.9**	**68.3**	**69.0**
White, total	67.7	68.7	69.1	69.3	70.0	70.5	71.1	71.6	71.8	71.7	72.1	72.8
Non-Hispanic white	70.0	70.9	71.7	72.0	72.6	73.2	73.8	74.3	74.5	74.7	75.4	76.0
Black,total	42.3	42.7	44.1	44.8	45.6	46.3	47.2	47.7	47.3	47.4	48.1	49.1
All other races, total	47.7	47.2	51.0	52.5	53.0	53.7	53.5	54.2	54.7	54.5	56.0	58.6
American Indian or Alaskan Native	51.7	55.8	51.6	51.7	54.3	56.1	56.2	55.4	54.6	54.0	54.3	55.6
Asian or Native Hawaiian/Pacific Islander	51.3	50.8	50.8	52.8	52.6	53.1	52.8	53.9	54.7	54.6	56.3	59.8
Other	36.1	37.4	NA	NA	NA	NA	NA	NA	NA	NA		
Hispanic or Latino	41.2	42.1	42.8	43.3	44.7	45.5	46.3	47.3	48.2	47.0	46.7	48.1
Non-Hispanic	65.9	66.7	67.4	67.8	68.3	68.9	69.5	69.9	70.0	70.2	70.8	71.5

	2005	2006	2007	2008	2009	2010	2011	2012	2013	2014	2015	2016
U.S. total	**68.9**	**68.8**	**68.1**	**67.8**	**67.4**	**66.9**	**66.1**	**65.4**	**65.1**	**64.5**	**63.7**	**63.4**
White alone, total	72.7	72.6	72.0	71.7	71.4	71.0	70.3	69.8	69.6	68.9	68.2	68.2
Non-Hispanic white alone	75.8	75.8	75.2	75.0	74.8	74.4	73.8	73.5	73.3	72.6	71.9	71.9
Black alone, total	48.2	47.9	47.2	47.4	46.2	45.4	44.9	43.9	43.1	43.0	42.3	41.6
All other races alone, total[b]	59.2	59.9	59.2	58.5	57.8	57.0	56.4	55.0	55.1	55.0	53.8	52.8
American Indian or Alaskan Native alone	58.2	58.2	56.9	56.5	56.2	52.3	53.5	51.1	51.0	52.2	50.3	47.6
Asian or Native Hawaiian/Pacific Islander alone	60.1	60.8	60.0	59.5	59.3	58.9	58.0	56.6	57.4	57.3	56.1	55.4
Hispanic or Latino	49.5	49.7	49.7	49.1	48.4	47.5	46.9	46.1	46.1	45.4	45.6	46.0
Non-Hispanic	71.2	71.2	70.5	70.3	69.8	69.4	68.7	68.2	67.9	67.3	66.4	66.1

NA = Not applicable.

[a]From 1996 to 2002, those answering 'other' for race were allocated to one of the 4 race categories.

[b]White, black, American Indian, Aleut. or Eskimo (one category), or Asian or Native Hawaiian.

[b]Asian, Native Hawaiian or other Pacific Islander, American Indian or Alaska Native (only one race reported) and two or more races.

[c]Revised based on the 2000 Census.

SOURCE: "Table 22. Homeownership Rates by Race and Ethnicity of Householder: 1994 to 2016," in *Housing Vacancies and Homeownership Annual Statistics, 2016*, U.S. Census Bureau, February 21, 2017, https://www.census.gov/housing/annual16/ann16t_22.xlsx (accessed September 4, 2017)

were in decline across all groups, a trend that would continue into 2013.

By mid-2008 Fannie Mae and Freddie Mac were nearly in ruins. In September 2008 the director of the Federal Housing Finance Agency announced that Fannie Mae and Freddie Mac, which together guaranteed about half of the U.S. mortgage market, would be put into a conservatorship of the agency. Dawn Kopecki and Alison Vekshin note in "Frank to Recommend Replacing Fannie Mae, Freddie Mac" (Bloomberg.com, January 22, 2010) that the companies, which were essentially bailed out by the federal government, received $110.6 billion in taxpayer-funded aid between 2008 and 2009.

In "Real Estate Matters: Is the Housing Crisis Over? Maybe Not for Minorities" (WashingtonPost.com, June 11, 2013), Ilyce R. Glink and Samuel J. Tamkin report that between 2008 and 2013 foreclosure proceedings were completed on roughly 4.4 million U.S. homes. Foreclosures tend to drive down the value of other homes in the same neighborhood, effectively making all of the other homeowners in the area less wealthy. Glink and Tamkin note that "homeowners in Detroit and other communities with significant minority populations lost an average of $2,008 in net worth" in 2012 due to foreclosures, an amount that was higher than the national average. Robert Jablon reports in "LA Sues Wells Fargo, Citigroup over Foreclosures" (Associated Press, December 5, 2013) that

the city of Los Angeles sued the lenders Wells Fargo and Citigroup in 2013. The city's suit alleged that minority borrowers were targeted for risky, subprime loans in the years leading up to the mortgage crisis. After the crisis hit, many of these borrowers lost their homes to foreclosure.

According to Ben Lane, in "Court of Appeals Hands Wells Fargo Victory over Los Angeles in Fair Housing Lawsuit" (HousingWire.com, May 30, 2017), in 2015 a district judge dismissed the lawsuit filed against Wells Fargo by the city of Los Angeles, citing a lack of evidence that the bank had engaged in discriminatory lending practices. Although the city promptly filed an appeal, the ruling was upheld two years later by the U.S. Court of Appeals for the Ninth Circuit. Despite this setback, a new avenue for seeking redress against lenders emerged in May 2017, when the U.S. Supreme Court ruled in *Bank of America Corp. v. City of Miami, Florida* (No. 15-1111) that federal housing laws gave cities the right to sue banks for unfair lending practices. In "Supreme Court Clears the Way for Cities, Including L.A., to Sue Banks over Foreclosure Crisis" (LATimes.com, May 1, 2017), David G. Savage explains that the decision expanded the antidiscrimination clause in the Fair Housing Act, enabling cities to claim to be an "aggrieved person" when discriminatory lending practices have a negative financial impact on municipal budgets. According to Savage, other cities, including Miami, Florida, and San Francisco, California, were poised to file lawsuits against major banks in the wake of the verdict.

In the meantime, some banks began implementing new rules designed to ease lending requirements for minority home buyers. Joe Light reports in "Fannie Mae Unveils Mortgage Program to Help Minority Borrowers" (WSJ.com, August 25, 2015) that in August 2015 Fannie Mae introduced a program aimed at strengthening the financial credentials of low-income borrowers. Under the terms of the new regulations, Fannie Mae allowed prospective borrowers to include income from nonborrowers living in their household when seeking to qualify for home loans. Citing an email written by a spokesperson for the Federal Housing Finance Agency, which regulates Fannie Mae, Light observes that the program was designed to "reflect today's economic reality, where many people live in non-traditional households with multi-generational family members, friends, and/or boarders."

CHAPTER 3
EDUCATION

In *The Condition of Education 2005* (June 2005, https://nces.ed.gov/pubs2005/2005094.pdf), the National Center for Education Statistics (NCES) reports that two factors—rising immigration and the baby boom echo—boosted public school enrollment beginning in the latter part of the 1980s. According to Grace Kena et al., in *The Condition of Education 2016* (May 2016, https://nces.ed.gov/pubs2016/2016144.pdf), public school enrollment reached 50 million students during the 2013–14 academic year, and was projected to continue to set new enrollment records each year through 2025–26, with a projected enrollment of 51.4 million students in that year.

Along with this increase in enrollment came an increase in the proportion of public school students who were considered to be part of a minority group, due largely to the growth in the Hispanic public school population. In 2013, 49.7% of public school students enrolled in elementary through 12th grade belonged to a minority group. (See Table 3.1.) Hispanics (12.5 million; 24.9%) and African Americans (7.8 million; 15.6%) accounted for the largest number of minority students in public schools. These figures represented a significant increase since 1995, when white students made up 64.8% and minority students only 35.2% of the public school population. However, minority enrollment in public schools varies from region to region. As Figure 3.1 shows, minorities constituted a significantly larger portion of the public school population in the South and West than in the Midwest and Northeast. According to Kena et al., between 2003 and 2013 white enrollment declined in all four regions of the country, while the proportion of Hispanic students rose in all four regions during this span. The largest increase occurred in the South, where Hispanic enrollment in public schools rose seven percentage points between 2003 and 2013. In the West, Kena et al. explain, Hispanic enrollment (42%) exceeded white enrollment (39%) in 2013.

RISK FACTORS IN EDUCATION

In the United States education is often viewed as a way out of poverty to a better life. Many observers believe education is the key to narrowing the economic gap between the races. Although many individual minority students strive for, and achieve, great educational success, on average minority students perform less well than white students in school and are generally more likely than their white counterparts to drop out of school. Asian Americans are the exception to this rule. Many Asian American students accomplish stunning academic achievements. Educators point with pride to these high-achieving students, who have often overcome both language and cultural barriers. Why are some groups more at risk of failure, and other groups more likely to succeed in school?

The Early Childhood Longitudinal Study, Birth Cohort, a study by the NCES, attempts to begin answering this question by assessing preschoolers' readiness for school. The study collected information on a cohort (a group of individuals with several characteristics in common) of children born in 2001 and followed them through 2007, focusing on the children's early development and how parents prepared their children for school. Although at nine months of age little variation in mental and motor skills was found by race or ethnic group, several demographic characteristics were related to the likelihood of families engaging in activities that help prepare children for school. These characteristics include reading or telling children stories, singing to them, taking them on errands, playing peek-a-boo, and allowing them to play outside. The NCES indicates in *Condition of Education 2005* that in 2001–02 Asian American families were more likely than other minority groups to read to their children (26%), tell them stories (25%), and play peek-a-boo (73%), although they were less likely to facilitate outside playing (43%) and significantly less likely to take their children on errands (38%) than were other minority families.

TABLE 3.1

Number and percentage distribution of public elementary and high school students, by race/ethnicity, selected years 1995–2025

Region and year	Enrollment (in thousands)							Percentage distribution						
	Total	White	Black	Hispanic	Asian/Pacific Islander	American Indian/ Alaska Native	Two or more races	Total	White	Black	Hispanic	Asian/Pacific Islander	American Indian/ Alaska Native	Two or more races
United States														
1995	44,840	29,044	7,551	6,072	1,668	505	a	100.0	64.8	16.8	13.5	3.7	1.1	b
2000	47,204	28,878	8,100	7,726	1,950	550	a	100.0	61.2	17.2	16.4	4.1	1.2	b
2001	47,672	28,735	8,177	8,169	2,028	564	a	100.0	60.3	17.2	17.1	4.3	1.2	b
2002	48,183	28,618	8,299	8,594	2,088	583	a	100.0	59.4	17.2	17.8	4.3	1.2	b
2003	48,540	28,442	8,349	9,011	2,145	593	a	100.0	58.6	17.2	18.6	4.4	1.2	b
2004	48,795	28,318	8,386	9,317	2,183	591	a	100.0	58.0	17.2	19.1	4.5	1.2	b
2005	49,113	28,005	8,445	9,787	2,279	598	a	100.0	57.0	17.2	19.9	4.6	1.2	b
2006	49,316	27,801	8,422	10,166	2,332	595	a	100.0	56.4	17.1	20.6	4.7	1.2	b
2007	49,291	27,454	8,392	10,454	2,396	594	a	100.0	55.7	17.0	21.2	4.9	1.2	b
2008	49,266	27,057	8,358	10,563	2,451	589	247c	100.0	54.9	17.0	21.4	5.0	1.2	0.5c
2009	49,361	26,702	8,245	10,991	2,484	601	338c	100.0	54.1	16.7	22.3	5.0	1.2	0.7c
2010	49,484	25,933	7,917	11,439	2,466	566	1,164	100.0	52.4	16.0	23.1	5.0	1.1	2.4
2011	49,522	25,602	7,827	11,759	2,513	547	1,272	100.0	51.7	15.8	23.7	5.1	1.1	2.6
2012	49,771	25,386	7,803	12,104	2,552	534	1,393	100.0	51.0	15.7	24.3	5.1	1.1	2.8
2013	50,045	25,160	7,805	12,452	2,593	523	1,511	100.0	50.3	15.6	24.9	5.2	1.0	3.0
2014d	50,132	25,007	7,828	12,740	2,637	516	1,404	100.0	49.9	15.6	25.4	5.3	1.0	2.8
2015d	50,268	24,789	7,817	13,030	2,678	508	1,445	100.0	49.3	15.6	25.9	5.3	1.0	2.9
2016d	50,385	24,566	7,806	13,306	2,723	499	1,484	100.0	48.8	15.5	26.4	5.4	1.0	2.9
2017d	50,477	24,340	7,796	13,563	2,769	490	1,519	100.0	48.2	15.4	26.9	5.5	1.0	3.0
2018d	50,528	24,128	7,776	13,791	2,799	483	1,552	100.0	47.8	15.4	27.3	5.5	1.0	3.1
2019d	50,618	23,993	7,754	13,964	2,846	472	1,590	100.0	47.4	15.3	27.6	5.6	0.9	3.1
2020d	50,774	23,882	7,756	14,142	2,892	463	1,638	100.0	47.0	15.3	27.9	5.7	0.9	3.2
2021d	50,928	23,777	7,774	14,300	2,934	457	1,685	100.0	46.7	15.3	28.1	5.8	0.9	3.3
2022d	51,084	23,686	7,799	14,437	2,979	451	1,731	100.0	46.4	15.3	28.3	5.8	0.9	3.4
2023d	51,225	23,614	7,819	14,541	3,029	447	1,777	100.0	46.1	15.3	28.4	5.9	0.9	3.5
2024d	51,338	23,544	7,832	14,615	3,083	443	1,821	100.0	45.9	15.3	28.5	6.0	0.9	3.5
2025d	51,420	23,465	7,836	14,677	3,139	439	1,863	100.0	45.6	15.2	28.5	6.1	0.9	3.6

aNot available.
bNot applicable.
cFor this year, data on students of two or more races were reported by only a small number of states. Therefore, the data are not comparable to figures for 2010 and later years.
dProjected.

Note: Race categories exclude persons of Hispanic ethnicity. Enrollment data for students not reported by race/ethnicity were prorated by state and grade to match state totals. Prior to 2008, data on students of two or more races were not collected. Some data have been revised from previously published figures. Detail may not sum to totals because of rounding.

SOURCE: Adapted from Thomas D. Snyder, Cristobal de Brey, and Sally A. Dillow, "Table 203.50. Enrollment and Percentage Distribution of Enrollment in Public Elementary and Secondary Schools, by Race/Ethnicity and Region: Selected Years, Fall 1995 through Fall 2025," in *Digest of Educational Statistics 2015*, U.S. Department of Education, Institute of Education Sciences, National Center for Education Statistics, December 2016, https://nces.ed.gov/programs/digest/d15/tables/xls/tabn203.50.xls (accessed September 4, 2017)

FIGURE 3.1

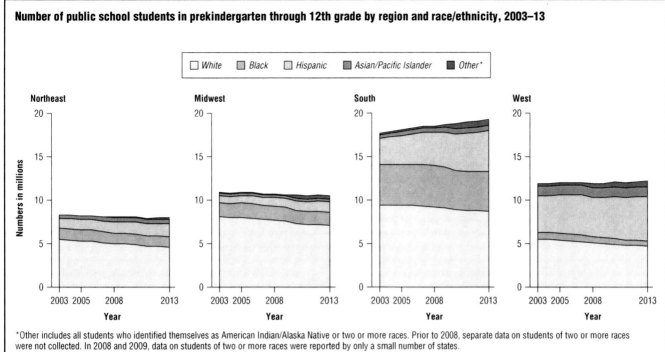

Number of public school students in prekindergarten through 12th grade by region and race/ethnicity, 2003–13

*Other includes all students who identified themselves as American Indian/Alaska Native or two or more races. Prior to 2008, separate data on students of two or more races were not collected. In 2008 and 2009, data on students of two or more races were reported by only a small number of states.
Note: Race categories exclude persons of Hispanic ethnicity.

SOURCE: Grace Kena et al., "Figure 2. Number of Students Enrolled in Public Elementary and Secondary Schools, by Region and Race/Ethnicity: Fall 2003–Fall 2013," in *The Condition of Education 2016*, U.S. Department of Education, Institute of Education Sciences, National Center for Education Statistics, May 2016, https://nces.ed.gov/pubs2016/2016144.pdf (accessed September 4, 2017)

In contrast, both African American and Hispanic families were less likely to read to (23% and 21%, respectively) and tell their children stories (24% and 21%, respectively), and more likely to sing to them (73% and 70%, respectively) and play peek-a-boo (61% and 64%, respectively) than were white families in 2001–02. This may be partly because poor families are much less likely to read to their children or tell them stories than are nonpoor families, and African American and Hispanic families are disproportionately poor. African American families, white families, and Hispanic families were about equally likely to take their children on errands and facilitate outside playing.

In its third wave, the Early Childhood Longitudinal Study, Birth Cohort, collected more specific information about the readiness of preschoolers for school. Researchers assessed children between the ages of 48 and 57 months. In *Preschool: First Findings from the Preschool Follow-Up of the Early Childhood Longitudinal Study, Birth Cohort* (October 2007, https://nces.ed.gov/pubs 2008/2008025.pdf), Jodi Jacobson Chernoff et al. note that children's language knowledge—or ability to understand words or retell a story—varied by race and ethnicity, with non-Hispanic white children (9.2) scoring the highest, followed by non-Hispanic African American children (8), Asian American children (7.9), Native American or Alaskan Native children (7.9), and Hispanic

children (7.4). Overall literacy, such as letter recognition, and understanding aspects of reading, such as reading from left to right, also varied by race and ethnicity. Asian American children (17.5) scored the highest on overall literacy, followed by non-Hispanic white children (14.2), non-Hispanic African American children (12), Hispanic children (10.7), and Native American or Alaskan Native children (9.6). Asian American preschoolers (26.3) also scored the highest on mathematics knowledge and skills, followed by non-Hispanic white preschoolers (24.2), non-Hispanic African American preschoolers (20.6), Hispanic preschoolers (20.1), and Native American or Alaskan Native preschoolers (17.6). Therefore, overall, Native American or Alaskan Native, Hispanic, and non-Hispanic African American children were less prepared for school than were either non-Hispanic white or Asian American children.

Kristin Denton Flanagan and Cameron McPhee note in *The Children Born in 2001 at Kindergarten Entry: First Findings from the Kindergarten Data Collections of the Early Childhood Longitudinal Study, Birth Cohort* (October 2009, https://nces.ed.gov/pubs2010/2010005.pdf) that by the time these children entered school, the average early reading scale scores varied considerably by race and ethnicity. Asian American children (51.9) scored the highest, followed by non-Hispanic white children (46.4), non-Hispanic African American children (41.1), Hispanic children (39.4), and Native American or Alaskan Native children (37.1). Mathematics scale scores also varied by race and ethnic group, although less dramatically. Asian American children (48.7) scored the highest and non-Hispanic white children (46.5) scored the second highest. Non-Hispanic African American children (40.4), Hispanic children (40.3), and Native American or Alaskan Native children (37.3) scored substantially lower.

A subsequent longitudinal study conducted by the NCES examined children who first entered kindergarten during the 2010–11 school year. As in the previous study, reading and math scores varied according to racial and ethnic backgrounds. Gail M. Mulligan et al. reveal in *Findings from the First-Grade Rounds of the Early Childhood Longitudinal Study, Kindergarten Class of 2010–11* (November 2014, https://nces.ed.gov/pubs2015/2015019.pdf) the results of reading and math testing among first graders during the 2011–12 school year. In reading, Asian American (74.9) and non-Hispanic white (73.3) students produced the highest scores, followed by Native Hawaiian or Pacific Islander (69.9), Native American or Alaskan Native (68.3), non-Hispanic African American (67.9), and Hispanic (65.8) students. Asian Americans (68.1) and non-Hispanic whites (67.5) also scored highest in math among first graders that year, followed by Native Hawaiians or Pacific Islanders (62.4), Native Americans or Alaskan Natives (62), Hispanics (58.7), and non-Hispanic African Americans (57.8). Mulligan et al. reveal in *Findings from the Third-Grade Round of the Early Childhood Longitudinal Study, Kindergarten Class of 2010–11* (May 2016, https://nces.ed.gov/pubs2016/2016094.pdf) that these tendencies shifted somewhat when the children in this age group reached the third grade. During the 2013–14 school year non-Hispanic white (114.3) and Asian American (113.9) third graders again scored highest in reading, followed by Native American or Alaskan Native (111.2), Native Hawaiian or Pacific Islander (109.3), Hispanic (107.6), and non-Hispanic African American (107) third graders. Asian American third graders (104.3) scored highest in math during the 2013–14 school year, followed by non-Hispanic white (102.9), Native American or Alaskan Native (99.2), Native Hawaiian or Pacific Islander (97.1), Hispanic (94.3), and non-Hispanic African American (90.2) third graders.

PREPRIMARY EDUCATION

One activity that can help preschoolers prepare for elementary school is attending center-based early childhood programs. In *Status and Trends in the Education of Racial and Ethnic Minorities* (September 2007, https://nces.ed.gov/pubs2007/2007039.pdf), Angelina Kewal-Ramani et al. state that "research has suggested that intensive, high-quality preschool programs can have positive effects on the cognitive and academic development of low-income minority children, both in the short- and long-term." Kena et al. report in *Condition of Education 2016* that 59% of all four-year-olds who were not yet enrolled in kindergarten were enrolled in center-based preschools in October 2014. In addition, 41% of three-year-olds, along with 14% of five-year-olds who were not yet enrolled in kindergarten, were enrolled in center-based preschools. Among children between the ages of three and five years who were not yet enrolled in kindergarten in October 2014, whites (41%) were the most likely to be attending center-based preschools, followed by Asian Americans (40%), African Americans (39%), Hispanics (32%), and Native Americans or Alaskan Natives (31%). (See Figure 3.2.)

KINDERGARTEN, ELEMENTARY, AND SECONDARY SCHOOL

According to Kena et al., in *Condition of Education 2016*, approximately 80% of children aged three to five years were enrolled in kindergarten full-time in 2014. Overall, there were 50 million students enrolled in public school at the beginning of the 2013–14 school year. Half (25.2 million) of these students were white; 12.5 million (25%) were Hispanic, 7.8 million (16%) were African American, 2.6 million (5%) were Asian or Pacific Islander, and 500,000 (1%) were Native American or Alaskan Native. (See Figure 3.3.) As Figure 3.3 shows, the proportion of Hispanic students in American public schools was expected to rise to 29% by 2025, while the proportion of white students was projected to shrink to 46%. Much of this shift can be attributed to broader changes in the U.S. population. As Table 1.3 in Chapter 1 shows, the nation's Hispanic population was projected to grow 11.98% between 2015 and 2020 and 10.84% between 2020 and 2025. By contrast, the non-Hispanic white population was projected to grow 0.53% between 2015 and 2020 and 0.23% between 2020 and 2025.

Educational Progress

READING PERFORMANCE. The ability to read is fundamental to most aspects of education. When students cannot read well, they usually cannot succeed in other subject areas and will eventually have additional problems in a society that requires increasingly sophisticated job skills.

The National Assessment of Educational Progress (NAEP) measures reading and mathematics proficiency at four levels. A rating of basic indicates that students have achieved partial mastery of fundamental knowledge and skills at their grade level; below level indicates less than this level. Proficient indicates solid mastery of knowledge and skills, and advanced indicates superior achievement and performance.

Thomas D. Snyder, Cristobal de Brey, and Sally A. Dillow report in *Digest of Education Statistics 2015* (December 2016, https://nces.ed.gov/pubs2016/2016014.pdf) that in

FIGURE 3.2

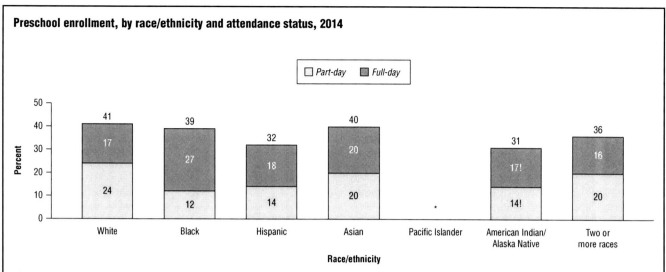

Preschool enrollment, by race/ethnicity and attendance status, 2014

*Reporting standards not met.
!Interpret data with caution. The coefficient of variation (CV) for this estimate is between 30 and 50 percent.
Note: Race categories exclude persons of Hispanic ethnicity. Enrollment data include only those children in preschool programs and do not include those enrolled in kindergarten or primary programs. Data are based on sample surveys of the civilian noninstitutionalized population. Detail may not sum to totals because of rounding.

SOURCE: Grace Kena et al., "Figure 4. Percentage of 3- to 5-Year-Old Children Enrolled in Preschool Programs, by Race/Ethnicity and Attendance Status: October 2014," in *The Condition of Education 2016*, U.S. Department of Education, Institute of Education Sciences, National Center for Education Statistics, May 2016, https://nces.ed.gov/pubs2016/2016144.pdf (accessed September 4, 2017)

FIGURE 3.3

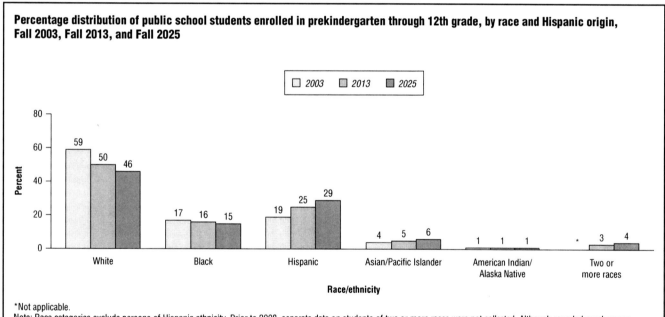

Percentage distribution of public school students enrolled in prekindergarten through 12th grade, by race and Hispanic origin, Fall 2003, Fall 2013, and Fall 2025

*Not applicable.
Note: Race categories exclude persons of Hispanic ethnicity. Prior to 2008, separate data on students of two or more races were not collected. Although rounded numbers are displayed, the figures are based on unrounded estimates. Detail may not sum to totals because of rounding. Data for 2025 are projected.

SOURCE: Grace Kena et al., "Figure 1. Percentage Distribution of Students Enrolled in Public Elementary and Secondary Schools, by Race/Ethnicity: Fall 2003, Fall 2013, and Fall 2025," in *The Condition of Education 2016*, U.S. Department of Education, Institute of Education Sciences, National Center for Education Statistics, May 2016, https://nces.ed.gov/pubs2016/2016144.pdf (accessed September 4, 2017)

2015 the average NAEP reading scale score for fourth graders was 221, while for eighth graders it was 264. Table 3.2 offers a breakdown of average reading scale scores for the years 2013 and 2015, by race and ethnicity, as well as for select cities. It shows that Asian American and white fourth graders scored substantially higher than both African American and Hispanic fourth graders in both years. In 2015 Asian American fourth graders had an average scale reading score of 240, compared with 232 for whites, 208 for Hispanics, and 206 for African Americans. Similar differences existed for eighth

TABLE 3.2

Average National Assessment of Educational Progress reading scores of 4th- and 8th-grade students, by race, Hispanic origin, jurisdiction, and major urban school district, 2009, 2011, 2013, and 2015

Grade level and jurisdiction or specific urban district	Average reading scale score[a]												Percent of students 2015	
	2009	2011	2013					2015					At or above basic[b]	At or above proficient[c]
	All students	All students	All students	White	Black	Hispanic	Asian	All students	White	Black	Hispanic	Asian		
4th grade														
United States	220	220	221	231	205	207	237	221	232	206	208	240	68	35
All large cities[d]	210	211	212	235	202	204	229	214	235	204	206	233	59	27
Selected urban districts														
Albuquerque (NM)	e	209	207	232	f	199	f	207	227	f	202	f	54	24
Atlanta (GA)	209	212	214	252	204	208	f	212	251	202	205	f	54	26
Austin (TX)	220	224	221	250	206	208	f	220	248	†	207	†	65	35
Baltimore City (MD)	202	200	204	233	201	f	234	199	217	196	200	230	40	11
Boston (MA)	215	217	214	237	205	210	238	219	241	214	214	246	65	29
Charlotte (NC)	225	224	226	245	215	212	235	226	245	216	212	248	72	39
Chicago (IL)	202	203	206	239	198	203	f	213	250	205	205	f	58	27
Cleveland (OH)	194	193	190	206	185	191	f	197	210	193	199	f	39	11
Dallas (TX)	204	204	205	231	201	204	f	204	240	202	200	f	47	17
Detroit (MI)	187	191	190	f	188	199	f	186	f	184	195	f	27	6
District of Columbia (DC)	203	201	206	260	192	211	e	214	262	202	206	f	56	30
Duval County (FL)	e	e	225	e	e	e	e	225	236	212	225	f	73	35
Fresno (CA)	197	194	196	218	187	192	199	199	220	186	196	207	42	13
Hillsborough County (FL)		231	228	237	214	223	247	230	242	216	221	f	76	41
Houston (TX)	211	213	208	238	202	204	245	210	246	207	204	f	54	23
Jefferson County (KY)	219	223	221	233	203	221	f	222	232	208	217	f	67	36
Los Angeles (CA)	197	201	205	237	204	199	222	204	233	202	197	237	50	21
Miami-Dade (FL)	221	221	223	239	209	225	f	226	239	210	229	e	74	39
Milwaukee (WI)	196	195	199	223	190	200	201	e	e	e	e	e	e	e
New York City (NY)	217	216	216	231	210	208	233	214	233	206	205	236	59	26
Philadelphia (PA)	195	199	200	214	196	193	215	201	216	198	188	221	44	14
San Diego (CA)	213	215	218	240	205	204	229	216	240	201	204	223	61	30
8th grade														
United States	262	264	266	275	250	255	280	264	273	247	253	280	75	33
All large cities[d]	252	255	258	276	246	253	273	257	277	246	251	272	67	25
Selected urban districts														
Albuquerque (NM)	e	254	256	275	f	250	f	251	267	f	246	f	62	19
Atlanta (GA)	250	253	255	294	249	254	f	252	290	246	258	f	61	20
Austin (TX)	261	261	261	286	245	251	f	261	290	241	249	f	70	33
Baltimore City (MD)	245	246	252	275	249	f	f	243	268	240	246	f	51	13
Boston (MA)	257	255	257	281	247	250	278	258	282	250	249	281	67	28

TABLE 3.2

Average National Assessment of Educational Progress reading scores of 4th- and 8th-grade students, by race, Hispanic origin, jurisdiction, and major urban school district, 2009, 2011, 2013, and 2015 [CONTINUED]

Grade level and jurisdiction or specific urban district	Average reading scale score[a]													Percent of students 2015	
	2009	2011	2013					2015						At or above basic[b]	At or above proficient[c]
	All students	All students	All students	White	Black	Hispanic	Asian	All students	White	Black	Hispanic	Asian			
Charlotte (NC)	259	265	266	286	253	259	f	263	284	251	254	f		73	33
Chicago (IL)	249	253	253	279	244	255	278	257	289	247	257	f		67	24
Cleveland (OH)	242	240	239	250	235	241	f	240	251	238	238	f		48	11
Dallas (TX)	e	248	251	f	244	253	f	250	f	241	251	f		60	17
Detroit (MI)	232	237	239	f	239	242	f	237	f	235	245	f		44	7
District of Columbia (DC)	240	237	245	301	237	247	f	245	299	236	244	f		52	19
Duval County (FL)	e	e	e	e	e	e	e	264	272	254	262	f		75	31
Fresno (CA)	240	238	245	265	236	241	247	242	256	238	238	249		51	13
Hillsborough County (FL)	e	264	267	277	252	263	f	261	274	246	254	f		71	29
Houston (TX)	252	252	252	284	245	250	284	252	280	246	247	f		61	20
Jefferson County (KY)	259	260	261	271	243	258	f	261	271	247	260	f		70	31
Los Angeles (CA)	244	246	250	276	240	245	272	251	273	248	246	274		62	20
Miami-Dade (FL)	261	260	259	278	245	261	f	265	279	254	266	f		77	32
Milwaukee (WI)	241	238	242	262	232	253	f	e	e	e	e	e		e	e
New York City (NY)	252	254	256	274	253	249	271	258	276	247	254	270		67	27
Philadelphia (PA)	247	247	249	261	244	243	265	248	263	240	244	276		58	16
San Diego (CA)	254	256	260	281	244	247	266	262	283	252	248	266		73	32

aScale ranges from 0 to 500.

bBasic denotes partial mastery of prerequisite knowledge and skills that are fundamental for proficient work at a given grade.

cProficient represents solid academic performance. Students reaching this level have demonstrated competency over challenging subject matter.

dIncludes public school students from all cities in the nation with populations of 250,000 or more, including the participating districts.

eNot available.

fReporting standards not met (too few cases for a reliable estimate).

Note: Race categories exclude persons of Hispanic ethnicity. Totals include racial/ethnic groups not shown separately.

SOURCE: Thomas D. Snyder, Cristobal de Brey, and Sally A. Dillow, "Table 221.80. Average National Assessment of Educational Progress (NAEP) Reading Scale Scores of 4th- and 8th-Grade Public School Students and Percentage Attaining Selected Reading Achievement Levels, by Race/Ethnicity and Jurisdiction or Specific Urban District: 2009, 2011, 2013, and 2015," in Digest of Educational Statistics 2015. U.S. Department of Education, Institute of Education Sciences, National Center for Education Statistics, December 2016, https://nces.ed.gov/programs/digest/d15/tables/xls/tabn221.80.xls (accessed September 4, 2017).

graders in 2015, when Asian Americans again had the highest average scale reading score (280), followed by whites (273), Hispanics (253), and African Americans (247).

SCIENCE AND MATHEMATICS PERFORMANCE. Since 1971 the NAEP has tested students to determine their mathematical knowledge, skills, and aptitudes. The measurement assesses students in five content areas: number sense, properties, and operations; measurement; geometry and spatial sense; data analysis, statistics, and probability; and algebra and functions. The NAEP also tests students on their knowledge of facts, understanding of concepts, and ability to reason in the life, physical, and earth sciences.

According to Snyder, de Brey, and Dillow, in *Digest of Education Statistics 2015*, the average NAEP mathematics scale score for fourth graders was 240 in 2015, while for eighth graders it was 281. (See Table 3.3.) Asian Americans outperformed all other racial and ethnic groups in mathematics for each grade that year, with an average scale score of 259 for fourth graders and 307 for eighth graders. In contrast, African American students scored the lowest in both grades, with average scale scores of 224 for fourth graders and 260 for eighth graders. Among 12th graders in 2009 (the date for which the most recent data were available), white students scored highest out of students whose most advanced mathematics course in school was algebra I or below, while Asian or Pacific Islander students scored highest among students who had taken calculus. (See Figure 3.4.)

Table 3.4 shows the results of the NAEP's science testing for 2009 and 2011. White students had the highest average score in the fourth and eighth grades, followed closely by Asian or Pacific Islander students. On the 12th-grade assessment Asian or Pacific Islander students slightly outscored white students on average. On the other side of the spectrum, African American students posted the lowest average scale scores in all three grades, while Hispanics posted the second-lowest average scale scores.

The consistently below-average scores of African American and Hispanic students in math and science has contributed to the underrepresentation of these groups in the growing number of jobs that require knowledge of science, technology, engineering, and mathematics (STEM). Chad Brooks reports in "Women and Minorities Underrepresented in STEM Jobs" (BusinessNewsDaily.com, September 10, 2013) that in 2011 African Americans held only 6% of all jobs in STEM-related fields, while Hispanics filled only 7% of all STEM jobs.

Dropping Out

When students drop out or fail to complete high school, both the individual and society suffer. Dropping out of school often results in limited occupational and economic opportunities for these individuals. Kewal-Ramani et al. note in *Status and Trends in the Education of Racial and Ethnic Minorities* that individuals who drop out of school have higher unemployment rates and lower earnings than individuals who graduate from high school. For society, high dropout rates may result in increased costs of government assistance programs for these individuals and their families, costly public training programs, and higher crime rates.

In 2014, 6.5% of all 16- to 24-year-olds had dropped out of high school. (See Table 3.5.) The dropout rate was highest among Hispanics (10.6%), followed by African Americans (7.4%) and whites (5.2%). However, since 1990 the percentage of dropouts in this age group has decreased for all race and ethnic groups, especially among Hispanics. (See Figure 3.5.)

In 2014 more than one out of five (20.8%) of foreign-born Hispanics dropped out of high school, compared with 7.6% of those born in the United States. (See Figure 3.6.) In *The Higher Dropout Rate of Foreign-Born Teens: The Role of Schooling Abroad* (November 1, 2005, http://www.pewhispanic.org/files/reports/55.pdf), the most recent report on this subject as of November 2017, Richard Fry of the Pew Hispanic Center notes that "foreign-born school dropout rates strongly depend on two linked factors: the age at which the teen migrated and the country that initially educated the teen." According to Fry, foreign-born students who have received inadequate educational opportunities prior to immigrating to the United States are considerably less likely to graduate from high school than native-born students. Based on the data relating to dropout rates for foreign-born Hispanics, these findings would suggest that many of these students received insufficient educational opportunities in their native countries.

Beginning in 2001 advocacy groups urged Congress to pass the Development, Relief, and Education for Alien Minors (DREAM) Act. The act would have allowed students to remain in the United States for up to six years after high school graduation, as long as they either attended college or joined the military. The act would also have allowed these students to pay in-state tuition rates for college in the state in which they had resided for at least five years. At the end of this period, students who completed the two-year college or military requirement would be allowed to become permanent residents. In 2006 the act passed the U.S. Senate as part of the Comprehensive Immigration Reform Act of 2006; however, in October 2007 it fell eight votes short of the 60 votes necessary to bring the bill up for full debate. The act was introduced again in the 110th Congress, where it died in committee, and in the 111th Congress, where it was again referred to committee. The administration of President Barack Obama (1961–) promoted passage of the DREAM Act as part of the National Defense Authorization

TABLE 3.3

Average National Assessment of Educational Progress mathematics scores of 4th- and 8th-grade students, by race, Hispanic origin, jurisdiction, and major urban school district, 2009, 2011, 2013, and 2015

Grade level and jurisdiction or specific urban district	2009 All students	2011 All students	Average mathematics scale score[a] 2013 All students	2013 White	2013 Black	2013 Hispanic	2013 Asian	2015 All students	2015 White	2015 Black	2015 Hispanic	2015 Asian	Percent of students 2015 At or above basic[b]	At or above proficient[c]
4th grade														
United States	239	240	241	250	224	230	260	240	248	224	230	259	81	39
All large cities[d]	231	233	235	254	223	229	258	234	251	222	230	253	75	32
Selected urban districts														
Albuquerque (NM)	—	235	235	253	—	229	—	231	249	—	226	—	72	28
Atlanta (GA)	225	228	233	269	222	233	—	228	267	218	225	—	65	26
Austin (TX)	240	245	245	264	228	237	—	246	268	226	237	—	85	47
Baltimore City (MD)	222	226	223	250	220	227	259	215	232	212	223	259	51	12
Boston (MA)	236	237	237	255	228	233	255	236	253	228	230	268	78	33
Charlotte (NC)	245	247	247	264	235	242	256	248	264	236	243	265	87	51
Chicago (IL)	222	224	231	261	221	230	—	232	262	221	230	—	71	30
Cleveland (OH)	213	216	216	233	210	221	—	219	233	215	221	—	58	13
Dallas (TX)	—	233	234	—	226	235	—	238	259	228	238	—	82	34
Detroit (MI)	200	203	204	—	201	214	—	205	—	202	215	—	36	5
District of Columbia (DC)	220	222	229	277	218	226	—	232	275	220	233	—	68	33
Duval County (FL)	—	—	—	—	—	—	—	243	254	230	240	—	86	41
Fresno (CA)	219	218	220	241	211	217	221	218	235	213	214	226	55	14
Hillsborough County (FL)	—	243	243	254	227	238	263	244	253	230	237	—	86	43
Houston (TX)	236	237	236	261	227	235	—	239	266	231	235	—	80	36
Jefferson County (KY)	233	235	234	245	220	224	—	236	245	225	226	—	77	34
Los Angeles (CA)	222	223	228	254	223	224	252	224	247	216	218	—	64	22
Miami-Dade (FL)	236	236	237	251	227	238	—	242	257	230	243	255	86	41
Milwaukee (WI)	220	220	221	246	209	227	234	—	—	—	—	—	—	—
New York City (NY)	237	234	236	251	225	228	257	231	242	220	226	254	73	26
Philadelphia (PA)	222	225	223	237	218	217	246	217	235	211	211	246	54	15
San Diego (CA)	236	239	241	260	228	228	253	233	254	217	222	243	73	31
8th grade														
United States	282	283	284	293	263	271	308	281	291	260	269	307	70	32
All large cities[d]	271	274	276	295	261	269	301	274	296	258	268	301	62	26
Selected urban districts														
Albuquerque (NM)	—	275	274	295	—	267	—	271	289	—	264	—	61	21
Atlanta (GA)	259	266	267	311	261	262	—	266	318	258	271	—	51	20
Austin (TX)	287	287	285	312	267	273	—	284	313	260	271	—	70	35
Baltimore City (MD)	257	261	260	286	257	—	—	255	281	251	261	—	41	12
Boston (MA)	279	282	283	309	271	275	318	281	311	269	271	318	67	34

TABLE 3.3

Average National Assessment of Educational Progress mathematics scores of 4th- and 8th-grade students, by race, Hispanic origin, jurisdiction, and major urban school district, 2009, 2011, 2013, and 2015 [CONTINUED]

Grade level and jurisdiction or specific urban district	Average mathematics scale score[a]												Percent of students 2015	
	2009	2011	2013					2015					At or above basic[b]	At or above proficient[c]
	All students	All students	All students	White	Black	Hispanic	Asian	All students	White	Black	Hispanic	Asian		
Charlotte (NC)	283	285	289	313	271	279	314	286	312	268	275	314	71	39
Chicago (IL)	264	270	269	294	259	270	306	275	317	262	275	[f]	62	25
Cleveland (OH)	256	256	253	265	249	252	[f]	254	273	249	257	[f]	40	9
Dallas (TX)	[e]	274	275	304	263	277	[f]	271	[f]	261	272	[f]	60	20
Detroit (MI)	238	246	240	[f]	239	243	[f]	244	[f]	242	253	[f]	27	4
District of Columbia (DC)	251	255	260	315	253	262	[f]	258	314	248	263	298	46	17
Duval County (FL)	[e]	[e]	[e]	[e]	[e]	[e]	[e]	275	285	264	266	270	64	22
Fresno (CA)	258	256	260	279	247	256	270	257	281	242	252	[f]	44	12
Hillsborough County (FL)	[e]	282	284	296	264	278	[f]	276	290	260	266	[f]	64	27
Houston (TX)	277	279	280	312	271	279	314	276	313	265	273	319	65	27
Jefferson County (KY)	271	274	273	285	257	265	[f]	272	285	252	266	[f]	58	26
Los Angeles (CA)	258	261	264	293	256	258	298	263	285	255	259	296	52	15
Miami-Dade (FL)	273	272	274	295	259	275	[f]	274	299	255	277	[f]	64	26
Milwaukee (WI)	251	254	257	282	247	266	[e]	[e]	[e]	[e]	[e]	[e]	[e]	[e]
New York City (NY)	273	272	274	301	263	263	304	275	294	261	267	303	62	27
Philadelphia (PA)	265	265	266	287	258	261	297	267	282	257	259	303	53	20
San Diego (CA)	280	278	277	300	260	260	294	280	302	261	266	293	70	32

[a] Scale ranges from 0 to 500.

[b] *Basic* denotes partial mastery of the knowledge and skills that are fundamental for proficient work at a given grade.

[c] *Proficient* represents solid academic performance. Students reaching this level have demonstrated competency over challenging subject matter.

[d] Includes public school students from all cities in the nation with populations of 250,000 or more, including the participating districts.

[e] Not available.

[f] Reporting standards not met (too few cases for a reliable estimate).

Note: Race categories exclude persons of Hispanic ethnicity. Totals include racial/ethnic groups not shown separately.

SOURCE: Thomas D. Snyder, Cristobal de Brey, and Sally A. Dillow, "Table 222.80. Average National Assessment of Educational Progress (NAEP) Mathematics Scale Scores of 4th- and 8th-Grade Public School Students and Percentage Attaining Achievement Levels, by Race/Ethnicity and Jurisdiction or Specific Urban District: 2009, 2011, 2013, and 2015," in *Digest of Educational Statistics 2015*, U.S. Department of Education, Institute of Education Sciences, National Center for Education Statistics, December 2016, https://nces.ed.gov/programs/digest/d15/tables/xls/tabn222.80.xls (accessed September 4, 2017)

FIGURE 3.4

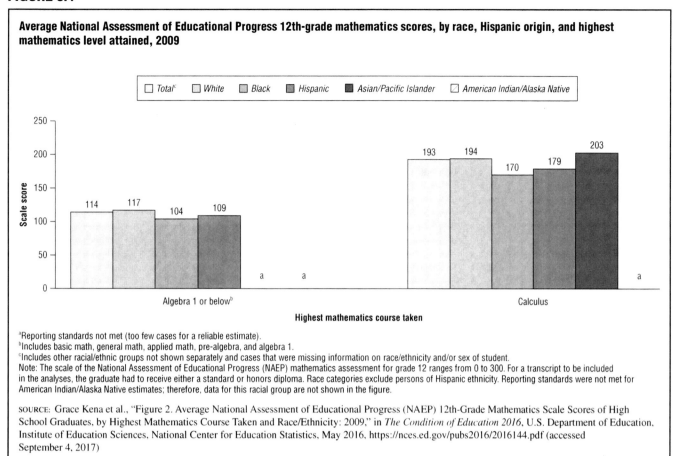

Average National Assessment of Educational Progress 12th-grade mathematics scores, by race, Hispanic origin, and highest mathematics level attained, 2009

□ Total[c]   □ White   ▨ Black   ▨ Hispanic   ■ Asian/Pacific Islander   □ American Indian/Alaska Native

[a]Reporting standards not met (too few cases for a reliable estimate).
[b]Includes basic math, general math, applied math, pre-algebra, and algebra 1.
[c]Includes other racial/ethnic groups not shown separately and cases that were missing information on race/ethnicity and/or sex of student.
Note: The scale of the National Assessment of Educational Progress (NAEP) mathematics assessment for grade 12 ranges from 0 to 300. For a transcript to be included in the analyses, the graduate had to receive either a standard or honors diploma. Race categories exclude persons of Hispanic ethnicity. Reporting standards were not met for American Indian/Alaska Native estimates; therefore, data for this racial group are not shown in the figure.

SOURCE: Grace Kena et al., "Figure 2. Average National Assessment of Educational Progress (NAEP) 12th-Grade Mathematics Scale Scores of High School Graduates, by Highest Mathematics Course Taken and Race/Ethnicity: 2009," in *The Condition of Education 2016*, U.S. Department of Education, Institute of Education Sciences, National Center for Education Statistics, May 2016, https://nces.ed.gov/pubs2016/2016144.pdf (accessed September 4, 2017)

Act in 2010; the bill, however, was filibustered in the Senate and died without a 60-vote majority in December of that year.

After the DREAM Act failed to pass, the Obama administration began seeking other ways to extend legal protections for undocumented immigrant minors, now commonly referred to as Dreamers. In June 2012 Janet Napolitano (1957–), the secretary of the U.S. Department of Homeland Security, introduced a new policy known as Deferred Action for Childhood Arrivals (DACA), which allowed Dreamers between the ages of 15 and 31 years to apply for a two-year deferral of deportation proceedings. According to the U.S. Citizenship and Immigration Services, in "Consideration of Deferred Action for Childhood Arrivals" (2017, https://www.uscis.gov/archive/consideration-deferred-action-childhood-arrivals-daca), the policy required Dreamers to be in school, to have received a high school diploma or general education development certificate, or to have completed military service in the United States, in addition to having no significant criminal record. Dreamers were also required to have arrived in the country prior to their 16th birthday and to have lived in the United States for at least five consecutive years. The American Immigration Council notes in "The Dream Act, DACA, and Other Policies Designed to Protect Dreamers" (September

6, 2017, https://www.americanimmigrationcouncil.org/research/dream-act-daca-and-other-policies-designed-protect-dreamers) that DACA ultimately enabled approximately 800,000 undocumented minors and young adults to continue to work or attend school in the United States without fear of deportation.

DACA remained in effect until September 2017, when President Donald Trump (1946–), in his first year in office, ordered an end to the policy. In "Trump Moves to End DACA and Calls on Congress to Act" (NYTimes.com, September 5, 2017), Michael D. Shear and Julie Hirschfeld Davis report that Trump's action would allow legal protections provided under DACA to expire by March 2018, unless Congress passed a new law in the interim. As of November 2017, no significant legislative action aimed at protecting Dreamers had been taken by Congress.

MINORITY STUDENTS IN SCHOOL

Asian American Students Often Excel

Andrew Lam observes in "SAT Scores and Asian American Academic Achievements" (HuffingtonPost.com, September 10, 2013) that on average Asian American students outperform students from all other racial and ethnic groups in academic achievement. There are a

TABLE 3.4

Average science scale scores by sex, grade, race, and Hispanic origin, 2009 and 2011

Selected characteristic, percentile, and achievement level	Grade 4 2009 Total, all students	Male	Female	Grade 8 2009 Total, all students	Male	Female	Grade 8 2011 Total, all students	Male	Female	Grade 12 2009 Total, all students	Male	Female
	Average science scale score[a]											
All students	**150**	**151**	**149**	**150**	**152**	**148**	**152**	**154**	**149**	**150**	**153**	**147**
Race/ethnicity												
White	163	164	162	162	164	160	163	166	161	159	162	156
Black	127	126	128	126	125	126	129	130	128	125	127	123
Hispanic	131	132	130	132	134	130	137	140	134	134	138	130
Asian/Pacific Islander	160	159	160	160	162	158	159	161	157	164	161	166
American Indian/Alaska Native	135	135	135	137	141	133	141	143	139	144	‡	‡
Highest education level of either parent												
Did not finish high school	—	—	—	131	135	128	132	136	130	131	136	128
Graduated high school	—	—	—	139	141	137	140	143	138	138	140	136
Some education after high school	—	—	—	152	154	150	153	156	151	147	150	144
Graduated college	—	—	—	161	162	159	162	164	160	161	163	159
Eligibility for free or reduced-price lunch												
Eligible	134	134	133	133	135	131	137	139	135	132	135	130
Not eligible	163	164	163	161	163	159	164	166	161	157	159	154
Unknown	162	163	161	164	167	161	164	168	159	156	156	156
School type												
Public	149	149	148	149	151	147	151	153	148	—	—	—
Private	163	165	162	164	167	161	163	168	158	—	—	—
School locale												
City	142	142	142	142	144	141	144	146	142	146	148	144
Suburban	154	154	153	154	155	152	155	158	153	154	157	150
Town	150	151	149	149	152	147	153	155	150	150	153	146
Rural	155	156	154	154	156	152	156	159	153	150	153	146
Percentile[b]												
10th	104	103	104	103	103	103	106	107	105	104	106	103
25th	128	128	128	128	130	127	131	133	129	126	128	125
50th	153	154	152	153	156	151	155	158	152	151	154	148
75th	175	176	174	175	178	172	176	179	173	174	178	171
90th	192	194	191	192	195	188	193	196	189	194	198	190
	Standard deviation of the science scale score[c]											
All students	35	36	34	35	36	34	34	35	33	35	36	34
	Percent of students attaining science achievement levels											
Achievement level												
Below *basic*[d]	28	27	28	37	35	38	35	32	37	40	37	42
At or above *basic*	72	73	72	63	65	62	65	68	63	60	63	58
At or above *proficient*[e]	34	35	32	30	34	27	32	35	28	21	24	18
At *advanced*[f]	1	1	1	2	2	1	2	2	1	1	2	1

—Not available.

‡Reporting standards not met (too few cases for a reliable estimate).

[a]Scale ranges from 0 to 300 for all three grades, but scores cannot be compared across grades. For example, the average score of 163 for white 4th-graders does not denote higher performance than the score of 159 for white 12th-graders.

[b]The percentile represents a specific point on the percentage distribution of all students ranked by their science score from low to high. For example, 10 percent of students scored at or below the 10th percentile score, while 90 percent of students scored above it.

[c]The standard deviation provides an indication of how much the test scores varied. The lower the standard deviation, the closer the scores were clustered around the average score. About two-thirds of the student scores can be expected to fall within the range of one standard deviation above and one standard deviation below the average score. For example, the average score for all 4th-graders was 150, and the standard deviation was 35. This means that we would expect about two-thirds of the students to have scores between 185 (one standard deviation above the average) and 115 (one standard deviation below). Standard errors also must be taken into account when making comparisons of these ranges.

[d]*Basic* denotes partial mastery of the knowledge and skills that are fundamental for proficient work.

[e]*Proficient* represents solid academic performance. Students reaching this level have demonstrated competency over challenging subject matter.

[f]*Advanced* signifies superior performance.

Note: In 2011, only 8th-grade students were assessed in science. Includes students tested with accommodations (7 to 11 percent of all students, depending on grade level and year); excludes only those students with disabilities and English language learners who were unable to be tested even with accommodations (2 to 3 percent of all students). Race categories exclude persons of Hispanic ethnicity.

SOURCE: Thomas D. Snyder, Cristobal de Brey, and Sally A. Dillow, "Table 223.10. Average National Assessment of Educational Progress (NAEP) Science Scale Score, Standard Deviation, and Percentage of Students Attaining Science Achievement Levels, by Grade Level, Selected Student and School Characteristics, and Percentile: 2009 and 2011," in *Digest of Educational Statistics 2015*, U.S. Department of Education, Institute of Education Sciences, National Center for Education Statistics, December 2016, https://nces.ed.gov/programs/digest/d15/tables/xls/tabn223.10.xls (accessed September 4, 2017)

number of factors behind this phenomenon. In "Academic Expectations as Sources of Stress in Asian Students" (*Social Psychology of Education: An International Journal*, vol. 14, no. 3, September 2011), Joyce Beiyu Tan and

TABLE 3.5

Percentage of 16- to 24-year-olds who were high school dropouts, by sex, race, and Hispanic origin, selected years 1970–2014

Year	Total status dropout rate				Male status dropout rate				Female status dropout rate			
	All races[a]	White	Black	Hispanic	All races[a]	White	Black	Hispanic	All races[a]	White	Black	Hispanic
1970[b]	15.0	13.2	27.9	—	14.2	12.2	29.4	—	15.7	14.1	26.6	—
1975	13.9	11.4	22.9	29.2	13.3	11.0	23.0	26.7	14.5	11.8	22.9	31.6
1980	14.1	11.4	19.1	35.2	15.1	12.3	20.8	37.2	13.1	10.5	17.7	33.2
1985	12.6	10.4	15.2	27.6	13.4	11.1	16.1	29.9	11.8	9.8	14.3	25.2
1990	12.1	9.0	13.2	32.4	12.3	9.3	11.9	34.3	11.8	8.7	14.4	30.3
1995[c]	12.0	8.6	12.1	30.0	12.2	9.0	11.1	30.0	11.7	8.2	12.9	30.0
2000[c]	10.9	6.9	13.1	27.8	12.0	7.0	15.3	31.8	9.9	6.9	11.1	23.5
2005[c, d]	9.4	6.0	10.4	22.4	10.8	6.6	12.0	26.4	8.0	5.3	9.0	18.1
2010[c, d]	7.4	5.1	8.0	15.1	8.5	5.9	9.5	17.3	6.3	4.2	6.7	12.8
2011[c, d]	7.1	5.0	7.3	13.6	7.7	5.4	8.3	14.6	6.5	4.6	6.4	12.4
2012[c, d]	6.6	4.3	7.5	12.7	7.3	4.8	8.1	13.9	5.9	3.8	7.0	11.3
2013[c, d]	6.8	5.1	7.3	11.7	7.2	5.5	8.2	12.6	6.3	4.7	6.6	10.8
2014[c, d]	6.5	5.2	7.4	10.6	7.1	5.7	7.1	11.8	5.9	4.8	7.7	9.3

—Not available.

[a]Includes other racial/ethnic categories not separately shown.

[b]For 1967 through 1971, White and Black include persons of Hispanic ethnicity.

[c]Because of changes in data collection procedures, data may not be comparable with figures for years prior to 1992.

[d]White and black exclude persons of two or more races.

Note: "Status" dropouts are 16- to 24-year-olds who are not enrolled in school and who have not completed a high school program, regardless of when they left school. People who have received GED credentials are counted as high school completers. All data are based on October counts. Data are based on sample surveys of the civilian noninstitutionalized population, which excludes persons in prisons, persons in the military, and other persons not living in households. Race categories exclude persons of Hispanic ethnicity except where otherwise noted.

SOURCE: Adapted from Thomas D. Snyder, Cristobal de Brey, and Sally A. Dillow, "Table 128. Percentage of High School Dropouts among Persons 16 to 24 Years Old (Status Dropout Rate), by Sex and Race/Ethnicity: Selected Years, 1960 through 2014," in *Digest of Educational Statistics 2015*, U.S. Department of Education, Institute of Education Sciences, National Center for Education Statistics, December 2016, https://nces.ed.gov/programs/digest/d15/tables/xls/tabn219.70.xls (accessed September 4, 2017)

FIGURE 3.5

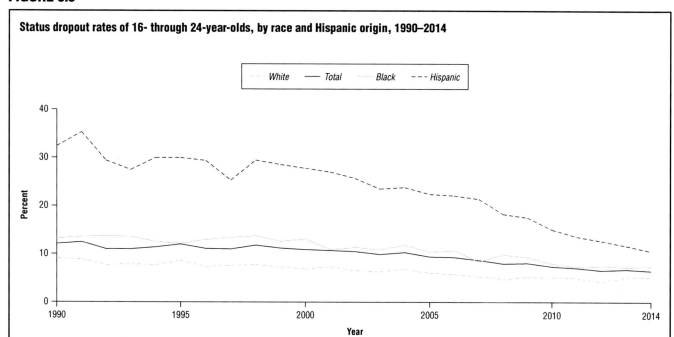

Status dropout rates of 16- through 24-year-olds, by race and Hispanic origin, 1990–2014

Note: The "status dropout rate" is the percentage of 16- to 24-year-olds who are not enrolled in school and have not earned a high school credential (either a diploma or an equivalency credential such as a GED certificate). Data are based on sample surveys of the civilian noninstitutionalized population, which excludes persons in prisons, persons in the military, and other persons not living in households. Data for all races include other racial/ethnic categories not separately shown. Race categories exclude persons of Hispanic ethnicity.

SOURCE: Grace Kena et al., "Figure 2. Status Dropout Rates of 16- to 24-Year-Olds, by Race/Ethnicity: 1990 through 2014," in *The Condition of Education 2016*, U.S. Department of Education, Institute of Education Sciences, National Center for Education Statistics, May 2016, https://nces.ed.gov/pubs2016/2016144.pdf (accessed September 4, 2017)

Shirley Yates note that education is highly valued in Asian cultures with a Confucian heritage, such as Chinese culture, and that Asian parents often have high educational aspirations and expectations of their children. According to

FIGURE 3.6

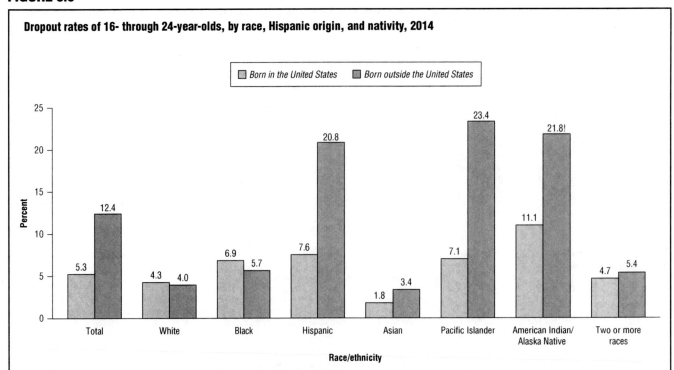

Dropout rates of 16- through 24-year-olds, by race, Hispanic origin, and nativity, 2014

!Interpret data with caution. The coefficient of variation (CV) is between 30 and 50 percent.
Note: United States refers to the 50 states, the District of Columbia, Puerto Rico, American Samoa, Guam, the U.S. Virgin Islands, and the Northern Marianas. The status dropout rate is the percentage of 16- to 24-year-olds who are not enrolled in school and have not earned a high school credential (either a diploma or an equivalency credential such as a GED certificate). Data are based on sample surveys of persons living in households and noninstitutionalized group quarters (such as college or military housing). Among those counted in noninstitutionalized group quarters in the American Community Survey, only the residents of military barracks are not included in the civilian noninstitutionalized population in the Current Population Survey. Race categories exclude persons of Hispanic ethnicity.

SOURCE: Grace Kena et al., "Figure 7. Status Dropout Rates of 16- to 24-Year-Olds, by Race/Ethnicity and Nativity: 2014," in *The Condition of Education 2016*, U.S. Department of Education, Institute of Education Sciences, National Center for Education Statistics, May 2016, https://nces.ed.gov/pubs2016/2016144.pdf (accessed September 4, 2017)

Weihua Fan, Cathy M. Williams, and Christopher A. Wolters, in "Parental Involvement in Predicting School Motivation: Similar and Differential Effects across Ethnic Groups" (*Journal of Educational Research*, vol. 105, no. 1, 2012), parental advising and other involvement in their children's education is highly related to student school motivation. As a result, Asian parents tend to be particularly involved in their children's education.

Progress for African American Students

Although the average academic performance of African American students, in general, remains below that of white students, high school graduation rates among African Americans rose considerably during the second half of the 20th century and the early 21st century. Snyder, de Brey, and Dillow indicate in *Digest of Education Statistics 2015* that 42.6% of African American students and 38.5% of Hispanic students graduated from high school in 1975. The graduation rate has increased more dramatically for African American students since 1975 than it has for Hispanic students. In 2015, 87.7% of African Americans aged 25 years and older had earned a high school diploma, a lower percentage than that of whites (93.3%) but higher than that of Hispanics (66.7%).

However, as Figure 3.7 reveals, African Americans still experienced one of the highest dropout rates between the freshman and senior years of high school. During the 2013–14 school year, 73% of African Americans who had entered high school as freshmen four years earlier earned their diplomas, compared with 76% of Hispanics and 87% of whites.

SCHOOL SEGREGATION. One reason African American children have historically lagged behind white children in educational achievement has been the separate and inferior schools that they have been forced to attend. In 1954, in *Brown v. Board of Education of Topeka, Kansas* (347 U.S. 483), the U.S. Supreme Court declared that separate schools for African American children were inherently unequal and that schools had to desegregate. Nearly 60 years later, more and more school districts are questioning whether the federal courts need to continue supervising desegregation. However, despite regulations and busing, many inner-city schools are still not integrated, and academic achievement for African American children is still lagging. Many white students have moved (with their family's tax dollars) to the suburbs or transferred to private schools to avoid inner-city schools with high populations of minority students.

FIGURE 3.7

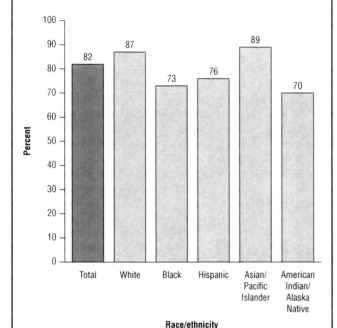

Public high school freshman graduation rates, by race and Hispanic origin, 2013–14

Note: The adjusted cohort graduation rate (ACGR) is the percentage of public high school freshmen who graduate with a regular diploma within 4 years of starting 9th grade. The Bureau of Indian Education and Puerto Rico were not included in United States 4-year Adjusted Cohort Gradutation Race (ACGR) estimates. Race categories exclude persons of Hispanic ethnicity.

SOURCE: Grace Kena et al., "Figure 3. Adjusted Cohort Graduation Rate (ACGR) for Public High School Students, by Race/Ethnicity: School Year 2013–14," in *The Condition of Education 2016*, U.S. Department of Education, Institute of Education Sciences, National Center for Education Statistics, May 2016, https://nces.ed.gov/pubs2016/2016144.pdf (accessed September 4, 2017)

Half a century after *Brown*, the Supreme Court restricted the use of plans that use race as a factor in assigning students to schools in an effort to promote racial diversity. The two cases, decided in a joint ruling in June 2007, were *Parents Involved in Community Schools v. Seattle School District* (551 U.S. 701) and *Meredith v. Jefferson County* (No. 05-915). The court did not, however, declare that race could never be used to achieve diversity. As of 2017, it was unclear whether the Supreme Court's decision had had a noticeable impact on racial diversity in the public school system.

In *Digest of Education Statistics 2015*, Snyder, de Brey, and Dillow report that during the 2013–14 school year 82.3% of white students attended public elementary or secondary schools where white students made up 50% or more of the students. By comparison, 12.6% of Asian American students, 22.8% of Native American or Alaskan Native students, 44.4% of African American students, and 56.6% of Hispanic students attended schools where at least half of the total student body belonged to their own race or ethnicity.

Hispanic Educational Attainment Increases

Although Hispanics made modest gains in education during the 1990s, low educational attainment has been a major hindrance to their economic advancement in the United States. Snyder, de Brey, and Dillow find in *Digest of Education Statistics 2015* that Hispanics continued to trail behind other groups in high school graduation rates in 2015. Only 66.7% of Hispanics aged 25 years and older had received high school diplomas, compared with 93.3% of whites and 87.7% of African Americans. Not surprisingly, in 2015 whites and African Americans were also more likely to have graduated from college than were Hispanics. (See Figure 3.8.)

However, there are some signs that the Hispanic population is making slow but steady progress in educational attainment in the United States. Snyder, de Brey, and Dillow indicate that the proportion of Hispanic adults aged 25 years and older with a high school diploma rose from 53.4% in 1995 to 66.7% in 2015. Likewise, the proportion of Hispanics with a bachelor's degree also rose, from 9% in 1995 to 16% in 2015. (See Figure 3.8.)

Native American Educational Attainment Remains Low

Native Americans have the lowest educational attainment of all minority groups, which is attributable in part to a high dropout rate. In *Digest of Education Statistics 2015*, Snyder, de Brey, and Dillow note that the dropout rate among Native Americans or Alaskan Natives who were aged 15 to 24 years and enrolled in grades 10 through 12 was 10.1% in 2014. This figure was nearly double the overall dropout rate of 5.2% for all other students in that age group.

Kristin Denton Flanagan and Jen Park indicate in *American Indian and Alaska Native Children: Findings from the Base Year of the Early Childhood Longitudinal Study, Birth Cohort* (August 2005, http://files.eric.ed.gov/fulltext/ED485835.pdf) that a high proportion of Native American children have certain risk factors that may affect their educational attainment. The Early Childhood Longitudinal Study, Birth Cohort, oversampled Native American children to better study their educational experiences. Fully one-third (34%) of Native American children lived below the poverty line, compared with 23% of all children. A quarter (24%) of all Native American children lived with a single parent, compared with 20% of all children. In addition, Native American parents had low educational attainment. One-third (34%) of the mothers and 27% of the fathers had not completed high school, compared with 27% of all mothers and 17% of all fathers. Furthermore, only 9% of Native American mothers and 6% of Native American fathers had earned a bachelor's degree or higher, compared with 24% of all mothers and 24% of all fathers.

FIGURE 3.8

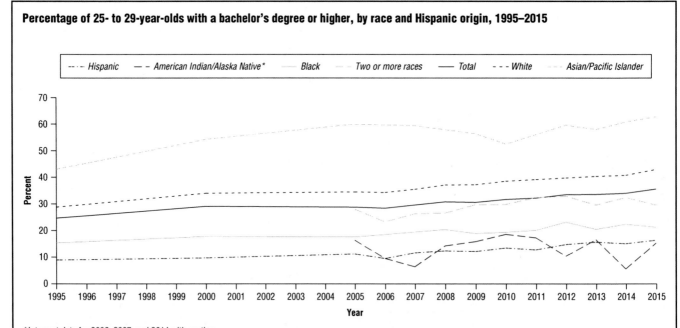

Percentage of 25- to 29-year-olds with a bachelor's degree or higher, by race and Hispanic origin, 1995–2015

*Interpret data for 2006, 2007, and 2014 with caution.

Note: Race categories exclude persons of Hispanic ethnicity. Prior to 2005, separate data on persons of two or more races were not available; data for American Indians/Alaska Natives are not shown prior to 2005.

SOURCE: Grace Kena et al., "Figure 4. Percentage of 25- to 29-Year-Olds Who Completed a Bachelor's or Higher Degree, by Race/Ethnicity: Selected Years, 1995–2015," in *The Condition of Education 2016*, U.S. Department of Education, Institute of Education Sciences, National Center for Education Statistics, May 2016, https://nces.ed.gov/pubs2016/2016144.pdf (accessed September 4, 2017)

REFORMING THE PUBLIC SCHOOL SYSTEM

No Child Left Behind

In January 2002 President George W. Bush (1946–) signed into law the No Child Left Behind (NCLB) Act, which was intended to improve the U.S. public school system and provide educational choice, especially for minority families. The law mandated that all public school students be proficient in reading and math by 2014, with progress measured by the administration of annual standardized tests. In addition, all subgroups (those with certain racial backgrounds, limited English proficiency, or disabilities or from low-income families) must meet the same performance standards as all students. Failure to make adequate yearly progress may result in escalating sanctions against the school, including the payment of transportation costs for students who wish to transfer to better-performing schools, extra tutoring for low-income students, replacement of the school staff, and potentially converting the school to a charter school or even turning to a private company to operate the school.

Although the NCLB was passed with bipartisan support, critics quickly emerged, including those who charged that the mandate was underfinanced by the Bush administration. Another problem was that because of the strict testing requirements, many schools that were regarded as successful by almost all objective measures found themselves designated as failing schools. In some cases a school failed to meet its goal simply because two or three students in a subgroup failed to take a standardized test. A further problem was that minority students who attended schools that were unquestionably substandard found that even if by law they had the right to transfer to another school, there were few places to go. In *Holding NCLB Accountable: Achieving Accountability, Equity, and School Reform* (2008), a multipart study that was conducted by the Civil Rights Project at Harvard University and edited by Gail L. Sunderman, the researchers find that no districts are able to approve all transfer requests. However well intentioned, the NCLB is proving difficult to implement, demonstrating once again that there are no easy answers to improving the U.S. educational system, especially for minority and low-income students.

Critics of the NCLB found an ally in the Obama administration. Under President Obama's direction, the U.S. Department of Education released *A Blueprint for Reform: The Reauthorization of the Elementary and Secondary Education Act* (March 2010, https://www2.ed.gov/policy/elsec/leg/blueprint/blueprint.pdf). The blueprint proposed increasing funding for states to broaden the assessments used to evaluate academic skills above basic levels, expanding requirements to include subjects other than reading and mathematics, relaxing the stringent accountability punishments, providing incentives to keep students in school, and narrowing the achievement gap. Cameron Brenchley reports in "We Can't Wait: 10 States

Approved for NCLB Flexibility" (February 9, 2012, https://blog.ed.gov/2012/02/we-cant-wait-10-states-approved-for-nclb-flexibility/) that in February 2012 President Obama announced that 10 states had been granted greater flexibility in exchange for implementing plans for comprehensive school reforms, including teacher and principal development, assessments and evaluations independent of test schools, and higher educational standards. In "Elementary & Secondary Education: ESEA Flexibility" (May 12, 2016, https://www2.ed.gov/policy/elsec/guid/esea-flexibility/index.html), the Department of Education indicates that as of May 2016, 45 states and the District of Columbia had received federal approval for flexible plans.

Meanwhile, in December 2015 President Obama signed the Every Student Succeeds Act (ESSA), a bipartisan program designed to address some of the deficiencies of the NCLB. The Department of Education explains in "Every Student Succeeds Act" (2017, https://www.ed.gov/essa?src=rn) that the new law placed greater emphasis on expanding equitable educational opportunities to the nation's most disadvantaged students, while increasing access to prekindergarten programs nationwide. Furthermore, the law required states to engage in outreach efforts with various communities, with the aim of ensuring that institutions, civil rights groups, and other local stakeholders had a voice in the development of educational initiatives tailored to meet the diverse needs of their students. According to the Department of Education, ESSA was also the first federal law to require public schools to ensure that students receive academic training specifically designed to enable them to attend college.

The election of President Trump brought significant changes to ESSA. In March 2017 the Republican-controlled Congress voted to weaken the accountability provision in ESSA, granting states greater flexibility in implementing the outreach provision of the law. In "Trump Education Dept. Releases New ESSA Guidelines" (EdWeek.org, March 13, 2017), Alyson Klein notes that following this action by Congress, the Trump administration issued its own revised ESSA guidelines, declaring that states were no longer required to report on their community outreach efforts. According to Klein, Betsy DeVos (1958–), the secretary of the U.S. Department of Education, explained in a speech to the Council of the Great City Schools in the District of Columbia in March 2017, "Too often the Department of Education has gone outside its established authority and created roadblocks, wittingly or unwittingly for parents and educators alike. This isn't right, nor is it acceptable. Under this administration, we will break this habit."

School "Choice"

SCHOOL VOUCHERS. Despite the Supreme Court's rejection of segregated schools, many minority students have been relegated to failing neighborhood public schools with little diversity. One proposed solution to this problem is the school voucher, a concept that was pioneered by the Nobel Prize–winning economist Milton Friedman (1912–2006) in 1955. According to the non-partisan group EdChoice (2017, https://www.edchoice.org), a voucher program provides parents with a predetermined amount of money—in essence a share of the tax dollars already collected by a community to be used for education—and allows parents to present that voucher to the public or private school of their choice. Proponents for vouchers believe that not only will minority children benefit from more options but also that public schools, fearful of losing tax revenues, will gain an incentive to improve. Opponents of vouchers, such as the National Education Association, in "Vouchers" (2017, http://www.nea.org/home/16378.htm), maintain that vouchers will simply drain money from the public schools and worsen their condition, while not providing real choice for students from impoverished or low-income families. Other critics charge that it is illegal to funnel government funds, in the form of vouchers, to private religious schools.

Vouchers have been used in various states and municipalities around the United States for decades, but the concept has been adopted on only a limited scale. According to the National Conference of State Legislatures, in "School Vouchers" 2017, http://www.ncsl.org/research/education/school-choice-vouchers.aspx), as of November 2017, 14 states and the District of Columbia had introduced voucher programs.

In some cases programs have been shut down after legal challenges or because of falling political support. For example, the Florida Supreme Court struck down that state's Opportunity Scholarship voucher system, saying that it violated the constitutional requirement of a uniform system of free public schools. (A second voucher program for disabled students remained in place.) The article "Topic A: Obama's Compromise on D.C.'s School Vouchers Program" (WashingtonPost.com, May 10, 2009) indicates that President Obama essentially ended the District of Columbia voucher program, established in 2004, when he signed a spending bill in 2009 that prevented new students from entering the program. However, funding for the voucher program was subsequently restored when Republican lawmakers introduced it into the federal budget negotiations of 2011. Chris Weller observes in "Trump's Education Secretary Supports School Vouchers—but Studies Suggest They Don't Help Students" (BusinessInsider.com, February 27, 2017) that DeVos has been a longtime advocate of school vouchers, suggesting that the program will become a priority during the Trump administration.

CHARTER SCHOOLS. Like vouchers, the idea of charter schools has also found proponents in the minority community. A charter school is publicly financed but operates independent of school districts, thereby combining the advantages of a private school with the free tuition of a public school. Parents, teachers, and other groups receive a charter from a state legislature to operate these schools, which in effect exist as independent school districts. They receive public funds and are accountable for both their financing and educational standards.

According to Robin J. Lake and Paul T. Hill, in *Hopes, Fears, and Reality: A Balanced Look at American Charter Schools in 2005* (November 2005, https://www.crpe.org/sites/default/files/hfrdec1_web_0.pdf), the charter school experiment started in Minnesota in 1992. Kena et al. report in *Condition of Education 2016* that by the 2013–14 school year, 6,465 charter schools taught 2.5 million students in 42 states and the District of Columbia. The Obama administration gave the charter school movement a boost when it pressured states to lift restrictions on the establishment and growth of charter schools as part of the American Recovery and Reinvestment Act of 2009.

However, one unintended consequence of charter schools is that they are more likely be categorized as high poverty than are their public school counterparts. Kena et al. note that during the 2013–14 academic year 39% of charter schools were considered high-poverty schools, compared with 24% of traditional public schools. Charter schools also had higher proportions of African American and Hispanic students than public schools that year. As Figure 3.9 reveals, in nearly a quarter (24%) of charter schools in 2013–14, African American students accounted for 50% or more of the total student population; by comparison, only 9% of traditional public schools had African American enrollment of 50% or higher. Similarly, 23% of charter schools had Hispanic enrollment of 50% or higher, whereas Hispanics constituted more than half of the total student population at only 15% of all traditional public schools.

Still, by 2013 charter schools had begun to demonstrate clear advantages for minority students. In *National Charter School Study 2013* (2013, http://credo.stanford.edu/documents/NCSS%202013%20Final%20Draft.pdf), the Center for Research on Education Outcomes at Stanford University indicates that, relative to their public school counterparts, minority charter school students achieved reading gains that were equivalent to eight

FIGURE 3.9

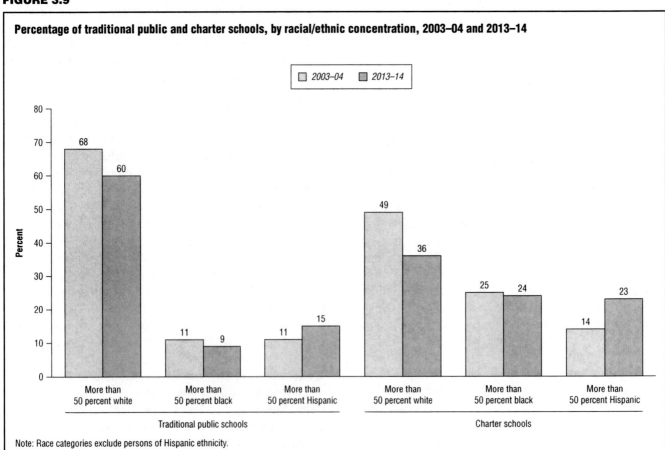

Percentage of traditional public and charter schools, by racial/ethnic concentration, 2003–04 and 2013–14

Note: Race categories exclude persons of Hispanic ethnicity.

SOURCE: Grace Kena et al., "Figure 2. Percentage of Traditional Public Schools and Charter Schools, by Racial/Ethnic Concentration: School Years 2003–2004 and 2013–2014," in *The Condition of Education 2016*, U.S. Department of Education, Institute of Education Sciences, National Center for Education Statistics, May 2016, https://nces.ed.gov/pubs2016/2016144.pdf (accessed September 4, 2017)

additional days of school. Among high-poverty African American students attending charter schools, gains were even more substantial. According to the center, in 2013 poor African American charter school students achieved reading gains equivalent to an additional 29 days of school and mathematics gains equivalent to an additional 36 days of school.

HIGHER EDUCATION
Preparation for College

HIGH SCHOOL COURSE TAKING. High school students are better prepared for college-level coursework if they take advanced courses while still in high school. Asian American students are more likely than other students to take advanced math and science courses in high school. White students, although less likely to take these courses than Asian American students, are significantly more likely than most minority students to take these courses. According to Snyder, de Brey, and Dillow, in *Digest of Education Statistics 2015*, in 2009, 42.2% of Asian or Pacific Islander high school graduates had taken calculus courses while in high school. This was far higher than the rates for any other group. Among white graduates, 17.5% had taken calculus in high school. By comparison, 6.1% of African American graduates, 6.3% of Native American or Alaskan Native graduates, and 8.6% of Hispanic graduates had taken calculus in 2009.

Snyder, de Brey, and Dillow report similar statistics for physics. In 2009, 61.1% of Asian or Pacific Islander graduates had taken physics in high school, compared with 37.6% of white graduates, 28.6% of Hispanic graduates, 26.9% of African American graduates, and 19.8% of Native American or Alaskan Native graduates. Asian or Pacific Islander high school graduates were also the most likely to have taken both biology and chemistry (82.7%), followed by white (68.9%), African American (64.3%), Hispanic (64.2%), and Native American or Alaskan Native (43.9%) graduates. In addition, more than half (54.4%) of Asian or Pacific Islander graduates had taken physics, biology, and chemistry in high school, compared with 31.4% of white graduates, 22.7% of Hispanic graduates, 21.9% of African American graduates, and 13.6% of Native American or Alaskan Native graduates.

However, Snyder, de Brey, and Dillow report that African American students earned more credits in English, on average, than did other students, followed closely by Hispanics and Native Americans or Alaskan Natives. In 2009 African American students earned, on average, 4.56 credits in English, Hispanic students earned 4.43 credits, and Native American or Alaskan Native students earned 4.39 credits. White students earned an average of 4.32 credits in English, while Asian or Pacific Islander students earned 4.19 credits. African Americans also earned the highest average number of history and social studies credits (4.26) in 2009, followed by whites (4.23), Asians or Pacific Islanders (4.13), Native Americans or Alaskan Natives (4.11), and Hispanics (4.04). Asian or Pacific Islander high school students earned the highest number, on average, of foreign language credits (2.98) in 2009, followed by Hispanics (2.34), whites (2.19), African Americans (1.87), and Native Americans or Alaskan Natives (1.56).

Advanced placement (AP) courses are college-level courses that are offered to students in high school. The College Board has developed tests for 38 courses in 20 subjects; college credit can be awarded for a qualifying score of 3.0 or better on a five-point scale. Students can also earn college credit through the International Baccalaureate (IB) program, which offers courses in six core subject areas. In *Status and Trends in the Education of Racial and Ethnic Groups 2017* (July 2017, https://nces.ed.gov/pubs2017/2017051.pdf), Lauren Musu-Gillette et al. provide a breakdown of students who earned credit in either AP or IB courses in 2013. That year, nearly three-quarters (72%) of Asian American students earned at least one credit in an AP course, compared with 40% of white students, 34% of Hispanic students, and 23% of African American students. (See Figure 3.10.) Nearly half (46%) of Asian American students earned AP credit in math in 2013. By contrast, only 17% of white students, 12% of Hispanic students, and 6% of African American students earned AP credit in math. This discrepancy was also observed in AP science courses. In 2013 two out of five (40%) Asian American students earned AP science credits, compared with 16% of white students, 10% of Hispanic students, and 8% of African American students.

SAT and ACT Scores

Students wishing to enter most colleges and universities in the United States must take the SAT (formerly the Scholastic Assessment Test) or the ACT (formerly the American College Test). These standardized tests measure verbal and mathematical ability to determine readiness for college-level work. Most students take the SAT. Performance on the SAT is measured in three areas, each on a scale of 200 to 800: critical reading, mathematics, and a written essay portion that was added to the SAT in 2005.

Historically, minority students have not scored as well on the SAT as white students, with the partial exception of Asians or Pacific Islanders. The College Board indicates in *2016 College-Bound Seniors: Total Group Profile Report* (2016, https://secure-media.collegeboard.org/digitalServices/pdf/sat/total-group-2016.pdf) that in 2016 the mean (average) score for the critical reading portion of the SAT among whites was 530, compared with 527 for Asian Americans, 470 for Native Americans or Alaskan Natives, 451 for Hispanics, 431 for Native Hawaiians or Pacific Islanders, and 425 for

FIGURE 3.10

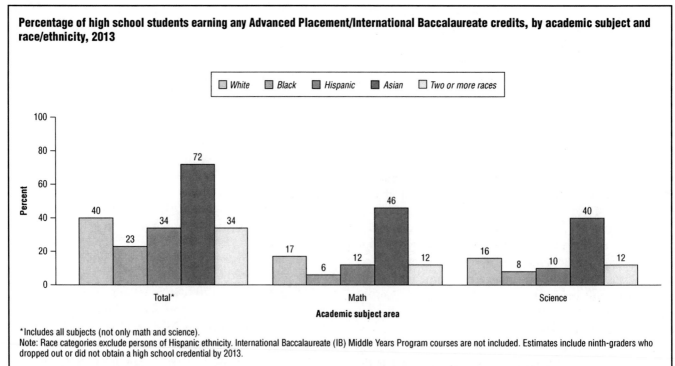

Percentage of high school students earning any Advanced Placement/International Baccalaureate credits, by academic subject and race/ethnicity, 2013

☐ White ☐ Black ☐ Hispanic ■ Asian ☐ Two or more races

*Includes all subjects (not only math and science).
Note: Race categories exclude persons of Hispanic ethnicity. International Baccalaureate (IB) Middle Years Program courses are not included. Estimates include ninth-graders who dropped out or did not obtain a high school credential by 2013.

SOURCE: Lauren Musu-Gillette et al., "Figure 13.1. Percentage of Fall 2009 Ninth-Graders Earning Any Credit in Advanced Placement (AP) or International Baccalaureate (IB) Courses, by Academic Subject Area and Race/Ethnicity: 2013," in *Status and Trends in the Education of Racial and Ethnic Groups 2017*, U.S. Department of Education, Institute of Education Sciences, National Center for Education Statistics, July 2017, https://nces.ed.gov/pubs2017/2017051.pdf (accessed September 4, 2017)

African Americans. As Table 3.6 shows, the mean critical reading scores either rose or stayed the same for most groups between 1986–87 and 2014–15, but declined for both Mexican Americans and the Other Hispanic category.

The College Board reports that in 2016 Asian Americans scored the highest by far on the math portion of the test, with a mean score of 614. Whites scored a mean of 550, Hispanics scored 468, Native Americans or Alaskan Natives scored 450, Native Hawaiians or Pacific Islanders scored 450, and African Americans scored 430. All groups saw their math SAT scores increase between 1986–87 and 2014–15 except for the Other Hispanic category. (See Table 3.6.)

The writing portion of the SAT was a relatively new part of the test in 2016, having only been added by the College Board in 2005. The College Board indicates that in 2016 Asian Americans did the best on this portion of the test, with a mean score of 527. Whites averaged 504, Native Americans or Alaskan Natives averaged 440, Hispanics averaged 431, Native Hawaiians or Pacific Islanders averaged 414, and African Americans averaged 404.

Minority College Attendance

Generally, minority enrollment in colleges and universities has grown ever since racial and ethnic enrollment statistics were first reported in 1975. Although these gains are encouraging, they must be viewed in the context of overall participation rates in higher education and degree completion rates, given that white enrollment has also increased.

In *Digest of Education Statistics 2015*, Snyder, de Brey, and Dillow note that in 2014, 65.2% of Asian Americans aged 18 to 24 years old were enrolled in colleges and universities, the highest proportion of any racial or ethnic group. (See Table 3.7.) By comparison, 42.2% of whites aged 18 to 24 years were enrolled in colleges and universities, followed by 41% of Pacific Islanders, 35.4% of Native Americans or Alaskan Natives, 34.7% of Hispanics, and 32.6% of African Americans in this age group. Figure 3.11 shows that larger proportions of African Americans and Hispanics were enrolled in associate's degree programs than in bachelor's degree programs in 2013.

Earning a Bachelor's Degree

College participation rates are telling, but so, too, are college completion rates. A number of students begin college but drop out before receiving a bachelor's degree. Kena et al. indicate in *Condition of Education 2016* that in 2015 only 21% of African Americans between the ages of 25 and 29 years had earned a bachelor's degree or higher. (See Figure 3.8.) Among Hispanics in this age group, only 16% had received a bachelor's degree or higher. Among Asians or Pacific Islanders in this age group, 63% had received a bachelor's degree or higher—the highest completion rate of any race or ethnic group.

TABLE 3.6

Mean SAT scores of college-bound seniors, by race and Hispanic origin, 1986–87 to 2014–15

Race/ethnicity	1986–87	1990–91	1996–97	2000–01	2003–04	2004–05	2005–06	2006–07	2007–08	2008–09	2009–10	2010–11	2011–12	2012–13	2013–14	2014–15	Score change 1990–91 to 2004–05	Score change 2004–05 to 2014–15	Score change 2009–10 to 2014–15	Score change 2013–14 to 2014–15
1	2	3	4	5	6	7	8	9	10	11	12	13	14	15	16	17	18	19	20	21
SAT—Critical reading																				
All students	507	499	505	506	508	508	503	502	502	501	501	497	496	496	497	495	9	−13	−6	−2
White	524	518	526	529	528	532	527	527	528	528	528	528	527	527	529	529	14	−3	1	0
Black	428	427	434	433	430	433	434	433	430	429	429	428	428	431	431	431	6	−2	2	0
Mexican American	457	454	451	451	451	453	454	455	454	453	454	451	448	449	450	448	−1	−5	−6	−2
Puerto Rican	436	436	454	457	457	460	459	459	456	452	454	452	452	456	456	456	24	−4	2	0
Other Hispanic	464	458	466	460	461	463	458	459	455	455	454	451	447	450	451	449	5	−14	−5	−2
Asian/Pacific Islander	479	485	496	501	507	511	510	514	513	516	519	517	518	521	523	525	26	14	6	2
American Indian/Alaska Native	471	470	475	481	483	489	487	487	485	486	485	484	482	480	483	481	19	−8	−4	−2
Other	480	486	512	503	494	495	494	497	496	494	494	493	491	492	493	490	9	−5	−4	−3
SAT—Mathematics																				
All students	501	500	511	514	518	520	518	515	515	515	516	514	514	514	513	511	20	−9	−5	−2
White	514	513	526	531	531	536	536	534	537	536	536	535	536	534	534	534	23	−2	−2	0
Black	411	419	423	426	427	431	429	429	426	426	428	427	428	429	429	428	12	−3	0	−1
Mexican American	455	459	458	458	458	463	465	466	463	463	467	466	465	464	461	457	4	−6	−10	−4
Puerto Rican	432	439	447	451	452	457	456	454	453	450	452	452	452	453	450	449	18	−8	−3	−1
Other Hispanic	462	462	468	465	465	469	463	463	461	461	462	462	461	461	459	457	7	−12	−5	−2
Asian/Pacific Islander	541	548	560	566	577	580	578	578	581	587	591	595	595	597	598	598	32	18	7	0
American Indian/Alaska Native	463	468	475	479	488	493	494	494	491	493	492	488	489	486	484	482	25	−11	−10	−2
Other	482	492	514	512	508	513	513	512	512	514	514	517	516	519	520	519	21	6	5	−1
SAT—Writing																				
All students	*	*	*	*	*	*	497	494	494	493	492	489	488	488	487	484	*	*	−8	−3
White	*	*	*	*	*	*	519	518	518	517	516	516	515	515	513	513	*	*	−3	0
Black	*	*	*	*	*	*	428	425	424	421	420	417	417	418	418	418	*	*	−2	0
Mexican American	*	*	*	*	*	*	452	450	447	446	448	445	443	442	443	438	*	*	−10	−5
Puerto Rican	*	*	*	*	*	*	448	447	445	443	443	442	442	445	443	442	*	*	−1	−1
Other Hispanic	*	*	*	*	*	*	450	450	448	448	447	444	442	443	443	439	*	*	−8	−4
Asian/Pacific Islander	*	*	*	*	*	*	512	513	516	520	526	528	528	527	530	531	*	*	5	1
American Indian/Alaska Native	*	*	*	*	*	*	474	473	470	469	467	465	462	461	461	460	*	*	−7	−1
Other	*	*	*	*	*	*	493	493	494	493	492	492	491	490	491	487	*	*	−5	−4

*Not applicable.

Note: Data for 2009–10 and earlier years are for seniors who took the SAT any time during their high school years through June of their senior year. Data for 2010–11 onwards are for seniors who took the SAT any time during their high school years through March of their senior year. If a student took the SAT more than once, the most recent score on each section was used. Possible scores on each section of the SAT range from 200 to 800. Prior to 2006, the critical reading section was known as the verbal section. The writing section was introduced in March 2005. The SAT was formerly known as the Scholastic Assessment Test and the Scholastic Aptitude Test.

SOURCE: Thomas D. Snyder, Cristobal de Brey, and Sally A. Dillow, "Table 226.10. SAT Mean Scores of College-Bound Seniors, by Race/Ethnicity: Selected Years, 1986–87 through 2014–15," in *Digest of Educational Statistics 2015*, U.S. Department of Education, Institute of Education Sciences, National Center for Education Statistics, December 2016, https://nces.ed.gov/programs/digest/d15/tables/xls/tabn226.10.xls (accessed September 5, 2017). Data from College Entrance Examination Board, *College-Bound Seniors: Total Group Profile [National] Report*, selected years, 1986–87 through 2014–15, from https://secure-media.collegeboard.org/digitalServices/pdf/sat/total-group-2015.pdf.

TABLE 3.7

Enrollment rates of 18- to 24-year-olds in degree-granting institutions, by type of institution, sex, race, and Hispanic origin of student, selected years 1975–2014

Year	Total, all students	Level of institution		Sex		Race/ethnicity							Race/ethnicity, by sex					
		2-year	4-year	Male	Female	White	Black	Hispanic	Asian	Pacific Islander	American Indian/ Alaska Native	Two or more races	White Male	White Female	Black Male	Black Female	Hispanic Male	Hispanic Female
1975[a]	26.3	9.0	17.3	29.0	23.7	27.4	20.4	20.4	c	c	c	c	30.7	24.3	19.9	20.8	21.4	19.5
1980	25.7	7.1	18.6	26.4	25.0	27.3	19.4	16.1	c	c	c	c	28.4	26.3	17.5	20.9	15.9	16.2
1985	27.8	7.4	20.4	28.4	27.2	30.0	19.6	16.9	c	c	c	c	30.9	29.2	20.2	19.1	14.9	18.9
1990	32.0	8.7	23.3	32.3	31.8	35.1	25.4	15.8	56.9	c	15.8[d]	c	35.5	34.7	26.0	24.8	15.3	16.4
1995	34.3	8.9	25.4	33.1	35.5	37.9	27.5	20.7	54.6	c	27.6	c	37.0	38.8	26.0	28.7	18.7	23.0
2000	35.5	9.4	26.0	32.6	38.4	38.7	30.5	21.7	55.9	c	15.9	c	36.2	41.3	25.1	35.2	18.5	25.4
2005[a]	38.9	9.6	29.2	35.3	42.5	42.8	33.1	24.8	61.0	50.6	27.8	41.8	39.4	46.1	28.2	37.6	20.7	29.5
2010[a, b]	41.2	12.9	28.2	38.3	44.1	43.3	38.4	31.9	63.6	36.0	41.4	38.3	40.6	46.1	35.2	41.4	27.9	36.1
2011[a, b]	42.0	12.0	30.0	39.1	44.9	44.7	37.1	34.8	60.1	37.8	23.5	38.8	42.4	47.1	34.0	39.9	31.0	39.4
2012[a, b]	41.0	12.7	28.3	37.6	44.5	42.1	36.4	37.5	59.8	50.3	27.8	39.4	38.3	46.0	33.9	38.7	33.5	41.7
2013[a, b]	39.9	11.6	28.3	36.6	43.3	41.6	34.2	33.8	62.3	32.9	31.8	44.7	38.1	45.3	30.6	37.6	29.1	38.8
2014[a, b]	40.0	10.6	29.4	37.3	42.8	42.2	32.6	34.7	65.2	41.0	35.4	31.6	40.2	44.2	28.5	36.6	30.3	39.4

[a]After 2002, data for individual race categories exclude persons of two or more races.
[b]Beginning in 2010, standard errors were computed using replicate weights, which produced more precise values than the generalized variance function methodology used in prior years.
[c]Not available.
[d]Interpret data with caution. The coefficient of variation (CV) for this estimate is between 30 and 50 percent.
Note: Data are based on sample surveys of the civilian noninstitutionalized population. Totals include other racial/ethnic groups not separately shown. Race categories exclude persons of Hispanic ethnicity except where otherwise noted.

SOURCE: Adapted from Thomas D. Snyder, Cristobal de Brey, and Sally A. Dillow, "Table 302.60. Percentage of 18- to 24-Year-Olds Enrolled in Degree-Granting Postsecondary Institutions, by Level of Institution and Sex and Race/Ethnicity of Student: 1970 through 2014," in *Digest of Educational Statistics 2015*, U.S. Department of Education, Institute of Education Sciences, National Center for Education Statistics, December 2016, https://nces.ed.gov/programs/digest/d15/tables/xls/tabn302.60.xls (accessed September 4, 2017)

FIGURE 3.11

Undergraduate enrollment distribution, by institutional level and race/ethnicity, Fall 2013

[Postsecondary institution enrollment status]

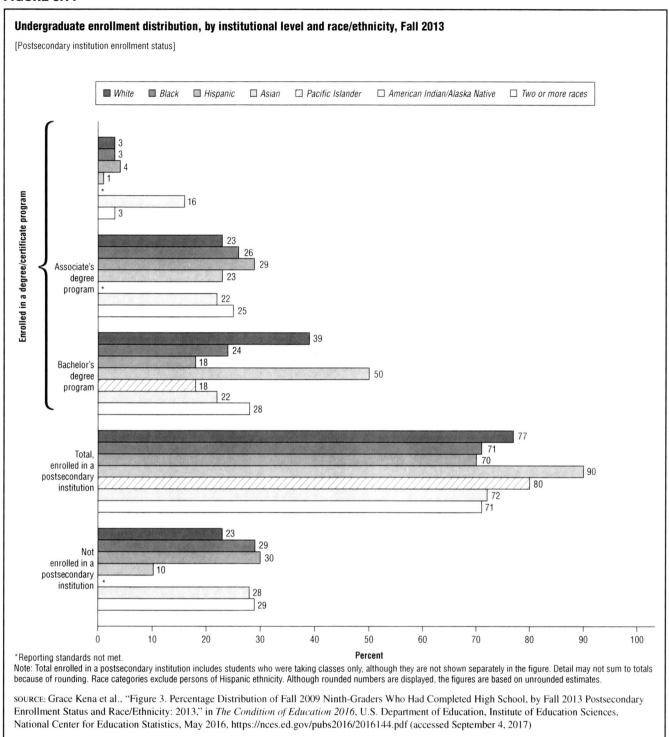

*Reporting standards not met.

Note: Total enrolled in a postsecondary institution includes students who were taking classes only, although they are not shown separately in the figure. Detail may not sum to totals because of rounding. Race categories exclude persons of Hispanic ethnicity. Although rounded numbers are displayed, the figures are based on unrounded estimates.

SOURCE: Grace Kena et al., "Figure 3. Percentage Distribution of Fall 2009 Ninth-Graders Who Had Completed High School, by Fall 2013 Postsecondary Enrollment Status and Race/Ethnicity: 2013," in *The Condition of Education 2016*, U.S. Department of Education, Institute of Education Sciences, National Center for Education Statistics, May 2016, https://nces.ed.gov/pubs2016/2016144.pdf (accessed September 4, 2017)

College completion rates among Asian Americans and Hispanics vary according to their country of origin. In *Status and Trends in the Education of Racial and Ethnic Groups 2016* (August 2016, https://nces.ed.gov/pubs2016/2016007.pdf), Musu-Gillette et al. report that among Hispanics aged 25 years and older in 2013, those who traced their roots to South America or Cuba had the highest completion rates, at 32% and 25%, respectively, followed by Puerto Ricans (18%) and Dominicans (17%).

A much lower proportion of Mexicans (10%) and Salvadorans (8%) had earned a bachelor's degree.

According to Musu-Gillette et al., among those of Asian origin, adults aged 25 years and older who traced their roots to India had the highest percentage of bachelor's degrees. Nearly three-quarters (73%) of Indians in this age group had a bachelor's degree in 2013, compared with 54% of Koreans, 52% of Chinese, 49% of Japanese, 48% of Filipinos, and 28% of Vietnamese.

By comparison, Musu-Gillette et al. indicate that 33% of whites aged 25 years and older held at least a bachelor's degree in 2013, as did 19% of African Americans.

Graduate School

Since the 1970s minorities have accounted for a steadily increasing proportion of students earning master's and doctoral degrees in the United States. Snyder, de Brey, and Dillow report in *Digest of Education, 2015* that African American students earned 88,515 out of the 754,475 master's degrees conferred during the 2013–14 academic year. Hispanic students earned 55,965 master's degrees that year, while Asian or Pacific Islander students earned 44,613 master's degrees, and Native American or Alaskan Native students earned 3,494 master's degrees. Combined, these groups accounted for more than a quarter (25.5%) of all the master's degrees earned in 2013–14. By comparison, in 1976–77 these groups earned only 10.4% of all master's degrees.

According to Snyder, de Brey, and Dillow, minority students accounted for a comparable proportion of

doctoral degrees in 2013–14. That year, Asians or Pacific Islanders earned 19,118 (10.8%) of the 177,580 doctoral degrees (including PhDs, M.D.s, and comparable degrees) conferred in the United States, African Americans earned 12,615 (7.1%), Hispanics earned 10,665 (6%), and Native Americans or Alaskan Natives earned 861 (0.5%). These figures represented a substantial improvement in the proportion of doctoral degrees granted to minorities in 1976–77, when African Americans earned 3.9%, Asians or Pacific Islanders earned 1.8%, Hispanics earned 1.7%, and Native Americans or Alaskan Natives earned 0.2% of all doctoral degrees.

In spite of this progress, in the early 21st century whites still earned the vast majority of graduate degrees in the United States, while also accounting for a majority of academic faculty positions at institutions of higher learning. (See Figure 3.12.) In 2013, in order to expand access to graduate education for minority students, the federal government launched a new initiative aimed at increasing funding to colleges and universities with large

FIGURE 3.12

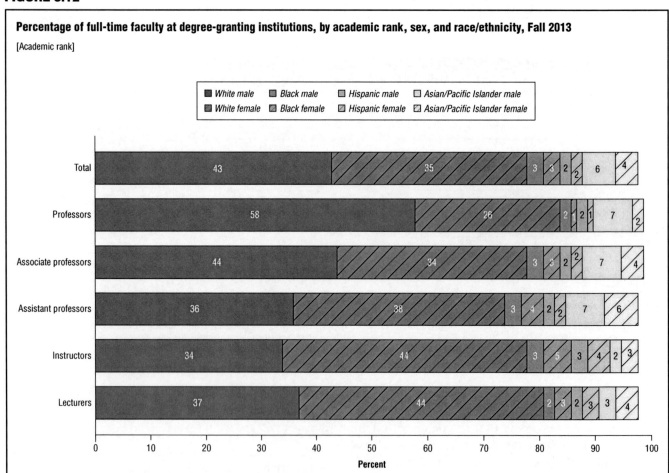

Percentage of full-time faculty at degree-granting institutions, by academic rank, sex, and race/ethnicity, Fall 2013

[Academic rank]

Note: Degree-granting institutions grant associate's or higher degrees and participate in Title IV federal financial aid programs. Race categories exclude persons of Hispanic ethnicity. Estimates are based on full-time faculty whose race/ethnicity was known. Detail may not sum to 100 percent because data on some racial/ethnic groups are not shown.

SOURCE: Grace Kena et al., "Figure 2. Percentage Distribution of Full-time Instructional Faculty in Degree-Granting Postsecondary Institutions, by Academic Rank, Selected Race/Ethnicity, and Sex: Fall 2013," in *The Condition of Education 2016*, U.S. Department of Education, Institute of Education Sciences, National Center for Education Statistics, May 2016, https://nces.ed.gov/pubs2016/2016144.pdf (accessed September 4, 2017)

minority student populations. The Department of Education reports in "Education Department Awards More than $2.7 Million to 12 Colleges to Strengthen Minority Participation in STEM-Related Fields" (September 18, 2013, http://www.ed.gov/news/press-releases/education-department-awards-more-27-million-12-colleges-strengthen-minority-part) that its Minority Science and Engineering Improvement Program awarded $2.7 million in grants, which were designed to encourage greater minority participation in STEM-related fields of study. At the same time, a number of individual colleges and universities launched similar programs aimed at improving minority access to graduate studies. In "UT's Intellectual Entrepreneurship Program Is Trying to Expand Minority Graduate School Enrollment" (DallasNews.com, October 11, 2013), Bill McKenzie explains that one notable initiative in 2013 was the Intellectual Entrepreneurship Program at the University of Texas, Austin, which aimed to expose minorities to academic disciplines and courses of study that they might not otherwise consider pursuing.

Affirmative Action in Higher Education

In the landmark 1978 affirmative action case *Regents of the University of California v. Bakke* (438 U.S. 265), the Supreme Court allowed race and ethnicity to be considered in college admissions in the interest of racial and ethnic diversity on U.S. college campuses. This led many schools to take special steps to boost the number of minorities that they admitted, a process commonly called affirmative action.

Over time, many people came to see affirmative action as a negative policy. Their reasons varied, but a common complaint was that affirmative action allowed some minority students to get into colleges even when their test scores and high school grades were below what those colleges would accept from white students. In June 1996 Pete Wilson (1933–), the governor of California, urged California voters to support the California Civil Rights Initiative (Proposition 209), a proposal to eliminate affirmative action in higher-education enrollment. In November 1996 California voters approved Proposition 209. Sheila O'Rourke of the University of California (UC) reports in "Strategies for Achieving Faculty Diversity at the University of California in a Post–Proposition 209 Legal Climate" (2002) that in 1997, the last year that UC considered race and ethnicity in its admissions process, 17.9% of the students who were admitted were from underrepresented minority groups (Native Americans, African Americans, and Hispanics). In 1998, the first year of admissions after Proposition 209 went into effect, the proportion of underrepresented minorities dropped to 15.5%.

In *Hopwood v. Texas* (78 F.3d 932 [1996]), the U.S. Court of Appeals for the Fifth Circuit unanimously ruled that the University of Texas (UT) School of Law was discriminating against white students by using race and ethnicity as a factor in admissions. Four white applicants charged that less-qualified African American and Hispanic students had been accepted instead of them because of racial preference on the part of UT. The appeals court ruled that colleges could not give preferences to minority students—even for what it called "the wholesome practice of correcting perceived racial imbalance in the student body." In the opinion of the appeals court, "any consideration of race or ethnicity by the law school for the purpose of achieving a diverse student body is not a compelling interest under the Fourteenth Amendment." The *Hopwood* decision applied to all public universities in Texas, Louisiana, and Mississippi. In Texas, Dan Morales (1956–), the attorney general of Texas, applied the admissions ruling to include financial aid and scholarships.

This decision negatively affected the number of underrepresented minority students at the UT School of Law. According to Lydia Lum, in "Minority Rolls Cut by Hopwood" (Chron.com, September 16, 1997), in 1997, following the decision affecting the law school, out of 500 incoming students, only four African American students and 26 Mexican Americans were enrolled, down from 31 African American students and 42 Mexican American students the previous year. At the undergraduate level, public universities throughout Texas also saw a drop in minority applications. Texas A&M University registered nearly 15% fewer Hispanics and 23% fewer African Americans that year.

PUBLIC UNIVERSITIES RESPOND. In 1998 the UT system became the first public university to grant automatic admission to first-time freshmen based on class rank. Under Texas Education Code 51.803, students who graduate in the top 10% of their class from an accredited Texas high school are guaranteed admission to UT. Because some high schools have large minority populations, state officials hoped that this policy would enable more minority students to attend state universities. After initial declines in minority enrollment, UT announced in early 2003 that Hispanic enrollment had returned to the pre-*Hopwood* level and that African American enrollment was nearing its 1996 level. However, James C. McKinley Jr. reports in "Texas Vote Curbs a College Admission Guarantee Meant to Bolster Diversity" (NYTimes.com, May 30, 2009) that in 2009 Texas legislators limited automatic college admissions to 75% of the incoming freshman class, although some state senators argued that such a limit would again depress minority enrollment. McKinley explains that this limit was put in place to give admissions officials more "latitude in putting together a class" and to lessen the so-called brain drain of students attending colleges and universities outside of the state.

In March 1999 UC regents approved a similar admissions policy called Eligibility in the Local Context (ELC). According to the University of California, in "Eligibility in the Local Context" (2014, admission.universityofcalifornia.edu/counselors/q-and-a/local/), as of 2014, students who graduated in the top 9% of their class from a California high school and who had completed a set of prerequisite courses were eligible for admission to one of UC's undergraduate campuses under the ELC program. The ELC was implemented starting with freshmen applicants during the fall of 2001. According to Rebecca Trounson, in "Admissions Studies Find Flaws" (LATimes.com, February 11, 2003), early reports did not find evidence, however, that the program boosted minority enrollment.

Catherine L. Horn and Stella M. Flores of Harvard University note in *Percent Plans in College Admissions: A Comparative Analysis of Three States' Experiences* (2003, http://civilrightsproject.ucla.edu/) that in November 1999 Florida implemented a similar plan called the Talented 20. Horn and Flores review the three admissions plans by Texas, California, and Florida and conclude that "any increases in racial/ethnic diversity on these campuses cannot be singularly attributed to percent plans because they have happened in the context of the extensive race-attentive efforts made by these schools."

Supreme Court Rulings

In June 2003 the Supreme Court made two separate rulings on the admissions practices at the University of Michigan's undergraduate college and law school. In an effort to achieve diversity in the student body, the undergraduate college used a point system by awarding points on a scale of 150 to African American, Hispanic, and Native American applicants. In *Gratz v. Bollinger* (539 U.S. 244), the court rejected this system, maintaining that it was too broad and too much like a quota, and ruled that it violated the equal protection clause in the 14th Amendment of the U.S. Constitution. By contrast, the University of Michigan law school weighed race and ethnicity along with a number of other admissions factors. In *Grutter v. Bollinger* (539 U.S. 306), the court deemed this approach legal because it furthered "a compelling interest in obtaining the educational benefits that flow from a diverse student body." As a result, the court upheld the concept of race-conscious admissions, but the nuanced approach to admissions that the court found acceptable left the door open for further lawsuits. Although smaller schools can devote more time and attention to individual applicants, larger institutions still face the problem of how to use race and ethnicity as a factor in screening many applications without assigning a numerical value to an individual's minority status.

Adam Liptak reports in "Justices Take up Race as a Factor in College Entry" (NYTimes.com, February 21, 2012) that in 2012 the Supreme Court agreed to hear a new challenge to affirmative action policies in higher education. After the 2003 Michigan rulings, education officials in Texas announced they would again use race as a factor for historically underrepresented minority groups. In 2008 Abigail Fisher, a white student from Sugar Land, Texas, was refused admission; she sued, alleging racial discrimination. After her claim was rejected by a federal judge and the U.S. Court of Appeals for the Fifth Circuit, the Supreme Court agreed to hear the case. In June 2013 the Supreme Court sent the case back to the Fifth Circuit Court of Appeals, on the grounds that the lower court had neglected to give full consideration to the university's affirmative action policies when rendering its decision. Two years later, after the Fifth Circuit Court of Appeals ruled against Fisher, the case once again found itself before the Supreme Court. According to Liptak, in "Supreme Court Upholds Affirmative Action Program at University of Texas" (NYTimes.com, June 23, 2016), the Supreme Court ruled in *Fisher v. University of Texas* (No. 14-981) that the affirmative action program at the University of Texas was constitutional, on the grounds that universities had the legal right to design admissions policies aimed at increasing diversity within the student body.

Meanwhile, in a separate case decided in April 2014, *Schuette v. Coalition to Defend Affirmative Action* (No. 12-682), the Supreme Court upheld an amendment to the Michigan constitution banning affirmative action in that state. Thus, as of 2017, Supreme Court rulings had indicated that affirmative action was legal when pursued correctly, but that there was nothing in the U.S. Constitution or federal law to prevent states from banning affirmative action.

Minority Education Advocacy

In the midst of the ongoing legal battle over affirmative action, the relative lack of quality educational opportunities for minorities continues to present a major concern to American educators. To address this ongoing issue, a number of organizations have emerged with the aim of improving minority access to education. Among the groups working toward this goal in 2017 was Quality Education for Minorities (2017, http://www.qem.org/), which aims to promote minority involvement in STEM-related courses of study. In addition, the Ad Council's Supporting Minority Education campaign (2017, https://www.adcouncil.org/Our-Campaigns/Education/Supporting-Minority-Education) has generated more than $4.3 billion in scholarship funding for African Americans over a 45-year period. Launched in Pittsburgh, Pennsylvania, in 1994, the Fund for Advancement of Minorities through Education (https://famefund.org/) is designed to guide African American students toward leadership positions in their communities by providing them with scholarships to attend leading independent schools.

Tribal Colleges

Special postsecondary institutions, collectively known as tribal colleges, have been established to prepare Native American or Alaskan Native students with the skills most needed on reservations, while at the same time preserving their culture. Usually situated in areas where the students cannot otherwise pursue education beyond high school without leaving the community, these colleges all offer associate's degrees. In addition, some offer bachelor's and master's degrees. Tribal colleges are located in Alaska, Arizona, Kansas, Michigan, Minnesota, Montana, Nebraska, New Mexico, North Dakota, Oklahoma, South Dakota, Washington, and Wisconsin.

Tribal colleges offer courses ranging from teaching and nursing to secretarial skills and computer science that meet the needs of specific communities. Tribal languages and other traditional subjects are a part of the curricula. For example, in *Salish Kootenai College 2016–2017 Catalog* (2017, https://www.skc.edu/wp-content/uploads/2016/08/SKC-2016_2017-Catalog.pdf), Salish Kootenai College in Montana indicates that a variety of tribal language and culture courses are offered, including "Coyote Stories," which covers morality tales that have important lessons of Native American life. "Tipi Setup" teaches students various techniques that are used by Montana tribes to erect tepees; "Hide Tanning" teaches students how to tan a fresh deer, elk, moose, or buffalo hide and turn it into buckskin; and "Stickgame" introduces students to the rules and techniques of this Native American game.

Christine A. Nelson and Joanna R. Frye report in *Tribal College and University Funding: Tribal Sovereignty at the Intersection of Federal, State, and Local Funding* (May 2016, http://www.acenet.edu/news-room/Documents/Tribal-College-and-University-Funding.pdf) that approximately 28,000 students were enrolled in tribal colleges in 2016. Of these, 84.2% were Native American or Alaskan Native.

Historically Black Colleges and Universities

According to the NCES, in "Historically Black Colleges and Universities" (2017, https://nces.ed.gov/fastfacts/display.asp?id=667), there were 102 historically black colleges and universities in the United States in 2015. Snyder, de Brey, and Dillow report in *Digest of Education, 2015* that 294,316 students, 254,589 of them African American, were enrolled in these institutions during the fall of 2014.

Historically black colleges and universities often offer unique courses and programs of study to students. For example, Howard University (2017, http://www.coas.howard.edu/afroamerican/courses.html), a traditionally black university that was founded in the District of Columbia in 1867, has an African American studies department that offers a major and a minor. Courses include "Black Philosophies of Education," which explores historical and contemporary theories of education of African American students; "Commercial Exploitation of the Third World," which examines colonial and imperialistic economies and explores the political and economic forces that influence people of color around the world; and both 19th- and 20th-century "Black Social and Political Thought," which examine influential political and social ideas that were supported by African American leaders in U.S. history. Florida A&M University (2017, http://famu.edu/index.cfm?histpol&AfricanAmericanStudies), which was founded in Tallahassee in 1887, also has an African American studies program. Majors are required to take courses such as "Blacks and the Political Process," "Black Psychology," and "Sociology of the Black Experience."

CHAPTER 4
MINORITIES IN THE LABOR FORCE

A HISTORICAL PERSPECTIVE

Members of minority groups have always been an important part of the U.S. labor force. In many instances groups were allowed and encouraged, or even forced, to immigrate to the United States (or, what would eventually become the United States) to fill specific labor needs. Perhaps the most obvious example is the involuntary immigration of Africans, who provided slave labor for southern plantations as early as the 17th century. Later, Asians and Hispanics were employed to mine resources, farm land, and build railroads.

African Americans

Since 1619, with the arrival of the first slave ships to North American shores, African Americans have been part of the labor force. Although most worked as unpaid slaves on southern plantations, a few were allowed to work for pay to purchase their freedom and that of their family, an effort that often took many years. Besides laboring on farms and in households, some enslaved people developed talents in masonry, music, or other skills and were hired out by their owners.

On January 1, 1863, during the Civil War (1861–1865), President Abraham Lincoln (1809–1865) issued the Emancipation Proclamation. This freed all slaves in the Confederacy, although the Confederate states did not recognize the authority of the Union government and blacks in the South remained enslaved. The proclamation did not free slaves who were being held in Northern states, where slavery remained legal unless it was abolished by state law. On January 31, 1865, Congress passed the 13th Amendment, which abolished slavery in the entire United States; it was ratified after the war. Then, on July 9, 1868, the 14th Amendment was ratified by three-fourths of the U.S. states, providing citizenship to African Americans, as it did to all immigrants born or naturalized in the United States. However, when the period of Reconstruction (1865–1877) came to an end, many southern states enacted so-called black codes, which were new laws that restricted the freedom of African Americans living in the South. These codes included provisions that forbade African Americans from leaving their jobs without permission. African Americans in the South labored under these codes for decades.

The Library of Congress (LOC) explains in "African Immigration" (2017, http://www.loc.gov/teachers/classroommaterials/presentationsandactivities/presentations/immigration/african.html) that because the best job prospects were in urban areas in the North and because the obstacles created by racial discrimination were the least burdensome there, hundreds of thousands of African Americans left their rural southern homes and migrated north and west before and during World War I (1914–1918) in search of unskilled work in factories and homes. During the 1940s arms production for World War II (1939–1945) again attracted hundreds of thousands of African Americans to the North, bringing about a moderate increase in the number of African American workers in these factories. These migrations of African Americans from the South to the North following both world wars were the largest movements of people within the United States in the country's history and did much to influence its future.

Asian Americans

In "Chinese Immigration to the United States, 1851–1900" (2017, http://www.loc.gov/teachers/classroommaterials/presentationsandactivities/presentations/timeline/riseind/chinimms/), the LOC notes that Chinese immigrants came to the United States during the 19th century because of the California gold rush but also to work on railroads, on farms, and in construction and manufacturing. This migration was largely ended by the federal Chinese Exclusion Act of 1882. Large-scale emigration from China to the United States would not resume until after World War II.

The LOC states in "Japanese Immigration" (2017, http://www.loc.gov/teachers/classroommaterials/presentationsandactivities/presentations/immigration/japanese.html) that between 1886 and 1911 more than 400,000 Japanese immigrants came to the United States, often to work on the rapidly expanding sugarcane plantations in Hawaii or on the fruit and vegetable farms in California. However, the Gentlemen's Agreement of 1907 between President Theodore Roosevelt (1858–1919) and the Japanese government stopped the flow of Japanese workers to the United States by withholding passports, thus cutting the flow to a trickle.

The most recent wave of Asian immigration to the United States took place during the 1970s and 1980s, when hundreds of thousands of refugees were admitted from Vietnam, Laos, and Cambodia following the Vietnam War (1954–1975). The first wave of refugees came from Vietnam when Saigon fell to the North Vietnamese communists in April 1975. More than 100,000 Vietnamese who had worked for the U.S. military during the war fled Vietnam for the United States, where they were resettled in communities around the nation. Subsequent waves of refugees fled Vietnam legally and illegally over the decades. According to the Southeast Asia Resource Action Center, in *Southeast Asian Americans at a Glance: Statistics on Southeast Asians Adapted from the American Community Survey* (October 6, 2011, http://www.searac.org/sites/default/files/STATISTICAL%20PROFILE%202010.pdf), as of 2010, the largest number of Vietnamese lived in California (647,589), Texas (227,968), Washington (75,843), Florida (65,772), and Virginia (59,984). When the Laotian government was toppled by a communist regime after the fall of South Vietnam in 1975, Laotian and Hmong refugees fled to Thailand and were then resettled in the United States. Likewise, when Cambodia was taken over by the Khmer Rouge in 1976, Cambodian refugees fled to Thailand and were then resettled in other countries, including the United States.

Hispanics

Many Hispanics can trace their roots to the time when the southwestern states were still a part of Mexico. The ancestors of most Hispanics, however, arrived after Mexico surrendered much of its territory following its defeat in the Mexican-American War (1846–1848). The U.S. policy toward Hispanic workers (mainly from Mexico) has alternately encouraged and discouraged immigration, reflecting the nation's changing needs for labor. In "Mexican Immigration" (2017, http://www.loc.gov/teachers/classroommaterials/presentationsandactivities/presentations/immigration/mexican.html), the LOC notes that before the 20th century, when there was little demand in the Southwest for Mexican labor, Mexicans moved back and forth across completely open borders to work in mines, on ranches, and on railroads.

However, as the Southwest began to develop and as Asian immigration slowed, the demand for Mexican labor increased. According to the LOC, "Between 1910 and

1930, the number of Mexican immigrants counted by the U.S. census tripled from 200,000 to 600,000." The need for Mexican labor was so great that during World War I the Immigration and Naturalization Service exempted many Mexicans from meeting most immigration conditions, such as head taxes (paying a small amount to enter the country) and literacy requirements. Although legal immigration rose, a large amount of illegal immigration also occurred. Historians estimate that during the 1920s there were as many illegal as legal Mexican immigrants in the country.

The LOC explains that during the Great Depression (1929–1939), when jobs became scarce, many Americans believed the nation's unemployment situation was significantly compounded by illegal immigrants working in the United States. As a result, hundreds of thousands of Mexican immigrants, including both legal and illegal immigrants, were repatriated (sent back) to Mexico.

Following the outbreak of World War II, the United States needed workers to help in its role as a supplier to the Allied countries. When the lure of better-paying factory jobs brought many rural workers to the city, the nation looked to Mexico to fill the need for agricultural workers. The Bracero Program (1942–1964) permitted the entry of Mexican farmworkers on a temporary contractual basis with U.S. employers. Although the program was considered to be an alternative to illegal immigration, it likely contributed to it because there were more workers who wanted to participate in the program than there were openings. According to the LOC, more than 5 million Mexican immigrants came to the United States during and after the war as part of the Bracero Program, and hundreds of thousands stayed.

Marc Perry et al. of the U.S. Census Bureau estimate in *Evaluating Components of International Migration: Legal Migrants* (December 2001, https://www.census.gov/population/www/documentation/twps0059/wtps0059.html) that more than 1 million undocumented Hispanics entered the United States during the early 1980s. A major downturn in the Mexican economy led to a surge in Mexican immigrants, and hundreds of thousands of other Hispanics arrived from Central America, most notably from El Salvador and Guatemala, to escape bloody civil wars and repressive regimes. Overall, Hispanics accounted for approximately one out of every three legal immigrants to the United States during this period. In 1986 the Immigration Reform and Control Act gave more than 2 million Mexicans legal status in the United States. Since that time, Hispanics from Cuba, Central and South America, and Mexico have continued to enter the United States, legally and illegally.

"GET TOUGH" POLICY. To stem the flow of undocumented workers, a "get tough" policy was initiated in 1994, but many critics believed that the money spent on installing infrared sensors, cameras, and stadium-level lighting along the U.S.-Mexican border was essentially wasted. Instead of crossing at more populated and better-secured areas, illegal immigrants crossed into the United States through mountains and deserts, facing dangerous conditions, and many died as a result.

In September 2006 Congress passed a bill that authorized the construction of a 700-mile (1,100-km) fence along the U.S.-Mexican border in California, Arizona, New Mexico, and Texas and the installation of a high-tech surveillance system to keep illegal Mexican immigrants from crossing into the United States. Jonathan Weisman reports in "With Senate Vote, Congress Passes Border Fence Bill" (WashingtonPost.com, September 30, 2006) that the fence would cost $6 billion to construct. Critics charged that the fence, as planned, would be impossible to construct across the rugged terrain and the borders of the Tohono O'odham Nation (who opposed the bill).

According to the U.S. Government Accountability Office (GAO), in *Secure Border Initiative: Technology Deployment Delays Persist and the Impact of Border Fencing Has Not Been Assessed* (September 2009, http://www.gao.gov/new.items/d09896.pdf), by June 2009, 661 miles (1,064 km) of the still-unfinished fence had been completed at a cost of $2.4 billion. The new fencing had been breached 3,363 times, requiring an average $1,300 repair for each breach, and the GAO estimated that the new fencing would cost $6.5 billion to maintain through 2029. CNN reports in "Homeland Security Chief Cancels Costly Virtual Border Fence" (CNN.com, January 14, 2011) that in January 2011 the U.S. Department of Homeland Security canceled the border fence program due to cost overruns and persistent technical issues.

Although arrests of illegal immigrants along the southwestern border increased after 1994, enforcement in the workplace was rare. In fact, the U.S. economy became so dependent on a pool of low-wage workers that mass deportation of undocumented workers was not a realistic option. In "Temporary Worker Program Is Explained" (WashingtonPost.com, October 19, 2005), Darryl Fears and Michael A. Fletcher note that in January 2004 President George W. Bush (1946–) proposed a guest-worker program that would grant a three-year work permit to millions of undocumented workers. This permit would be renewable for at least three more years, with a chance to apply for a green card to gain permanent residency. In addition, workers in other countries could apply for work permits to take jobs that no U.S. citizen wanted. That program was not approved, and since then various types of guest-worker programs have been introduced by many lawmakers.

Guest-worker programs have come under criticism because opponents argue they leave foreign workers vulnerable to exploitation. For example, the article "Broad Opposition to Guest Worker Program" (Associated Press,

October 21, 2009) indicates that a 2009 lawsuit alleged that a Tennessee company, the Cumberland Environmental Resources Company, abused the nonagricultural guest-worker program by lying about the availability of U.S. workers and failing to pay immigrants the prevailing wage required by law. The article also reports that a survey undertaken by the Economic Policy Institute in 2008 found that 98% of temporary workers "were paid less than the prevailing wage in occupations they commonly filled." According to Julia Preston, in "Suit Points to Guest Worker Program Flaws" (NYTimes.com, February 1, 2010), a 2007 lawsuit against a marine oil-rig company located in Mississippi alleged that Indian workers had been abused and discriminated against.

Farmworker Justice reports in "Labor Department Reverses Bush Administration Changes to Guestworker Program" (February 11, 2010, https://www.farmworkerjustice.org/sites/default/files/FJ%20Press%20Statement%20Solis%20Reversal%202010.pdf) that the Bush administration, having failed to expand the guest-worker programs already in place while in office, issued rules during its final days that reversed regulations, which had somewhat protected foreign workers in the H-2A program. These rules slashed minimum wages and reduced government oversight of the program. However, the following year the Obama administration restored the older minimum wage formula, reestablished the requirement that employers pay employees' transportation costs, and reinstated several government oversight regulations. In "Labor Dept. Issues New Rules for Guest Workers" (NYTimes.com, February 10, 2012), Preston notes that in February 2012 the U.S. Department of Labor issued important changes in the H-2B program that require businesses to hire qualified local workers if possible and that make it more difficult for businesses to exploit foreign workers by paying low wages.

STATE IMMIGRATION LAWS. In 2010 Arizona adopted the harshest immigration law in the United States, known as SB1070. This bill allowed police officers to ask about individuals' immigration status in the course of any contact with police. It also required officers to detain individuals who they suspected were illegal immigrants. Several of the law's most contentious provisions were blocked by federal courts, including provisions that required officers to check immigration status and that required immigrants to carry their immigration papers at all times. In April 2012 the U.S. Supreme Court heard arguments about whether to uphold the law or declare it unconstitutional. According to Dylan Smith, in "Supreme Court Strikes Down Most SB1070 Provisions" (TucsonSentinel.com, June 25, 2012), in June of that year the court invalidated several core provisions of the law, including those that made it a state crime for illegal immigrants to seek or engage in employment. At the same time, however, the court upheld the controversial provision that allowed police to verify the immigration status of individuals they suspected of having unlawfully entered the country.

IMMIGRATION AND THE 2016 PRESIDENTIAL ELECTION. In his 2016 presidential bid, the Republican candidate Donald Trump (1946–) made immigration a focal point of his campaign platform. Appealing to a segment of the American electorate that believed tackling the problem of illegal immigration should be a top priority of the federal government, Trump pledged to deport all of the estimated 11.3 million undocumented immigrants living in the United States in 2016. Trump later altered his stance, declaring that his administration would focus primarily on detaining and deporting illegal immigrants who had committed crimes. According to the article "Trump's Promises before and after the Election" (BBC.com, September 19, 2017), Trump contended that there were between 2 million and 3 million undocumented immigrants with criminal records in the United States in 2016. The article notes, however, that the Migration Policy Institute, a nonpartisan think tank based in the District of Columbia, estimated that the number of illegal immigrants with criminal records was closer to 890,000, a total that included people who had been charged with unlawfully entering the country.

Besides promising to increase deportations, Trump also pledged to implement other measures aimed at both curbing illegal immigration and enhancing national security. Among his proposed policies was the imposition of a travel ban on people trying to enter the United States from some Muslim countries, cutting funding to cities that refused to cooperate fully with federal immigration enforcement (known as "sanctuary cities"), and revoking President Obama's policy of Deferred Action for Childhood Arrivals (see Chapter 3). One of Trump's most controversial campaign promises included a plan to build a border wall between the United States and Mexico. Although Trump asserted that Mexico would pay for the project, the Mexican president Enrique Peña Nieto (1966–) continually denied that his government would fund Trump's border wall.

In the months after taking office in January 2017, President Trump introduced dramatic changes to the country's immigration policies. One of his first actions was in the form of an executive order that significantly expanded the nation's deportation efforts. Nigel Duara reports in "Arrests on Civil Immigration Charges Go Up 38% in the First 100 Days since Trump's Executive Order" (LATimes.com, May 17, 2017) that between January and May 2017 U.S. Immigration and Customs Enforcement officials arrested more than 40,000 undocumented immigrants, a 38% increase over the same period in 2016. Duara also notes that the Trump administration prioritized the removal of more than 8 million undocumented immigrants, nearly six times the 1.4 million illegal immigrants considered priorities for

deportation under President Obama. Meanwhile, Trump ordered a series of travel bans in 2017 that targeted emigrants from countries such as Syria, Iran, Yemen, and other countries the Trump administration considered to be security threats to the United States. These bans immediately became subject to legal challenges from the attorneys general of several states. In "Federal Judge Blocks Trump's Third Travel Ban" (WashingtonPost.com, October 17, 2017), Matt Zapotosky indicates that all three travel bans were ultimately deemed to exceed Trump's presidential authority by federal courts. As of November 2017, the Trump administration was expected to appeal these decisions.

LABOR FORCE PARTICIPATION AND UNEMPLOYMENT

Participation in the labor force means that a person is either employed or actively seeking employment. People who are not looking for work because they are going to school, retired, or disabled such that they are unable to work are not considered to be part of the labor force. The labor force increases with the long-term growth of the population. It responds to economic forces and social trends, and its size changes with the seasons.

To be classified as unemployed, a person must:

• Not have worked in the week specified for the survey

• Have actively sought work sometime during the four weeks preceding the survey

• Be currently available to take a suitable job

Due to the Great Recession (which lasted from late 2007 to mid-2009) the U.S. unemployment rate rose throughout much of 2008 and 2009, going from 4.7% in September 2007 to 10% in October 2009. (These statistics are "seasonally adjusted," meaning that the government has modified them to reflect predictable changes that occur over the course of a typical year. Unless otherwise noted, all employment statistics described in this chapter are seasonally adjusted.) This was the first time since 1983 that the unemployment rate reached double digits; it remained at or above 9% for another two years. According to the U.S. Bureau of Labor Statistics (BLS), in *The Employment Situation—August 2017* (September 1, 2017, https://www.bls.gov/news.release/pdf/empsit.pdf), in August 2017 the unemployment rate was 4.4%, down from 4.9% the previous year.

In spite of this recovery, some ethnic and racial groups were affected by lingering unemployment more than others. For example, in August 2017 more than 1.5 million African Americans in the civilian labor force were unemployed; this figure represented 7.7% of all African Americans in the civilian labor force. (See Table 4.1.) Their unemployment rate was nearly double that of the white population, at 3.9% (4.8 million). More than 1.4 million

TABLE 4.1

Employment status of the civilian population, by race, sex, and age, 2016–17

[Numbers in thousands]

Employment status, race, sex, and age	Not seasonally adjusted			Seasonally adjusted*					
	Aug. 2016	July 2017	Aug. 2017	Aug. 2016	Apr. 2017	May 2017	June 2017	July 2017	Aug. 2017
White									
Civilian noninstitutional population	198,380	198,974	199,082	198,380	198,685	198,775	198,872	198,974	199,082
Civilian labor force	124,998	126,046	125,280	124,736	124,925	124,481	124,890	124,968	125,037
Participation rate	63.0	63.3	62.9	62.9	62.9	62.6	62.8	62.8	62.8
Employed	119,477	121,029	120,365	119,269	120,142	119,896	120,091	120,262	120,209
Employment-population ratio	60.2	60.8	60.5	60.1	60.5	60.3	60.4	60.4	60.4
Unemployed	5,521	5,017	4,915	5,466	4,783	4,585	4,799	4,706	4,828
Unemployment rate	4.4	4.0	3.9	4.4	3.8	3.7	3.8	3.8	3.9
Not in labor force	73,382	72,928	73,802	73,644	73,760	74,294	73,982	74,006	74,046
Men, 20 years and over									
Civilian labor force	65,401	65,555	65,455	65,207	65,306	65,217	65,225	65,141	65,262
Participation rate	72.1	72.1	71.9	71.9	71.9	71.8	71.8	71.6	71.7
Employed	62,883	63,394	63,281	62,536	63,053	62,999	62,886	62,904	62,961
Employment-population ratio	69.4	69.7	69.5	69.0	69.4	69.3	69.2	69.2	69.2
Unemployed	2,518	2,161	2,174	2,671	2,253	2,218	2,339	2,238	2,301
Unemployment rate	3.8	3.3	3.3	4.1	3.4	3.4	3.6	3.4	3.5
Women, 20 years and over									
Civilian labor force	54,566	55,081	54,980	54,863	54,983	54,785	55,015	55,393	55,282
Participation rate	57.2	57.6	57.4	57.5	57.6	57.3	57.5	57.9	57.7
Employed	52,245	52,839	52,797	52,720	53,049	52,927	53,100	53,420	53,286
Employment-population ratio	54.8	55.2	55.2	55.3	55.5	55.4	55.5	55.8	55.7
Unemployed	2,321	2,242	2,183	2,143	1,935	1,858	1,915	1,973	1,996
Unemployment rate	4.3	4.1	4.0	3.9	3.5	3.4	3.5	3.6	3.6
Both sexes, 16 to 19 years									
Civilian labor force	5,031	5,411	4,845	4,665	4,635	4,479	4,650	4,433	4,492
Participation rate	40.7	43.8	39.3	37.8	37.5	36.3	37.7	35.9	36.4
Employed	4,349	4,796	4,288	4,013	4,040	3,970	4,105	3,938	3,962
Employment-population ratio	35.2	38.9	34.7	32.5	32.7	32.2	33.3	31.9	32.1
Unemployed	682	615	557	652	595	508	545	495	530
Unemployment rate	13.6	11.4	11.5	14.0	12.8	11.4	11.7	11.2	11.8
Black or African American									
Civilian noninstitutional population	31,945	32,260	32,296	31,945	32,161	32,193	32,226	32,260	32,296
Civilian labor force	19,840	20,309	20,142	19,767	20,110	20,075	20,002	20,096	20,092
Participation rate	62.1	63.0	62.4	61.9	62.5	62.4	62.1	62.3	62.2
Employed	18,167	18,719	18,542	18,170	18,514	18,560	18,576	18,617	18,544
Employment-population ratio	56.9	58.0	57.4	56.9	57.6	57.7	57.6	57.7	57.4
Unemployed	1,673	1,590	1,600	1,597	1,597	1,515	1,426	1,479	1,548
Unemployment rate	8.4	7.8	7.9	8.1	7.9	7.5	7.1	7.4	7.7
Not in labor force	12,106	11,951	12,154	12,178	12,051	12,118	12,224	12,163	12,204
Men, 20 years and over									
Civilian labor force	8,960	9,250	9,214	8,950	9,169	9,063	9,084	9,163	9,205
Participation rate	67.3	68.7	68.3	67.3	68.3	67.5	67.5	68.0	68.2
Employed	8,298	8,598	8,521	8,269	8,496	8,475	8,510	8,522	8,487
Employment-population ratio	62.4	63.8	63.2	62.2	63.3	63.1	63.3	63.3	62.9
Unemployed	661	652	693	680	673	588	574	641	718
Unemployment rate	7.4	7.0	7.5	7.6	7.3	6.5	6.3	7.0	7.8
Women, 20 years and over									
Civilian labor force	10,025	10,118	10,108	10,025	10,168	10,224	10,143	10,170	10,127
Participation rate	62.2	62.2	62.0	62.2	62.7	62.9	62.4	62.5	62.1
Employed	9,249	9,420	9,405	9,316	9,470	9,513	9,455	9,511	9,474
Employment-population ratio	57.4	57.9	57.7	57.8	58.4	58.6	58.1	58.4	58.1
Unemployed	776	698	703	709	698	712	689	660	653
Unemployment rate	7.7	6.9	7.0	7.1	6.9	7.0	6.8	6.5	6.4
Both sexes, 16 to 19 years									
Civilian labor force	855	941	820	792	773	787	774	763	760
Participation rate	34.0	37.5	32.7	31.5	30.8	31.3	30.8	30.4	30.3
Employed	619	701	617	585	547	572	611	585	583
Employment-population ratio	24.6	27.9	24.6	23.3	21.8	22.8	24.3	23.3	23.2
Unemployed	236	239	204	207	226	215	163	178	178
Unemployment rate	27.6	25.4	24.8	26.2	29.3	27.3	21.1	23.3	23.4

(5.2%) Hispanics in the civilian labor force were unemployed in August 2017. (See Table 4.2.) After white Americans, the lowest unemployment rate was among Asian Americans. Table 4.1 shows that in August 2017, 397,000 Asian Americans in the civilian labor force were unemployed, with an unemployment rate of 4%.

TABLE 4.1

Employment status of the civilian population, by race, sex, and age, 2016–17 [CONTINUED]

[Numbers in thousands]

Employment status, race, sex, and age	Not seasonally adjusted			Seasonally adjusted*					
	Aug. 2016	July 2017	Aug. 2017	Aug. 2016	Apr. 2017	May 2017	June 2017	July 2017	Aug. 2017
Asian									
Civilian noninstitutional population	15,304	15,290	15,341	15,304	15,389	15,433	15,367	15,290	15,341
Civilian labor force	9,705	9,866	9,894	9,702	9,761	9,826	9,792	9,789	9,886
Participation rate	63.4	64.5	64.5	63.4	63.4	63.7	63.7	64.0	64.4
Employed	9,298	9,467	9,498	9,293	9,446	9,471	9,443	9,418	9,489
Employment-population ratio	60.8	61.9	61.9	60.7	61.4	61.4	61.4	61.6	61.9
Unemployed	406	398	396	409	316	356	350	370	397
Unemployment rate	4.2	4.0	4.0	4.2	3.2	3.6	3.6	3.8	4.0
Not in labor force	5,600	5,424	5,446	5,603	5,628	5,607	5,575	5,502	5,455

*The population figures are not adjusted for seasonal variation; therefore, identical numbers appear in the unadjusted and seasonally adjusted columns.
Note: Updated population controls are introduced annually with the release of January data.

SOURCE: "Table A-2. Employment Status of the Civilian Population by Race, Sex, and Age," in *The Employment Situation—August 2017*, U.S. Department of Labor, Bureau of Labor Statistics, September 1, 2017, https://www.bls.gov/news.release/pdf/empsit.pdf (accessed September 5, 2017)

TABLE 4.2

Employment status of the Hispanic population, by sex and age, 2016–17

[Numbers in thousands]

Employment status, sex, and age	Not seasonally adjusted			Seasonally adjusted*					
	Aug. 2016	July 2017	Aug. 2017	Aug. 2016	Apr. 2017	May 2017	June 2017	July 2017	Aug. 2017
Hispanic or Latino ethnicity									
Civilian noninstitutional population	40,825	41,404	41,492	40,825	41,162	41,241	41,323	41,404	41,492
Civilian labor force	27,007	27,677	27,335	26,988	27,241	27,239	27,290	27,487	27,322
Participation rate	66.2	66.8	65.9	66.1	66.2	66.0	66.0	66.4	65.8
Employed	25,483	26,204	25,922	25,460	25,832	25,833	25,974	26,078	25,914
Employment-population ratio	62.4	63.3	62.5	62.4	62.8	62.6	62.9	63.0	62.5
Unemployed	1,524	1,473	1,413	1,528	1,410	1,405	1,315	1,409	1,408
Unemployment rate	5.6	5.3	5.2	5.7	5.2	5.2	4.8	5.1	5.2
Not in labor force	13,818	13,727	14,157	13,838	13,921	14,003	14,034	13,917	14,170
Men, 20 years and over									
Civilian labor force	14,912	15,146	15,038	14,895	14,927	14,936	14,976	15,085	15,017
Participation rate	81.0	81.2	80.5	80.9	80.5	80.4	80.5	80.9	80.4
Employed	14,252	14,537	14,367	14,176	14,297	14,304	14,414	14,425	14,298
Employment-population ratio	77.4	78.0	76.9	77.0	77.1	77.0	77.5	77.4	76.5
Unemployed	660	609	670	719	630	632	562	660	719
Unemployment rate	4.4	4.0	4.5	4.8	4.2	4.2	3.8	4.4	4.8
Women, 20 years and over									
Civilian labor force	10,903	11,121	11,028	10,957	11,086	11,062	11,030	11,176	11,091
Participation rate	58.5	58.8	58.2	58.8	59.0	58.7	58.4	59.1	58.5
Employed	10,238	10,486	10,481	10,322	10,493	10,461	10,451	10,580	10,570
Employment-population ratio	54.9	55.4	55.3	55.4	55.8	55.5	55.4	55.9	55.8
Unemployed	665	635	547	635	593	601	579	596	521
Unemployment rate	6.1	5.7	5.0	5.8	5.4	5.4	5.3	5.3	4.7
Both sexes, 16 to 19 years									
Civilian labor force	1,193	1,410	1,269	1,136	1,228	1,240	1,284	1,227	1,214
Participation rate	31.5	36.7	32.9	30.0	32.1	32.3	33.4	31.9	31.5
Employed	994	1,182	1,073	962	1,042	1,068	1,110	1,073	1,046
Employment-population ratio	26.2	30.7	27.9	25.4	27.2	27.8	28.9	27.9	27.1
Unemployed	199	229	196	174	186	172	174	154	169
Unemployment rate	16.7	16.2	15.4	15.3	15.2	13.9	13.6	12.5	13.9

*The population figures are not adjusted for seasonal variation; therefore, identical numbers appear in the unadjusted and seasonally adjusted columns.
Note: Persons whose ethnicity is identified as Hispanic or Latino may be of any race. Updated population controls are introduced annually with the release of January data.

SOURCE: "Table A-3. Employment Status of the Hispanic or Latino Population by Sex and Age," in *The Employment Situation—August 2017*, U.S. Department of Labor, Bureau of Labor Statistics, September 1, 2017, https://www.bls.gov/news.release/pdf/empsit.pdf (accessed September 5, 2017)

African Americans

Overall, there were 20.1 million African American men and women aged 16 years and older in the labor force in August 2017, for a participation rate of 62.2%. (See Table 4.1.) The comparable figures for whites were 125 million and 62.8%. Although unemployment rates rise and fall with the strength of the economy, for several decades the unemployment rates for African Americans have been nearly twice the rates for whites. Often having fewer marketable skills and less education than do whites, in addition to facing long-standing discrimination in the labor force, African Americans are more likely to remain unemployed for longer periods, especially during a recession. As a result, they are more likely to be labeled as "long-term unemployed" (those without work for at least 27 weeks).

In August 2017 the unemployment rate for African American men aged 20 years and older was 7.8% (718,000), which was more than double the rate for white men of the same age, 3.5% (2.3 million). (See Table 4.1.) African American women aged 20 years and older had an unemployment rate of 6.4% (653,000), compared with an unemployment rate of 3.6% (2 million) among white women of the same age.

Hispanics

The BLS began maintaining annual employment data on Hispanics in 1973. In August 2017, 27.3 million Hispanics were employed or actively looking for work, for a labor force participation rate of 65.8%. (See Table 4.2.) However, the labor force participation rate among Hispanic subgroups varies. In 2016 Mexican Americans had the highest overall participation rate among the three largest Hispanic groups in the United States. Roughly two out of three Mexican Americans (16.5 million, or 65.9%) aged 16 years and older participated in the civilian labor force, followed by Cuban Americans (1.1 million, or 63.2%) and Puerto Ricans (2.3 million, or 60.1%). (See Table 4.3.)

In all three Hispanic subgroups, men aged 20 years and older had a much higher labor force participation rate than did women of the same age. This difference in rates of labor force participation was especially pronounced for Mexican Americans. Among Mexican Americans, 9.3 million (82%) men and 6.3 million (57.2%) women participated in the labor force in 2016. (See Table 4.3.) Among Cuban Americans, 625,000 (74.9%) men and 508,000 (57.5%) women participated in the labor force. Among Puerto Ricans, 1.1 million (69.2%) men and 1.1 million (57.7%) women participated in the labor force.

Asian Americans

In August 2017 an unadjusted 9.9 million (64.5%) Asian Americans aged 16 years and older were in the civilian labor force. (See Table 4.1.) In 2016 an unadjusted 4.4 million (57.4%) Asian American women and 5 million (75.3%) Asian American men aged 20 years and older were in the labor force. (See Table 4.4.) In that year, a higher percentage of Asian American men aged 20 years and older was participating in the labor force than either white men (65.2 million, or 72%) or African American men (9 million, or 67.5%). Among women aged 20 years and older, the Asian American participation rate was lower than both that of white women (54.9 million, or 57.6%) and African American women (9.9 million, or 61.8%).

As of August 2017, the unemployment rate for Asian Americans was 4% (397,000). (See Table 4.1.) This was lower than the rate for any other racial or ethnic group. The low rate of unemployment among Asian Americans can be attributed, in part, to their high educational attainment and their commitment to small family businesses.

Native Americans or Alaskan Natives

Gathering accurate statistical data on the labor force participation rates of Native Americans is difficult. They are often counted as "other" in BLS and Census Bureau data, making specific information hard to obtain. In addition, the concepts that guide the assessment of labor force participation nationally are considered to be inappropriate for Native American population groups. For example, because few jobs are available on many reservations, many adults do not actively seek work—but to exclude these individuals from the statistics on the labor force results in a serious underestimation of unemployment of Native Americans.

In "American Indian and Alaska Native Heritage Month: November 2013" (October 31, 2013, https://www.census.gov/content/dam/Census/newsroom/facts-for-features/2013/cb13ff-26_aian.pdf), the most recent source of data as of November 2017, the Census Bureau calculates that 22% of Native Americans or Alaskan Natives lived in "American Indian areas" (reservations or trust lands) in 2010. The Bureau of Indian Affairs (BIA) notes in *2013 American Indian Population and Labor Force Report* (January 16, 2014, http://www.lb7.uscourts.gov/documents/14-10515.pdf) that in 2010 the civilian employment rates among tribal service populations 16 years of age and older averaged just over 49%, but varied greatly among tribal service areas. For example, employment rates were highest in tribal areas in Alabama and Kansas, where the BIA estimates that nearly 65% of the population aged 16 years and older was employed in 2010. That year employment rates hovered above 60% in tribal service areas in Massachusetts and Mississippi, and above 55% in Florida, Oklahoma, and Wyoming. Employment rates in tribal service areas were lowest in Arizona and Iowa, where employment rates for individuals aged 16 years and older were below 40% in 2010.

TABLE 4.3

Employment status of the Mexican, Puerto Rican, and Cuban populations in the United States, by sex and age, 2015–16

[Numbers in thousands]

| | Hispanic or Latino ethnicity | | | | | | | |
| Employment status, sex, and age | Total* | | Mexican | | Puerto Rican | | Cuban | |
	2015	2016	2015	2016	2015	2016	2015	2016
Total								
Civilian noninstitutional population	39,617	40,697	24,711	24,960	3,679	3,835	1,760	1,819
Civilian labor force	26,126	26,797	16,392	16,458	2,220	2,305	1,079	1,149
Participation rate	65.9	65.8	66.3	65.9	60.4	60.1	61.3	63.2
Employed	24,400	25,249	15,342	15,502	2,022	2,146	1,010	1,088
Employment-population ratio	61.6	62.0	62.1	62.1	55.0	56.0	57.4	59.8
Unemployed	1,726	1,548	1,050	955	198	159	69	61
Unemployment rate	6.6	5.8	6.4	5.8	8.9	6.9	6.4	5.3
Not in labor force	13,491	13,900	8,319	8,503	1,459	1,530	681	670
Men, 16 years and over								
Civilian noninstitutional population	19,745	20,266	12,476	12,594	1,756	1,833	883	882
Civilian labor force	15,054	15,396	9,675	9,718	1,172	1,196	610	632
Participation rate	76.2	76.0	77.5	77.2	66.7	65.3	69.1	71.6
Employed	14,111	14,563	9,099	9,199	1,062	1,114	566	597
Employment-population ratio	71.5	71.9	72.9	73.0	60.5	60.8	64.1	67.7
Unemployed	943	833	576	519	110	82	44	35
Unemployment rate	6.3	5.4	6.0	5.3	9.4	6.9	7.3	5.5
Not in labor force	4,691	4,870	2,801	2,876	584	636	273	250
Men, 20 years and over								
Civilian noninstitutional population	17,860	18,346	11,238	11,356	1,585	1,652	824	834
Civilian labor force	14,444	14,775	9,256	9,309	1,124	1,142	596	625
Participation rate	80.9	80.5	82.4	82.0	70.9	69.2	72.3	74.9
Employed	13,624	14,055	8,761	8,863	1,025	1,072	553	592
Employment-population ratio	76.3	76.6	78.0	78.0	64.6	64.9	67.0	71.0
Unemployed	820	720	495	446	99	70	43	33
Unemployment rate	5.7	4.9	5.3	4.8	8.8	6.2	7.2	5.2
Not in labor force	3,416	3,571	1,982	2,047	461	509	229	210
Women, 16 years and over								
Civilian noninstitutional population	19,872	20,430	12,234	12,366	1,923	2,002	876	936
Civilian labor force	11,072	11,401	6,716	6,740	1,048	1,108	468	517
Participation rate	55.7	55.8	54.9	54.5	54.5	55.4	53.5	55.2
Employed	10,289	10,686	6,243	6,304	961	1,032	444	491
Employment-population ratio	51.8	52.3	51.0	51.0	50.0	51.5	50.6	52.4
Unemployed	783	715	474	436	88	77	25	26
Unemployment rate	7.1	6.3	7.1	6.5	8.4	6.9	5.3	5.1
Not in labor force	8,800	9,029	5,518	5,626	874	894	408	419
Women, 20 years and over								
Civilian noninstitutional population	18,052	18,573	10,989	11,089	1,763	1,830	815	884
Civilian labor force	10,539	10,844	6,347	6,345	1,002	1,056	453	508
Participation rate	58.4	58.4	57.8	57.2	56.8	57.7	55.6	57.5
Employed	9,853	10,217	5,942	5,969	922	987	431	484
Employment-population ratio	54.6	55.0	54.1	53.8	52.3	53.9	52.9	54.7
Unemployed	686	627	404	376	79	69	22	24
Unemployment rate	6.5	5.8	6.4	5.9	7.9	6.5	4.9	4.8
Not in labor force	7,513	7,729	4,643	4,743	762	774	362	376
Both sexes, 16 to 19 years								
Civilian noninstitutional population	3,705	3,777	2,483	2,516	330	353	120	101
Civilian labor force	1,144	1,178	789	804	95	107	30	16
Participation rate	30.9	31.2	31.8	31.9	28.7	30.2	24.9	16.3
Employed	922	977	638	670	75	87	26	12
Employment-population ratio	24.9	25.9	25.7	26.6	22.8	24.6	21.7	12.3
Unemployed	221	201	151	133	20	20	4	4
Unemployment rate	19.3	17.1	19.1	16.6	20.7	18.6	—	—
Not in labor force	2,562	2,599	1,695	1,713	236	246	90	84

*Includes persons of Central or South American origin and of other Hispanic or Latino ethnicity, not shown separately.
Note: Persons whose ethnicity is identified as Hispanic or Latino may be of any race. Updated population controls are introduced annually with the release of January data. Dash indicates no data or data that do not meet publication criteria (values not shown where base is less than 35,000).

SOURCE: "6. Employment Status of the Hispanic or Latino Population by Sex, Age, and Detailed Ethnic Group," in *Current Population Survey*, U.S. Department of Labor, Bureau of Labor Statistics, February 8, 2017, http://www.bls.gov/cps/cpsaat06.pdf (accessed September 5, 2017)

In many cases reservations do not generate the jobs that are necessary to support Native American families. Even when Native Americans are employed, the BIA notes that

23.2% of families earn incomes that fall below the poverty guidelines. This fact helps explain why Native American tribes have been so willing to introduce or expand casino

TABLE 4.4

Employment status of the civilian noninstitutional population, by sex, age, and race, 2015–16

[Numbers in thousands]

Employment status, sex, and age	Total 2015	Total 2016	White 2015	White 2016	Black or African American 2015	Black or African American 2016	Asian 2015	Asian 2016
Total								
Civilian noninstitutional population	250,801	253,538	196,868	198,215	31,386	31,889	14,420	15,121
Civilian labor force	157,130	159,187	123,607	124,658	19,318	19,637	9,053	9,562
Participation rate	62.7	62.8	62.8	62.9	61.5	61.6	62.8	63.2
Employed	148,834	151,436	117,944	119,313	17,472	17,982	8,706	9,213
Employment-population ratio	59.3	59.7	59.9	60.2	55.7	56.4	60.4	60.9
Unemployed	8,296	7,751	5,662	5,345	1,846	1,655	347	349
Unemployment rate	5.3	4.9	4.6	4.3	9.6	8.4	3.8	3.6
Not in labor force	93,671	94,351	73,261	73,557	12,068	12,252	5,366	5,559
Men, 16 years and over								
Civilian noninstitutional population	121,101	122,497	96,147	96,861	14,268	14,525	6,737	7,064
Civilian labor force	83,620	84,755	67,018	67,564	9,099	9,315	4,811	5,091
Participation rate	69.1	69.2	69.7	69.8	63.8	64.1	71.4	72.1
Employed	79,131	80,568	63,892	64,612	8,164	8,471	4,620	4,915
Employment-population ratio	65.3	65.8	66.5	66.7	57.2	58.3	68.6	69.6
Unemployed	4,490	4,187	3,126	2,952	935	845	191	176
Unemployment rate	5.4	4.9	4.7	4.4	10.3	9.1	4.0	3.5
Not in labor force	37,481	37,743	29,129	29,297	5,169	5,209	1,925	1,973
Men, 20 years and over								
Civilian noninstitutional population	112,671	114,023	89,865	90,572	13,031	13,278	6,331	6,640
Civilian labor force	80,735	81,759	64,710	65,169	8,773	8,965	4,728	5,000
Participation rate	71.7	71.7	72.0	72.0	67.3	67.5	74.7	75.3
Employed	76,776	78,084	61,959	62,575	7,938	8,228	4,552	4,836
Employment-population ratio	68.1	68.5	68.9	69.1	60.9	62.0	71.9	72.8
Unemployed	3,959	3,675	2,751	2,594	835	737	176	164
Unemployment rate	4.9	4.5	4.3	4.0	9.5	8.2	3.7	3.3
Not in labor force	31,936	32,263	25,155	25,403	4,258	4,313	1,603	1,640
Women, 16 years and over								
Civilian noninstitutional population	129,700	131,040	100,720	101,354	17,118	17,365	7,683	8,057
Civilian labor force	73,510	74,432	56,589	57,095	10,218	10,321	4,242	4,471
Participation rate	56.7	56.8	56.2	56.3	59.7	59.4	55.2	55.5
Employed	69,703	70,868	54,052	54,701	9,308	9,511	4,086	4,298
Employment-population ratio	53.7	54.1	53.7	54.0	54.4	54.8	53.2	53.4
Unemployed	3,807	3,564	2,537	2,393	911	810	156	172
Unemployment rate	5.2	4.8	4.5	4.2	8.9	7.8	3.7	3.9
Not in labor force	56,190	56,608	44,132	44,260	6,899	7,043	3,441	3,586
Women, 20 years and over								
Civilian noninstitutional population	121,511	122,801	94,680	95,301	15,863	16,102	7,256	7,635
Civilian labor force	70,695	71,538	54,410	54,871	9,843	9,943	4,154	4,383
Participation rate	58.2	58.3	57.5	57.6	62.0	61.8	57.2	57.4
Employed	67,323	68,387	52,161	52,771	9,032	9,219	4,008	4,218
Employment-population ratio	55.4	55.7	55.1	55.4	56.9	57.3	55.2	55.2
Unemployed	3,371	3,151	2,249	2,100	811	724	146	165
Unemployment rate	4.8	4.4	4.1	3.8	8.2	7.3	3.5	3.8
Not in labor force	50,816	51,263	40,270	40,430	6,021	6,159	3,102	3,252
Both sexes, 16 to 19 years								
Civilian noninstitutional population	16,619	16,714	12,323	12,342	2,491	2,510	833	846
Civilian labor force	5,700	5,889	4,487	4,618	701	729	172	179
Participation rate	34.3	35.2	36.4	37.4	28.1	29.0	20.6	21.2
Employed	4,734	4,965	3,824	3,967	502	535	147	159
Employment-population ratio	28.5	29.7	31.0	32.1	20.1	21.3	17.7	18.8
Unemployed	966	925	662	651	199	194	25	20
Unemployment rate	16.9	15.7	14.8	14.1	28.4	26.7	14.4	10.9
Not in labor force	10,919	10,824	7,836	7,724	1,790	1,781	661	667

Note: Estimates for the above race groups will not sum to totals because data are not presented for all races. Updated population controls are introduced annually with the release of January data.

SOURCE: "5. Employment Status of the Civilian Noninstitutional Population by Sex, Age, and Race," in *Current Population Survey*, U.S. Department of Labor, Bureau of Labor Statistics, February 8, 2017, http://www.bls.gov/cps/cpsaat05.pdf (accessed September 5, 2017)

gambling on their reservations. According to the National Indian Gaming Commission, in "2016 Indian Gaming Revenues Increased 4.4%" (July 17, 2017, https://www.nigc.gov/news/detail/2016-indian-gaming-revenues-increased-4.4), in 2016, 244 Native American tribes engaged in gaming in 28 states and generated $31.2 billion in revenues.

DISCRIMINATORY EMPLOYMENT PRACTICES

Under Title VII of the Civil Rights Act of 1964, employers may not intentionally use race, skin color, age, gender, religious beliefs, or national origin as the basis for decisions relating to almost any aspect of the employment relationship, including hiring. Despite this law, African Americans, Hispanics, and other minority groups continue to suffer from discriminatory hiring practices as well as from other race- and ethnicity-based obstacles to finding employment.

In one of the highest profile workplace discrimination cases in recent years, civil rights attorneys filed a class action lawsuit in June 2003 against Abercrombie & Fitch, one of the nation's largest clothing retailers, for discriminating against people of Hispanic, Asian American, and African American descent. The young adults were represented by the Mexican American Legal Defense and Educational Fund, the Asian Pacific American Legal Center, the National Association for the Advancement of Colored People's Legal Defense and Educational Fund, and the law firm of Lieff Cabraser Heimann & Bernstein LLP. In "Abercrombie Fitch Race Discrimination" (2017, https://www.lieffcabraser.com/employment/abercrombie-fitch/), Lieff Cabraser Heimann & Bernstein explains that a settlement was approved in April 2005. The company agreed to pay $40 million to the applicants and employees who charged the company with discrimination and to comply with provisions related to the recruitment, hiring, job assignment, training, and promotion of minority employees. This was a prominent case brought to court; however, in general, discriminatory employment practices are difficult to prosecute effectively and remain pervasive in the United States.

In 2006 the federal government filed a lawsuit against a medical clinic in California because a manager used racial code words, including "reggin," which Barbara Feder Ostrov explains in "Discrimination at Work Growing Subtle" (MercuryNews.com, August 12, 2006) is an "infamous racial slur spelled backward." An African American file clerk was fired from her job after she complained about the racial slurs. The case underscored the changing nature of racial and ethnic discrimination in the workplace, as methods of intimidation become more subtle. This kind of subtle discrimination does not always lead to lawsuits. In fact, the Level Playing Field Institute reports in "The Cost of Employee Turnover Due Solely to Unfairness in the Workplace" (June 22, 2007, http://www.lpfi.org/wp-content/uploads/2015/05/cl-executive-summary.pdf) that each year 2 million professionals and managers leave their jobs because they are "pushed out by cumulative small comments, whispered jokes and not-so-funny emails."

The U.S. Equal Employment Opportunity Commission (EEOC) won a settlement in a racial harassment lawsuit against Lockheed Martin in 2008. In the press release "Lockheed Martin to Pay $2.5 Million to Settle Racial Harassment Lawsuit" (January 2, 2008, http://www.eeoc.gov/eeoc/newsroom/release/1-2-08.cfm), the EEOC notes that Charles Daniels, an African American electrician, was awarded $2.5 million after being harassed at job sites nationwide, including being threatened with lynching and other physical harm. Coworkers and a supervisor reportedly told Daniels that "we should do to blacks what Hitler did to the Jews" and "if the South had won then this would be a better country." The company failed to discipline the harassers when it was made aware of the situation.

Abercrombie & Fitch found itself at the center of another discrimination case in 2008, when the retailer refused to hire Samantha Elauf, a Muslim woman, after she wore a hijab (a head scarf) during her job interview. Although Abercrombie & Fitch claimed that its dress code prohibited the wearing of head scarves by employees, Elauf and the EEOC sued the company on grounds of religious discrimination. In "Muslim Woman Denied Job over Head Scarf Wins in Supreme Court" (NYTimes.com, June 1, 2015), Adam Liptak reports that in 2015 the Supreme Court ruled in Elauf's favor, asserting that Abercrombie & Fitch had violated her religious freedom in denying her employment.

In another high-profile case, in January 2012 Pepsi Beverages agreed to pay $3.1 million and to provide jobs and training to African American applicants for positions at the company. The EEOC explains in the press release "Pepsi to Pay $3.13 Million and Made Major Policy Changes to Resolve EEOC Finding of Nationwide Hiring Discrimination against African Americans" (January 11, 2012, http://www.eeoc.gov/eeoc/newsroom/release/1-11-12a.cfm) that Pepsi's use of the criminal background check policy discriminated against African Americans. The company used arrest records to bar applicants from jobs even if the applicants had never been convicted, a policy that disproportionally affected African Americans. Julie Schmid, the acting director of the EEOC's Minneapolis Area Office, stated, "When employers contemplate instituting a background check policy, the EEOC recommends that they take into consideration the nature and gravity of the offense, the time that has passed since the conviction and/or completion of the sentence, and the nature of the job sought in order to be sure that the exclusion is important for the particular position. Such exclusions can create an adverse impact based on race in violation of Title VII."

U.S. Equal Employment Opportunity Commission

In May 2000 the EEOC issued new guidelines to facilitate the settlement of federal-sector discrimination complaints, including claims brought under Title VII. Under the administration of Chair Ida L. Castro (1953–), the EEOC sought to reform its complaint process for federal employees. The new directive authorizes federal agencies to enter into settlement of bias claims, including monetary payment.

In fiscal year (FY) 2016 the EEOC received 32,309 charges under Title VII alleging race-based discrimination. (See Table 4.5.) That same year the EEOC resolved 33,936 charges (some of these cases were carried over from the previous fiscal year). Of those, 2,280 (6.7%) were settled. The percentage of settled cases was up substantially from FY 1997, when only 3.3% (1,206) were settled. In FY 2016 another 709 (2.1%) of the claims were found to have reasonable cause; 268 (0.8%) of these were charges with reasonable cause that closed after successful conciliation and 411 (1.3%) of them were charges with reasonable cause that closed after unsuccessful conciliation. Another 1,503 (4.4%) cases were withdrawn by the charging party on receipt of desired benefits ("withdrawals with benefits"). In other words, 4,903 cases of racial discrimination were found to have reasonable cause or were settled or withdrawn after the employer admitted culpability and submitted to a monetary settlement. Countless other incidents of racial discrimination in the workplace are never brought to the attention of the EEOC. Instead, victims suffer silently or leave their places of employment, as found by the Level Playing Field Institute Survey.

Views of Economic Opportunities

According to Jeffrey M. Jones of Gallup, Inc., in *As in 1963, Blacks Still Feel Disadvantaged in Getting Jobs* (August 28, 2013, http://www.gallup.com/poll/164153/1963-blacks-feel-disadvantaged-getting-jobs.aspx), in 2013 a majority (60%) of African Americans believed they had less of a chance than whites of getting a job for which they were qualified. This figure represented a decline from 1963, when nearly three-quarters (74%) of African Americans felt themselves at a disadvantage in the job market, but was an increase from 1995, when just over half (52%) of African Americans believed they were less likely to be hired than whites. In *Nearly Half of Blacks Treated Unfairly "in Last 30 Days"* (August 22, 2016, http://news.gallup.com/poll/194750/nearly-half-blacks-treated-unfairly-last-days.aspx), Jim Norman of Gallup reveals that African Americans also believed they were more likely to confront racial prejudice in the workplace. In 2016 nearly one out of five (19%) of African Americans had contended with racial discrimination at the their job during the previous month. Overall, more than half (52%) of African Americans believed they were treated unfairly at work because of their race. By contrast, only 17% of whites believed African Americans were treated unfairly at work due to racial discrimination.

WORKFORCE PROJECTIONS FOR 2024

In 2014, 16.3% of the workforce was Hispanic (and of any race), 12.1% was African American, and 5.6% was Asian American. (See Table 4.6.) More Hispanics than any other group are projected to enter the workforce through 2024, causing Hispanics to make up an increasingly large share of the workforce. By 2024 they will equal 19.8% of the workforce. The proportion of Asian Americans in the labor force is expected to grow to 6.6% by 2024, while the percentage of African Americans in the labor force is expected to increase slightly, to 12.7%. The proportion of non-Hispanic whites in the labor force is expected to decrease from 64.6% in 2014 to 59.6% in 2024. As recently as 1994, non-Hispanic whites made up more than three-quarters (76.7%) of the workforce.

The increasing share of the workforce that is projected to be Hispanic, Asian American, and African American reflects a combination of high fertility and immigration rates for these groups when compared with non-Hispanic whites. In addition, the share of non-Hispanic white men who participate in the labor force is projected to decline, which is a consequence of the aging of the white male labor force.

OCCUPATIONS
African Americans and Jobs

African Americans are much less likely than whites or Asian Americans to hold the jobs that require the most education and pay the highest salaries—those in management, professional, and related occupations. In 2016 just under 18 million African Americans accounted for 11.9% of the civilian labor force aged 16 years and older. (See Table 4.7.) Only 30.1% of employed African Americans held management, professional, or related occupations, compared with 40% of white workers. Women of both races were more likely to hold these positions, but only 34.8% of African American women were managers or professionals, compared with 44.4% of white women. As with labor force participation rates in general, fewer educational opportunities, a lack of marketable skills, and racial discrimination are likely factors preventing African Americans from obtaining equal access to professional and management positions.

African Americans were much more likely than whites to work in the poorly paid service occupations in 2016. That year, 25.1% of African Americans worked in service occupations. (See Table 4.7.) By contrast, 16.5% of white Americans worked in service occupations in 2016.

Any growth in professional employment for African Americans has generally occurred in fields at the lower end of the earnings scale. The BLS (February 8, 2017, https://www.bls.gov/cps/cpsaat11.htm) notes that 30.3% of all licensed practical and vocational nurses were African American in 2016, but only 11.9% of registered nurses, 8.5% of nurse practitioners, 7.5% of physicians and surgeons, and 3.2% of dentists were African American. The same pattern holds true for management positions. Although 15.4% of social and community service

TABLE 4.5

Race-based charges filed and resolved under Title VII of the Civil Rights Act of 1964, fiscal years 1997–2016

	FY 1997	FY 1998	FY 1999	FY 2000	FY 2001	FY 2002	FY 2003	FY 2004	FY 2005	FY 2006	FY 2007	FY 2008	FY 2009	FY 2010	FY 2011	FY 2012	FY 2013	FY 2014	FY 2015	FY 2016
Receipts	29,199	28,820	28,819	28,945	28,912	29,910	28,526	27,696	26,740	27,238	30,510	33,937	33,579	35,890	35,395	33,512	33,068	31,073	31,027	32,309
Resolutions	36,419	35,716	35,094	33,188	32,077	33,199	30,702	29,631	27,411	25,992	25,882	28,321	31,129	37,559	40,534	38,426	33,978	30,429	31,782	33,936
Resolutions by type																				
Settlements	1,206	1,460	2,138	2,802	2,549	3,059	2,890	2,927	2,801	3,039	2,945	3,069	3,065	3,325	3,307	3,020	2,709	2,274	2,610	2,280
	3.3%	4.1%	6.1%	8.4%	7.9%	9.2%	9.4%	9.9%	10.2%	11.7%	11.4%	10.8%	9.8%	8.9%	8.2%	7.9%	8.0%	7.5%	8.2%	6.7%
Withdrawals w/benefits	912	823	1,036	1,150	1,203	1,200	1,125	1,088	1,167	1,177	1,235	1,435	1,530	1,567	1,657	1,545	1,621	1,500	1,430	1,503
	2.5%	2.3%	3.0%	3.5%	3.8%	3.6%	3.7%	3.7%	4.3%	4.5%	4.8%	5.1%	4.9%	4.2%	4.1%	4.0%	4.8%	4.9%	4.5%	4.4%
Administrative closures	8,395	7,871	7,213	5,727	5,626	5,043	4,759	4,261	3,674	3,436	3,931	3,964	4,803	5,018	5,719	4,571	4,516	4,263	4,368	4,444
	23.1%	22.0%	20.6%	17.3%	17.5%	15.2%	15.5%	14.4%	13.4%	13.2%	15.2%	14.0%	15.4%	13.4%	14.1%	11.9%	13.3%	14.0%	13.7%	13.1%
No reasonable cause	24,988	24,515	23,148	21,319	20,302	21,853	20,506	20,166	18,608	17,324	16,773	18,792	20,530	26,319	28,602	28,111	24,175	21,737	22,696	25,000
	68.6%	68.6%	66.0%	64.2%	63.3%	65.8%	66.8%	68.1%	67.9%	66.7%	64.8%	66.4%	66.0%	70.1%	70.6%	73.2%	71.1%	71.4%	71.4%	73.7%
Reasonable cause	918	1,047	1,559	2,190	2,397	2,044	1,422	1,189	1,161	1,016	998	1,061	1,201	1,330	1,248	1,179	957	655	678	709
	2.5%	2.9%	4.4%	6.6%	7.5%	6.2%	4.6%	4.0%	4.2%	3.9%	3.9%	3.7%	3.9%	3.5%	3.1%	3.1%	2.8%	2.2%	2.1%	2.1%
Successful conciliations	248	287	382	529	691	580	392	330	377	292	285	355	392	377	322	450	424	215	254	268
	0.7%	0.8%	1.1%	1.6%	2.2%	1.7%	1.3%	1.1%	1.4%	1.1%	1.1%	1.3%	1.3%	1.0%	0.8%	1.2%	1.2%	0.7%	0.8%	0.8%
Unsuccessful conciliations	670	760	1,177	1,661	1,706	1,464	1,030	859	784	724	713	706	809	953	926	729	533	440	424	411
	1.8%	2.1%	3.4%	5.0%	5.3%	4.4%	3.4%	2.9%	2.9%	2.8%	2.8%	2.5%	2.6%	2.5%	2.3%	1.9%	1.6%	1.4%	1.3%	1.3%
Merit resolutions	3,036	3,330	4,733	6,142	6,149	6,303	5,437	5,204	5,129	5,232	5,178	5,565	5,796	6,222	6,212	5,744	5,287	4,429	4,718	4,492
	8.3%	9.3%	13.5%	18.5%	19.2%	19.0%	17.7%	17.6%	18.7%	20.1%	20.0%	19.6%	18.6%	16.6%	15.3%	14.9%	15.6%	14.6%	14.8%	13.2%
Monetary benefits (millions)*	$41.8	$32.2	$53.2	$61.7	$86.5	$81.1	$69.6	$61.1	$76.5	$61.4	$67.7	$79.3	$82.4	$84.4	$83.3	$100.9	$112.7	$74.9	$88.4	$79.0

FY = fiscal year

*Does not include monetary benefits obtained through litigation.

Notes: The data are compiled by the Office of Research, Information and Planning from data compiled from Equaly Employment Opportunity Commission's (EEOC) Charge Data System, and from fiscal year 2004 forward, EEOC's Integrated Mission System. This does not include charges filed with state or local Fair Employment Practices Agencies. The total of individual percentages may not always sum to 100% due to rounding. EEOC total workload includes charges carried over from previous fiscal years, new charge receipts and charges transferred to EEOC from Fair Employment Practice Agencies (FEPAs). Resolution of charges each year may therefore exceed receipts for that year because workload being resolved is drawn from a combination of pending, new receipts, and FEPA transfer charges rather than from new charges only.

SOURCE: "Race-Based Charges (Charges filed with EEOC) FY 1997–FY 2016," in *Enforcement and Litigation Statistics*, U.S. Equal Employment Opportunity Commission, Office of Research, Information, and Planning, 2016, https://www.eeoc.gov/eeoc/statistics/enforcement/race.cfm (accessed September 5, 2017)

TABLE 4.6

Civilian labor force, by age, sex, race, and ethnicity, 1994, 2004, 2014, and projected 2024

[Numbers in thousands]

Group	Level				Change			Percent change			Percent distribution				Annual growth rate (percent)		
	1994	2004	2014	2024	1994–2004	2004–2014	2014–2024	1994–2004	2004–2014	2014–2024	1994	2004	2014	2024	1994–2004	2004–2014	2014–2024
Total, 16 years and older	131,056	147,401	155,922	163,770	16,345	8,521	7,848	12.5	5.8	5.0	100.0	100.0	100.0	100.0	1.2	0.6	0.5
Age, years:																	
16 to 24	21,612	22,268	21,295	18,498	656	973	2,797	3.0	4.4	13.1	16.5	15.1	13.7	11.3	0.3	0.4	1.4
25 to 54	93,898	102,122	100,767	104,697	8,224	1,355	3,930	8.8	1.3	3.9	71.6	69.3	64.6	63.9	0.8	0.1	0.4
55 and older	15,547	23,011	33,860	40,575	7,464	10,849	6,715	48.0	47.1	19.8	11.9	15.6	21.7	24.8	4.0	3.9	1.8
Gender:																	
Men	70,817	78,980	82,882	86,524	8,163	3,902	3,642	11.5	4.9	4.4	54.0	53.6	53.2	52.8	1.1	0.5	0.4
Women	60,239	68,421	73,039	77,246	8,182	4,618	4,207	13.6	6.7	5.8	46.0	46.4	46.8	47.2	1.3	0.7	0.6
Race:																	
White	111,082	121,086	123,327	126,143	10,004	2,241	2,816	9.0	1.9	2.3	84.8	82.1	79.1	77.0	0.9	0.2	0.2
Black	14,502	16,638	18,873	20,772	2,136	2,235	1,899	14.7	13.4	10.1	11.1	11.3	12.1	12.7	1.4	1.3	1.0
Asian	5,473	6,271	8,760	10,792	798	2,489	2,032	14.6	39.7	23.2	4.2	4.3	5.6	6.6	1.4	3.4	2.1
All other groups*	—	3,406	4,961	6,063	—	1,555	1,102	—	45.7	22.2	—	2.3	3.2	3.7	—	3.8	2.0
Ethnicity:																	
Hispanic origin	11,975	19,272	25,370	32,486	7,297	6,098	7,116	60.9	31.6	28.0	9.1	13.1	16.3	19.8	4.9	2.8	2.5
Other than Hispanic origin	119,081	128,129	130,552	131,284	9,048	2,423	732	7.6	1.9	0.6	90.9	86.9	83.7	80.2	0.7	0.2	0.1
White non-Hispanic	100,462	103,202	100,661	97,622	2,740	2,541	3,039	2.7	2.5	3.0	76.7	70.0	64.6	59.6	0.3	0.2	0.3
Age of baby boomers	30 to 48	40 to 58	50 to 68	60 to 78													

*The "all other groups" category includes (1) those classified as being of multiple racial origin and (2) the racial categories of (2a) American Indian and Alaska Native and (2b) Native Hawaiian and other Pacific Islanders.

Note: Dash indicates no data collected for category. Details may not sum to totals because of rounding.

SOURCE: Mitra Toossi, "Table 1. Civilian Labor Force, by Age, Gender, Race, and Ethnicity, 1994, 2004, 2014, and Projected 2024," in "Labor Force Projections to 2024: The Labor Force Is Growing, but Slowly," *Monthly Labor Review*, December 2015, https://www.bls.gov/opub/mlr/2015/article/labor-force-projections-to-2024.htm (accessed September 5, 2017)

TABLE 4.7

Employed persons by occupation, race, Hispanic origin, and sex, 2015–16

[Percent distribution]

Occupation, race, and Hispanic or Latino ethnicity	Total		Men		Women	
	2015	2016	2015	2016	2015	2016
Total						
Total, 16 years and over (in thousands)	148,834	151,436	79,131	80,568	69,703	70,868
Percent of total employed	100.0	100.0	100.0	100.0	100.0	100.0
Management, professional, and related occupations	38.9	39.2	35.5	35.8	42.9	43.2
Management, business, and financial operations occupations	16.2	16.5	17.2	17.4	15.1	15.4
Professional and related occupations	22.7	22.8	18.3	18.4	27.8	27.8
Service occupations	17.4	17.7	14.2	14.4	21.1	21.4
Sales and office occupations	22.6	22.1	16.4	16.2	29.6	28.9
Sales and related occupations	10.5	10.5	10.1	10.0	11.1	11.0
Office and administrative support occupations	12.0	11.7	6.3	6.1	18.5	18.0
Natural resources, construction, and maintenance occupations	9.2	9.2	16.5	16.4	0.9	0.9
Farming, fishing, and forestry occupations	0.7	0.7	1.0	1.1	0.4	0.3
Construction and extraction occupations	5.1	5.2	9.4	9.5	0.3	0.3
Installation, maintenance, and repair occupations	3.4	3.2	6.1	5.8	0.3	0.2
Production, transportation, and material moving occupations	11.9	11.7	17.4	17.2	5.5	5.5
Production occupations	5.7	5.6	7.7	7.5	3.5	3.4
Transportation and material moving occupations	6.1	6.1	9.8	9.6	2.0	2.2
White						
Total, 16 years and over (in thousands)	117,944	119,313	63,892	64,612	54,052	54,701
Percent of total employed	100.0	100.0	100.0	100.0	100.0	100.0
Management, professional, and related occupations	39.6	40.0	36.0	36.3	44.0	44.4
Management, business, and financial operations occupations	17.0	17.3	18.2	18.4	15.6	16.0
Professional and related occupations	22.7	22.7	17.8	17.9	28.4	28.4
Service occupations	16.2	16.5	13.1	13.5	19.8	20.0
Sales and office occupations	22.6	22.1	16.2	15.9	30.1	29.5
Sales and related occupations	10.8	10.6	10.4	10.3	11.2	11.0
Office and administrative support occupations	11.8	11.5	5.8	5.6	18.9	18.5
Natural resources, construction, and maintenance occupations	10.2	10.1	17.9	17.9	1.0	1.0
Farming, fishing, and forestry occupations	0.8	0.8	1.1	1.2	0.4	0.4
Construction and extraction occupations	5.7	5.9	10.3	10.5	0.3	0.4
Installation, maintenance, and repair occupations	3.6	3.5	6.5	6.2	0.3	0.2
Production, transportation, and material moving occupations	11.4	11.3	16.8	16.4	5.1	5.1
Production occupations	5.6	5.5	7.6	7.5	3.2	3.1
Transportation and material moving occupations	5.8	5.7	9.2	8.9	1.9	2.0
Black or African American						
Total, 16 years and over (in thousands)	17,472	17,982	8,164	8,471	9,308	9,511
Percent of total employed	100.0	100.0	100.0	100.0	100.0	100.0
Management, professional, and related occupations	30.4	30.1	24.9	24.9	35.2	34.8
Management, business, and financial operations occupations	11.3	11.3	10.9	11.0	11.7	11.6
Professional and related occupations	19.1	18.8	14.0	13.9	23.6	23.2
Service occupations	24.8	25.1	21.6	20.9	27.7	28.8
Sales and office occupations	23.7	23.5	17.4	18.2	29.2	28.3
Sales and related occupations	9.5	9.7	8.1	8.5	10.7	10.8
Office and administrative support occupations	14.2	13.8	9.3	9.7	18.5	17.5
Natural resources, construction, and maintenance occupations	5.7	5.7	11.5	11.2	0.6	0.7
Farming, fishing, and forestry occupations	0.3	0.3	0.5	0.5	0.1	0.2
Construction and extraction occupations	3.0	3.0	6.2	6.1	0.2	0.2
Installation, maintenance, and repair occupations	2.4	2.4	4.8	4.7	0.2	0.3
Production, transportation, and material moving occupations	15.4	15.6	24.7	24.8	7.3	7.4
Production occupations	6.1	6.1	8.4	8.4	4.1	4.0
Transportation and material moving occupations	9.3	9.5	16.3	16.4	3.2	3.4
Asian						
Total, 16 years and over (in thousands)	8,706	9,213	4,620	4,915	4,086	4,298
Percent of total employed	100.0	100.0	100.0	100.0	100.0	100.0
Management, professional, and related occupations	51.3	52.3	52.3	53.4	50.2	51.0
Management, business, and financial operations occupations	17.3	17.9	17.1	18.0	17.5	17.8
Professional and related occupations	33.9	34.4	35.1	35.4	32.6	33.2
Service occupations	16.1	16.1	12.7	12.4	20.0	20.3
Sales and office occupations	19.9	18.9	17.0	16.1	23.2	22.1
Sales and related occupations	10.2	9.8	10.2	10.0	10.2	9.6
Office and administrative support occupations	9.7	9.1	6.8	6.1	13.0	12.5

managers and 14.3% of education administrators were African American in 2016, only 7.1% of general and operations managers, 3.8% of construction managers, and 3.4% of chief executives were African American.

TABLE 4.7

Employed persons by occupation, race, Hispanic origin, and sex, 2015–16 [CONTINUED]

[Percent distribution]

Occupation, race, and Hispanic or Latino ethnicity	Total		Men		Women	
	2015	2016	2015	2016	2015	2016
Natural resources, construction, and maintenance occupations	3.1	3.4	5.4	5.7	0.4	0.7
Farming, fishing, and forestry occupations	0.2	0.2	0.2	0.2	0.2	0.2
Construction and extraction occupations	1.1	1.5	2.1	2.5	0.1	0.2
Installation, maintenance, and repair occupations	1.8	1.7	3.2	3.0	0.2	0.2
Production, transportation, and material moving occupations	9.6	9.3	12.6	12.3	6.2	5.9
Production occupations	6.0	5.4	6.6	6.2	5.4	4.6
Transportation and material moving occupations	3.6	3.9	6.0	6.2	0.8	1.2
Hispanic or Latino ethnicity						
Total, 16 years and over (in thousands)	**24,400**	**25,249**	**14,111**	**14,563**	**10,289**	**10,686**
Percent of total employed	**100.0**	**100.0**	**100.0**	**100.0**	**100.0**	**100.0**
Management, professional, and related occupations	21.5	22.0	17.8	18.3	26.6	27.0
Management, business, and financial operations occupations	9.3	9.7	9.1	9.5	9.7	10.0
Professional and related occupations	12.2	12.3	8.7	8.8	16.9	17.0
Service occupations	24.9	25.4	19.9	20.3	31.8	32.2
Sales and office occupations	21.1	20.8	14.3	14.3	30.4	29.6
Sales and related occupations	9.7	9.8	7.8	8.2	12.2	12.1
Office and administrative support occupations	11.4	10.9	6.5	6.1	18.2	17.5
Natural resources, construction, and maintenance occupations	16.3	16.3	26.7	26.8	2.0	2.1
Farming, fishing, and forestry occupations	2.0	2.0	2.6	2.6	1.2	1.1
Construction and extraction occupations	10.4	10.7	17.6	18.0	0.6	2.7
Installation, maintenance, and repair occupations	3.9	3.7	6.5	6.2	0.3	0.3
Production, transportation, and material moving occupations	16.1	15.6	21.3	20.3	9.1	9.1
Production occupations	7.8	7.5	9.1	8.7	5.9	5.7
Transportation and material moving occupations	8.4	8.1	12.2	11.6	3.2	3.4

Note: Estimates for the above race groups (white, black or African American, and Asian) do not sum to totals because data are not presented for all races. Persons whose ethnicity is identified as Hispanic or Latino may be of any race. Updated population controls are introduced annually with release of January data.

SOURCE: "10. Employed Persons by Occupation, Race, Hispanic or Latino Ethnicity, and Sex," in *Current Population Survey*, U.S. Department of Labro, Bureau of Labor Statistics, February 8, 2017, https://www.bls.gov/cps/cpsaat10.pdf (accessed September 5, 2017)

Hispanics and Jobs

Overall, Hispanics are less likely than any other group to hold professional and management positions. In 2016 only 22% of employed Hispanics held management, professional, and related occupations, compared with 30.1% of African Americans, who had the next-lowest representation in this area. (See Table 4.7.) As with African Americans, Hispanics were hindered by a lack of access to educational and training opportunities in their pursuit of these types of positions. The largest percentage of Hispanics worked in service occupations (25.4%), where they are seriously overrepresented, compared with 17.7% of workers overall in these low-paying occupations. More than one out of five (20.8%) Hispanic workers worked in sales and office occupations.

In 2016, 25.2 million Hispanics worked, making up 16.7% of the workforce. (See Table 4.7.) According to the BLS (February 8, 2017, https://www.bls.gov/cps/cpsaat11 .htm), Hispanics were concentrated in low-paying jobs. In 2016 they made up 32.8% of janitors and building cleaners, 43.1% of grounds maintenance workers, and 47.3% of maids and housekeeping cleaners. They also made up 25.8% of the food preparation and serving related occupations, including 27.8% of dining room and cafeteria attendants and bartender helpers, 35% of cooks, and 35.4% of dishwashers. By contrast, they made up only 17.6% of first-line supervisors of food preparation and serving workers and 17% of bartenders.

Significant occupational differences exist among Hispanic subgroups. Cuban Americans have traditionally done better in securing higher-paying jobs because they are often well educated. In 2016, 385,000 out of 1.1 million (35.4%) Cuban Americans in the workforce held management, professional, and related occupations. (See Table 4.8.) In contrast, 623,000 out of 2.1 million (29%) Puerto Ricans in the workforce and 2.9 million out of 15.5 million (18.9%) Mexican Americans in the workforce held management, professional, and related occupations. Mexican Americans were more likely to work in service occupations (4 million, or 25.6%) than in other occupations, especially in food preparation and serving related occupations and building and grounds cleaning and maintenance occupations.

Asian Americans and Jobs

The high educational attainment of many Asian Americans is a likely explanation for the fact that a larger proportion of them work in higher-paying jobs than do other racial and ethnic groups. In 2016 more than half (52.3%) of all Asian Americans worked in management, professional, and related occupations: 34.4% in professional and related occupations and 17.9% in management, business, and financial operations occupations. (See Table 4.7.) By comparison, only 40% of whites worked in these occupations. The BLS (February 8, 2017, https://www.bls.gov/cps/cpsaat11.htm)

TABLE 4.8

Employed Hispanic workers by sex, occupation, class of workers, full- or part-time status, and detailed ethnic group, 2015–16

[In thousands]

Category	Total[a] 2015	Total[a] 2016	Mexican 2015	Mexican 2016	Puerto Rican 2015	Puerto Rican 2016	Cuban 2015	Cuban 2016
Total, 16 years and over	**24,400**	**25,249**	**15,342**	**15,502**	**2,022**	**2,146**	**1,010**	**1,088**
Men	14,111	14,563	9,099	9,199	1,062	1,114	566	597
Women	10,289	10,686	6,243	6,304	961	1,032	444	491
Occupation								
Management, professional, and related occupations	5,249	5,551	2,872	2,929	624	623	354	385
Management, business, and financial operations occupations	2,278	2,456	1,250	1,343	254	241	152	162
Management occupations	1,650	1,720	924	970	172	154	119	117
Business and financial operations occupations	628	735	327	373	82	86	33	45
Professional and related occupations	2,971	3,095	1,621	1,586	370	382	202	223
Computer and mathematical occupations	297	315	145	143	34	31	25	21
Architecture and engineering occupations	241	273	135	155	25	30	18	23
Life, physical, and social science occupations	98	112	50	52	14	15	4	7
Community and social service occupations	277	317	147	171	44	46	15	14
Legal occupations	135	151	67	71	22	22	11	13
Education, training, and library occupations	884	895	508	503	104	111	58	51
Arts, design, entertainment, sports, and media occupations	328	329	183	143	32	34	16	23
Healthcare practitioner and technical occupations	710	703	386	347	95	92	55	70
Service occupations	6,084	6,403	3,835	3,964	452	494	180	198
Healthcare support occupations	580	601	317	328	65	65	31	29
Protective service occupations	433	438	246	246	67	69	32	20
Food preparation and serving related occupations	2,057	2,200	1,396	1,459	141	147	47	54
Building and grounds cleaning and maintenance occupations	2,171	2,217	1,408	1,404	105	117	45	63
Personal care and service occupations	842	947	469	528	75	96	25	33
Sales and office occupations	5,150	5,243	3,164	3,158	522	564	238	253
Sales and related occupations	2,363	2,486	1,469	1,468	208	251	121	124
Office and administrative support occupations	2,787	2,758	1,695	1,690	314	313	118	129
Natural resources, construction, and maintenance occupations	3,980	4,119	2,808	2,880	172	202	105	117
Farming, fishing, and forestry occupations	490	493	436	442	3	2	2	1
Construction and extraction occupations	2,546	2,696	1,749	1,851	80	101	58	71
Installation, maintenance, and repair occupations	944	929	622	588	88	99	45	45
Production, transportation, and material moving occupations	3,937	3,933	2,663	2,571	252	263	133	136
Production occupations	1,898	1,884	1,344	1,284	116	111	46	45
Transportation and material moving occupations	2,039	2,050	1,320	1,287	137	151	87	90
Class of worker[b]								
Agriculture								
Wage and salary workers[c]	560	576	502	513	5	2	4	2
Self-employed workers, unincorporated	19	27	14	24	1	0	0	0
Nonagricultural industries								
Wage and salary workers[c]	22,266	23,095	13,841	14,023	1,942	2,054	929	1,013
Government	2,333	2,437	1,408	1,443	303	314	110	111
Private industries	19,933	20,657	12,433	12,579	1,639	1,740	819	901
Private households	306	279	173	142	5	6	8	15
Other industries	19,628	20,378	12,260	12,437	1,634	1,734	811	886
Self-employed workers, unincorporated	1,541	1,540	974	932	75	91	77	74
Full- or part-time status[d]								
Full-time workers	20,056	20,813	12,605	12,735	1,646	1,752	867	945
Part-time workers	4,344	4,436	2,737	2,767	376	394	143	143

[a]Includes persons of Central or South American origin and of other Hispanic or Latino ethnicity, not shown separately.
[b]Unpaid family workers are included in total employed, but are not shown separately.
[c]Includes self-employed workers whose businesses are incorporated.
[d]Employed persons are classified as full- or part-time workers based on their usual weekly hours at all jobs regardless of the number of hours they are at work during the reference week. Persons absent from work also are classified according to their usual status. Full time is 35 hours or more per week; part time is less than 35 hours.
Note: Persons whose ethnicity is identified as Hispanic or Latino may be of any race. Updated population controls are introduced annually with the release of January data.

SOURCE: "13. Employed Hispanic or Latino Workers by Sex, Occupation, Class of Worker, Full- or Part-Time Status, and Detailed Ethnic Group," in *Current Population Survey*, U.S. Department of Labor, Bureau of Labor Statistics, February 8, 2017, https://www.bls.gov/cps/cpsaat13.pdf (accessed September 5, 2017)

indicates that although only 6.1% of the workforce was of Asian origin, 8.1% of managers and professionals were Asian American, and they were especially overrepresented among computer hardware engineers (29.2%); medical scientists

(37.3%); and software developers, applications workers, and systems software workers (35.7%)—three highly paid occupations.

Native Americans or Alaskan Natives and Jobs

As stated previously, detailed data on Native American or Alaskan Native workers are difficult to obtain. The EEOC, however, keeps some basic data on job patterns for minorities in private industry that includes Native Americans or Alaskan Natives as a separate category. In 2015 Native Americans made up only 0.55% of the total workforce. (See Table 4.9.) They made up only 0.31% of all executives and senior-level managers, 0.37% of all first- and midlevel officials and managers, and only 0.35% of professionals. Nonetheless, Native Americans were overrepresented among craft workers (0.86%), operatives (0.65%), sales workers (0.6%), and technicians (0.6%).

MINORITIES AND THE FEDERAL GOVERNMENT

Traditionally, white men have held most of the higher-level positions in the federal government. Along with cabinet members selected by the president, these high-level officials wield much of the power in the federal government. This holds true for many agencies, including the Federal Bureau of Investigation, the U.S. Immigration and Customs Enforcement, and the U.S. Customs and Border Protection.

In *Federal Equal Opportunity Recruitment Program (FEORP), Fiscal Year 2014* (February 2016, https://www.opm.gov/policy-data-oversight/diversity-and-inclusion/reports/feorp-2014.pdf), the U.S. Office of Personnel Management finds that in FY 2014 minorities were overrepresented in the federal workforce with the exception of Hispanics, who were significantly underrepresented in federal jobs. African Americans represented 18.1% of the federal workforce in FY 2014, but only 10.4% of the total civilian labor force. Native Americans represented 1.7% of the federal workforce, but only 1% of the total civilian labor force. Asian Americans represented 5.6% of the federal workforce, compared with 4.8% of the civilian workforce. Meanwhile, Hispanics represented 8.4% of the federal workforce, but 14.6% of the total civilian workforce in FY 2014. The federal government's Senior Executive Service remained predominantly (79.3%) white.

MINORITIES IN BUSINESS
Minority Set-Aside Programs

Many levels of government, including the federal government, have set-aside programs that award a certain percentage of contracts to minority- and women-owned businesses. These programs were developed to remedy the effects of past discrimination and to address the difficulties these firms faced in competing with larger, more established firms for government contracts.

One of the first federal initiatives designed to assist minority-owned businesses was the Office of Minority Business Enterprise (later renamed the Minority Business Development Agency [https://www.mbda.gov]), a program created by President Richard M. Nixon (1913–1994) in 1969. Over a decade later, Congress established the Disadvantaged Business Enterprise (DBE) program as part of the Surface Transportation Act of 1982. In "Definition of a Disadvantaged Business Enterprise" (2017, https://www.transportation.gov/civil-rights/disadvantaged-business-enterprise/definition-disadvantaged-business-enterprise), the U.S. Department of Transportation (DOT) defines a DBE as a company in which "socially and economically disadvantaged individuals own at least a 51% interest and also control management and daily business operations." Furthermore, the DOT explains in "History of the DOT DBE Program" (January 5, 2016, https:// www.transportation.gov/civil-rights/disadvantaged-business-enterprise/history-dot-dbe-program) that it pursues "a single DBE goal, encompassing both firms owned by women and minority group members." According to the requirements of the program, the DOT awards a minimum of 10% of all agency funding to DBEs.

Minority businesses are often newer and smaller and have difficulty competing with older, larger businesses that know the process and can afford to make lower bids. Acquiring government contracts can be involved and confusing for businesses that are unfamiliar with the process. Governments, especially the federal government, are often slow to pay their bills, so businesses frequently have to borrow money to bridge the gap between the delivery of goods and services that must be paid for and the time it takes the government to pay them.

The U.S. Supreme Court has ruled that the use of racial classifications is suspect and subject to strict judicial scrutiny. As a result, set-aside programs came under increasing attack during the 1990s and at the turn of the 21st century.

In *Richmond v. J. A. Croson Co.* (488 U.S. 469 [1989]), the Supreme Court struck down a Richmond, Virginia, city ordinance that reserved 30% of city-financed construction contracts for minority-owned businesses. The court ruled that the ordinance violated equal protection because there was no "specific" and "identified" evidence of past discrimination, "public or private," against the Richmond Minority Business Enterprise in city contracting. The majority opinion, written by Justice Sandra Day O'Connor (1930–), also noted that the city had failed to "narrowly tailor" the remedy to accomplish any objective "except perhaps outright racial balancing." The opinion further stated that it was a "completely unrealistic" assumption that a 30% assignment to minority business enterprises in a particular trade would be a fair representation of the community.

In a similar case, Adarand Constructors, a white-owned company, sued the federal government, claiming

TABLE 4.9

Occupational employment in private industry, by race, ethnicity, sex, and industry, 2015

Racial/ethnic group and sex	Total employment	Executive/senior level officials & managers	First/mid-level officials & managers	Professionals	Technicians	Sales workers	Office & clerical workers	Craft workers	Operatives
				Participation rate					
All employees	**100.00**	**100.00**	**100.00**	**100.00**	**100.00**	**100.00**	**100.00**	**100.00**	**100.00**
Men	52.15	70.27	60.76	46.59	49.51	46.48	25.92	92.79	76.74
Women	47.85	29.73	39.24	53.41	50.49	53.52	74.08	7.21	23.26
White	**62.28**	**85.99**	**76.74**	**72.14**	**66.56**	**63.68**	**61.47**	**68.74**	**56.91**
Men	33.15	61.28	47.31	33.83	33.95	31.63	15.44	64.52	45.27
Women	29.13	24.71	29.43	38.31	32.62	32.06	46.03	4.22	11.65
Minority	**37.72**	**14.01**	**23.26**	**27.86**	**33.44**	**36.32**	**38.53**	**31.26**	**43.09**
Men	19.00	8.99	13.45	12.76	15.56	14.85	10.48	28.27	31.47
Women	18.72	5.02	9.81	15.10	17.88	21.47	28.05	2.99	11.61
Black	**14.80**	**3.18**	**7.17**	**7.75**	**13.94**	**14.76**	**17.67**	**9.16**	**18.44**
Men	6.68	1.62	3.56	2.58	5.03	5.59	4.33	8.03	13.52
Women	8.12	1.56	3.61	5.17	8.92	9.17	13.33	1.13	4.92
Hispanic	**14.11**	**4.55**	**7.71**	**6.01**	**10.28**	**14.25**	**13.56**	**17.16**	**18.14**
Men	7.74	2.93	4.73	2.74	5.68	6.14	3.86	15.93	13.49
Women	6.37	1.61	2.98	3.27	4.60	8.11	9.70	1.23	4.65
Asian American	**6.16**	**5.00**	**6.61**	**12.02**	**6.70**	**3.92**	**4.14**	**2.76**	**4.35**
Men	3.28	3.65	4.17	6.49	3.60	1.70	1.35	2.32	2.82
Women	2.88	1.35	2.44	5.53	3.10	2.21	2.80	0.44	1.53
American Indian	**0.55**	**0.31**	**0.37**	**0.35**	**0.60**	**0.60**	**0.55**	**0.86**	**0.65**
Men	0.28	0.19	0.23	0.16	0.29	0.24	0.15	0.80	0.49
Women	0.26	0.12	0.15	0.19	0.31	0.36	0.41	0.06	0.16
Hawaiian	**0.45**	**0.20**	**0.28**	**0.33**	**0.44**	**0.44**	**0.49**	**0.39**	**0.46**
Men	0.23	0.13	0.16	0.15	0.24	0.18	0.14	0.36	0.34
Women	0.22	0.07	0.12	0.19	0.21	0.26	0.34	0.04	0.12
Two or more races	**1.66**	**0.78**	**1.11**	**1.39**	**1.47**	**2.35**	**2.11**	**0.92**	**1.05**
Men	0.79	0.47	0.60	0.64	0.73	1.00	0.65	0.83	0.80
Women	0.86	0.31	0.51	0.75	0.74	1.35	1.47	0.09	0.24

SOURCE: Adapted from "2015 EEO-1 National Aggregate Report," in *2015 Job Patterns for Minorities and Women in Private Industry (EEO-1)*, U.S. Equal Employment Opportunity Commission, 2015, https://www1.eeoc.gov/eeoc/statistics/employment/jobpat-eeo1/2015/index.cfm#select_label (accessed September 5, 2017)

the company failed to receive a government contract because racial preferences had violated the owner's right to equal protection under the Fifth Amendment. In 1989 the DOT awarded a contract for a federal highway project to a construction firm that in turn subcontracted the job to a DBE in compliance with the Subcontractor Compensation Clause. In *Adarand Constructors Inc. v. Peña* (515 U.S. 200 [1995]), the Supreme Court expressed doubt in the validity of the affirmative action programs, which were based on the Surface Transportation and Uniform Relocation Assistance Act of 1987 that channeled $10 billion per year in construction contracts to women- and minority-owned businesses. The court, citing the need for stricter and narrower standards in determining racial preferences when awarding contracts, returned the case to the district court for review.

In June 2000 a federal court decided in *Associated General Contractors of Ohio v. Sandra A. Drabik* (No. 98-4393) that the Ohio State program of setting aside 5% of state construction projects for minority-owned businesses was unconstitutional. Although that court had upheld the state's program in 1983, subsequent U.S. Supreme Court decisions required the federal court to apply a more stringent standard of judicial review and no longer allowed legislatures to use "implicit fact-finding of discrimination" to justify racial preferences and affirmative action programs such as set-aside programs.

In the meantime, the federal government created a new set-aside program in 1993 called the Small and Disadvantaged Business (SDB) Set-Aside Program. This program supplemented other set-aside programs by allowing agencies to set aside some competitions solely for small and disadvantaged businesses with awards made through the agencies rather than through the government. The U.S. Small Business Administration notes in "Small Disadvantaged Businesses" (2017, https://www.sba.gov/contracting/government-contracting-programs/small-disadvantaged-businesses) that beginning in 2008 the program established guidelines enabling a small business to self-represent its status as an SDB, without submitting an application to the Small Business Administration.

TRIBAL CASINOS: A MATTER OF SELF-RULE

The Indian Gaming Regulatory Act of 1988 gives tribes "the exclusive right to regulate gaming on Indian lands if the gaming activity is not specifically prohibited by federal law and is conducted within a State which does not, as a matter of criminal law and public policy, prohibit such gaming activity." The law requires that only tribes, not individuals, run gaming operations. The tribes do not need state approval for class-two casinos, which are supposedly bingo halls but which in many cases have slot machine parlors that skirt the law. Class-three casinos offer slots, roulette, craps, and poker, and they require state approval. Thus, governors make deals with tribes,

granting class-three approval in exchange for a share of the profits going to the state treasury. With many states facing severe budget problems, tribal gaming has become an attractive source of revenue. As a result, tribal gaming has gained considerable political influence. In "2016 Indian Gaming Revenues Increased 4.4%" (July 17, 2017, https://www.nigc.gov/news/detail/2016-indian-gaming-revenues-increased-4.4), the National Indian Gaming Commission reports that 244 out of 567 federally recognized Native American tribes were engaged in gaming in 2016.

Donald L. Barlett and James B. Steele provide in "Wheel of Misfortune" (Time.com, December 16, 2002) a scathing and controversial review of tribal gaming. According to Barlett and Steele, when tribal gaming emerged during the late 1980s "in a frenzy of cost cutting and privatization, Washington perceived gaming on reservations as a cheap way to wean tribes from government handouts, encourage economic development and promote tribal self-sufficiency." However, the 1988 Indian Gaming Regulatory Act "was so riddled with loopholes, so poorly written, so discriminatory and subject to such conflicting interpretations that 14 years later, armies of high-priced lawyers are still debating the definition of a slot machine." Barlett and Steele maintain that only a handful of tribal gaming establishments, those operating close to major population centers, are successful, whereas the overwhelming majority are either too small or too remote in location: "Casinos in California, Connecticut and Florida—states with only 3% of the Indian population—haul in 44% of all revenue, an average of $100,000 per Indian." Barlett and Steele state that in 2002 "290 Indian casinos in 28 states pulled in at least $12.7 billion in revenue. Of that sum, ... the casinos kept more than $5 billion as profit. That would place overall Indian gaming among *Fortune* magazine's 20 most profitable U.S. corporations." However, "just 39 casinos generated $8.4 billion. In short, 13% of the casinos accounted for 66% of the take."

Also controversial was the authenticity of the tribes that were involved in gaming. According to Barlett and Steele, leaders of tribes involved in gaming "are free to set their own whimsical rules for admission, without regard to Indian heritage. They may exclude rivals, potential whistle-blowers and other legitimate claimants. The fewer tribe members, the larger the cut for the rest. Some tribes are booting out members, while others are limiting membership." Moreover, many "long-defunct tribes and extended families" have attempted to gain congressional certification to become involved in tribal gaming. In New York State some tribes that are not even recognized as New York tribes, including tribes from Oklahoma and Wisconsin, have teamed with area developers to buy land in the Catskills and elsewhere in the state in hopes of building casinos.

By contrast, many proponents point out the positive effects of tribal gaming, arguing that it spurs economic development and helps tribes solidify tribal sovereignty. The immediate effect of tribal gaming seems to have done just that. For example, Thaddieus W. Conner and William A. Taggart studied tribal gaming in New Mexico and published their findings in "The Impact of Gaming on the Indian Nations in New Mexico" (*Social Science Quarterly*, vol. 90, no. 1, March 2009). The researchers find that gaming tribes have higher incomes, lower poverty, and improvement in some social areas when compared with nongaming tribes. In "The Political Economy of American Indian Gaming" (*Annual Review of Law and Social Science*, vol. 4, December 2008), Stephen Cornell of the University of Arizona points out that tribal gaming has had positive economic, political, and social effects on both gaming and nongaming Native American reservations. Taggart and Conner note in "Indian Gaming and Tribal Revenue Allocation Plans: A Case of 'Play to Pay'" (*Gaming Law Review and Economics*, vol. 15, no. 6, June 2011) that evidence suggests that tribal gaming has allowed tribes to provide for their members' general welfare, to fund tribal government operations, and to spur economic development.

Proponents of tribal gaming also point to a number of success stories. For example, in "Lands of Opportunity: Social and Economic Effects of Tribal Gaming on Localities" (*Policy Matters*, vol. 1, no. 4, Summer 2007), Mindy Marks and Kate Spilde Contreras of the University of California, Riverside, find that in 2007 tribal gaming reduced poverty and improved employment and income in the communities near the California casinos. The Oneidas of Wisconsin took advantage of a bingo hall to lower the tribe's unemployment rate during the early 1990s and used proceeds to build an elementary school and subsidize a Head Start program. The Suquamish in Washington State used gambling profits to buy back former reservation land. Only a handful of tribal casinos generate large revenues, but even those operations that break even create jobs that benefit many Native Americans. Furthermore, tribes not able to take advantage of gambling can benefit from revenue-sharing programs, such as the one that was set up in California.

Tribal Casinos and the Global Economic Recession

Interestingly, tribal casinos were much less affected by the global economic recession than were nontribal casinos. According to Howard Stutz, in "Gaming Revenue Tight in 2008" (*Las Vegas Review-Journal*, December 10, 2009), tribal casinos collected $26.8 billion in gaming revenue in 2008, a 1.5% increase over the previous year.

Regardless, wary that the future might see the curtailment in revenues, some tribes began to diversify by expanding their facilities into full-fledged resorts, whereas others started investing proceeds into nongaming businesses, thereby establishing an economic base independent of gambling.

CHAPTER 5

MONEY, INCOME, AND POVERTY STATUS

Income greatly influences where people live, what they eat, how they dress, what cars they drive or transportation they take, and what schools their children can attend. How much money and income people have is usually determined by their occupation, which is often directly related to their level of education. Racial and ethnic backgrounds can play a big role in all these factors as well.

INCOME DIFFERENCES

All Households

A household consists of a person or people who occupy the same housing unit and may have just one person (the householder who owns or rents the house). It may also consist of related family members (family household) or unrelated people (nonfamily household).

The median income (half of all households earned more and half earned less) of U.S. households in 2015, including money income before taxes but excluding the value of noncash benefits such as food assistance, Medicare (a federal health insurance program for people aged 65 years and older and people with disabilities), Medicaid (a state and federal health insurance program for low-income people), public housing, and employer-provided benefits, was $56,516, up from $53,718 in 2014. (See Table 5.1.) The median income varied substantially between races and ethnic groups. The median income of non-Hispanic white households was $62,950, which was considerably higher than that of Hispanic households ($45,148) and African American households ($36,898). However, non-Hispanic white income was significantly less than the median household income of Asian Americans ($77,166).

Married-Couple Households

In 2015 there were 60.3 million married-couple households in the United States (see Table 5.1), representing 47.9% of all households and 73.3% of all family households. Married couples tend to have a higher household income than do single householders, because often both the husband and wife work outside of the home. In 2015 married-couple households had a median income of $84,626. The median income for female-headed households with no husband present was substantially lower, at $37,797 (only 44.7% of the median income of married-couple households). The median income for male-headed households with no wife present was also lower than the married-couple median but substantially higher than the median income for female-headed households, at $55,861.

Minority Incomes

HISPANIC INCOME. As shown in Table 5.1, Hispanic households earned an average median income of $45,148 in 2015, up from $42,540 in 2014, but the financial situation among Hispanic subgroups tends to vary. The U.S. Census Bureau notes in *The Hispanic Population in the United States: 2013* (January 5, 2017, https://www.census.gov/data/tables/2013/demo/hispanic-origin/2013-cps.html) that in 2012 more than three out of 10 (31.3%) Hispanic households had money income under $25,000 per year, compared with just 21% of non-Hispanic white households. Among family households, more than a quarter (26.4%) of Hispanic families earned under $25,000 per year, compared with just 11.1% of non-Hispanic white families.

Hispanic incomes are relatively low for a variety of reasons, including language barriers and discrimination in the workplace. However, the lack of educational attainment is a major reason for low Hispanic incomes. In *Hispanic Population in the United States: 2014* (August 23, 2017, https://www.census.gov/data/tables/2014/demo/hispanic-origin/2014-cps.html), the Census Bureau indicates that in 2014, 18.5% of all Hispanics aged 25 years and older had less than a ninth-grade education, another 15% did not have a high school diploma, and only 10.8% had a bachelor's degree or higher.

AFRICAN AMERICAN INCOME. African American households had the lowest median income in 2015, at

TABLE 5.1

Median household and per capita income by selected characteristics, 2014 and 2015

	2014			2015			2016 Percentage change* in real median income (2015 less 2014)	
	Number (thousands)	Median income (dollars)		Number (thousands)	Median income (dollars)			
Characteristic		Estimate	Margin of error[a] (±)		Estimate	Margin of error[a] (±)	Estimate	Margin of error[a] (±)
Households								
All households	124,587	53,718	645	125,819	56,516	528	5.2*	1.60
Type of household								
Family households	81,716	68,504	815	82,184	72,165	608	5.3*	1.46
Married-couple	60,010	81,118	677	60,251	84,626	983	4.3*	1.32
Female householder, no husband present	15,544	36,192	682	15,622	37,797	995	4.4*	3.17
Male householder, no wife present	6,162	53,746	1,644	6,310	55,861	1,595	3.9	4.37
Nonfamily households	42,871	32,084	466	43,635	33,805	776	5.4*	2.82
Female householder	22,728	26,703	523	23,093	29,022	822	8.7*	3.74
Male householder	20,143	39,226	1,118	20,542	40,762	745	3.9*	3.51
Race[b] and hispanic origin of householder								
White	98,679	56,932	585	99,313	60,109	627	5.6*	1.58
White, not Hispanic	84,228	60,325	606	84,445	62,950	892	4.4*	1.76
Black	16,437	35,439	759	16,539	36,898	845	4.1*	2.96
Asian	6,040	74,382	3,470	6,328	77,166	2,791	3.7	5.47
Hispanic (any race)	16,239	42,540	849	16,667	45,148	1,012	6.1*	2.97
Nativity of householder								
Native born	106,191	54,741	713	107,081	57,173	558	4.4*	1.68
Foreign born	18,396	49,649	1,142	18,738	52,295	1,126	5.3*	3.23
Naturalized citizen	9,735	59,329	2,239	9,856	61,982	1,325	4.5	4.55
Not a citizen	8,661	40,842	780	8,881	45,137	1,722	10.5*	4.39
Residence[c]								
Inside metropolitan statistical areas	104,009	55,920	582	107,615	59,258	780	N	N
Inside principal cities	40,578	47,905	974	42,615	51,378	646	N	N
Outside principal cities	63,431	61,671	626	65,000	64,144	952	N	N
Outside metropolitan statistical areas[d]	20,578	45,534	859	18,204	44,657	1,543	N	N
Earnings of full-time, year-round workers								
Men with earnings	62,455	50,441	218	63,887	51,212	225	1.5*	0.60
Women with earnings	46,226	39,667	719	47,211	40,742	241	2.7*	1.86
Female-to-male earnings ratio	X	0.79	0.014	X	0.80	0.005	1.2	1.80

*An asterisk following an estimate indicates change is statistically different from zero at the 90 percent confidence level.

X Not applicable.

N Not comparable.

[a]A margin of error is a measure of an estimate's variability. The larger the margin of error in relation to the size of the estimate, the less reliable the estimate. This number, when added to and subtracted from the estimate, forms the 90 percent confidence interval. Margins of error shown in this table are based on standard errors calculated using replicate weights.

[b]Federal surveys give respondents the option of reporting more than one race. Therefore, two basic ways of defining a race group are possible. A group such as Asian may be defined as those who reported Asian and no other race (the race-alone or single-race concept) or as those who reported Asian regardless of whether they also reported another race (the race-alone-or-in-combination concept). This table shows data using the first approach (race alone). The use of the single-race population does not imply that it is the preferred method of presenting or analyzing data. The Census Bureau uses a variety of approaches. Information on people who reported more than one race, such as white *and* American Indian and Alaska Native or Asian *and* black or African American, is available from Census 2010 through American FactFinder. About 2.9 percent of people reported more than one race in Census 2010. Data for American Indians and Alaska Natives, Native Hawaiians and other Pacific Islanders, and those reporting two or more races are not shown separately.

[c]Once a decade, the CPS ASEC (Current Population Survey, American Savings Education Council) transitions to a new sample design and updates all metropolitan statistical area delineations. As a result, the metropolitan/nonmetropolitan estimates for 2014 and 2015 are not comparable Users may want to use the American Community Survey estimates for metropolitan/nonmetropolitan comparisons.

[d]The "outside metropolitan statistical areas" category includes both micropolitan statistical areas and territory outside of metropolitan and micropolitan statistical areas.

SOURCE: Adapted from Bernadette D. Proctor, Jessica L. Semega, and Melissa A. Kollar, "Table 1. Income and Earnings Summary Measures by Selected Characteristics: 2014 and 2015," in *Income and Poverty in the United States: 2015*, U.S. Census Bureau, September 2016, https://www.census.gov/content/dam/Census/library/publications/2016/demo/p60-256.pdf (accessed September 5, 2017)

$36,898. (See Table 5.1.) As noted earlier, households that are headed by an unmarried adult have a substantially lower income than do married-couple households. This puts African Americans at a disadvantage because among those over the age of 15 years, African Americans are far more likely than whites, Hispanics, or Asian Americans to have never married. According to the Census Bureau, in *Historical Marriage Tables* (April 4, 2017, https://www.census.gov/data/tables/time-series/demo/families/marital.html), 49% of African Americans aged 15 years and older had never been married in 2016, compared with 40.2% of Hispanics, 30.3% of Asian Americans, and 29.1% of whites.

ASIAN AMERICAN INCOME. Conversely, Asian American households tend to have higher incomes than comparable non-Hispanic white households. As Table 5.1 shows, Asian American households had an average annual income of $77,166 in 2015. This higher median income is considered directly related to the higher educational attainment of Asian Americans. In *The Asian Alone Population in the United*

States: 2014 (August 23, 2017, https://www.census.gov/data/tables/2014/demo/race/ppl-aa14.html), the Census Bureau reports that 53.1% of Asian Americans aged 25 years and older had a bachelor's degree or higher in 2015, compared with 35.6% of non-Hispanic whites in the same age group.

Minorities and Retirement

Members of racial and ethnic minority groups also encounter greater challenges than whites when it comes to saving money for retirement. Mikki Waid of the AARP Public Policy Institute notes in *Social Security: A Key Retirement Income Source for Older Minorities* (March 2016, http://www.aarp.org/content/dam/aarp/ppi/2016-03/social-security-a-key-income-source-for-older-minorities-aarp-ppi.pdf) that African American and Hispanic senior citizens are significantly more dependent on Social Security benefits for their retirement income than white seniors. According to Waid, in 2014 nearly one-third of African American (32.5%) and Hispanic (31.2%) seniors received 90% or more of their retirement income from Social Security, compared with 23.5% of white seniors and 22.1% of Asian American seniors.

Waid also finds significant racial disparities among seniors, with regard to pensions, retirement savings, and assets. As Figure 5.1 shows, 52.9% of retired whites drew income from pensions and retirement savings in 2014, compared with 34% of African Americans, 29.5% of Asian Americans, and 23.2% of Hispanics. Meanwhile, African American and Hispanic retirees were less likely than white and Asian American seniors to draw income from assets. In 2014, 45.7% of African Americans and 43.3% of Hispanics received income from assets, compared with 72.3% of

whites and 63.3% of Asian Americans. Hispanic (18.1%) and African American (19.1%) seniors were also considerably more likely than Asian American (14.5%) or white (7.8%) seniors to live below the poverty line in 2014.

POVERTY STATUS OF MINORITIES

Every year the Census Bureau establishes poverty thresholds that determine the distribution of different welfare benefits. In 2017 the poverty threshold ranged from $12,060 for single people to $41,320 for families with eight members. (See Table 5.2.) In 2015, 43.1 million people, or 13.5% of the U.S. population, were in poverty. (See Figure 5.2.) The number of people in poverty and the poverty rate rose sharply after 2007, when the United States entered the Great Recession, the worst economic downturn since the Great Depression (1929–1939). Both the number of impoverished people and the poverty rate continued to climb, even after the recession had officially ended in 2009.

In 2015, 24.1% of African Americans and 21.4% of Hispanics lived in poverty. (See Table 5.3.) Asian Americans had a relatively low rate of poverty, at 11.4%, although it was still higher than the poverty rate of non-Hispanic whites, at 9.1%. As Table 5.3 shows, poverty rates fell slightly for every racial and ethnic group between 2014 and 2015, as the economy continued its slow recovery from the Great Recession.

The poverty rate varies among Hispanic subgroups. The Census Bureau notes in *Hispanic Population in the United States: 2013* that in 2013 Puerto Ricans were the most likely to live in poverty, at 28.3%. Mexicans and Central Americans also had relatively high poverty rates,

FIGURE 5.1

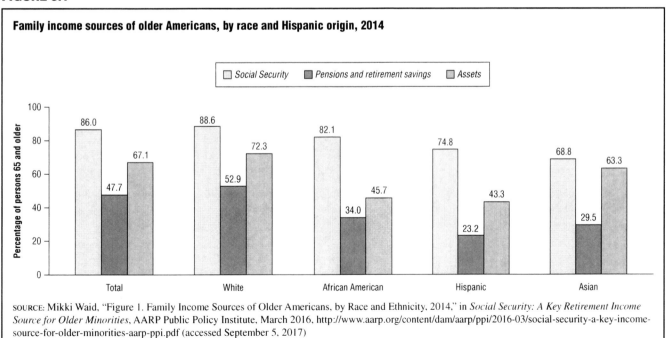

Family income sources of older Americans, by race and Hispanic origin, 2014

SOURCE: Mikki Waid, "Figure 1. Family Income Sources of Older Americans, by Race and Ethnicity, 2014," in *Social Security: A Key Retirement Income Source for Older Minorities*, AARP Public Policy Institute, March 2016, http://www.aarp.org/content/dam/aarp/ppi/2016-03/social-security-a-key-income-source-for-older-minorities-aarp-ppi.pdf (accessed September 5, 2017)

at 26.7% and 26.3%, respectively. By contrast, Cubans and South Americans had the lowest poverty rates, at 19.1% and 15.3%, respectively. Cubans and South Americans tend to be better educated than other Hispanic subgroups, which partially explains the income disparities between the groups.

TABLE 5.2

Poverty guidelines, 2017

Persons in family/household	Poverty guideline
1	$12,060
2	16,240
3	20,420
4	24,600
5	28,780
6	32,960
7	37,140
8	41,320

SOURCE: "2017 Poverty Guidelines for the 48 Contiguous States and the District of Columbia," "2017 Poverty Guidelines for Alaska," and "2017 Poverty Guidelines for Hawaii," in "Annual Update of the HHS Poverty Guidelines," *Federal Register*, vol. 82, no. 19, January 31, 2017, https://www.gpo.gov/fdsys/pkg/FR-2017-01-31/pdf/2017-02076.pdf (accessed September 5, 2017)

Depth of Poverty

Although measuring the proportions of people in various groups who are above and below the poverty threshold provides one measure of poverty, it does not account for the levels of poverty. Some people below the poverty level are moderately poor, whereas others are extremely poor. Some households with incomes above the poverty threshold are just above it and barely getting by. The ratio of income to poverty compares a family's income with its poverty threshold, providing one way to measure how poor a family actually is.

Table 5.4 shows income-to-poverty ratios by race and Hispanic origin, with people under 0.50 of the poverty threshold (in other words, people who earn less than 50% of the income designating the poverty level, also known as extreme poverty) and people between 1.25 and 2.00 of the poverty threshold (people who earn between 1.25 and two times the income designating the poverty level, also known as low income). In 2015, 10.9% of African Americans lived on incomes under 0.50 of the poverty threshold. Among Hispanics, 8.5% lived in extreme poverty, compared with 6.2% of Asian Americans and 4.3% of non-Hispanic whites.

FIGURE 5.2

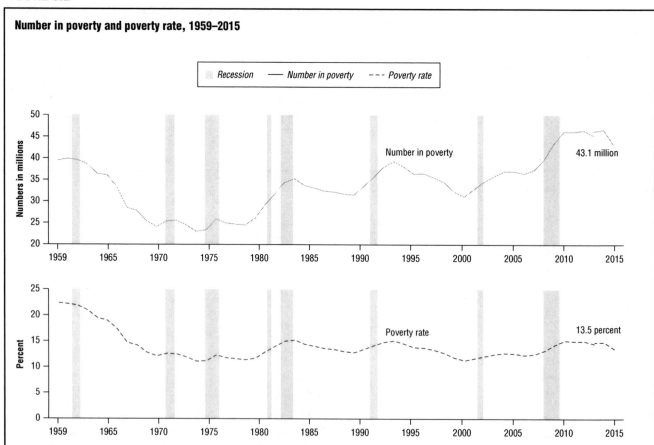

Number in poverty and poverty rate, 1959–2015

Note: The data for 2013 and beyond reflect the implementation of the redesigned income questions. The data points are placed at the midpoints of the respective years.

SOURCE: Bernadette D. Proctor, Jessica L. Semega, and Melissa A. Kollar, "Figure 4. Number in Poverty and Poverty Rate: 1959–2015," in *Income and Poverty in the United States: 2015*, U.S. Census Bureau, September 2016, https://www.census.gov/content/dam/Census/library/publications/2016/demo/p60-256.pdf (accessed September 5, 2017)

TABLE 5.3

People and families in poverty by selected characteristics, 2014 and 2015

Characteristic	2014			2015			Change in poverty (2015 less 2014)[a, *]	
	Total	Below poverty		Total	Below poverty		Number	Percent
		Number	Percent		Number	Percent		
People								
Total	315,804	46,657	14.8	318,454	43,123	13.5	−3,534*	−1.2*
Family status								
In families	256,308	32,615	12.7	258,121	29,893	11.6	−2,722*	−1.1*
Householder	81,730	9,467	11.6	82,199	8,589	10.4	−879*	−1.1*
Related children under age 18	72,383	14,987	20.7	72,558	13,962	19.2	−1,025*	−1.5*
Related children under age 6	23,470	5,504	23.5	23,459	4,923	21.0	−582*	−2.5*
In unrelated subfamilies	1,558	668	42.9	1,344	559	41.6	−109	−1.3
Reference person	652	266	40.8	563	231	41.0	−35	0.1
Children under age 18	832	388	46.6	701	321	45.9	−67	−0.8
Unrelated individuals	57,937	13,374	23.1	58,988	12,671	21.5	−702*	−1.6*
Race[b] and Hispanic origin								
White	244,253	31,089	12.7	245,536	28,566	11.6	−2,523*	−1.1*
White, not Hispanic	195,208	19,652	10.1	195,450	17,786	9.1	−1,867*	−1.0*
Black	41,112	10,755	26.2	41,625	10,020	24.1	−735*	−2.1*
Asian	17,790	2,137	12.0	18,241	2,078	11.4	−59	−0.6
Hispanic (any race)	55,504	13,104	23.6	56,780	12,133	21.4	−971*	−2.2*
Sex								
Male	154,639	20,708	13.4	156,009	19,037	12.2	−1,671*	−1.2*
Female	161,164	25,949	16.1	162,445	24,086	14.8	−1,863*	−1.3*
Age								
Under age 18	73,556	15,540	21.1	73,647	14,509	19.7	−1,031*	−1.4*
Aged 18 to 64	196,254	26,527	13.5	197,260	24,414	12.4	−2,114*	−1.1*
Aged 65 and older	45,994	4,590	10.0	47,547	4,201	8.8	−389*	−1.1*
Nativity								
Native born	273,628	38,871	14.2	275,398	35,973	13.1	−2,898*	−1.1*
Foreign born	42,175	7,786	18.5	43,056	7,150	16.6	−636*	−1.9*
Naturalized citizen	19,731	2,347	11.9	20,084	2,255	11.2	−92	−0.7
Not a citizen	22,444	5,439	24.2	22,973	4,895	21.3	−544*	−2.9*
Region								
Northeast	55,725	7,020	12.6	55,779	6,891	12.4	−129	−0.2
Midwest	67,130	8,714	13.0	67,030	7,849	11.7	−865*	−1.3*
South	118,193	19,531	16.5	119,955	18,305	15.3	−1,227*	−1.3*
West	74,756	11,391	15.2	75,690	10,079	13.3	−1,312*	−1.9*
Residence[c]								
Inside metropolitan statistical areas	265,788	38,416	14.5	274,046	35,718	13.0	N	N
Inside principal cities	99,182	18,708	18.9	103,617	17,368	16.8	N	N
Outside principal cities	166,606	19,708	11.8	170,429	18,350	10.8	N	N
Outside metropolitan statistical areas[d]	50,016	8,241	16.5	44,408	7,405	16.7	N	N
Work experience								
Total, aged 18 to 64	196,254	26,527	13.5	197,260	24,414	12.4	−2,114	−1.1
All workers	147,712	10,155	6.9	150,229	9,457	6.3	−698*	−0.6*
Worked full-time, year-round	103,379	3,091	3.0	105,695	2,537	2.4	−554*	−0.6*
Less than full-time, year-round	44,332	7,064	15.9	44,534	6,920	15.5	−144*	−0.4*
Did not work at least 1 week	48,542	16,372	33.7	47,031	14,957	31.8	−1,415*	−1.9*

Children Living in Poverty

According to the Federal Interagency Forum on Child and Family Statistics, in *America's Children: Key National Indicators of Well-Being, 2017* (July 2017, https://www.childstats.gov/pdf/ac2017/ac_17.pdf), in 2015 non-Hispanic African American and Hispanic children were significantly more likely to live in poverty than non-Hispanic white children. More than one out of three (33.6%) non-Hispanic African American children and more than one out of four (28.9%) Hispanic children lived in poverty, whereas 12.1% of non-Hispanic white children lived in poverty. (See Table 5.5.)

Family type affected children's risk of poverty. In families that were headed by married couples, only 6% of non-Hispanic white children lived in poverty in 2015. (See Table 5.5.) The non-Hispanic African American poverty rate of children living in married-couple families was significantly lower than for all non-Hispanic African American children, at 11%, but still nearly double the poverty rate of non-Hispanic white children in married-couple families. Hispanic children living in married-couple families did not have as significant a drop in their poverty rates; 19.5% of Hispanic children living with married parents lived in poverty. Children were particularly at risk in households that were headed

TABLE 5.3

People and families in poverty by selected characteristics, 2014 and 2015 [CONTINUED]

| | | 2014 | | | 2015 | | Change in poverty (2015 less 2014)[a],* | |
| | | Below poverty | | | Below poverty | | | |
Characteristic	Total	Number	Percent	Total	Number	Percent	Number	Percent
Disability status[e]								
Total, aged 18 to 64	196,254	26,527	13.5	197,260	24,414	12.4	−2,114*	−1.1*
With a disability	15,429	4,403	28.5	15,276	4,358	28.5	−45	Z
With no disability	179,905	22,055	12.3	181,069	20,000	11.0	−2,056*	−1.2*
Educational attainment								
Total, aged 25 and older	212,132	25,163	11.9	215,015	22,957	10.7	−2,207*	−1.2*
No high school diploma	24,582	7,098	28.9	23,453	6,171	26.3	−928*	−2.6*
High school, no college	62,575	8,898	14.2	62,002	8,016	12.9	−882*	−1.3*
Some college, no degree	56,031	5,719	10.2	57,660	5,550	9.6	−169*	−0.6*
Bachelor's degree or higher	68,945	3,449	5.0	71,900	3,221	4.5	−228*	−0.5*

*An asterisk following an estimate indicates change is statistically different from zero at the 90 percent confidence level.
N Not comparable.
[a]Details may not sum to totals because of rounding.
[b]Federal surveys give respondents the option of reporting more than one race. Therefore, two basic ways of defining a race group are possible. A group such as Asian may be defined as those who reported Asian and no other race (the race-alone or single-race concept) or as those who reported Asian regardless of whether they also reported another race (the race-alone-or-in-combination concept). This table shows data using the first approach (race alone). The use of the single-race population does not imply that it is the preferred method of presenting or analyzing data. The Census Bureau uses a variety of approaches. Information on people who reported more than one race, such as white *and* American Indian and Alaska Native or Asian *and* black or African American, is available from Census 2010 through American FactFinder. About 2.9 percent of people reported more than one race in Census 2010. Data for American Indians and Alaska Natives, Native Hawaiians and other Pacific Islanders, and those reporting two or more races are not shown separately.
[c]Once a decade, the CPS ASEC (Current Population Survey, American Savings Education Council) transitions to a new sample design and updates all metropolitan statistical area delineations. As a result, the metropolitan/nonmetropolitan estimates for 2014 and 2015 are not comparable. Users may want to use the American Community Survey estimates for metropolitan/nonmetropolitan comparisons.
[d]The "outside metropolitan statistical areas" category includes both micropolitan statistical areas and territory outside of metropolitan and micropolitan statistical areas.
[e]The sum of those with and without a disability does not equal the total because disability status is not defined for individuals in the armed forces.

SOURCE: Bernadette D. Proctor, Jessica L. Semega, and Melissa A. Kollar, "Table 3. People in Poverty by Selected Characteristics: 2014 and 2015," in *Income and Poverty in the United States: 2015*, U.S. Census Bureau, September 2016, https://www.census.gov/content/dam/Census/library/publications/2016/demo/p60-256.pdf (accessed September 5, 2017)

---

by a single female. Nearly half of Hispanic children (48.7%) and non-Hispanic African American children (46.9%) living in female-headed families lived in poverty. Slightly more than one out of three (34.8%) non-Hispanic white children living in female-headed families lived in poverty.

The Federal Interagency Forum on Child and Family Statistics notes that non-Hispanic African American children were also much more likely to live in extreme poverty than non-Hispanic white children in 2015; 16.2% of non-Hispanic African American children lived in families with incomes below 50% of the poverty threshold, compared with 11.5% of Hispanic children and 5.8% of non-Hispanic white children. (See Table 5.5.) More than one out of five (23.1%) non-Hispanic African American children and more than one out of four (25.9%) Hispanic children living in female-householder families lived below 50% of the poverty threshold, compared with 18.1% of non-Hispanic white children living in female-householder families.

The National School Lunch Program provides free or reduced-price meals to children from low-income families. Researchers consider the percentage of students eligible for free or reduced-price lunch under this program as a proxy measure for the concentration of low-income students within a school. Schools in which 25% or fewer of students qualify for free or reduced-price lunch are designated as low poverty, while schools in which 75% or more of students qualify are designated as high poverty. In *The Condition of Education*

2017 (May 2017, https://nces.ed.gov/pubs2017/2017144.pdf), Joel McFarland et al. note that African American and Hispanic students are much more concentrated in high-poverty schools than their white peers. Indeed, 45% of all African American public school students and 46% of all Hispanic public school students attended high-poverty schools, compared with 8% of white students. By contrast, 29% of white students attended low-poverty schools, compared with 7% of African American students and 8% of Hispanic students. Asian American students were much more likely to attend low-poverty schools (37%) than high-poverty schools (15%). The reverse was true among Native American or Alaskan Native students—33% attended high-poverty schools and 12% attended low-poverty schools.

GOVERNMENT PROGRAMS

Because minorities are disproportionately poor, they have long accounted for a major portion of the welfare rolls across the United States. The U.S. government offers various forms of assistance to people living with economic hardship. Some of these programs are federally operated, and others are run at the state level. In many cases states administer federally mandated government programs, which can make tracking them complicated.

In 1996 Congress enacted the Personal Responsibility and Work Opportunity Reconciliation Act to reform the welfare system. The primary goal of the legislation was to get as

TABLE 5.4

People with income below specified ratios of their poverty thresholds, by selected characteristics, 2015

Characteristic	Total	Income-to-poverty ratio							
		Under 0.50		Under 1.25		Under 1.50		Under 2.00	
		Number	Percent	Number	Percent	Number	Percent	Number	Percent
All people	**318,454**	**19,444**	**6.1**	**56,912**	**17.9**	**71,681**	**22.5**	**100,894**	**31.7**
Age									
Under age 18	73,647	6,537	8.9	18,725	25.4	23,117	31.4	30,756	41.8
Aged 18 to 64	197,260	11,572	5.9	31,632	16.0	39,226	19.9	55,348	28.1
Aged 65 and older	47,547	1,335	2.8	6,556	13.8	9,338	19.6	14,789	31.1
Sex									
Male	156,009	8,484	5.4	25,208	16.2	31,989	20.5	45,868	29.4
Female	162,445	10,960	6.7	31,705	19.5	39,693	24.4	55,025	33.9
Race* and Hispanic origin									
White	245,536	12,555	5.1	38,504	15.7	49,245	20.1	71,104	29.0
White, not Hispanic	195,450	8,355	4.3	24,091	12.3	31,256	16.0	46,475	23.8
Black	41,625	4,549	10.9	12,538	30.1	15,180	36.5	19,843	47.7
Asian	18,241	1,133	6.2	2,638	14.5	3,275	18.0	4,465	24.5
Hispanic (any race)	56,780	4,839	8.5	16,328	28.8	20,278	35.7	27,921	49.2
Family status									
In families	258,121	12,464	4.8	40,272	15.6	51,477	19.9	74,400	28.8
Householder	82,199	3,666	4.5	11,603	14.1	14,822	18.0	21,812	26.5
Related children under age 18	72,558	6,121	8.4	18,106	25.0	22,399	30.9	29,927	41.2
Related children under age 6	23,459	2,341	10.0	6,296	26.8	7,747	33.0	10,291	43.9
In unrelated subfamilies	1,344	396	29.4	662	49.3	791	58.8	961	71.5
Unrelated individuals	58,988	6,585	11.2	15,978	27.1	19,414	32.9	25,532	43.3

*Federal surveys give respondents the option of reporting more than one race. Therefore, two basic ways of defining a race group are possible. A group such as Asian may be defined as those who reported Asian and no other race (the race-alone or single-race concept) or as those who reported Asian regardless of whether they also reported another race (the race-alone-or-in-combination concept). This table shows data using the first approach (race alone). The use of the single-race population does not imply that it is the preferred method of presenting or analyzing data. The Census Bureau uses a variety of approaches. Information on people who reported more than one race, such as white **and** American Indian and Alaska Native or Asian **and** black or African American, is available from Census 2010 through American FactFinder. About 2.9 percent of people reported more than one race in Census 2010. Data for American Indians and Alaska Natives, Native Hawaiian and other Pacific Islanders, and those reporting two or more races are not shown separately.

Note: Details may not sum to totals because of rounding.

SOURCE: Bernadette D. Proctor, Jessica L. Semega, and Melissa A. Kollar, "Table 5. People with Income below Specified Ratios of Their Poverty Thresholds by Selected Characteristics: 2015," in *Income and Poverty in the United States: 2015*, U.S. Census Bureau, September 2016, https://www.census.gov/content/dam/Census/library/publications/2016/demo/p60-256.pdf (accessed September 5, 2017)

many people as possible into the paid labor force and off the welfare rolls. The law set limits on how long people could receive welfare benefits. Aid to Families with Dependent Children (AFDC), a guaranteed assistance program for low-income families, was eliminated and replaced in 1996 with the Temporary Assistance for Needy Families (TANF) program. According to the Office of Family Assistance, in "About TANF" (June 28, 2017, https://www.acf.hhs.gov/ofa/programs/tanf/about), TANF has four specific purposes:

- Provide assistance to needy families so that children can be cared for in their own homes

- Reduce the dependency of needy parents by promoting job preparation, work, and marriage

- Prevent and reduce the incidence of out-of-wedlock pregnancies

- Encourage the formation and maintenance of two-parent families

The U.S. House of Representatives Committee on Ways and Means reports in *The Green Book* (December 2016, https://greenbook-waysandmeans.house.gov/2016-green-book) that the number of families receiving welfare dropped from more than 5.1 million in March 1994 to 1.9 million in December 2011, a decrease of 62.7%. In *Characteristics and Financial Circumstances of TANF Recipients, Fiscal Year (FY) 2016* (October 26, 2017, https://www.acf.hhs.gov/sites/default/files/ofa/fy16_characteristics.pdf), the Office of Family Assistance notes that the total number of families receiving welfare was down to 1.2 million in fiscal year 2016.

Besides TANF, two other means-tested government programs also extend benefits to needy individuals and families. Established in 1974, the Supplemental Security Income Program provides stipends to low-income people who are 65 years of age or older and to those who are blind or disabled. Originally created under the Food Stamp Act of 1964 and renamed in 2008, the Supplemental Nutrition Assistance Program (SNAP) helps low-income families purchase food, with an emphasis on healthy and nutritious choices.

Gilbert Crouse and Suzanne Macartney of the U.S. Department of Health and Human Services note in *Welfare Indicators and Risk Factors: Fifteenth Report to Congress* (2016, https://aspe.hhs.gov/system/files/pdf/206736/WelfareIndicators15thReport.pdf) that in 2013, 41.2% of all

TABLE 5.5

Percentage of children under age 18 living below selected poverty levels, by age, family structure, race, and Hispanic origin, selected years 1980–2015

Characteristic	1980	1985	1990	1995	2000	2005	2010	2013[a]	2014	2015
Below 100% poverty										
Total	**18.3**	**20.7**	**20.6**	**20.8**	**16.2**	**17.6**	**22.0**	**21.5**	**21.1**	**19.7**
Gender										
Male	18.1	20.3	20.5	20.4	16.0	17.4	22.2	21.5	21.2	19.5
Female	18.6	21.1	20.8	21.2	16.3	17.8	21.9	21.5	21.1	19.9
Age										
Ages 0–5	20.7	23.0	23.6	24.1	18.3	20.2	25.8	24.1	23.9	21.3
Ages 6–17	17.3	19.5	19.0	19.1	15.2	16.3	20.2	20.3	19.8	19.0
Race and Hispanic origin[b]										
White, non-Hispanic	11.8	12.8	12.3	11.2	9.1	10.0	12.3	13.4	12.3	12.1
Black, non-Hispanic	42.3	43.3	44.5	41.5	31.0	34.5	39.1	33.4	37.3	33.6
Hispanic	33.2	40.3	38.4	40.0	28.4	28.3	34.9	33.0	31.9	28.9
Region[c]										
Northeast	16.3	18.5	18.4	19.0	14.5	15.5	18.5	18.2	17.8	18.4
South	22.5	22.8	23.8	23.5	18.4	19.7	24.3	24.2	23.8	22.1
Midwest	16.3	20.7	18.8	16.9	13.1	15.9	20.5	20.1	18.8	17.2
West	16.1	19.3	19.8	22.1	16.9	17.5	22.2	20.8	21.2	19.0
Children in married-couple families, total	10.1	11.4	10.3	10.0	8.0	8.5	11.6	10.1	10.6	9.8
Ages 0–5	11.6	12.9	11.7	11.1	8.7	9.9	13.4	11.5	11.6	10.1
Ages 6–17	9.4	10.5	9.5	9.4	7.7	7.7	10.7	9.4	10.2	9.6
White, non-Hispanic	7.5	8.2	6.9	6.0	4.7	4.5	6.4	6.6	6.4	6.0
Black, non-Hispanic	19.7	17.2	17.8	12.0	8.5	12.4	16.0	10.3	13.3	11.0
Hispanic	23.0	27.2	26.6	28.4	20.8	20.1	25.1	19.6	21.2	19.5
Children in female-householder families, no husband present, total	51.4	54.1	54.2	50.7	40.5	43.1	47.1	47.4	46.4	42.6
Ages 0–5	65.4	65.7	65.9	61.9	50.7	52.9	58.7	55.3	55.1	49.5
Ages 6–17	46.2	49.1	48.4	45.2	36.3	38.9	41.9	43.8	42.4	39.5
White, non-Hispanic	38.6	39.1	41.4	34.9	29.3	33.8	36.0	39.6	35.7	34.8
Black, non-Hispanic	64.9	66.7	65.1	61.5	48.9	50.2	52.6	49.9	52.9	46.9
Hispanic	64.8	73.0	68.9	66.0	50.5	51.0	56.8	53.2	53.3	48.7
Below 50% poverty										
Total	**6.9**	**8.6**	**8.8**	**8.5**	**6.7**	**7.7**	**9.9**	**9.9**	**9.3**	**8.9**
Gender										
Male	6.9	8.6	8.8	8.4	6.6	7.3	10.0	10.1	9.3	8.8
Female	6.9	8.6	8.8	8.5	6.8	8.1	9.8	9.7	9.3	9.0
Age										
Ages 0–5	8.3	10.0	10.7	10.8	8.1	9.1	12.0	12.0	11.2	10.2
Ages 6–17	6.2	7.8	7.8	7.2	6.0	7.0	8.9	8.9	8.4	8.3
Race and Hispanic origin[b]										
White, non-Hispanic	4.3	5.0	5.0	3.9	3.7	4.1	5.1	6.3	5.4	5.8
Black, non-Hispanic	17.7	22.1	22.7	20.5	14.9	17.3	20.1	16.6	18.5	16.2
Hispanic	10.8	14.1	14.2	16.3	10.2	11.5	15.0	14.6	12.9	11.5
Region[c]										
Northeast	4.7	6.5	7.6	8.6	6.4	7.5	8.9	7.7	7.7	7.9
South	9.7	10.9	11.3	10.1	7.9	9.0	10.5	11.0	10.9	10.3
Midwest	6.3	9.5	8.9	6.6	5.5	6.5	9.8	10.2	7.8	7.6
West	5.1	5.6	6.1	7.8	6.2	7.0	9.8	9.6	9.0	8.3
Children in married-couple familes, total	3.1	3.5	2.7	2.6	2.2	2.4	3.5	3.1	3.1	3.0
Ages 0–5	3.7	4.0	3.2	2.9	2.2	2.8	4.1	3.7	3.6	3.1
Ages 6–17	2.8	3.1	2.4	2.5	2.2	2.2	3.2	2.8	2.9	3.0
White, non-Hispanic	2.5	2.6	2.0	1.5	1.5	1.2	1.8	2.6	2.1	2.4
Black, non-Hispanic	4.2	5.2	3.9	2.5	2.9	4.5	5.7	2.1	4.0	4.2
Hispanic	6.2	7.4	6.7	8.6	4.5	5.2	7.5	4.8	5.4	4.4
Children in female-householder families, no husband present, total	22.3	27.0	28.7	24.4	19.7	22.5	25.3	25.5	23.9	22.1
Ages 0–5	31.4	35.8	37.7	34.3	28.4	29.4	33.3	33.7	30.6	29.0
Ages 6–17	18.8	23.2	24.2	19.7	16.1	19.6	21.7	21.8	20.8	19.0
White, non-Hispanic	15.3	17.5	21.1	14.5	13.4	16.4	18.6	20.3	18.0	18.1
Black, non-Hispanic	31.0	38.0	37.1	32.6	23.9	26.5	28.2	26.7	27.5	23.1
Hispanic	24.7	31.1	33.1	33.1	26.0	29.1	31.5	30.5	28.1	25.9

SOURCE: Adapted from "Table ECON1.A. Child Poverty: Percentage of All Children Ages 0–17 Living below Selected Poverty Thresholds by Selected Characteristics, Selected Years 1980–2015," in *America's Children: Key National Indicators of Well-Being, 2017*, Federal Interagency Forum on Child and Family Statistics, July 2017, https://www.childstats.gov/pdf/ac2017/ac_17.pdf (accessed September 5, 2017).

non-Hispanic African Americans received some portion of their total annual family income from means-tested assistance programs (i.e., 58.8% did not receive benefits; see Table 5.6). More than one out of three (37.6%) Hispanics received means-tested assistance, whereas 16.3% of non-Hispanic whites received such assistance. Moreover, 12% of non-Hispanic African Americans received more than half of their total annual family income from means-tested assistance programs, compared with 7% of Hispanics and 3.1% of non-Hispanic whites.

Therefore, Crouse and Macartney indicate that non-Hispanic African Americans are the most likely to receive means-tested assistance, especially SNAP benefits. Nearly one-third (32.7%) of non-Hispanic African Americans received SNAP benefits, either alone or in combination with another program, in 2013, compared with 25.5% of Hispanics and 11.9% of non-Hispanic whites. (See Table 5.7.) In addition, non-Hispanic African Americans are more likely than Hispanics or non-Hispanic whites to receive assistance from multiple programs. Of the 32.7% of non-Hispanic African Americans who received means-tested assistance in 2013, 3% of them received both TANF and SNAP, compared with 2.3% of Hispanics and 0.4% of non-Hispanic whites.

The high number of female-headed families among non-Hispanic African Americans may partly account for the high rate of receipt of means-tested assistance among that population. According to Crouse and Macartney, more than four out of 10 (42.8%) individuals in female-headed families received means-tested assistance in 2013, compared with only 10% of individuals in married-couple families.

(See Table 5.7.) In addition, individuals in female-headed families were the most likely to receive more than half of the annual family income from these programs; in 2013, 15.8% did so, compared with only 1.6% of individuals living in married-couple families. (See Table 5.6.) These percentages suggest that it is particularly difficult for single women with children to make ends meet without turning to government programs for assistance.

The TANF program has been criticized since its inception in 1996. Critics maintain that the drop in the number of recipients cannot measure success. Caseloads initially decreased simply because the eligibility requirements were stiffened. As a result, many immigrants, especially Hispanics who were working poor, were denied aid, adversely affecting their children, who were U.S. citizens. Moreover, the type of work available to individuals on welfare was generally low paying, offered no health insurance or other benefits, and did little to lift welfare-to-work participants above the poverty level. Thus, poverty levels, rather than numbers of TANF recipients, may provide a more telling portrayal of the program's progress. (See Figure 5.2 and Table 5.3.)

In *TANF Reaching Few Poor Families* (March 30, 2017, https://www.cbpp.org/sites/default/files/atoms/files/6-16-15tanf.pdf), Ife Floyd, Ladonna Pavetti, and Liz Schott of the Center on Budget and Policy Priorities (CBPP), a nonpartisan research and policy institute, note that the annual TANF budget has remained frozen since 1996, without even increases to keep pace with inflation. The American Recovery and Reinvestment Act, which was signed into law by President Barack Obama (1961–) in February 2009,

TABLE 5.6

Percentage of total family income from means-tested assistance programs, by race, Hispanic origin, and age, 2013

	0%	>0% to 25%	>25% to 50%	>50% to 75%	>75% to 100%	Total >50%
All persons	76.5	14.4	4.1	1.7	3.4	5.0
Age categories						
Children ages 0–17	64.7	20.3	7.3	3.1	4.5	7.7
Adults ages 18 to 64	78.7	13.4	3.4	1.3	3.3	4.6
Adults ages 65 and over	86.5	9.1	2.0	0.7	1.8	2.4
Racial/ethnic categories						
Non-Hispanic White	83.7	10.7	2.5	1.0	2.2	3.1
Non-Hispanic Black	58.8	20.9	8.3	4.3	7.7	12.0
Hispanic	62.4	23.3	7.2	2.5	4.6	7.0
Family categories						
Persons in married-couple families	84.6	11.4	2.4	0.7	1.0	1.6
Persons in single female families	44.3	27.7	12.3	6.4	9.4	15.8
Persons in single male families	64.0	24.2	6.5	1.6	3.7	5.3
Unrelated persons	80.7	10.1	2.2	0.9	6.1	7.0

Note: Income includes cash income from TANF (Temporary Assistance for Needy Families), SSI (Supplemental Security Income) and the value of SNAP (Supplemental Nutrition Assistance Program) benefits. Means-tested assistance includes TANF through federally-funded and state-separate programs, but does not include other cash benefits, such as state-local "general assistance" or solely-state-funded programs providing benefits to families who previously would have received TANF in some states. Total >50% includes all persons with more than 50 percent of their total annual income from these programs.
Beginning in 2002 persons who reported more than one race are included in the total for all persons but are not shown under either race category. Due to small sample size, American Indians/Alaska Natives, Asians and Native Hawaiians/Other Pacific Islanders are not shown separately. Hispanic persons may be of any race.

SOURCE: Gilbert Crouse and Suzanne Macartney, "Table 3 Indicator 1. Percentage of Total Income from TANF, SNAP and/or SSI Programs by Selected Characteristics: 2013," in *Welfare Indicators and Risk Factors: Fifteenth Report to Congress*, U.S. Department of Health and Human Services, 2016, https://aspe.hhs.gov/system/files/pdf/206736/WelfareIndicators15thReport.pdf (accessed September 5, 2017)

TABLE 5.7

Percentage of population receiving assistance from Temporary Assistance for Needy Families, Supplemental Nutrition Assistance Program, and/or Supplemental Security Income, by race, Hispanic origin, and age, 2013

	Any receipt	One program only			Two programs	
		TANF	SNAP	SSI	TANF & SNAP	SNAP & SSI
All persons	**17.0**	**0.1**	**13.2**	**1.0**	**1.1**	**1.6**
Racial/ethnic categories						
Non-Hispanic white	11.9	0.1	9.5	0.7	0.4	1.3
Non-Hispanic black	32.7	0.2	24.6	1.4	3.0	3.5
Hispanic	25.5	0.2	19.7	1.6	2.3	1.7
Age categories						
Children ages 0–5	32.5	0.4	26.6	0.6	4.3	0.6
Children ages 6–10	30.7	0.3	24.6	0.9	3.6	1.3
Children ages 11–15	26.1	0.3	21.0	1.0	2.7	1.1
Women ages 16–64	15.9	0.1	12.5	0.7	0.9	1.7
Men ages 16–64	13.0	0.0	10.2	0.9	0.3	1.6
Adults ages 65 and over	10.0	0.0	5.4	2.2	0.0	2.4
Family categories						
Persons in:						
Marrried couple families	10.0	0.1	8.4	0.6	0.4	0.6
Single female families	42.8	0.3	32.0	1.9	5.3	3.2
Single male families	23.6	0.2	18.3	2.2	1.2	1.7
Unrelated persons	16.5	0.0	11.5	1.2	0.0	3.8

TANF = Temporary Assistance for Needy Families
SNAP = Supplemental Nutrition Assistance Program
SSI = Supplemental Security Income
Note: Data is an average monthly percentage of the population. Categories are mutually exclusive. TANF and SNAP receipt are based on the family or recipient unit while SSI receipt is based on individuals. Individuals do not tend to receive both TANF and SSI; hence, no individual receives benefits from all three programs. The percentage of individuals receiving assistance from any one program in an average month (shown here) is lower than the percentage residing in families receiving assistance at some point over the course of a year. Persons who reported more than one race are not included the race categories above. Due to small sample sizes, American Indians/Alaska Natives, Asians and Native Hawaiians/other Pacific Islanders are not shown separately. Hispanic persons may be of any race.

SOURCE: Gilbert Crouse and Suzanne Macartney, "Table 15 Indicator 5. Percentage of Recipients Receiving Assistance from One Program or Multiple Programs in an Average Month among TANF, SSI and SNAP by Selected Characteristics: 2013," in *Welfare Indicators and Risk Factors: Fifteenth Report to Congress*, U.S. Department of Health and Human Services, 2016, https://aspe.hhs.gov/system/files/pdf/206736/WelfareIndicators15thReport.pdf (accessed September 5, 2017)

contained a provision for a TANF emergency fund of $5 billion for fiscal years 2009 and 2010, but the emergency fund was allowed to expire in September 2010, and TANF funding returned to its original level.

Floyd, Pavetti, and Schott indicate that in 2015 only 23 of every 100 families in poverty received cash assistance from TANF, down 66.2% since 1996, when TANF was first enacted. Furthermore, they explain that TANF has been far less effective than the AFDC (its predecessor program) for lifting families out of deep poverty. In 1995, 2 million children were lifted out of deep poverty by the AFDC. By comparison, in 2010 only 635,000 children were lifted out of deep poverty by TANF.

It appeared that TANF would be further weakened under the administration of President Donald Trump (1946–), who took office in January 2017. Tazra Mitchell of the CBPP reports in "President Trump's Budget Cuts TANF Despite Stated Goal to Reduce Poverty, Boost Work" (May 24, 2017, https://www.cbpp.org/blog/president-trumps-budget-cuts-tanf-despite-stated-goal-to-reduce-poverty-boost-work) that Trump's proposed 2018 budget would cut TANF funding by 10%, from $16.5 billion to $14.9 billion. Furthermore,

the new budget would discontinue the TANF Contingency Fund, which is an additional resource for states in hard economic times. In all, Trump intended to cut TANF by $2.2 billion in 2018 and by $22 billion over 10 years. The Republican-controlled Congress was expected to pass Trump's budget in December 2017.

Minority families living below the poverty line endured further reductions to their benefits with the passage of the Agriculture Act of 2014 (also known as the Farm Bill). According to Ron Nixon, in "House Approves Farm Bill, Ending a 2-Year Impasse" (NYTimes.com, January 29, 2014), the 2014 Farm Bill slashed $8 billion from SNAP, cuts that were expected to affect 850,000 families nationwide. With Congress due to pass a new Farm Bill for 2018, SNAP—which is the primary driver of farm bill spending—appeared to be facing even more drastic cuts. In "Trump's Budget Takes Aim at SNAP, Crop Insurance" (Politico.com, May 23, 2017), Helena Bottemiller Evich, Catherine Boudreau, and Jenny Hopkinson report that President Trump's initial 2018 budget proposal called on Congress to slash SNAP spending by 25%—reducing program benefits by more than $190 billion over 10 years.

CHAPTER 6

HEALTH

The demographic profiles of African Americans, Hispanics, Asian Americans, Pacific Islanders, Native Americans, and Alaskan Natives differ considerably from those of the majority population in the United States. Because a high percentage of minorities live in urban areas, they are exposed to a greater number of environmental hazards, including pollution, traffic hazards, substandard and/or overcrowded housing, and crime. Occupational risks are also greater for minorities because a greater percentage of them are employed in potentially dangerous jobs. Poverty, which is experienced disproportionately by African Americans, Hispanics, and Native Americans and Alaskan Natives, leads to poor nutrition, poor housing conditions, and poor access to health care. In addition, the stress that is involved in facing daily discrimination and changing cultural environments as well as the lack of resources for solving stressful situations can play a critical role in the mental and physical health of minority groups.

As a whole, Hispanics enjoy better health on a variety of measures than do non-Hispanic whites, despite Hispanics' disadvantaged position, higher poverty rates, lower educational attainment, and the obstacles to health care that they encounter. This is likely due in part to the fact that the average age of Hispanics in the United States is younger than the average age of the non-Hispanic white population. As Table 6.1 shows, 33.1% of the Hispanic population was under the age of 18 years in 2014, compared with 19.7% of the non-Hispanic white population. Conversely, only 6.3% of Hispanics were aged 65 years and older, compared with 17.8% of non-Hispanic whites.

This age differential is partly due to the higher fertility rate of Hispanics and partly to the higher percentage among them of recent immigrants. (Younger people are more likely to immigrate.) Antonio Flores, Gustavo López, and Jynnah Radford of the Pew Research Center report in *Facts on U.S. Latinos, 2015* (September 18, 2017, http://www.pewhispanic.org/2017/09/18/facts-on-u-s-latinos-current-data/) that an estimated 36.2% of Hispanics in the United States in 2015 were born in other countries. According to Flores, López, and Radford, at the time they were surveyed Hispanic women were more likely to have given birth in the previous year than were other women in the United States, and foreign-born Hispanic women were more likely than U.S.-born Hispanic women to have given birth that year. In 2015 an estimated 6.7% of Hispanic women (and 7.7% of foreign-born Hispanic women) aged 15 to 44 years had given birth within the past year, compared with 5.8% of non-Hispanic Asian women, 5.9% of non-Hispanic white women, and 6% of non-Hispanic African American women.

Flores, López, and Radford further report that Hispanics and other minorities accounted for a disproportionately large number of births in 2015. Hispanics comprised 17% of the total U.S. population in 2015 but accounted for more than one-fifth (22.5%) of all births. Non-Hispanic African Americans made up 12.3% of the population and 13.9% of births; non-Hispanic Asians were 5.3% of the population and 6.2% of births; non-Hispanic people of other races comprised 3.3% of the population and 3.6% of births. Only non-Hispanic whites accounted for a disproportionately smaller number of births in 2015. That year non-Hispanic whites made up 61.5% of the population but accounted for just 53.8% of births.

HEALTH CARE
Quality of Care

In *2016 National Healthcare Quality and Disparities Report* (July 2017, https://www.ahrq.gov/sites/default/files/wysiwyg/research/findings/nhqrdr/nhqdr16/2016qdr.pdf), the U.S. Department of Health and Human Services (HHS) outlines a number of core measures, assessing both quality and access, that compare the health care that is received across racial and ethnic groups. These measures assess such areas as person-centered care, patient safety, healthy living, effective treatment, care coordination, and care affordability. The HHS finds that minorities often

TABLE 6.1

Population by sex, age, race, and Hispanic origin, 2014

[Numbers in thousands. Civilian noninstitutionalized population.[a]]

					Hispanic origin and race[b]							
							Non-Hispanic					
	Total		Hispanic		Total		White alone		All other races			
Sex and age	Number	Percent	Number	Percent	Number	Percent	Number	Percent	Number	Percent		
Both sexes	313,401	100.0	54,268	100.0	259,134	100.0	195,489	100.0	63,644	100.0		
Under 15 years	61,029	19.5	15,088	27.8	45,941	17.7	31,394	16.1	14,548	22.9		
15 years and over	252,372	80.5	39,180	72.2	213,192	82.3	164,096	83.9	49,097	77.1		
Under 16 years	65,158	20.8	16,025	29.5	49,133	19.0	33,671	17.2	15,462	24.3		
16 years and over	248,243	79.2	38,242	70.5	210,001	81.0	161,819	82.8	48,182	75.7		
Under 18 years	73,953	23.6	17,971	33.1	55,982	21.6	38,550	19.7	17,432	27.4		
18 years and over	239,448	76.4	36,296	66.9	203,152	78.4	156,940	80.3	46,212	72.6		
Under 21 years	86,202	27.5	20,677	38.1	65,525	25.3	45,167	23.1	20,358	32.0		
21 years and over	227,199	72.5	33,591	61.9	193,608	74.7	150,323	76.9	43,286	68.0		
Under 65 years	268,924	85.8	50,863	93.7	218,062	84.2	160,638	82.2	57,423	90.2		
65 years and over	44,477	14.2	3,405	6.3	41,072	15.8	34,851	17.8	6,221	9.8		
Male	153,595	100.0	27,382	100.0	126,212	100.0	96,134	100.0	30,078	100.0		
Under 15 years	31,182	20.3	7,687	28.1	23,495	18.6	16,097	16.7	7,398	24.6		
15 years and over	122,413	79.7	19,695	71.9	102,717	81.4	80,037	83.3	22,680	75.4		
Under 16 years	33,285	21.7	8,176	29.9	25,109	19.9	17,264	18.0	7,846	26.1		
16 years and over	120,310	78.3	19,207	70.1	101,103	80.1	78,871	82.0	22,232	73.9		
Under 18 years	37,714	24.6	9,172	33.5	28,542	22.6	19,712	20.5	8,830	29.4		
18 years and over	115,881	75.4	18,210	66.5	97,671	77.4	76,422	79.5	21,248	70.6		
Under 21 years	43,936	28.6	10,555	38.5	33,381	26.4	23,121	24.1	10,261	34.1		
21 years and over	109,659	71.4	16,827	61.5	92,831	73.6	73,013	75.9	19,818	65.9		
Under 65 years	133,863	87.2	25,915	94.6	107,948	85.5	80,468	83.7	27,480	91.4		
65 years and over	19,731	12.8	1,467	5.4	18,264	14.5	15,666	16.3	2,598	8.6		
Female	159,806	100.0	26,885	100.0	132,921	100.0	99,355	100.0	33,566	100.0		
Under 15 years	29,847	18.7	7,401	27.5	22,446	16.9	15,296	15.4	7,150	21.3		
15 years and over	129,959	81.3	19,484	72.5	110,475	83.1	84,059	84.6	26,416	78.7		
Under 16 years	31,873	19.9	7,850	29.2	24,023	18.1	16,407	16.5	7,616	22.7		
16 years and over	127,933	80.1	19,035	70.8	108,898	81.9	82,948	83.5	25,950	77.3		
Under 18 years	36,239	22.7	8,799	32.7	27,440	20.6	18,838	19.0	8,602	25.6		
18 years and over	123,567	77.3	18,086	67.3	105,481	79.4	80,517	81.0	24,964	74.4		
Under 21 years	42,266	26.4	10,122	37.6	32,144	24.2	22,046	22.2	10,098	30.1		
21 years and over	117,541	73.6	16,763	62.4	100,777	75.8	77,309	77.8	23,468	69.9		
Under 65 years	135,061	84.5	24,947	92.8	110,114	82.8	80,171	80.7	29,943	89.2		
65 years and over	24,745	15.5	1,938	7.2	22,808	17.2	19,185	19.3	3,623	10.8		

[a]Plus armed forces living off post or with their families on post.
[b]Hispanic refers to people whose origin is Mexican, Puerto Rican, Cuban, Spanish-speaking Central or South American countries, or other Hispanic/Latino, regardless of race.
Note: Details may not sum to totals because of rounding.
The 2014 CPS ASEC included redesigned questions for income and health insurance coverage. All of the approximately 98,000 addresses were selected to receive the improved set of health insurance coverage items. The improved income questions were implemented using a split panel design. Approximately 68,000 addresses were selected to receive a set of income questions similar to those used in the 2013 CPS ASEC. The remaining 30,000 addresses were selected to receive the redesigned income questions. The source of data for this table is the CPS ASEC sample of 98,000 addresses.

SOURCE: Adapted from "Table 1. Population by Sex, Age, Hispanic Origin, and Race: 2014," in *The Hispanic Population in the United States: 2014*, U.S. Census Bureau, 2017, https://www2.census.gov/programs-surveys/demo/tables/hispanic-origin/2014/cps-2014-hispanic-tab1.xls (accessed September 6, 2017)

receive a poorer quality of care than do non-Hispanic whites. Between 2013 and 2015, African Americans received poorer quality of care than whites for roughly 77 out of 182 (42.3%) core quality measures, Hispanics for 65 out of 168 (38.7%) core quality measures, Native Americans and Alaskan Natives for 31 out of 93 (33.3%) core quality measures, Native Hawaiians and Pacific Islanders for 14 out of 50 (28%) core quality measures, and Asian Americans for 32 out of 163 (19.6%) core quality measures. (See Figure 6.1.) Poor people received lower quality of care than high-income people (family incomes above 400% of the poverty level) in 60% of core quality measures. (It should be noted that people from minority groups are disproportionally poor.)

Access to Care

In *2016 National Healthcare Quality and Disparities Report*, the HHS measures access to health care, finding that minorities, particularly those of low socioeconomic status, face barriers to accessing health care that make receiving basic health services a struggle. Access is measured in several ways, including ability to get into the health care system, to get care within the health care system, and to find providers to meet their needs.

The HHS finds that between 2013 and 2015, Hispanics had worse access to care than non-Hispanic whites for 15 out of 20 (75%) core access measures. (See Figure 6.2.) African Americans had worse access to care for 10 out of

FIGURE 6.1

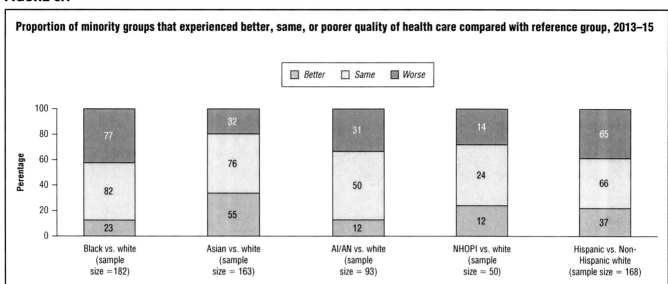

Proportion of minority groups that experienced better, same, or poorer quality of health care compared with reference group, 2013–15

Key: AI/AN = American Indian or Alaska Native; NHOPI = Native Hawaiian or other Pacific Islander.

SOURCE: "Figure 15. Number and Percentage of Quality Measures for Which Members of Selected Groups Experienced Better, Same, or Worse Quality of Care Compared with Reference Group (White) in 2013–2015," in *2016 National Healthcare Quality and Disparities Report*, U.S. Department of Health and Human Services, Agency for Healthcare Research and Quality, July 2017, https://www.ahrq.gov/sites/default/files/wysiwyg/research/findings/nhqrdr/nhqdr16/2016qdr.pdf (accessed September 6, 2017)

FIGURE 6.2

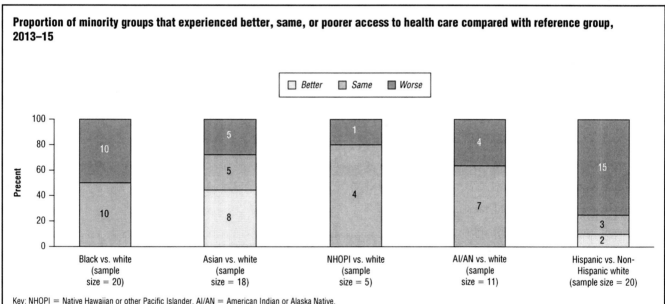

Proportion of minority groups that experienced better, same, or poorer access to health care compared with reference group, 2013–15

Key: NHOPI = Native Hawaiian or other Pacific Islander. AI/AN = American Indian or Alaska Native.
Note: The number of measures is based on the measures that have data for each population group.

SOURCE: Adapted from "Figure 10. Number and Percentage of Access Measures for Which Members of Selected Groups Experienced Better, Same, or Worse Access to Care Compared with Reference Group, 2013–2015," in *2016 National Healthcare Quality and Disparities Report*, U.S. Department of Health and Human Services, Agency for Healthcare Research and Quality, July 2017, https://www.ahrq.gov/sites/default/files/wysiwyg/research/findings/nhqrdr/nhqdr16/2016qdr.pdf (accessed September 6, 2017)

20 (50%) core access measures, Native Americans and Alaskan Natives had worse access to care for 4 out of 11 (36.4%) core access measures, and Native Hawaiians and Pacific Islanders for 1 out of 5 (20%) core access measures. Asian Americans had worse access to care than non-Hispanic whites for 5 out of 18 (27.8%) of the core access measures,

while having better access to care than non-Hispanic whites for 8 out of 18 (44.4%) core access measures. Part of these differences in access to care for minority groups had to do with socioeconomics; people below the poverty level had worse access to care than did high-income people for every one of the access measures.

HEALTH INSURANCE. Lack of health insurance is one formidable barrier to receiving health care. Jessica C. Barnett and Marina S. Vornovitsky of the U.S. Census Bureau indicate in *Income, Poverty, and Health Insurance Coverage in the United States: 2015* (September 2016, https://www.census.gov/content/dam/Census/library/publications/2016/demo/ p60- 257.pdf) that 29 million people (9.1% of the population) were uninsured in 2015. Although this figure represented a steep decline from the 41.8 million people without insurance in 2013, lack of insurance coverage remains a significant barrier for people seeking basic health care services. The HHS emphasizes in *2016 National Healthcare*

Quality and Disparities Report that uninsured people are more likely to have a poor health status and to die early because it is more difficult for the uninsured to get health care, and therefore they are diagnosed at later disease stages and receive less therapeutic care.

In 2015 African Americans and Hispanics were much less likely to carry health insurance coverage than were their non-Hispanic white and Asian American counterparts. (See Figure 6.3.) According to Barnett and Vornovitsky, 6.7% of non-Hispanic whites and 7.5% of Asian Americans lacked health insurance in 2015; by contrast, 11.1% of

FIGURE 6.3

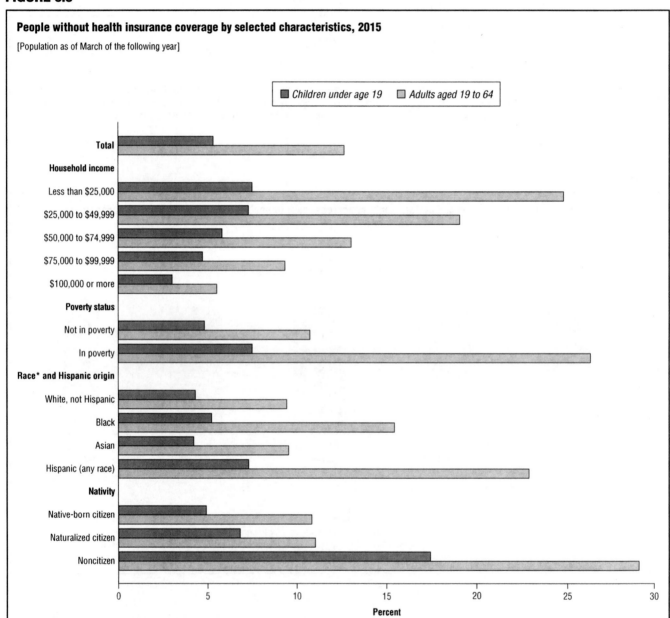

People without health insurance coverage by selected characteristics, 2015

[Population as of March of the following year]

*Federal surveys give respondents the option of reporting more than one race. This figure shows data using the race-alone concept. For example, Asian refers to people who reported Asian and no other race.

SOURCE: Jessica C. Barnett and Marina S. Vornovitsky, "Figure 6. Children Under Age 19 and Adults Aged 19 to 64 without Health Insurance Coverage by Selected Characteristics: 2015," in *Health Insurance Coverage in the United States: 2015*, U.S. Census Bureau, September 2016, https://www.census.gov/content/dam/Census/library/publications/2016/demo/p60-257.pdf (accessed September 6, 2017)

African Americans and 16.2% of Hispanics were uninsured that year. These discrepancies narrowed somewhat among children 18 years of age and younger; 5.2% of African American children and 7.3% of Hispanic children lacked coverage in 2015. (See Figure 6.3.) Meanwhile, 4.3% of non-Hispanic white children and 4.2% of Asian American children lacked health insurance coverage that year.

Those minorities who do have health insurance are more likely than non-Hispanic whites to be covered by government programs rather than by private health insurance. In 2015 members of all minority groups were more likely to be covered by Medicaid (the federally funded health care program for low-income people) than were non-Hispanic whites. In that year Medicaid covered 17.9% of non-Hispanic whites and 16.5% of Asian Americans. (See Table 6.2.) By comparison, Medicaid covered 34.3% of African Americans, 34.3% of Native Americans or Alaskan Natives, and 33.5% of Hispanics in 2015. Among Hispanics, Puerto Ricans were the most likely (38.9%) and Cubans were the least likely (22.8%) to be covered by Medicaid. The large proportion of minorities on Medicaid is in part explained by eligibility requirements; only poor and low-income people qualify, and members of minority groups are disproportionately poor.

Nearly all people aged 65 years and older are covered by health insurance largely due to Medicare (the federally administered system of health insurance for people aged 65 years and older and people with disabilities). Medicaid, however, additionally covers a much higher proportion of minorities of this age, whereas non-Hispanic whites tend to be covered by private insurance. For example, in 2013 4.9% of non-Hispanic whites aged 65 years and older were covered by Medicaid, compared with 17.8% of non-Hispanic African Americans and 20.1% of Hispanics. (See Table 6.3.) In 2013 non-Hispanic whites aged 65 years and older were more likely to be covered either by an employer-sponsored plan (29.5%) or by a Medigap plan (22.1%), both of which are forms of private health insurance, although in both cases the percentages covered by private plans had been dropping steadily since 1992. Nevertheless, lower proportions of minority groups were covered by private plans. In 2013, 26.7% of non-Hispanic African Americans and 13.9% of Hispanics were covered by an employer-sponsored plan, and 5.3% and 5.6%, respectively, were covered by a Medigap plan.

TABLE 6.2

Medicaid coverage among persons under 65 years of age, by race and Hispanic origin, selected years 1984–2015

[Data are based on household interviews of a sample of the civilian noninstitutionalized population]

Characteristic	1984[a]	1997	2000[b]	2005[c]	2010[c]	2012[c]	2013[c]	2014[c]	2015[c]
Race[d]									
White only	4.6	7.4	7.1	11.0	14.5	15.5	15.6	16.9	17.9
Black or African American only	20.5	22.4	21.2	24.9	30.4	31.6	31.6	34.1	34.3
American Indian or Alaska Native only	28.2*	19.6	15.1	24.2	21.6	36.5	32.0	35.5	34.3
Asian only	8.7*	9.6	7.5	8.2	12.0	13.0	13.2	14.7	16.5
Native Hawaiian or other Pacific Islander only	—	—	*	*	*	*	*	*	*
2 or more races	—	—	19.1	22.0	27.4	29.1	30.4	30.2	31.5
Hispanic origin and race[d]									
Hispanic or Latino	13.3	17.6	15.5	22.9	28.6	30.5	29.5	31.3	33.5
Mexican	12.2	17.2	14.0	23.0	29.5	31.0	29.8	32.1	34.2
Puerto Rican	31.5	31.0	29.4	31.9	35.7	35.3	36.9	35.7	38.9
Cuban	4.8*	7.3	9.2	17.7	17.3	22.9	23.3	22.4	22.8
Other Hispanic or Latino	7.9	15.3	14.5	19.7	24.5	28.3	27.0	28.6	30.7
Not Hispanic or Latino	6.2	8.7	8.5	11.1	14.4	15.2	15.5	16.9	17.5
White only	3.7	6.1	6.1	8.5	11.0	11.5	11.9	13.0	13.6
Black or African American only	20.7	22.1	21.0	24.8	30.0	31.3	31.3	33.4	33.6

—Data not available.

*Estimates are considered unreliable. Data followed by an asterisk have a relative standard error (RSE) of 20%–30%. Data not shown have an RSE greater than 30%.

[a]Data prior to 1997 are not strictly comparable with data for later years due to the 1997 questionnaire redesign.

[b]Estimates for 2000–2002 were calculated using 2000-based sample weights and may differ from estimates in other reports that used 1990-based sample weights for 2000–2002 estimates.

[c]Beginning in quarter 3 of the 2004 NHIS, persons under age 65 with no reported coverage were asked explicitly about Medicaid coverage. Estimates were calculated without and with the additional information from this question in the columns labeled 2004(1) and 2004(2) (in spreadsheet version), respectively, and estimates were calculated with the additional information starting with 2005 data.

[d]The race groups, white, black, American Indian or Alaska Native, Asian, Native Hawaiian or other Pacific Islander, and 2 or more races, include persons of Hispanic and non-Hispanic origin. Persons of Hispanic origin may be of any race. Starting with 1999 data, race-specific estimates are tabulated according to the 1997 *Revisions to the Standards for the Classification of Federal Data on Race and Ethnicity* and are not strictly comparable with estimates for earlier years. The five single-race categories plus multiple-race categories shown in the table conform to the 1997 Standards. Starting with 1999 data, race-specific estimates are for persons who reported only one racial group; the category 2 or more races includes persons who reported more than one racial group. Prior to 1999, data were tabulated according to the 1977 Standards with four racial groups, and the Asian only category included Native Hawaiian or Other Pacific Islander. Estimates for single-race categories prior to 1999 included persons who reported one race or, if they reported more than one race, identified one race as best representing their race. Starting with 2003 data, race responses of other race and unspecified multiple race were treated as missing, and then race was imputed if these were the only race responses. Almost all persons with a race response of other race were of Hispanic origin.

SOURCE: Adapted from "Table 104. Medicaid Coverage among Persons under Age 65, by Selected Characteristics: United States, Selected Years 1984–2015," in *Health, United States, 2016: With Chartbook on Long-term Trends in Health*, Centers for Disease Control and Prevention, National Center for Health Statistics, May 2017, https://www.cdc.gov/nchs/data/hus/hus16.pdf (accessed September 6, 2017)

TABLE 6.3

Health insurance coverage of noninstitutionalized Medicare beneficiaries 65 years of age and over, by type of coverage and race and Hispanic origin, selected years 1992–2013

[Data are based on household interviews of a sample of noninstitutionalized Medicare beneficiaries]

Characteristic	Medicare Advantage plan[a]					Medicaid[b]				
	1992	1995	2000	2012	2013	1992	1995	2000	2012	2013
Age					Number, in millions					
65 years and over	1.1	2.6	5.9	12.4	13.8	2.7	2.8	2.7	3.6	3.6
					Percent distribution					
65 years and over	3.9	8.9	19.3	29.1	31.2	9.4	9.6	9.0	8.5	8.1
65–74 years	4.2	9.5	20.6	29.1	30.3	7.9	8.8	8.5	7.6	7.2
75–84 years	3.7	8.3	18.5	30.1	33.8	10.6	9.6	8.9	9.2	8.6
85 years and over	*	7.3	16.3	26.3	29.4	16.6	13.6	11.2	10.3	11.4
Race and Hispanic origin										
White, not Hispanic or Latino	3.6	8.4	18.4	26.9	29.1	5.6	5.4	5.1	5.1	4.9
Black, not Hispanic or Latino	*	7.9	20.7	30.3	33.4	28.5	30.3	23.6	19.0	17.8
Hispanic	*	15.5	27.5	45.5	46.7	39.0	40.5	28.7	20.2	20.1

Characteristic	Employer-sponsored plan[c]					Medigap[d]				
	1992	1995	2000	2012	2013	1992	1995	2000	2012	2013
Age					Number, in millions					
65 years and over	12.5	11.3	10.7	12.0	12.1	9.9	9.5	7.6	8.0	8.2
					Percent distribution					
65 years and over	42.8	38.6	35.2	28.1	27.4	33.9	32.5	25.0	18.9	18.7
65–74 years	46.9	41.1	36.6	29.8	29.5	31.4	29.9	21.7	17.5	17.5
75–84 years	38.2	37.1	35.0	25.9	24.4	37.5	35.2	27.8	20.2	19.8
85 years and over	31.6	30.2	29.4	26.1	24.9	38.3	37.6	31.1	22.1	21.1
Race and Hispanic origin										
White, not Hispanic or Latino	45.9	41.3	38.6	30.6	29.5	37.2	36.2	28.3	22.4	22.1
Black, not Hispanic or Latino	25.9	26.7	22.0	27.4	26.7	13.6	10.2	7.5	5.7	5.3
Hispanic	20.7	16.9	15.8	13.1	13.9	15.8	10.1	11.3	6.3	5.6

Characteristic	Medicare fee-for-service only or Other[e]				
	1992	1995	2000	2012	2013
Age			Number, in millions		
65 years and over	2.9	3.1	3.5	6.6	6.4
			Percent distribution		
65 years and over	9.9	10.5	11.5	15.5	14.6
65–74 years	9.7	10.7	12.6	16.0	15.5
75–84 years	10.1	9.9	9.9	14.6	13.5
85 years and over	10.8	11.3	12.1	15.1	13.3
Race and Hispanic origin					
White, not Hispanic or Latino	7.7	8.7	9.6	15.1	14.3
Black, not Hispanic or Latino	26.7	25.0	26.1	17.6	16.8
Hispanic	18.3	17.1	16.7	14.9	13.7

*Estimates are considered unreliable if the sample cell size is 50 or fewer.
—Data not available.
[a]Enrollee has a Medicare Advantage plan regardless of other insurance. Medicare Advantage plans include health maintenance organizations, preferred provider organizations, private fee-for-service plans, special needs plans, and Medicare medical savings account plans. Starting with 2013 data, the term Medicare Risk Health Maintenance Organization was replaced with Medicare Advantage plan.
[b]Enrolled in Medicaid and not enrolled in a Medicare Advantage plan.
[c]Private insurance plans purchased through employers (own, current, or former employer, family business, union, or former employer or union of spouse) and not enrolled in a Medicare Advantage plan or Medicaid.
[d]Supplemental insurance purchased privately or through organizations such as American Association of Retired Persons or professional organizations, and not enrolled in a Medicare Advantage plan, Medicaid, or employer-sponsored plan.
[e]Medicare fee-for-service only or other public plans (except Medicaid).

SOURCE: Adapted from "Table 106. Health Insurance Coverage of Noninstitutionalized Medicare Beneficiaries Aged 65 and over, by Type of Coverage and Selected Characteristics: United States, Selected Years 1992–2013," in *Health, United States, 2016: With Chartbook on Long-term Trends in Health*, Centers for Disease Control and Prevention, National Center for Health Statistics, May 2017, https://www.cdc.gov/nchs/data/hus/hus16.pdf (accessed September 6, 2017)

THE AFFORDABLE CARE ACT. In March 2010 President Barack Obama (1961–) signed into law the Affordable Care Act (ACA), the nation's most sweeping piece of health care legislation since the launch of the Medicare and Medicaid programs in the 1960s. Often referred to as "Obamacare," the law was designed to help uninsured Americans gain access to health care coverage, regardless of their prior medical history or ability to afford monthly premiums. Because minorities constituted a disproportionate number of the uninsured population in the United States, the ACA also included a number of programs aimed at addressing disparities in health care access among various races and ethnicities. Janell Ross writes in "Supreme Court Upholds Affordable Care Act, a Boon to Minority Health in the U.S." (HuffingtonPost.com, June 28, 2012) that African Americans, Asian Americans, and Hispanics were roughly 27 million of the estimated 50 million Americans without health insurance in 2010, the year of the law's passage. According to Ross, 16 million Hispanics, or 33% of the Hispanic population in the United States, had no health insurance before the passage of the ACA; 7 million African Americans, or 22% of the African American population, were also without coverage.

Ross reports in "Affordable Care Act May Help Close Gap on Health Disparities" (NationalJournal.com, April 9, 2014) that the ACA aimed to address these disparities through a number of key initiatives. These measures included an expansion of existing Medicaid programs, increased investment in community health clinics, and the designation of additional funding for the National Health Service Corps, an organization that provides health care to underserved communities nationwide. In addition, the ACA authorized the Office of Minority Health (https://www.minorityhealth.hhs.gov), to establish six new branches within six federal agencies, with the goal of developing new policies aimed at improving health care for racial and ethnic minorities.

Despite fierce opposition to the law from Republican lawmakers and conservative political groups, the ACA survived a series of legal challenges at both the state and federal level, and was finally upheld by the U.S. Supreme Court in June 2012. Jeff Mason and Mark Felsenthal report in "Obamacare Enrollment Exceeds Seven Million Target Despite Setback" (Reuters, April 1, 2014) that by April 2014 roughly 7.1 million Americans had enrolled in the new health care program. Over the next three years, the ACA played a critical role in expanding health coverage to previously uninsured Americans. In "Census: Uninsured Rate Dropped to 8.8 Percent Last Year" (Politico.com, September 12, 2017), Paul Demko reports that 13.3% of Americans had no health insurance prior to full implementation of the ACA. By 2016, this figure had fallen to 8.8%. The decline in the uninsured rate was even more pronounced among African Americans and Hispanics. Namrata Uberoi, Kenneth Finegold, and Emily Gee report in *Health Insurance Coverage and the Affordable Care Act, 2010–2016* (March 3, 2016, https://aspe.hhs.gov/system/files/pdf/187551/ACA2010-2016.pdf) that in 2013 nearly one-quarter (22.4%) of African Americans had no health insurance; by 2016, this figure had dropped to 10.4%. Meanwhile, the uninsured rate among Hispanics fell from 41.8% to 30.5% over this same period.

Following the election of President Donald Trump (1946–) in 2016, the Republican-led Congress again launched a series of attempts to repeal the ACA. Samantha Artige, Petry Ubri, and Julia Foutz of the Henry J. Kaiser Family Foundation report in "What Is at Stake for Health and Health Care Disparities under ACA Repeal?" (March 20, 2017, https://www.kff.org/disparities-policy/issue-brief/what-is-at-stake-for-health-and-health-care-disparities-under-aca-repeal/) that disparities in access to health insurance among minority groups, which had been reduced under the ACA, would likely increase again if the law were repealed. As of November 2017, efforts to replace the ACA with an alternative health plan had stalled in Congress.

DOCTOR VISITS. Another measure of a group's access to care is the number of doctor visits that are made annually. Since the 1980s, as more outpatient clinics and other outreach health facilities have opened, Americans have had increased opportunities to seek medical help. However, in 2015 almost all minority groups were more likely than non-Hispanic whites to have not visited a doctor's office or emergency department in the previous 12 months. In that year, 22.3% of Hispanics, 20.6% of Native Americans or Alaskan Natives, and 18.2% of Asian Americans had not visited a health care provider. (See Table 6.4.) Non-Hispanic African Americans (14.7%) were slightly less likely than non-Hispanic whites (12.7%) to have not visited a health care provider in 2015.

INDIAN HEALTH SERVICE. Federal funding for Native American health care is provided through the Indian Health Service (2017, http://www.ihs.gov/), whose mission is "to raise the physical, mental, social, and spiritual health of American Indians and Alaskan Natives to the highest level." The delivery of health care to Native Americans is complicated by the lack of services and the long distances that sometimes must be traveled to receive care. Alaskan Natives are often able to get preventive medical care only by flying to a medical facility, and although transportation costs are covered for emergency care, they are not provided for routine care.

Many Native American tribes have invested some of the money earned from casinos to improve health services. For example, Herman Williams Jr. explains in "Gambling Expansion Advocates Ignore the Facts about Tribal Gaming" (*Tulalip–Quil Ceda Messenger*, March 2003) that the Tulalip Tribes in Washington State were able to build a new state-of-the-art health center as well as improve other social services and reduce unemployment with proceeds from tribal gaming. In "Tribes Hit the Jackpot" (*New Mexico Resources*, Fall 2003), Kevin Robinson-Avila reports that the Sandia Pueblo in New Mexico built a wellness center that provides free medical care to all tribe members as well as child care, education, and training. Barbara Wolfe et al.

TABLE 6.4

Health care visits to doctor offices, emergency departments, and home visits within the past 12 months, by race, Hispanic origin, and poverty level, selected years 1997, 2010, 2015

[Data are based on household interviews of a sample of the civilian noninstitutionalized population]

| | Number of health care visits[a] | | | | | | | | | | | |
| | None | | | 1–3 visits | | | 4–9 visits | | | 10 or more visits | | |
Characteristic	1997	2010	2015	1997	2010	2015	1997	2010	2015	1997	2010	2015
						Percent distribution						
Race[b, c]												
White only	16.0	15.3	14.8	46.1	44.9	47.8	23.9	26.1	24.0	14.0	13.7	13.4
Black or African American only	16.8	15.7	14.5	46.1	47.2	50.2	23.2	24.7	24.1	13.9	12.4	11.2
American Indian or Alaska Native only	17.1	19.4	20.6	38.0	40.3	39.0	24.2	28.1	23.3	20.7	12.2	17.1
Asian only	22.8	20.4	18.2	49.1	49.9	54.7	19.7	22.1	18.7	8.3	7.6	8.5
Native Hawaiian or other Pacific Islander only	—	*	*	—	*	*	—	*	*	—	*	*
2 or more races	—	13.9	17.3	—	42.3	41.5	—	25.2	25.0	—	18.6	16.2
Hispanic origin and race[b, c]												
Hispanic or Latino	24.9	23.5	22.3	42.3	43.2	45.9	20.3	22.6	21.9	12.5	10.7	9.9
Mexican	28.9	25.2	24.8	40.8	43.3	44.8	18.5	21.4	20.7	11.8	10.1	9.7
Not Hispanic or Latino	15.4	14.0	13.4	46.7	45.8	49.0	24.0	26.5	24.1	13.9	13.7	13.5
White only	14.7	13.2	12.7	46.6	45.3	48.1	24.4	27.1	24.7	14.3	14.4	14.5
Black or African American only	16.9	15.6	14.7	46.1	47.3	50.5	23.1	24.9	23.8	13.8	12.2	11.0
Percent of poverty level[b, d]												
Below 100%	20.6	20.4	19.0	37.8	37.5	39.9	22.7	25.1	23.9	18.9	17.0	17.1
100%–199%	20.1	20.8	18.4	43.3	42.1	45.1	21.7	23.1	22.9	14.9	13.9	13.6
200%–399%	16.4	16.2	15.9	47.2	46.3	49.5	23.6	25.4	22.8	12.8	12.1	11.8
400% or more	12.8	10.2	11.2	49.8	49.4	51.8	24.9	27.6	24.7	12.5	12.7	12.3
Hispanic origin and race and percent of poverty level[b, c, d]												
Hispanic or Latino:												
Below 100%	30.2	28.7	26.3	34.8	36.5	38.3	19.9	22.5	22.7	15.0	12.3	12.7
100%–199%	28.7	27.7	25.1	39.7	42.7	45.1	20.4	19.9	21.0	11.2	9.8	8.8
200%–399%	20.7	21.6	22.2	47.4	45.0	49.5	19.8	23.1	20.2	12.1	10.3	8.2
400% or more	15.2	11.3	13.3	50.4	51.1	50.2	22.6	26.1	25.1	11.8	11.5	11.4
Not Hispanic or Latino:												
White only:												
Below 100%	17.0	15.0	15.2	38.3	37.0	38.3	23.9	27.4	25.6	20.9	20.6	20.9
100%–199%	17.3	18.4	15.7	44.1	40.4	43.6	22.2	24.7	23.7	16.3	16.5	17.0
200%–399%	15.4	14.7	13.7	46.9	46.0	48.6	24.3	26.3	24.0	13.4	13.0	13.7
400% or more	12.5	9.9	10.6	49.1	48.2	51.1	25.5	28.4	25.2	13.0	13.5	13.2
Black or African American only:												
Below 100%	17.4	18.4	16.2	38.5	39.8	42.9	23.4	25.0	25.1	20.7	16.8	15.7
100%–199%	18.8	17.6	14.6	43.7	45.7	47.6	22.9	24.3	25.2	14.5	12.5	12.6
200%–399%	16.6	15.1	15.6	49.7	49.0	54.0	22.9	25.7	22.3	10.8	10.2	8.0
400% or more	14.0	10.0	11.7	54.3	58.2	55.9	22.7	22.5	23.2	9.0	9.3	9.2
Percent of poverty level and health insurance status prior to interview[d, e, f]												
Under 65 years:												
Below 100%:												
Insured continuously all 12 months	13.8	12.7	14.3	39.7	39.5	42.3	25.2	27.5	25.9	21.4	20.3	17.5
Uninsured for any period up to 12 months	19.7	16.9	21.8	37.6	43.0	45.6	21.9	25.0	19.0	20.9	15.1	13.7
Uninsured more than 12 months	41.2	45.0	48.8	39.9	38.1	36.9	12.2	13.6	10.6	6.6	3.3	3.8*
100%–199%:												
Insured continuously all 12 months	16.0	14.8	13.3	46.4	44.4	49.1	21.9	24.8	23.8	15.8	16.0	13.8
Uninsured for any period up to 12 months	18.8	21.0	25.6	45.1	46.0	41.9	21.0	20.6	19.4	15.0	12.4	13.0
Uninsured more than 12 months	38.7	43.2	48.8	41.0	39.4	37.6	14.0	12.4	11.1	6.3	5.0	*

report in "The Income and Health Effects of Tribal Casino Gaming on American Indians" (*La Follette Policy Report*, vol. 19, no. 2, Spring 2010) that when one or more gaming tribes is present in a county, Native Americans residing in the area are more likely to carry health insurance and less likely to forgo health care when needed.

PREGNANCY AND BIRTH

Prenatal Care

The importance of early prenatal care cannot be over-emphasized, as doctors are now better able to detect, and often correct, potential problems early in pregnancy. Every pregnant woman should receive prenatal care, and the

TABLE 6.4

Health care visits to doctor offices, emergency departments, and home visits within the past 12 months, by race, Hispanic origin, and poverty level, selected years 1997, 2010, 2015 [CONTINUED]

[Data are based on household interviews of a sample of the civilian noninstitutionalized population]

Characteristic	Number of health care visits[a]											
	None			1–3 visits			4–9 visits			10 or more visits		
	1997	2010	2015	1997	2010	2015	1997	2010	2015	1997	2010	2015
	Percent distribution											
200%–399%:												
Insured continuously all 12 months	15.1	13.6	14.0	49.4	49.4	53.5	23.4	25.3	22.0	12.1	11.7	10.5
Uninsured for any period up to 12 months	17.9	18.8	19.8	49.3	49.7	49.0	20.0	19.7	21.1	12.8	11.8	10.0
Uninsured more than 12 months	37.0	43.8	50.7	43.8	40.7	38.5	12.6	13.3	8.7	6.6	2.2*	2.2*
400% or more:												
Insured continuously all 12 months	12.4	9.7	11.4	52.2	51.8	54.3	23.9	26.8	23.5	11.5	11.6	10.8
Uninsured for any period up to 12 months	17.2	16.6	16.6	50.0	53.5	54.1	24.2	23.9	20.2	8.5*	6.0*	9.0
Uninsured more than 12 months	35.1	39.2	39.3	44.1	46.0	41.1	15.1	8.8*	*	5.7*	*	*

—Data not available.

*Estimates are considered unreliable. Data followed by an asterisk have a relative standard error (RSE) of 20%–30%. Data not shown have an RSE greater than 30%.

[a]This table presents a summary measure of the number of visits to hospital emergency departments, home visits by a nurse or other health care professional, and visits to doctor offices, clinics, or some other place during a 12-month period.

[b]Estimates are age-adjusted to the year 2000 standard population using six age groups: Under 18 years, 18–44 years, 45–54 years, 55–64 years, 65–74 years, and 75 years and over. The disability measure is age-adjusted using the five adult age groups.

[c]The race groups, white, black, American Indian or Alaska Native, Asian, Native Hawaiian or Other Pacific Islander, and 2 or more races, include persons of Hispanic and non-Hispanic origin. Persons of Hispanic origin may be of any race. Starting with 1999 data, race-specific estimates are tabulated according to the 1997 *Revisions to the Standards for the Classification of Federal Data on Race and Ethnicity* and are not strictly comparable with estimates for earlier years. The five single-race categories plus multiple-race categories shown in the table conform to the 1997 standards. Starting with 1999 data, race-specific estimates are for persons who reported only one racial group; the category 2 or more races includes persons who reported more than one racial group. Prior to 1999, data were tabulated according to the 1977 standards with four racial groups, and the Asian only category included Native Hawaiian or Other Pacific Islander. Estimates for single-race categories prior to 1999 included persons who reported one race or, if they reported more than one race, identified one race as best representing their race. Starting with 2003 data, race responses of other race and unspecified multiple race were treated as missing, and then race was imputed if these were the only race responses. Almost all persons with a race response of other race were of Hispanic origin.

[d]Percent of poverty level is based on family income and family size and composition using U.S. Census Bureau poverty thresholds. Missing family income data were imputed for 1997 and beyond.

[e]Estimates for persons under age 65 are age-adjusted to the year 2000 standard population using four age groups: Under 18 years, 18–44 years, 45–54 years, and 55–64 years.

[f]Health insurance categories are mutually exclusive. Persons who reported both Medicaid and private coverage are classified as having private coverage. Starting with 1997 data, state-sponsored health plan coverage is included as Medicaid coverage. Starting with 1999 data, coverage by the Children's Health Insurance Program (CHIP) is included with Medicaid coverage. In addition to private and Medicaid, the insured category also includes military plans, other government-sponsored health plans, and Medicare, not shown separately. Persons not covered by private insurance, Medicaid, CHIP, state-sponsored or other government-sponsored health plans (starting in 1997), Medicare, or military plans are considered to have no health insurance coverage. Persons with only Indian Health Service coverage are considered to have no health insurance coverage.

SOURCE: Adapted from "Table 65. Health Care Visits to Doctor Offices, Emergency Departments, and Home Visits within the Past 12 months, by Selected Characteristics: United States, Selected Years 1997–2015," in *Health, United States, 2016: With Chartbook on Long-term Trends in Health*, Centers for Disease Control and Prevention, National Center for Health Statistics, May 2017, https://www.cdc.gov/nchs/data/hus/hus16.pdf (accessed September 6, 2017)

National Center for Health Statistics (NCHS) believes the United States is capable of guaranteeing that more than 90% of pregnant women receive prenatal care during their first trimester of pregnancy.

The Child Trends Databank reports in "Late or No Prenatal Care" (December 2015, https://www.childtrends.org/wp-content/uploads/2014/07/25_Prenatal_Care.pdf) that in 2014, 4.3% of non-Hispanic white mothers received either no prenatal care or received prenatal care only late in their pregnancy. By comparison, 10.8% of Native Americans or Alaskan Natives, 9.7% of African Americans, 7.5% of Hispanics, and 5.7% of Asian Americans or Pacific Islanders received late or no prenatal care that year. These figures represented notable increases for all groups compared with 2000, when 2.3% of non-Hispanic whites, 3.3% of Asian Americans or Pacific Islanders, 6.3% of Hispanics, 6.7% of African Americans, and 8.6% of Native Americans or Alaskan Natives received no or late prenatal care during their pregnancies.

Births and Fertility

In "Births: Final Data for 2015" (*National Vital Statistics Reports*, vol. 66, no. 1, January 5, 2017), Joyce A. Martin et al. of the NCHS report that, of the nearly 4 million births in 2015, just over 2.1 million were to non-Hispanic white mothers, 924,048 were to Hispanic mothers (who may be of any race), 589,047 were to non-Hispanic black mothers, 281,264 were to Asian or Pacific Islander mothers, and 44,299 were to Native American or Alaskan Native mothers. The birth rate (live births per 1,000 population in a specified group) was highest among Hispanics (16.3; Hispanics may be of any race), followed by non-Hispanic African Americans (14.2) and Asian Americans or Pacific Islanders (14). Non-Hispanic whites (10.7 per 1,000) and Native Americans or Alaskan Natives (9.7) had the lowest birth rates.

The fertility rate refers to the number of live births per 1,000 women aged 15 to 44 years in a specified group. According to Martin et al., in 2015 Hispanic women, who may be of any race, had the highest fertility rate (71.7 per 1,000), followed by non-Hispanic African American women (64.1), non-Hispanic white women (59.3), and Asian or Pacific Islander women (58.5). Native American or Alaskan Native women (43.9 per 1,000) had the lowest fertility rates.

Low Birth Weight and Infant Mortality

The percentage of babies that were born with low birth weights increased steadily between 1980 and 2005, decreased between 2010 and 2014, and then rose slightly in 2015, as reported by the NCHS in *Health, United States, 2016: With Chartbook on Long-Term Trends in Health* (May 2017, https://www.cdc.gov/nchs/data/hus/hus16.pdf). (See Table 6.5.) Low birth weight is defined as weighing between 3 pounds, 4 ounces and 5 pounds, 8 ounces (1,500 g and 2,500 g). Very low birth weight is less than 3 pounds, 4 ounces (1,500 g). Low-birth-weight babies, as well as premature babies (born before 37 weeks of gestation), often suffer serious health problems and encounter developmental problems later in life. In 2015, 13.4% of non-Hispanic African American babies were born with low birth weights, whereas 8.4% of Asian or Pacific Islander babies, 7.5% of Native American or Alaskan Native babies, 7.2% of Hispanic babies, and 6.9% of non-Hispanic white babies were born with low birth weights. (See Table 6.5.) The percentage of very low-birth-weight live births also increased between 1980 to 2005, from nearly 1.2% to 1.5%, before gradually declining between 2010 and 2015. Again, non-Hispanic African American mothers (2.9%) were more likely to give birth to a very low-birth-weight baby than were all other mothers (1.4%).

As Table 6.6 shows, the infant mortality rate (the rate of deaths before one year of age) fell from 6.9 infant deaths per 1,000 live births in 2000 to 5.8 infant deaths per 1,000 live births in 2014. The infant mortality rate is much higher

TABLE 6.5

Low-birthweight live births, by detailed race and Hispanic origin of mother, selected years 1970–2015

[Data are based on birth certificates]

Birthweight, maternal race, and Hispanic origin	1970	1975	1980	1990	2000	2005	2010	2013	2014	2015
Low birthweight (less than 2,500 grams)					Percent of live births[a]					
All races	7.93	7.38	6.84	6.97	7.57	8.19	8.15	8.02	8.00	8.07
White	6.85	6.27	5.72	5.70	6.55	7.16	7.08	7.00	6.98	7.00
Black or African American	13.90	13.19	12.69	13.25	12.99	13.59	13.21	12.76	12.83	13.03
American Indian or Alaska Native	7.97	6.41	6.44	6.11	6.76	7.36	7.61	7.48	7.65	7.53
Asian or Pacific Islander[b]	—	—	6.68	6.45	7.31	7.98	8.49	8.34	8.05	8.40
Hispanic or Latina[c]	—	—	6.12	6.06	6.41	6.88	6.97	7.09	7.05	7.21
Mexican	—	—	5.62	5.55	6.01	6.49	6.49	6.62	6.58	6.81
Puerto Rican	—	—	8.95	8.99	9.30	9.92	9.55	9.38	9.54	9.42
Cuban	—	—	5.62	5.67	6.49	7.64	7.30	7.35	7.48	7.16
Central and South American	—	—	5.76	5.84	6.34	6.78	6.55	6.85	6.68	6.74
Other and unknown Hispanic or Latina	—	—	6.96	6.87	7.84	8.27	8.38	7.99	7.94	8.13
Not Hispanic or Latina:[c]										
White	—	—	5.69	5.61	6.60	7.29	7.14	6.98	6.96	6.93
Black or African American	—	—	12.71	13.32	13.13	14.02	13.53	13.08	13.17	13.35
Very low birthweight (less than 1,500 grams)										
All races	1.17	1.16	1.15	1.27	1.43	1.49	1.45	1.41	1.40	1.40
White	0.95	0.92	0.90	0.95	1.14	1.20	1.17	1.14	1.14	1.12
Black or African American	2.40	2.40	2.48	2.92	3.07	3.15	2.90	2.82	2.79	2.81
American Indian or Alaska Native	0.98	0.95	0.92	1.01	1.16	1.17	1.28	1.32	1.27	1.27
Asian or Pacific Islander[b]	—	—	0.92	0.87	1.05	1.14	1.17	1.18	1.15	1.13
Hispanic or Latina[c]	—	—	0.98	1.03	1.14	1.20	1.20	1.21	1.23	1.23
Mexican	—	—	0.92	0.92	1.03	1.12	1.09	1.13	1.13	1.13
Puerto Rican	—	—	1.29	1.62	1.93	1.87	1.82	1.65	1.86	1.73
Cuban	—	—	1.02	1.20	1.21	1.50	1.42	1.27	1.45	1.38
Central and South American	—	—	0.99	1.05	1.20	1.19	1.09	1.15	1.12	1.13
Other and unknown Hispanic or Latina	—	—	1.01	1.09	1.42	1.36	1.46	1.37	1.38	1.44
Not Hispanic or Latina:[c]										
White	—	—	0.87	0.93	1.14	1.21	1.16	1.11	1.10	1.09
Black or African American	—	—	2.47	2.93	3.10	3.27	2.98	2.90	2.87	2.89

—Data not available.

[a]Excludes live births with unknown birthweight. Percentage based on live births with known birthweight.

[b]Estimates are not available for Asian or Pacific Islander subgroups because not all states have adopted the 2003 revision of the U.S. Standard Certificate of Live Birth.

[c]Prior to 1993, data from states that did not report Hispanic origin on the birth certificate were excluded. Data for non-Hispanic white and non-Hispanic black women for years prior to 1989 are not nationally representative and are provided solely for comparison with Hispanic data.

Notes: The race groups, white, black, American Indian or Alaska Native, and Asian or Pacific Islander, include persons of Hispanic and non-Hispanic origin. Persons of Hispanic origin may be of any race. Starting with 2003 data, some states reported multiple-race data. The multiple-race data for these states were bridged to the single-race categories of the 1977 Office of Management and Budget standards, for comparability with other states. Data for additional years are available.

SOURCE: "Table 5. Low Birthweight Live Births, by Detailed Race and Hispanic Origin of Mother: United States, Selected Years 1970–2015," in *Health, United States, 2016: With Chartbook on Long-term Trends in Health*, Centers for Disease Control and Prevention, National Center for Health Statistics, May 2017, https://www.cdc.gov/nchs/data/hus/hus16.pdf (accessed September 6, 2017)

TABLE 6.6

Infant, neonatal, and postneonatal mortality rates, by detailed race and Hispanic origin of mother, selected years 1983–2014

[Data are based on linked birth and death certificates for infants and fetal death records]

Maternal race and Hispanic origin	1983[a]	1985[a]	1990[a]	1995[b]	2000[b]	2005[b]	2010[b]	2013[b]	2014[b]
	Infant[c] deaths per 1,000 live births								
All mothers	10.9	10.4	8.9	7.6	6.9	6.9	6.1	6.0	5.8
White	9.3	8.9	7.3	6.3	5.7	5.7	5.2	5.1	4.9
Black or African American	19.2	18.6	16.9	14.6	13.5	13.3	11.2	10.8	10.7
American Indian or Alaska Native	15.2	13.1	13.1	9.0	8.3	8.1	8.3	7.6	7.6
Asian or Pacific Islander[d]	8.3	7.8	6.6	5.3	4.9	4.9	4.3	4.1	3.9
Hispanic or Latina[e, f]	9.5	8.8	7.5	6.3	5.6	5.6	5.3	5.0	5.0
Mexican	9.1	8.5	7.2	6.0	5.4	5.5	5.1	4.9	4.8
Puerto Rican	12.9	11.2	9.9	8.9	8.2	8.3	7.1	5.9	7.2
Cuban	7.5	8.5	7.2	5.3	4.6	4.4	3.8	3.0	3.9
Central and South American	8.5	8.0	6.8	5.5	4.6	4.7	4.4	4.3	4.3
Other and unknown Hispanic or Latina	10.6	9.5	8.0	7.4	6.9	6.4	6.1	5.9	5.4
Not Hispanic or Latina:[f]									
White	9.2	8.6	7.2	6.3	5.7	5.8	5.2	5.1	4.9
Black or African American	19.1	18.3	16.9	14.7	13.6	13.6	11.5	11.1	10.9
	Neonatal[c] deaths per 1,000 live births								
All mothers	7.1	6.8	5.7	4.9	4.6	4.5	4.0	4.0	3.9
White	6.1	5.8	4.6	4.1	3.8	3.8	3.5	3.4	3.3
Black or African American	12.5	12.3	11.1	9.6	9.1	8.9	7.3	7.3	7.3
American Indian or Alaska Native	7.5	6.1	6.1	4.0	4.4	4.0	4.3	4.1	4.1
Asian or Pacific Islander[d]	5.2	4.8	3.9	3.4	3.4	3.4	3.0	3.0	2.8
Hispanic or Latina[e, f]	6.2	5.7	4.8	4.1	3.8	3.9	3.6	3.6	3.5
Mexican	5.9	5.4	4.5	3.9	3.6	3.8	3.5	3.5	3.5
Puerto Rican	8.7	7.6	6.9	6.1	5.8	5.9	4.8	4.2	5.0
Cuban	5.0*	6.2	5.3	3.6*	3.2*	3.1*	2.9*	2.3*	2.6
Central and South American	5.8	5.6	4.4	3.7	3.3	3.2	3.0	3.1	3.1
Other and unknown Hispanic or Latina	6.4	5.6	5.0	4.8	4.6	4.3	4.0	4.0	3.7
Not Hispanic or Latina:[f]									
White	5.9	5.6	4.5	4.0	3.8	3.7	3.4	3.3	3.2
Black or African American	12.0	11.9	11.0	9.6	9.2	9.1	7.5	7.5	7.4
	Postneonatal[c] deaths per 1,000 live births								
All mothers	3.8	3.6	3.2	2.6	2.3	2.3	2.1	1.9	1.9
White	3.2	3.1	2.7	2.2	1.9	2.0	1.8	1.6	1.6
Black or African American	6.7	6.3	5.9	5.0	4.3	4.3	3.9	3.5	3.4
American Indian or Alaska Native	7.7	7.0	7.0	5.1	3.9	4.0	4.0	3.5	3.5
Asian or Pacific Islander[d]	3.1	2.9	2.7	1.9	1.4	1.5	1.3	1.1	1.0
Hispanic or Latina[e, f]	3.3	3.2	2.7	2.1	1.8	1.8	1.7	1.5	1.5
Mexican	3.2	3.2	2.7	2.1	1.8	1.7	1.6	1.4	1.4
Puerto Rican	4.2	3.5	3.0	2.8	2.4	2.4	2.3	1.7	2.2
Cuban	2.5*	2.3*	1.9*	1.7*	*	1.4*	*	*	1.3*
Central and South American	2.6	2.4	2.4	1.9	1.4	1.5	1.4	1.2	1.1
Other and unknown Hispanic or Latina	4.2	3.9	3.0	2.6	2.3	2.1	2.1	1.9	1.7
Not Hispanic or Latina:[f]									
White	3.2	3.0	2.7	2.2	1.9	2.1	1.8	1.7	1.7
Black or African American	7.0	6.4	5.9	5.0	4.4	4.5	4.0	3.7	3.5

*Estimates are considered unreliable. Rates followed by an asterisk are based on fewer than 50 deaths in the numerator. Rates not shown are based on fewer than 20 deaths in the numerator.

—Data not available.

[a]Rates based on unweighted birth cohort data.

[b]Rates based on a period file using weighted data.

[c]Infant (under 1 year of age), neonatal (under 28 days), and postneonatal (28 days–11 months).

[d]Estimates are not available for Asian or Pacific Islander subgroups because not all states have adopted the 2003 revision of the U.S. Standard Certificate of Live Birth.

[e]Persons of Hispanic origin may be of any race.

[f]Prior to 1995, data are shown only for states with an Hispanic-origin item on their birth certificates.

Notes: The race groups, white, black, American Indian or Alaska Native, and Asian or Pacific Islander include persons of Hispanic and non-Hispanic origin. Starting with 2003 data, some states reported multiple-race data. The multiple-race data for these states were bridged to the single-race categories of the 1977 Office of Management and Budget standards, for comparability with other states. Data for additional years are available.

SOURCE: Adapted from "Table 10. Infant, Neonatal, Postneonatal, Fetal, and Perinatal Mortality Rates, by Detailed Race and Hispanic Origin of Mother: United States, Selected Years 1983–2014," in *Health, United States, 2016: With Chartbook on Long-term Trends in Health*, Centers for Disease Control and Prevention, National Center for Health Statistics, May 2017, https://www.cdc.gov/nchs/data/hus/hus16.pdf (accessed September 6, 2017)

for some race and ethnicity groups than for others. In 2014 non-Hispanic African Americans suffered the highest rate of infant mortality, with 10.9 infant deaths per 1,000 live births. This rate was more than double the rate of 4.9 infant deaths per 1,000 live births for non-Hispanic whites. Native Americans or Alaskan Natives also had a relatively high rate of infant deaths, at 7.6 per 1,000 live births. By comparison, Hispanics (5 deaths per 1,000 live births) and Asian or Pacific Islanders (3.9 deaths per 1,000 live births) had much lower infant mortality rates.

DISEASES AND MINORITY POPULATIONS

Cancer

Cancer is the uncontrolled spread of abnormal cells and can lead to death if left unchecked. Cancer incidence varies according to racial and ethnic background. Risk factors such as occupation, use of tobacco and alcohol, sexual and reproductive behaviors, and nutritional and dietary habits influence the development of cancer. Cancer screening, treatment, and mortality rates also vary by race and ethnicity.

The incidence rates of cancer declined for all racial and ethnic groups between 2005 and 2014. (See Table 6.7.) This decline was highest among African Americans, whose annual percent change during this period was −1.5%. The annual percent change for Native Americans and Alaskan Natives was −1.4%; for Hispanics, −1.3%; for Asian Americans and Pacific Islanders, −1.2%; and for whites, −1.1%. The death rates also declined for all groups. Again, the most pronounced annual percent change was among African Americans (−2%), followed by Asians and Pacific Islanders (−1.4%) and whites (−1.4%), Hispanics (−1.3%), and Native Americans and Alaskan Natives (−1.2%). (See Table 6.8.)

BREAST CANCER. Although a smaller proportion of African American women than non-Hispanic white women were diagnosed with breast cancer between 2000 and 2014, during that span a higher proportion of African American women died of the disease than did white women. (See Figure 6.4.) For years, experts assumed that the difference in mortality rates was due to poor health care and late treatment for African American women. Rob Stein, however, reports in "Blacks Getting Equal Health Care Are Still More Likely to Die from Some Cancers" (WashingtonPost.com, July 8, 2009) that a large study involving 20,000 cancer patients finds that despite equal care, African American women with breast or ovarian cancer were more likely than white women with these cancers to die of the disease. The researcher Kathy S. Albain of Loyola University stated, "This is almost certainly related to a mix of factors across races pertaining to tumor biology and inherited factors." After peaking during the mid-1990s, the death rate from breast cancer for African American women declined steadily between 1995 and 2010. (See Figure 6.4.) Hispanics, Asians and Pacific Islanders, and Native Americans and Alaskan Natives are less likely to be diagnosed with breast cancer or to die from breast cancer than whites or African Americans.

PROSTATE CANCER. African American men have a particularly high incidence of prostate cancer and a high mortality rate for that disease. Nadia Howlader et al. of the National Cancer Institute report in *SEER Cancer Statistics Review, 1975–2014* (June 28, 2017, https://seer.cancer.gov/csr/1975_2014/results_merged/sect_23_prostate.pdf) that between 2010 and 2014 the prostate cancer incidence rate among African American men was 188.7 cases per 100,000 population, compared with a rate of 116 cases per 100,000

population among non-Hispanic whites. Although the incidence and mortality rates for prostate cancer decreased for both groups between the early 1990s and 2014, the incidence and mortality rates for African American men remained substantially higher than for all other groups. (See Figure 6.5.)

Hispanics, Asians and Pacific Islanders, and Native Americans and Alaskan Natives have lower rates of prostate cancer incidence and lower rates of prostate cancer mortality than do African Americans or non-Hispanic whites. (See Figure 6.5.) Howlader et al. report that the incidence rates of prostate cancer between 2010 and 2014 were 98.3 per 100,000 Hispanic men, 62.9 per 100,000 Asian American and Pacific Islander men, and 59.9 per 100,000 Native American and Alaskan Native men. The mortality rate of prostate cancer was lowest for Asian American and Pacific Islander males, at 8.8 per 100,000 males, whereas the mortality rates for Hispanic and non-Hispanic whites were much higher at 16.5 per 100,000 males and 18.7 per 100,000 males, respectively. African American men experienced by far the highest mortality rate from prostate cancer, 42 per 100,000 males.

LUNG AND BRONCHUS CANCER. According to Howlader et al., lung cancer is the deadliest cancer in the United States; the five-year survival rate for all races was only 19.5% of those diagnosed between 2007 and 2013. African Americans have a particularly high incidence of lung cancer and mortality rate compared with other groups. (See Figure 6.6.) Between 2010 and 2014 the lung cancer incidence rate among African Americans was 63 cases per 100,000 population, compared with a rate of 61.8 cases per 100,000 non-Hispanic whites, 37.4 cases per 100,000 Native Americans and Alaskan Natives, 35.7 cases per 100,000 Asian Americans and Pacific Islanders, and 28.8 cases per 100,000 Hispanics.

COLON AND RECTUM CANCER. Colon and rectum cancer is the fourth-most frequently diagnosed cancer in the United States after prostate cancer, breast cancer, and lung and bronchus cancer; it is also the second-most deadly. African Americans are diagnosed at a higher rate than other groups. Howlader et al. report that between 2010 and 2014 African Americans had an incidence of 48.7 cases per 100,000 population, compared with a rate of 40.2 per 100,000 non-Hispanic whites. African Americans had the highest mortality rate from colon and rectum cancer between 2010 and 2014, at 12.4 deaths per 100,000 population, compared with 11.4 deaths per 100,000 non-Hispanic whites. As Figure 6.7 shows, African American mortality rates from colon and rectum cancer were higher than those for all other racial and ethnic groups.

Heart Disease and Stroke

Heart disease includes coronary and hypertensive heart diseases and heart failure. According to the NCHS, in *Tables of Summary Health Statistics* (January 24, 2017,

TABLE 6.7

Cancer incidence rates and trends for the top 15 cancer sites[a], by race and Hispanic origin, 2010–14

All races	Rate[a] 2010–2014	APC[b] 2005–2014
All sites	442.7	1.1
Breast	67.0	0.0
Lung and bronchus	55.8	2.3
Prostate[e]	54.7	4.8
Colon and rectum	40.1	2.8
Melanoma of the skin	22.3	1.1
Urinary bladder	19.8	1.2
Non-Hodgkin lymphoma	19.5	0.5
Kidney and renal pelvis	15.6	0.7
Thyroid	14.2	4.0
Leukemia	13.7	0.5
Corpus and uterus, NOS[e]	13.6	1.2
Pancreas	12.5	0.5
Oral cavity and pharynx	11.2	0.7
Liver & IBD[f]	8.6	2.6
Stomach	7.3	0.9

White	Rate[a] 2010–2014	APC[b] 2005–2014
All sites	451.8	1.1
Breast	67.8	0.1
Lung and bronchus	57.3	2.2
Prostate[e]	52.1	5.2
Colon and rectum	39.3	2.8
Melanoma of the skin	26.6	1.1
Urinary bladder	21.7	1.2
Non-Hodgkin lymphoma	20.4	0.6
Kidney and renal pelvis	16.1	0.7
Thyroid	14.9	3.9
Leukemia	14.5	0.4
Corpus and uterus, NOS[e]	13.8	0.9
Pancreas	12.5	0.6
Oral cavity and pharynx	11.7	1.0
Liver & IBD[f]	7.8	3.4
Brain and ONS[i]	7.0	0.5

Black	Rate[a] 2010–2014	APC[b] 2005–2014
All sites	459.3	1.5
Prostate[e]	80.7	4.5
Breast	71.1	0.5
Lung and bronchus	63.0	2.5
Colon and rectum	48.7	3.3
Kidney and renal pelvis	18.0	1.0
Pancreas	15.5	0.5
Non-Hodgkin lymphoma	14.6	0.3
Corpus and uterus, NOS[e]	14.0	2.3
Myeloma	13.2	0.8
Urinary bladder	12.5	0.9
Leukemia	10.9	1.2
Stomach	10.2	3.0
Liver & IBD[f]	10.1	2.5
Oral cavity and pharynx	9.1	1.5
Thyroid	8.7	4.4

Asian/Pacific Islander	Rate[a] 2010–2014	APC[b] 2005–2014
All sites	298.8	1.2
Breast	54.1	0.9
Lung and bronchus	35.7	1.8
Colon and rectum	33.8	2.8
Prostate[e]	27.5	6.4
Thyroid	13.7	3.3
Non-Hodgkin lymphoma	13.5	0.2
Liver & IBD[f]	13.2	2.2
Corpus and uterus, NOS[e]	11.2	2.1
Stomach	10.6	3.2
Pancreas	10.0	0.5
Urinary bladder	8.7	1.9
Kidney and renal pelvis	8.2	0.5
Leukemia	7.8	0.5
Oral cavity and pharynx	7.7	0.5
Ovary[e, g]	5.2	0.7

American Indian/Alaska Native[c]	Rate[a] 2010–2014	APC[b] 2005–2014
All sites	316.0	1.4
Breast	44.1	0.0
Colon and rectum	41.1	0.6
Lung and bronchus	37.4	3.8
Prostate[e]	26.5	6.3
Kidney and renal pelvis	17.2	3.2
Liver & IBD[f]	13.3	2.2
Non-Hodgkin lymphoma	12.1	2.0
Stomach	10.6	0.5
Corpus and uterus, NOS[e]	10.5	0.8
Pancreas	9.6	2.9
Thyroid	9.3	5.0
Oral cavity and pharynx	8.9	1.4
Urinary bladder	8.5	0.4
Leukemia	8.1	0.7
Ovary[e, g]	5.1	3.6

Hispanic[d]	Rate[a] 2010–2014	APC[b] 2005–2014
All sites	340.6	1.3
Breast	49.8	0.1
Prostate[e]	43.7	5.6
Colon and rectum	33.9	2.5
Lung and bronchus	28.8	2.5
Non-Hodgkin lymphoma	17.8	0.2
Kidney and renal pelvis	15.4	0.6
Liver & IBD[f]	13.2	1.9
Thyroid	12.3	4.2
Corpus and uterus, NOS[e]	11.6	2.5
Pancreas	11.1	0.2
Urinary bladder	11.0	1.7
Leukemia	10.6	0.2
Stomach	10.5	1.7
Oral cavity and pharynx	6.6	0.1
Myeloma	6.1	0.9

https://ftp.cdc.gov/pub/Health_Statistics/NCHS/NHIS/SHS/2015_SHS_Table_A-1.pdf), approximately 14.9 million American adults aged 18 years and older suffered from coronary heart disease in 2015. Adult Native Americans and Alaskan Natives (7.2%) had the highest recorded incidence of coronary disease in 2015, followed by non-Hispanic whites (7.1%), non-Hispanic African Americans (5.2%), Hispanics (3.8%), and Asian Americans (3.1%); data were not reported for Native Hawaiians and Pacific Islanders in 2015.

HIGH BLOOD PRESSURE. Emelia J. Benjamin et al. explain in "Heart Disease and Stroke Statistics—2017 Update" (*Circulation*, October 31, 2017) that the prevalence

TABLE 6.7

[a]Rates are per 100,000 and age-adjusted to the 2000 US Std Population (19 age groups—Census P25–1130).
[b]The APC is the Annual Percent Change over the time interval. Trends are based on rates age-adjusted to the 2000 US Std Population (19 age groups—Census P25–1130).
[c]Rates for American Indian/Alaska Native are based on the CHSDA (Contract Health Service Delivery Area) counties.
[d]Hispanic is not mutually exclusive from whites, blacks, Asian/Pacific Islanders, and American Indians/Alaska Natives. Incidence data for Hispanics are based on NHIA and exclude cases from the Alaska Native Registry.
[e]The rates for sex-specific cancer sites are calculated using the population for both sexes combined.
[f]IBD Intrahepatic Bile Duct. ONS Other Nervous System.
[g]Ovary excludes borderline cases or histologies 8442, 8451, 8462, 8472, and 8473.
–Statistic not shown. Rate based on less than 16 cases for the time interval. Trend based on less than 10 cases for at least one year within the time interval.
Notes: Top 15 cancer sites selected based on 2010–2014 age-adjusted rates for the race/ethnic group.

SOURCE: N. Howlader et al., eds., "Table 1.24. Age-Adjusted SEER Incidence Rates and Trends for the Top 15 Cancer Sites by Race/Ethnicity, Both Sexes," in *SEER Cancer Statistics Review, 1975–2014*, National Cancer Institute, June 28, 2017, https://seer.cancer.gov/csr/1975_2014/results_merged/topic_inc_trends .pdf (accessed September 6, 2017)

of high blood pressure (hypertension) in both non-Hispanic African American men and women is significantly higher than in non-Hispanic white men and women. Among adults aged 20 years and older, 34.5% of non-Hispanic white males and 32.3% of non-Hispanic white females had high blood pressure between 2011 and 2014; 45% of African American males and 46.3% of non-Hispanic African American females had high blood pressure during that same span. The rates of high blood pressure among Native Americans and Alaskan Natives (26.4%), Asian American men (28.8%) and women (25.7%), and Hispanic men (28.9%) and women (30.7%) were all lower.

DEATHS FROM HEART DISEASE. The NCHS indicates in *Health, United States, 2016* that the death rate from heart disease was higher for males (when compared with females) among all racial and ethnic groups (at 211.8 per 100,000 and 133.6 per 100,000, respectively), but that the rate declined between 1990 and 2015 for all groups. African American males had the highest death rate from heart disease in 2015, at 258.6 deaths per 100,000 population, down from 485.4 deaths per 100,000 population in 1990. Native American and Alaskan Native males (148 deaths per 100,000 population), Hispanic males (146.4), and Asian and Pacific Islander males (109.7) all had lower death rates from heart disease than did non-Hispanic white males (216.3).

The NCHS reports that females die of heart disease at high rates as well, although not at the rate that males do. In 2015 African American females had the highest death rate for heart disease of all racial and ethnic groups, at 155.7 deaths per 100,000 population, down significantly from the 1990 rate of 327.5 deaths per 100,000 population. Non-Hispanic white females had the next highest death rate from heart disease, at 135.6 deaths per 100,000 population. Native American and Alaskan Native females (94 deaths per 100,000 population), Hispanic females (93), and Asian and Pacific Islander females (68.5) all had lower death rates from heart disease than did African American and non-Hispanic white women. The death rates for all females from heart disease had declined since 1990.

Alzheimer's Disease

Alzheimer's disease is a progressive brain disorder that gradually destroys a person's memory and ability to reason, communicate, and carry out daily activities. As it progresses, it also tends to affect personality and behavior and may result in anxiety, paranoia, and delusions or hallucinations. The disease can last from three to 20 years, and eventually the loss of brain function will cause death. Although the underlying causes of Alzheimer's disease remain unclear, some research indicates that minorities, particularly African Americans, are at a greater risk of developing the disease.

The Alzheimer's Association emphasizes in *2017 Alzheimer's Disease Facts and Figures* (2017, https://www.alz .org/documents_custom/2017-facts-and-figures.pdf) that African Americans have about twice the risk of whites to develop Alzheimer's disease or another form of dementia, whereas Hispanics are about 1.5 times as likely as whites to develop these diseases. Since the start of the 21st century, discoveries of risk factors for Alzheimer's disease (high blood pressure and high cholesterol) have begun to provide some explanation for this increased risk, as these risk factors are disproportionately present in the African American and Hispanic communities. The Alzheimer's Association stresses the importance of getting effective medical therapies for vascular disease and its risk factors, as these drugs could potentially protect against Alzheimer's disease as well.

Diabetes

Diabetes is a chronic disease in which the body does not produce or use insulin properly, leading to cells being starved for sugar and often resulting in damage to the heart, kidneys, and eyes. Diabetes is a dangerous disease because it can cause many different complications, including heart disease, kidney failure, and loss of circulation in the extremities. The lack of circulation in the lower limbs can lead to infection of small wounds and gangrene, which can eventually require leg amputation. Diabetes requires effective management of hemoglobin A1c and lipids, as well as regular examination of the eyes and feet and yearly influenza immunizations. In

TABLE 6.8

Cancer mortality rates and trends for the top 15 cancer sites[a], by race and Hispanic origin, 2010–14

All races	Rate[a] 2010–2014	APC[b] 2005–2014	White	Rate[a] 2010–2014	APC[b] 2005–2014
All sites	166.1	1.5	All sites	166.2	1.4
Lung and bronchus	44.7	2.5	Lung and bronchus	45.5	2.4
Colon and rectum	14.8	2.5	Colon and rectum	14.4	2.4
Breast	11.8	1.9	Breast	11.4	1.9
Pancreas	10.9	0.1	Pancreas	10.8	0.2
Prostate[e]	8.1	2.6	Prostate[e]	7.5	2.4
Leukemia	6.8	0.9	Leukemia	7.1	0.9
Liver & IBD[f]	6.3	2.7	Non-Hodgkin lymphoma	6.1	2.2
Non-Hodgkin lymphoma	5.9	2.3	Liver & IBD[f]	5.8	2.9
Urinary bladder	4.4	0.1	Brain and ONS[f]	4.7	0.4
Brain and ONS[f]	4.3	0.4	Urinary bladder	4.6	0.1
Esophagus	4.1	1.1	Esophagus	4.3	0.6
Ovary[e]	4.1	2.5	Ovary[e]	4.2	2.6
Kidney and renal pelvis	3.9	0.8	Kidney and renal pelvis	4.0	0.7
Myeloma	3.3	0.6	Myeloma	3.1	0.7
Stomach	3.2	2.3	Melanoma of the skin	3.1	0.3

Black	Rate[a] 2010–2014	APC[b] 2005–2014	Asian/Pacific Islander	Rate[a] 2010–2014	APC[b] 2005–2014
All sites	194.2	2.0	All sites	102.8	1.4
Lung and bronchus	48.0	2.8	Lung and bronchus	23.7	1.7
Colon and rectum	20.0	3.3	Colon and rectum	10.3	2.0
Breast	17.1	1.7	Liver & IBD[f]	9.7	0.5
Prostate[e]	15.2	3.8	Pancreas	7.7	0.0
Pancreas	13.4	0.5	Breast	6.4	0.7
Liver & IBD[f]	8.2	2.5	Stomach	5.5	4.2
Myeloma	6.3	0.3	Non-Hodgkin lymphoma	4.0	1.1
Stomach	5.9	3.1	Leukemia	3.9	0.4
Leukemia	5.7	1.3	Prostate[e]	3.5	3.3
Corpus and uterus, NOS[e]	4.8	1.8	Ovary[e]	2.5	2.2
Non-Hodgkin lymphoma	4.3	1.6	Brain and ONS[f]	2.1	1.5
Ovary[e]	3.8	1.5	Oral cavity and pharynx	1.9	1.2
Esophagus	3.7	4.4	Kidney and renal pelvis	1.8	1.1
Kidney and renal pelvis	3.7	1.3	Urinary bladder	1.7	0.1
Urinary bladder	3.6	0.8	Esophagus	1.7	1.7

American Indian/Alaska Native[c]	Rate[a] 2010–2014	APC[b] 2005–2014	Hispanic[d]	Rate[a] 2010–2014	APC[b] 2005–2014
All sites	152.4	1.2	All sites	116.2	1.3
Lung and bronchus	37.5	1.5	Lung and bronchus	19.3	2.5
Colon and rectum	16.4	0.3	Colon and rectum	11.7	2.0
Liver & IBD[f]	10.5	3.0	Liver & IBD[f]	9.1	1.2
Pancreas	9.0	1.2	Pancreas	8.5	0.4
Breast	7.9	3.9	Breast	8.0	0.7
Prostate[e]	7.9	2.0	Prostate[e]	6.6	3.0
Kidney and renal pelvis	6.3	0.3	Stomach	5.3	2.0
Stomach	5.4	1.2	Non-Hodgkin lymphoma	5.0	1.5
Leukemia	4.4	1.9	Leukemia	4.9	0.2
Non-Hodgkin lymphoma	4.2	2.7	Kidney and renal pelvis	3.5	0.9
Ovary[e]	3.5	2.5	Ovary[e]	3.0	2.0
Esophagus	3.4	1.7	Brain and ONS[f]	2.9	0.4
Myeloma	3.0	0.3	Myeloma	2.8	0.8
Brain and ONS[f]	2.5	0.9	Urinary bladder	2.3	0.9
Urinary bladder	2.3	0.4	Esophagus	2.2	1.5

recent years, the death rate due to diabetes has been on the rise at the same time that the death rates due to other diseases such as cancer and heart disease have been declining.

In *National Diabetes Statistics Report, 2017* (2017, https://www.cdc.gov/diabetes/pdfs/data/statistics/national-diabetes-tatistics-report.pdf), the Centers for Disease Control and Prevention (CDC) reports that, between 2013 and 2015, Native Americans and Alaskan Native women (15.1%) were more likely than any other racial or ethnic group to be diagnosed with diabetes. Native American and Alaskan Native women (15.3%) were slightly more likely than Native American and Alaskan Native men (14.9%) to be diagnosed with diabetes

[a]Rates are per 100,000 and age-adjusted to the 2000 US Std Population.
[b]The APC is the Annual Percent Change over the time interval. Trends are based on rates age-adjusted to the 2000 US Std Population.
[c]Rates for American Indian/Alaska Native are based on the CHSDA (Contract Health Service Delivery Area) counties.
[d]Hispanic is not mutually exclusive from whites, blacks, Asian/Pacific Islanders, and American Indians/Alaska Natives.
[e]The rates for sex-specific cancer sites are calculated using the population for both sexes combined.
[f]IBD = Intrahepatic Bile Duct. ONS = Other Nervous System.
–Statistic not shown. Rate based on less than 16 cases for the time interval. Trend based on less than 10 cases for at least one year within the time interval.
Notes: Top 15 cancer sites selected based on 2010–2014 age-adjusted rates for the race/ethnic group.

SOURCE: N. Howlader et al., eds., "Table 1.27. Age-Adjusted U.S. Death Rates and Trends for the Top 15 Cancer Sites by Race/Ethnicity, Both Sexes," in *SEER Cancer Statistics Review, 1975–2014*, National Cancer Institute, June 28, 2017, https://seer.cancer.gov/csr/1975_2014/results_merged/topic_mor_trends .pdf (accessed September 6, 2017)

during that period. Between 2013 and 2015, 12.2% of African American males and 13.2% of African American females, 12.6% of Hispanic males and 11.7% of Hispanic females, 9% of Asian American males and 7.3% of Asian American females, and 8.1% of white males and 6.8% of white females were diagnosed with diabetes. As shown in Figure 6.8, rates overall and for non-Hispanic whites, non-Hispanic blacks, and people of Mexican origin have risen significantly since the late 1980s.

Mental Health and Minorities

The Office of Minority Health reports in "National Minority Mental Health Awareness Month" (July 7, 2017, https://www.minorityhealth.hhs.gov/omh/content.aspx?ID =9447) that more than one in five adults in the United States, and 10% of all children, struggle with mental illness. Because poverty and drug addiction are especially prevalent among minority groups (notably among African Americans, Hispanics, and Native Americans), mental illness has a disproportionately negative impact on minority communities. These issues are further exacerbated by the relative lack of access minorities have to quality health care, particularly when compared with non-Hispanic whites, making minority individuals less likely to seek and receive necessary treatment for psychological disorders. In 2008, in order to increase public awareness of mental health issues that affect minority communities, Congress declared July to be annually celebrated as Bebe Moore Campbell National Minority Mental Health Awareness Month.

In "Mental Health and African Americans" (September 15, 2017, https://www.minorityhealth.hhs.gov/omh/ browse .aspx?lvl=4&lvlid=24), the Office of Minority Health compares the prevalence of mental health issues among African Americans and non-Hispanic whites. In 2013–14, 3.4% of non-Hispanic African American adults reported suffering from "serious psychological distress," compared with 3.2% of non-Hispanic whites. At the same time, African Americans were considerably less likely than non-Hispanic whites to seek mental health counseling or receive prescription medication for psychological disorders. According to the Office of Minority Health, 9.4% of African American adults

received treatment for mental health issues in 2014, compared with 18.8% of non-Hispanic whites; that year, only 6.6% of African American adults received prescription medication for mental health issues, compared with 15.7% of non-Hispanic whites. The Office of Minority Health indicates in "Mental Health and Hispanics" (February 24, 2017, https://www.minorityhealth.hhs.gov/omh/ browse.aspx?lvl=4&lvlid=69) that Hispanics (4.5%) were also more likely than non-Hispanic whites (3.2%) to report suffering from "serious psychological distress" in 2013–14. Native Americans and Alaskan Natives (5.4%) also experienced higher rates of "serious psychological distress" than non-Hispanic whites in 2013–14, according to "Mental Health and American Indians/Alaskan Natives" (February 24, 2017, https://www.minorityhealth.hhs.gov/omh/browse .aspx?lvl=4&lvlid=39). By contrast, as the Office of Minority Health reports in "Mental Health and Asian Americans" (February 24, 2017, https://www.minorityhealth .hhs.gov/omh/browse.aspx?lvl=4&lvlid=54), Asian Americans (1.9%) were the least likely to report suffering from serious mental health issues during the same period.

AIDS

The acquired immunodeficiency syndrome (AIDS) is caused by a virus that affects the body's immune system, making it difficult to fight invasions from infection or other foreign substances. As a result, people who have AIDS are subject to a number of opportunistic infections, primarily *Pneumocystis carinii* pneumonia and Kaposi's sarcoma, a form of skin cancer. AIDS, which is caused by the human immunodeficiency virus (HIV), is not transmitted casually, but only through the transfer of bodily fluids, such as blood, semen, and vaginal secretions. There are only four methods of transmission: contaminated blood, sexual transmission, contaminated syringes from injection drug use, and perinatal (around the time of birth) transmission from a mother to her child or through breast milk.

Minorities have been especially hard hit by the AIDS epidemic. The CDC notes in *HIV Surveillance Report, 2015* (November 2016, https://www.cdc.gov/hiv/pdf/library/ reports/surveillance/cdc-hiv-surveillance-report-2015-vol-27

FIGURE 6.4

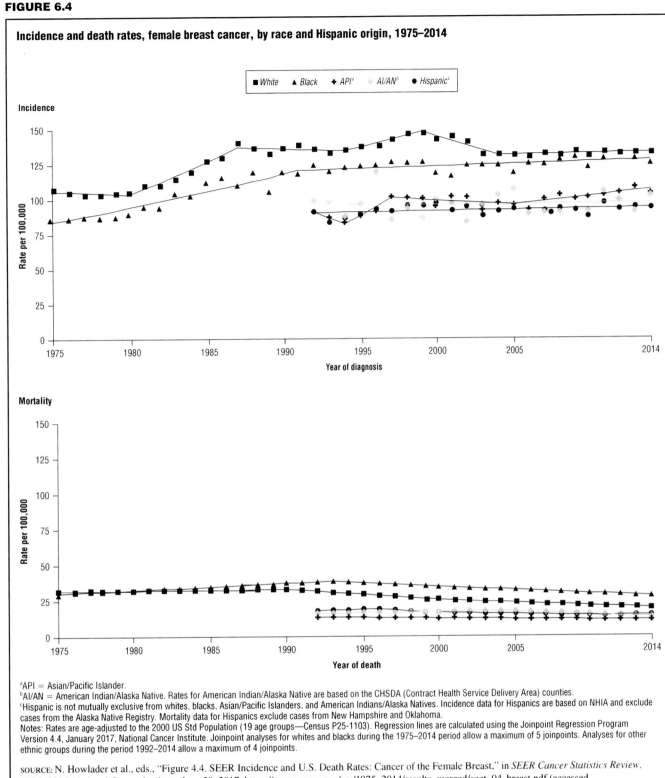

Incidence and death rates, female breast cancer, by race and Hispanic origin, 1975–2014

■ *White* ▲ *Black* ✚ *API[a]* ◆ *AI/AN[b]* ● *Hispanic[c]*

Incidence

Year of diagnosis

Mortality

Year of death

[a]API = Asian/Pacific Islander.

[b]AI/AN = American Indian/Alaska Native. Rates for American Indian/Alaska Native are based on the CHSDA (Contract Health Service Delivery Area) counties.

[c]Hispanic is not mutually exclusive from whites, blacks, Asian/Pacific Islanders, and American Indians/Alaska Natives. Incidence data for Hispanics are based on NHIA and exclude cases from the Alaska Native Registry. Mortality data for Hispanics exclude cases from New Hampshire and Oklahoma.

Notes: Rates are age-adjusted to the 2000 US Std Population (19 age groups—Census P25-1103). Regression lines are calculated using the Joinpoint Regression Program Version 4.4, January 2017, National Cancer Institute. Joinpoint analyses for whites and blacks during the 1975–2014 period allow a maximum of 5 joinpoints. Analyses for other ethnic groups during the period 1992–2014 allow a maximum of 4 joinpoints.

SOURCE: N. Howlader et al., eds., "Figure 4.4. SEER Incidence and U.S. Death Rates: Cancer of the Female Breast," in *SEER Cancer Statistics Review, 1975–2014*, National Cancer Institute, June 28, 2017, https://seer.cancer.gov/csr/1975_2014/results_merged/sect_04_breast.pdf (accessed September 6, 2017)

.pdf) that of the estimated 955,081 people living with HIV in 2014, 405,321 (42.4%) were African American, 300,156 (31.4%) were white, and 198,456 (20.8%) were Hispanic. Asian Americans (12,328, or 1.3%) and Native Americans and Alaskan Natives (2,908, or 0.3%) were the least likely groups to be living with HIV. Of the

405,321 African Americans who were HIV positive in 2014, 64,755 (16%) were between the ages of 50 and 54. (See Table 6.9.) An estimated 521,002 individuals were living with AIDS at year-end 2014 across the nation. Again, African Americans (218,041, or 41.9%) were disproportionately represented. (See Table 6.10.)

FIGURE 6.5

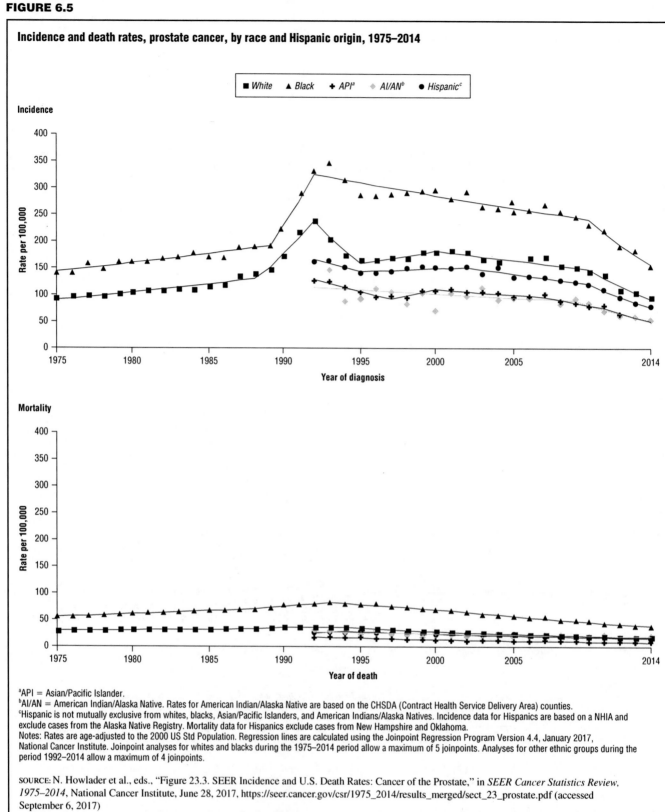

Incidence and death rates, prostate cancer, by race and Hispanic origin, 1975–2014

■ White ▲ Black ✚ API[a] ◆ AI/AN[b] ● Hispanic[c]

[a]API = Asian/Pacific Islander.
[b]AI/AN = American Indian/Alaska Native. Rates for American Indian/Alaska Native are based on the CHSDA (Contract Health Service Delivery Area) counties.
[c]Hispanic is not mutually exclusive from whites, blacks, Asian/Pacific Islanders, and American Indians/Alaska Natives. Incidence data for Hispanics are based on a NHIA and exclude cases from the Alaska Native Registry. Mortality data for Hispanics exclude cases from New Hampshire and Oklahoma.
Notes: Rates are age-adjusted to the 2000 US Std Population. Regression lines are calculated using the Joinpoint Regression Program Version 4.4, January 2017, National Cancer Institute. Joinpoint analyses for whites and blacks during the 1975–2014 period allow a maximum of 5 joinpoints. Analyses for other ethnic groups during the period 1992–2014 allow a maximum of 4 joinpoints.

SOURCE: N. Howlader et al., eds., "Figure 23.3. SEER Incidence and U.S. Death Rates: Cancer of the Prostate," in *SEER Cancer Statistics Review, 1975–2014*, National Cancer Institute, June 28, 2017, https://seer.cancer.gov/csr/1975_2014/results_merged/sect_23_prostate.pdf (accessed September 6, 2017)

In "HIV among Pregnant Women, Infants, and Children" (September 14, 2017, https://www.cdc.gov/hiv/group/gender/pregnantwomen/index.html), the CDC explains that children primarily get HIV in utero from infected mothers. Far more AIDS cases have been diagnosed among African American children than among children of other racial or ethnic backgrounds. Through 2015, an estimated 5,624 cases among African American children, 1,965 cases among Hispanic children, and 1,537 cases among white children had been diagnosed. (See Table 6.11.) Only

FIGURE 6.6

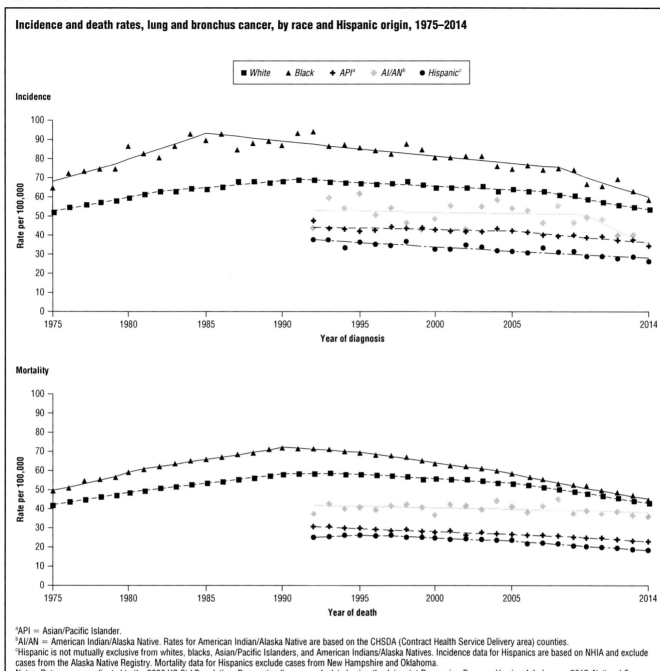

Incidence and death rates, lung and bronchus cancer, by race and Hispanic origin, 1975–2014

■ *White* ▲ *Black* ✛ *API*[a] ◆ *AI/AN*[b] ● *Hispanic*[c]

Incidence

Rate per 100,000

Year of diagnosis

Mortality

Rate per 100,000

Year of death

[a]API = Asian/Pacific Islander.

[b]AI/AN = American Indian/Alaska Native. Rates for American Indian/Alaska Native are based on the CHSDA (Contract Health Service Delivery area) counties.

[c]Hispanic is not mutually exclusive from whites, blacks, Asian/Pacific Islanders, and American Indians/Alaska Natives. Incidence data for Hispanics are based on NHIA and exclude cases from the Alaska Native Registry. Mortality data for Hispanics exclude cases from New Hampshire and Oklahoma.

Notes: Rates are age-adjusted to the 2000 US Std Population. Regression lines are calculated using the Joinpoint Regression Program Version 4.4, January 2017, National Cancer Institute. Joinpoint analyses for whites and blacks during the 1975–2014 period allow a maximum of 5 joinpoints. Analyses for other ethnic groups during the period 1992–2014 allow a maximum of 4 joinpoints.

SOURCE: N. Howlader et al., eds., "Figure 15.4. SEER Incidence and U.S. Death Rates: Cancer of the Lung and Bronchus, Both Sexes," in *SEER Cancer Statistics Review, 1975–2014*, National Cancer Institute, June 28, 2017, http://seer.cancer.gov/csr/1975_2014/results_merged/sect_15_lung_bronchus.pdf (accessed September 6, 2017)

49 cases had been diagnosed among Asian American children; 27 cases had been diagnosed among Native American and Alaskan Native children, and 6 cases had been diagnosed among Native Hawaiian and Pacific Islander children. The use of antiretroviral drugs has greatly diminished the rate of infection of the children of HIV-positive mothers. The use of these drugs reduces the rate of transmission from 25% to about 2%. The rate of diagnosis among African American children dropped from 13 cases in 2010 to five in 2013 (a decrease of 61.5%) rose to 53 in 2014, and declined to 19 in 2015. Only five cases were diagnosed among Hispanic children, two cases among Asian American children, and two cases among white children in 2015.

The methods of transmission of HIV among the adolescent and adult population remain roughly consistent across all races and ethnicities. Of the 31,991 men diagnosed with HIV in 2015, 26,375 (82.4%) contracted

FIGURE 6.7

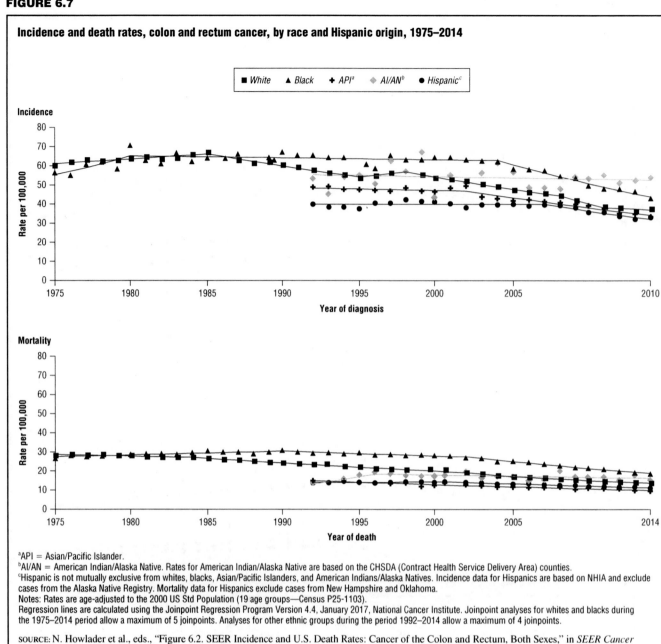

Incidence and death rates, colon and rectum cancer, by race and Hispanic origin, 1975–2014

◼ *White*   ▲ *Black*   ✦ *API*[a]   ◈ *AI/AN*[b]   ● *Hispanic*[c]

Incidence

Rate per 100,000

Year of diagnosis

Mortality

Rate per 100,000

Year of death

[a]API = Asian/Pacific Islander.

[b]AI/AN = American Indian/Alaska Native. Rates for American Indian/Alaska Native are based on the CHSDA (Contract Health Service Delivery Area) counties.

[c]Hispanic is not mutually exclusive from whites, blacks, Asian/Pacific Islanders, and American Indians/Alaska Natives. Incidence data for Hispanics are based on NHIA and exclude cases from the Alaska Native Registry. Mortality data for Hispanics exclude cases from New Hampshire and Oklahoma.

Notes: Rates are age-adjusted to the 2000 US Std Population (19 age groups—Census P25-1103).

Regression lines are calculated using the Joinpoint Regression Program Version 4.4, January 2017, National Cancer Institute. Joinpoint analyses for whites and blacks during the 1975–2014 period allow a maximum of 5 joinpoints. Analyses for other ethnic groups during the period 1992–2014 allow a maximum of 4 joinpoints.

SOURCE: N. Howlader et al., eds., "Figure 6.2. SEER Incidence and U.S. Death Rates: Cancer of the Colon and Rectum, Both Sexes," in *SEER Cancer Statistics Review, 1975–2014*, National Cancer Institute, June 28, 2017, http://seer.cancer.gov/csr/1975_2014/results_merged/sect_06_colon_rectum.pdf (accessed September 6, 2017)

the disease through homosexual (male-to-male sexual) contact. (See Table 6.12.) Among white males, an estimated 7,570 out of 9,060 (83.6%) contracted HIV in this way. (See Table 6.12.) Among Asian American men who were diagnosed with HIV in 2015, 726 of 816 cases (89%) had contracted the disease through male-to-male sexual contact. Male-to-male sexual contact was also the method of transmission for large majorities of African American men (10,315 of 13,070, or 78.9%) and Hispanic men (7,013 of 8,147, or 86.1%). Another sizable proportion of African American men with HIV had contracted the disease through high-risk heterosexual (male-to-female sexual) contact (1,926 of 13,070, or 14.7%).

Most men who contracted AIDS in 2015 had done so through male-to-male sexual contact. Among white men who were diagnosed with AIDS in that year, 79.4% (3,096 of 3,901) had contracted the disease through homosexual contact, as had 84.5% (229 of 271) of Asian American men, 75.2% (2,430 of 3,233) of Hispanic men, and 66.8% (3,928 of 5,879) of African American men. (See Table 6.13.)

The transmission patterns of HIV and AIDS are quite different among women. In 2015 most cases of HIV had been transmitted to women through heterosexual contact with an infected partner. About 67.6% (968 of 1,431) of white women, 89.3% (1,010 of 1,131) of

FIGURE 6.8

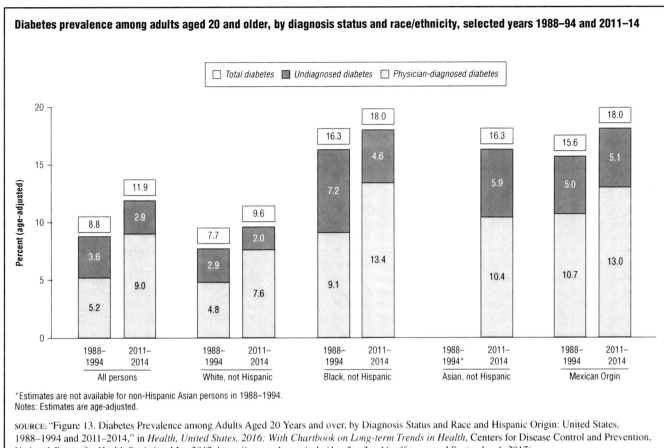

Diabetes prevalence among adults aged 20 and older, by diagnosis status and race/ethnicity, selected years 1988–94 and 2011–14

*Estimates are not available for non-Hispanic Asian persons in 1988–1994.

Notes: Estimates are age-adjusted.

SOURCE: "Figure 13. Diabetes Prevalence among Adults Aged 20 Years and over, by Diagnosis Status and Race and Hispanic Origin: United States, 1988–1994 and 2011–2014," in *Health, United States, 2016: With Chartbook on Long-term Trends in Health*, Centers for Disease Control and Prevention, National Center for Health Statistics, May 2017, https://www.cdc.gov/nchs/data/hus/hus16.pdf (accessed September 6, 2017)

Hispanic women, 91.6% (4,142 of 4,524) of African American women, and 94.7% (125 of 132) of Asian American women contracted HIV in this way. (See Table 6.12.) These patterns were similar among women who were diagnosed with AIDS in 2015. (See Table 6.13.)

Sickle-Cell Disease in African Americans

In "Facts about Sickle Cell Disease" (November 17, 2016, https://www.cdc.gov/ncbddd/sicklecell/facts.html), the CDC explains that sickle-cell anemia, a hereditary disease that primarily strikes African American people, is a blood disorder in which defective hemoglobin causes red blood cells to become sickle shaped, rather than round. This can create blockages in small arteries and can result in many problems, including chronic anemia, episodes of intense pain, strokes, and death. Scientists believe the genetic trait arose randomly in Africa and survived as a defense against malaria. The disease can be inherited only when both parents have the sickle-cell trait and the child inherits the defective gene from both parents. The CDC notes in "Data & Statistics" (August 31, 2016, https://www.cdc.gov/NCBDDD/sicklecell/data.html) that an estimated 1 out of every 13 African Americans is a carrier for sickle-cell anemia, and about 1 out of every 365 African American infants is born with it.

BEHAVIORS THAT THREATEN HEALTH

Cigarette Smoking

Nicotine is the drug in tobacco that causes addiction; cigarette smoking is the most popular method of taking nicotine in the United States. The National Institutes of Health indicates in the press release "Most Behaviors Preceding Major Causes of Preventable Death Have Begun by Young Adulthood" (January 11, 2006, https://www.nih.gov/news-events/news-releases/most-behaviors-preceding-major-causes-preventable-death-have-begun-young-adulthood) that tobacco use is the leading cause of preventable death in the United States. According to the CDC, in "Trends in the Prevalence of Tobacco Use" (2017, https://www.cdc.gov/healthyyouth/data/yrbs/pdf/trends/2015_us_tobacco_trend_yrbs.pdf), the national Youth Risk Behavior Survey finds that on three key measures smoking among teens had decreased between 1991 and 2015: those who had ever tried cigarette smoking (decreased from 70.1% to 32.3%), those who smoked cigarettes on at least one day in the past 30 days (decreased from 27.5% to 10.8%), and those who smoked cigarettes on 20 or more days in the past 30 days (decreased from 12.7% to 3.4%). Nevertheless, a significant proportion of young people still smoke. Smoking during pregnancy causes an increased risk of stillbirth, premature birth, low birth weight, and sudden infant death syndrome. The tar in

TABLE 6.9

Persons living with a diagnosis of HIV infection, by race and Hispanic origin and selected characteristics, 2014

	American Indian/Alaska Native		Asian[a]		Black/African American		Hispanic/Latino[b]		Native Hawaiian/other Pacific Islander		White		Multiple races		Total	
	No.	Rate[c]	No.	Rate[c]	No.	Rate[c]	No.	Rate[c]	No.	Rate[c]	No.	Rate[c]	No.	Rate[c]	No.	Rate[c]
Age at end of year																
Under 13	10	2.2	90	3.6	1,593	22.1	319	2.4	5	4.8	332	1.2	128	5.6	2,477	4.7
13–14	2	2.7	14	3.5	472	39.8	138	7.2	0	0.0	86	1.9	33	11.3	745	8.9
15–19	12	6.6	54	5.4	3,418	113.8	1,059	22.8	2	5.0	543	4.7	233	35.1	5,321	25.2
20–24	106	52.5	362	29.1	19,036	552.4	6,294	132.0	26	54.1	4,619	36.5	1,332	231.6	31,775	138.6
25–29	207	117.1	903	63.6	33,131	1,113.0	13,239	298.0	64	126.8	11,503	92.0	2,575	591.3	61,622	280.1
30–34	301	186.6	1,230	84.5	34,702	1,258.7	18,565	418.6	97	203.6	17,000	138.1	3,045	813.5	74,940	347.8
35–39	301	208.0	1,626	118.4	37,211	1,468.5	22,216	537.0	107	264.7	21,074	185.0	3,365	1,087.8	85,900	430.9
40–44	402	275.8	2,189	158.2	45,883	1,768.8	26,796	694.0	130	352.8	31,623	257.1	4,129	1,488.2	111,152	539.5
45–49	481	321.3	1,981	165.7	59,706	2,295.4	33,676	993.1	131	381.8	50,652	381.4	5,798	2,395.9	152,425	729.6
50–54	499	304.4	1,518	136.2	64,755	2,375.8	32,025	1,088.7	120	351.2	64,032	417.1	6,064	2,516.6	169,013	748.8
55–59	280	187.5	1,047	104.2	50,700	2,030.7	21,343	917.8	89	307.0	45,592	298.1	4,205	1,989.0	123,256	573.0
60–64	181	151.6	665	77.7	30,945	1,556.3	12,158	702.3	54	239.2	28,225	206.3	2,421	1,485.3	74,649	402.1
Over 65	126	54.4	649	34.7	23,769	592.3	10,628	299.1	36	84.6	24,875	68.8	1,723	531.0	61,806	133.8
Transmission category[d]																
Male adult or adolescent																
Male-to-male sexual contact	1,434	—	8,277	—	157,758	—	109,857	—	605	—	212,558	—	18,187	—	508,676	—
Injection drug use	219	—	429	—	39,419	—	21,581	—	25	—	14,480	—	2,545	—	78,699	—
Male-to-male sexual contact and injection drug use	293	—	356	—	16,162	—	10,514	—	36	—	21,896	—	3,099	—	52,357	—
Heterosexual contact[e]	172	—	876	—	47,771	—	14,382	—	36	—	9,457	—	2,184	—	74,879	—
Perinatal	6	—	25	—	2,649	—	1,097	—	1	—	555	—	195	—	4,528	—
Other[f]	13	—	71	—	911	—	454	—	3	—	1,534	—	120	—	3,106	—
Subtotal	**2,136**	**229.8**	**10,036**	**149.2**	**264,670**	**1,738.4**	**157,885**	**742.4**	**706**	**317.7**	**260,481**	**311.2**	**26,330**	**1,329.7**	**722,244**	**555.3**
Female adult or adolescent																
Injection drug use	239	—	181	—	27,036	—	9,524	—	24	—	12,501	—	2,507	—	52,013	—
Heterosexual contact[e]	502	—	1,929	—	108,102	—	29,294	—	124	—	25,728	—	5,791	—	171,470	—
Perinatal	8	—	22	—	3,042	—	1,128	—	1	—	578	—	218	—	4,997	—
Other[f]	13	—	70	—	878	—	305	—	1	—	536	—	77	—	1,880	—
Subtotal	**762**	**78.5**	**2,202**	**29.0**	**139,058**	**813.4**	**40,252**	**192.7**	**150**	**68.2**	**39,343**	**45.1**	**8,593**	**403.6**	**230,360**	**169.2**
Child (<13 years at end of year)																
Perinatal	8	—	62	—	1,288	—	294	—	5	—	226	—	112	—	1,995	—
Other[f]	2	—	28	—	305	—	25	—	0	—	106	—	16	—	482	—
Subtotal	**10**	**2.2**	**90**	**3.6**	**1,593**	**22.1**	**319**	**2.4**	**5**	**4.8**	**332**	**1.2**	**128**	**5.6**	**2,477**	**4.7**
Region of residence																
Northeast	165	130.8	2,730	76.6	94,730	1,500.3	68,613	885.8	57	273.2	57,159	152.4	12,174	1,373.6	235,628	419.5
Midwest	366	90.8	1,135	55.4	49,277	702.9	12,534	245.5	38	125.6	45,832	88.2	4,390	360.1	113,572	167.6
South	709	91.1	2,380	61.5	231,653	1,016.6	61,813	303.6	128	152.7	111,767	160.0	13,864	664.1	422,314	352.5
West	1,668	160.0	6,083	82.6	29,661	866.1	55,496	250.1	638	154.9	85,398	221.5	4,623	210.6	183,567	244.2
Total	**2,908**	**123.7**	**12,328**	**73.2**	**405,321**	**1,025.2**	**198,456**	**358.3**	**861**	**157.4**	**300,156**	**151.7**	**35,051**	**548.7**	**955,081**	**299.5**

TABLE 6.9

Persons living with a diagnosis of HIV infection, by race and Hispanic origin and selected characteristics, 2014 [CONTINUED]

[a]Includes Asian/Pacific Islander legacy cases.
[b]Hispanics/Latinos can be of any race.
[c]Rates are per 100,000 population. Rates are not calculated by transmission category because of the lack of denominator data.
[d]Data have been statistically adjusted to account for missing transmission category.
[e]Heterosexual contact with a person known to have, or to be at high risk for, HIV infection.
[f]Includes hemophilia, blood transfusion, and risk factor not reported or not identified.
Notes: HIV = human immunodeficiency virus. Data include persons with a diagnosis of HIV infection regardless of stage of disease at diagnosis. Data are based on address of residence at the end of the specified year (i.e., most recent known address). Numbers less than 12, and rates based on these numbers, should be interpreted with caution.

SOURCE: "Table 20a. Persons Living with Diagnosed HIV Infection, by Race/Ethnicity and Selected Characteristics, Year-End 2014—United States," in *HIV Surveillance Report, 2015*, vol. 27, U.S. Department of Health and Human Services, Centers for Disease Control and Prevention, November 2016, https://www.cdc.gov/hiv/pdf/library/reports/surveillance/cdc-hiv-surveillance-report-2015-vol-27.pdf (accessed September 6, 2017)

TABLE 6.10

Persons living with an AIDS diagnosis, by race and Hispanic origin and selected characteristics, 2014

	American Indian/ Alaska Native		Asian[a]		Black/African American		Hispanic/Latino[b]		Native Hawaiian/ other Pacific Islander		White		Multiple races		Total	
	No.	Rate[c]	No.	Rate[c]	No.	Rate[c]	No.	Rate[c]	No.	Rate[c]	No.	Rate[c]	No.	Rate[c]	No.	Rate[c]
Age at end of year																
<13	2	0.4	5	0.2	200	2.8	44	0.3	2	1.9	34	0.1	21	0.9	308	0.6
13–14	1	1.4	4	1.0	88	7.4	25	1.3	0	0.0	14	0.3	4	1.4	136	1.6
15–19	2	1.1	10	1.0	887	29.5	239	5.2	1	2.5	104	0.9	64	9.6	1,307	6.2
20–24	19	9.4	44	3.5	4,795	139.1	1,501	31.5	6	12.5	767	6.1	400	69.5	7,532	32.9
25–29	50	28.3	207	14.6	10,258	344.6	4,002	90.1	15	29.7	2,503	20.0	866	198.9	17,901	81.4
30–34	118	73.1	388	26.6	13,521	490.4	7,412	167.1	36	75.6	4,915	39.9	1,261	336.9	27,651	128.3
35–39	122	84.3	664	48.3	17,669	697.3	10,811	261.3	52	128.7	7,992	70.1	1,750	565.7	39,060	196.0
40–44	233	159.9	1,095	79.1	25,111	968.1	15,228	394.4	64	173.7	14,966	121.7	2,509	904.3	59,206	287.4
45–49	272	181.7	1,142	95.5	35,874	1,379.2	21,361	629.9	93	271.0	27,676	208.4	3,813	1,575.7	90,231	431.9
50–54	309	188.5	953	85.5	40,813	1,497.4	21,980	747.2	82	240.0	38,368	249.9	4,293	1,781.6	106,798	473.1
55–59	188	125.9	709	70.6	32,868	1,316.4	15,011	645.5	51	175.9	28,299	185.0	3,027	1,431.8	80,153	372.6
60–64	111	93.0	470	54.9	20,317	1,021.8	8,820	509.5	27	119.6	17,941	131.1	1,773	1,087.7	49,459	266.4
Over 65	88	38.0	474	25.3	15,640	389.7	7,771	218.7	28	65.8	16,023	44.3	1,236	380.9	41,260	89.3
Transmission category[d]																
Male adult or adolescent																
Male-to-male sexual contact	705	—	3,990	—	76,832	—	58,382	—	322	—	110,438	—	10,061	—	260,730	—
Injection drug use	132	—	258	—	25,971	—	15,051	—	13	—	9,294	—	1,908	—	52,628	—
Male-to-male sexual contact and injection drug use	191	—	224	—	10,734	—	7,040	—	22	—	13,277	—	2,154	—	33,643	—
Heterosexual contact[e]	101	—	566	—	28,431	—	9,636	—	21	—	5,554	—	1,451	—	45,761	—
Perinatal	3	—	11	—	1,448	—	597	—	1	—	278	—	116	—	2,454	—
Other[f]	10	—	54	—	516	—	316	—	2	—	1,124	—	81	—	2,104	—
Subtotal	1,143	123.0	5,103	75.9	143,933	945.4	91,023	428.0	382	171.9	139,965	167.2	15,771	796.5	397,320	305.5
Female adult or adolescent																
Injection drug use	120	—	94	—	16,823	—	6,208	—	15	—	6,868	—	1,740	—	31,867	—
Heterosexual contact[e]	236	—	907	—	54,906	—	16,112	—	57	—	12,121	—	3,315	—	87,655	—
Perinatal	5	—	7	—	1,677	—	616	—	1	—	273	—	125	—	2,704	—
Other[f]	9	—	48	—	503	—	202	—	0	—	341	—	45	—	1,148	—
Subtotal	370	38.1	1,057	13.9	73,908	432.3	23,138	110.8	73	33.2	19,603	22.5	5,225	245.4	123,374	90.6
Child (<13 years at end of year)																
Perinatal	0	—	3	—	181	—	40	—	2	—	30	—	19	—	275	—
Other[f]	2	—	2	—	19	—	4	—	0	—	4	—	2	—	33	—
Subtotal	2	0.4	5	0.2	200	2.8	44	0.3	2	1.9	34	0.1	21	0.9	308	0.6
Region of residence																
Northeast	82	65.0	1,341	37.6	55,030	871.6	41,357	533.9	22	105.4	30,950	82.5	7,731	872.3	136,513	243.0
Midwest	177	43.9	514	25.1	25,044	357.2	6,940	136.0	17	56.2	23,308	44.9	2,519	206.6	58,519	86.4
South	321	41.3	1,061	27.4	121,649	533.8	33,609	165.1	47	56.1	58,061	83.1	8,176	391.6	222,924	186.1
West	935	89.7	3,249	44.1	16,318	476.5	32,299	145.6	371	90.1	47,283	122.6	2,591	118.0	103,046	137.1
Total	1,515	64.5	6,165	36.6	218,041	551.5	114,205	206.2	457	83.6	159,602	80.7	21,017	329.0	521,002	163.4

TABLE 6.10

Persons living with an AIDS diagnosis, by race and Hispanic origin and selected characteristics, 2014 [CONTINUED]

[a]Includes Asian/Pacific Islander legacy cases.
[b]Hispanics/Latinos can be of any race.
[c]Rates are per 100,000 population. Rates are not calculated by transmission category because of the lack of denominator data.
[d]Data have been statistically adjusted to account for missing transmission category.
[e]Heterosexual contact with a person known to have, or to be at high risk for, HIV infection.
[f]Includes hemophilia, blood transfusion, and risk factor not reported or not identified.
AIDS = acquired immune deficiency syndrome.
Notes: Data are based on address of residence at the end of the specified year (i.e., most recent known address). Numbers less than 12, and rates based on these numbers, should be interpreted with caution.

SOURCE: "Table 21a. Persons Living with Diagnosed HIV Infection Ever Classified as Stage 3 (AIDS), by Race/Ethnicity and Selected Characteristics, Year-End 2014—United States," in *HIV Surveillance Report, 2015,* vol. 27, U.S. Department of Health and Human Services, Centers for Disease Control and Prevention, November 2016, https://www.cdc.gov/hiv/pdf/library/reports/surveillance/cdc-hiv-surveillance-report-2015-vol-27.pdf (accessed September 6, 2017)

TABLE 6.11

AIDS diagnoses among children less than 13 years of age, by race and Hispanic origin, 2010–15 and cumulative

Race/ethnicity	2010		2011		2012		2013		2014		2015		Cumulative[a]
	No.	Rate[b]	No.	Rate[b]	No.	Rate[b]	No.	Rate[b]	No.	Rate[b]	No.	Rate[b]	No.
American Indian/Alaska Native	0	0.0	0	0.0	0	0.0	0	0.0	1	0.2	0	0.0	27
Asian[c]	1	0.0	1	0.0	0	0.0	0	0.0	1	0.0	2	0.1	49
Black/African American	13	0.2	12	0.2	9	0.1	5	0.1	53	0.7	19	0.3	5,624
Hispanic/Latino[d]	4	0.0	2	0.0	1	0.0	2	0.0	12	0.1	5	0.0	1,965
Native Hawaiian/other Pacific Islander	0	0.0	0	0.0	0	0.0	0	0.0	0	0.0	0	0.0	6
White	3	0.0	2	0.0	1	0.0	0	0.0	6	0.0	2	0.0	1,537
Multiple races	0	0.0	0	0.0	0	0.0	2	0.1	4	0.2	1	0.0	258
Total	**21**	**0.0**	**17**	**0.0**	**11**	**0.0**	**9**	**0.0**	**77**	**0.1**	**29**	**0.1**	**9,466**

AIDS = acquired immune deficiency syndrome.
[a]From the beginning of the epidemic through 2015.
[b]Rates are per 100,000 population.
[c]Includes Asian/Pacific Islander legacy cases.
[d]Hispanics/Latinos can be of any race.
Notes: Data for the year 2015 are preliminary (subject to change) because they are based on only a 6-month reporting delay. Data for the year 2015 should not be used when assessing trends. Numbers less than 12, and rates and trends based on these numbers, should be interpreted with caution. The criteria for stage 3 (AIDS) classification among pediatric cases were expanded in 2014.

SOURCE: "Table 8a. Stage 3 (AIDS) among Children Aged <13 Years, by Race/Ethnicity, 2010–2015 and Cumulative—United States," in *HIV Surveillance Report, 2015*, vol. 27, U.S. Department of Health and Human Services, Centers for Disease Control and Prevention, November 2016, https://www.cdc.gov/hiv/pdf/library/reports/surveillance/cdc-hiv-surveillance-report-2015-vol-27.pdf (accessed September 6, 2017)

cigarettes increases the user's risk of lung cancer and other bronchial diseases, and the carbon monoxide in the smoke increases the chance of cardiovascular diseases.

In 2015 non-Hispanic whites accounted for 71.2% (121.9 million of 171.1 million) of all people aged years 12 and older who had ever used tobacco. (See Table 6.14.) Hispanics (22.3 million) accounted for 13% of all lifetime tobacco users that year, whereas African Americans (17.2 million) accounted for just over 10%. The Substance Abuse and Mental Health Services Administration (SAMHSA) reports in *Results from the 2015 National Survey on Drug Use and Health: Detailed Tables* (September 8, 2016, https://pep-c.rti.org/HERO/KB/Documents/NSDUH-DetTabs-2015.pdf) that non-Hispanic whites aged 12 years and older also had the highest lifetime prevalence of using tobacco, at 71.5%. Native Americans and Alaskan Natives (42.8%) were the most likely to report having used tobacco in the previous year. Asian Americans were the least likely either to have ever used tobacco during their lifetimes (35.4%) or in the previous year (15%).

Obesity and Poor Nutrition

In "Adult Obesity Facts" (August 21, 2017, https://www.cdc.gov/obesity/data/adult.html), the CDC reports that obesity can put people at risk for a variety of diseases, including type 2 diabetes, cardiovascular disease, high blood pressure, some forms of cancer, and stroke. Although rates of obesity are high among the entire U.S. population, obesity is more likely among some groups. The CDC estimates that more than one-third (36.5%) of all American adults are obese. These figures are higher for non-Hispanic African Americans (48.1%) and Hispanics (42.5%), and significantly lower among non-Hispanic Asian Americans

(11.7%). The CDC estimates that roughly one-third (34.5%) of non-Hispanic whites are obese.

The CDC reports in "Childhood Obesity Facts" (April 10, 2017, https://www.cdc.gov/obesity/data/childhood.html) that roughly 17% of American children between the ages of two and 19 years were obese between 2011 and 2014. As with adult obesity trends, the prevalence of obesity in young people tended to be higher among African Americans and Hispanics, and lower among Asian Americans. According to the CDC, more than one in five (21.9%) Hispanics between the ages of two and 19 years was obese during this period; a similar proportion of African American youth (19.5%) were obese over that span. By contrast, 14.7% of non-Hispanic white youth and 8.6% of non-Hispanic Asian Americans were obese during the period between 2011 and 2014.

Drug Abuse

ALCOHOL. Alcohol depresses the central nervous system. The consumption of small amounts of alcohol can actually have a beneficial effect on the body. However, when consumed in larger amounts, alcohol impairs judgment and increases reaction time, can interfere with prescription and nonprescription medications in adverse ways, and can cause serious damage to developing fetuses. Chronic health consequences of excessive drinking include increased risk of liver cirrhosis, pancreatitis, certain types of cancer, high blood pressure, and psychological disorders. Addiction to alcohol is a chronic disease that is often progressive and sometimes fatal.

In 2015 non-Hispanic whites (57%) aged 12 years and older were the most likely to report having used alcohol in the past month, followed by African Americans (43.8%), Hispanics (42.4%), Asian Americans (39.7%), Native

TABLE 6.12

Diagnoses of HIV infection, by race, Hispanic origin, age, and transmission category, 2015

	American Indian/Alaska Native		Asian		Black/African American		Hispanic/Latino[a]		Native Hawaiian/other Pacific Islander		White		Multiple races		Total	
	No.	Rate[b]	No.	Rate[b]	No.	Rate[b]	No.	Rate[b]	No.	Rate[b]	No.	Rate[b]	No.	Rate[b]	No.	Rate[b]
Age at diagnosis (year)																
<13	2	0.4	7	0.3	76	1.1	12	0.1	0	0.0	18	0.1	5	0.2	120	0.2
13–14	0	0.0	1	0.2	21	1.8	1	0.1	0	0.0	2	0.0	0	0.0	25	0.3
15–19	9	4.9	29	2.8	1,082	36.2	332	7.0	4	9.9	204	1.8	38	5.5	1,698	8.0
20–24	42	21.1	147	11.7	3,778	111.2	1,624	33.7	15	32.0	1,300	10.5	178	29.6	7,084	31.2
25–29	39	21.3	206	13.9	3,496	112.2	1,795	39.6	15	28.8	1,783	14.1	176	38.1	7,510	33.4
30–34	33	20.3	142	9.4	2,140	77.3	1,500	33.7	13	26.7	1,497	12.1	112	29.2	5,437	25.1
35–39	26	17.6	115	8.1	1,643	63.0	1,221	28.8	8	18.9	1,106	9.5	75	23.1	4,194	20.6
40–44	13	9.1	114	8.1	1,306	51.2	875	22.3	6	16.1	1,051	8.9	53	19.0	3,418	16.9
45–49	17	11.6	83	6.6	1,258	48.7	781	22.3	6	17.2	1,111	8.5	46	18.5	3,302	15.8
50–54	13	8.0	54	4.7	1,162	42.8	575	18.9	5	14.4	1,144	7.6	57	23.6	3,010	13.5
55–59	11	7.2	26	2.5	849	33.2	306	12.5	6	19.7	634	4.1	28	12.8	1,860	8.5
60–64	2	1.6	16	1.8	473	23.0	126	6.9	1	4.2	362	2.6	16	9.3	996	5.2
Over 65	2	0.8	15	0.7	386	9.2	142	3.8	0	0.0	297	0.8	17	4.9	859	1.8
Transmission category[c]																
Male adult or adolescent																
Male-to-male sexual contact	120	—	726	—	10,315	—	7,013	—	62	—	7,570	—	570	—	26,375	—
Injection drug use	10	—	19	—	538	—	328	—	3	—	493	—	22	—	1,412	—
Male-to-male sexual contact and injection drug use	11	—	17	—	262	—	264	—	1	—	605	—	42	—	1,202	—
Heterosexual contact[d]	11	—	53	—	1,926	—	533	—	5	—	381	—	40	—	2,948	—
Other[e]	0	—	2	—	29	—	9	—	0	—	12	—	1	—	53	—
Subtotal	152	16.2	816	11.7	13,070	84.8	8,147	37.4	71	31.2	9,060	10.8	675	32.9	31,991	24.4
Female adult or adolescent																
Injection drug use	15	—	6	—	363	—	115	—	2	—	458	—	20	—	980	—
Heterosexual contact[d]	40	—	125	—	4,142	—	1,010	—	6	—	968	—	100	—	6,391	—
Other[e]	0	—	0	—	19	—	5	—	0	—	5	—	1	—	31	—
Subtotal	55	5.6	132	1.7	4,524	26.2	1,131	5.3	8	3.5	1,431	1.6	121	5.5	7,402	5.4
Child (<13 years at diagnosis)																
Perinatal	2	—	4	—	54	—	10	—	0	—	11	—	5	—	86	—
Other[f]	0	—	3	—	22	—	2	—	0	—	7	—	0	—	34	—
Subtotal	2	0.4	7	0.3	76	1.1	12	0.1	0	0.0	18	0.1	5	0.2	120	0.2
Region of residence																
Northeast	8	6.3	168	4.6	2,745	43.3	1,844	23.3	4	18.8	1,531	4.1	216	23.8	6,516	11.6
Midwest	20	4.9	110	5.2	2,425	34.5	594	11.4	3	9.5	1,877	3.6	128	10.2	5,157	7.6
South	70	8.9	255	6.3	11,143	48.3	4,014	19.2	26	29.8	4,576	6.5	324	15.0	20,408	16.8
West	111	10.6	422	5.6	1,357	39.1	2,838	12.6	46	11.0	2,525	6.5	133	5.9	7,432	9.8
Total	209	8.8	955	5.5	17,670	44.3	9,290	16.4	79	14.1	10,509	5.3	801	12.2	39,513	12.3

TABLE 6.12

Diagnoses of HIV infection, by race, Hispanic origin, age, and transmission category, 2015 [CONTINUED]

[a]Hispanics/Latinos can be of any race.
[b]Rates are per 100,000 population. Rates are not calculated by transmission category because of the lack of denominator data.
[c]Data have been statistically adjusted to account for missing transmission category.
[d]Heterosexual contact with a person known to have, or to be at high risk for, HIV infection.
[e]Includes hemophilia, blood transfusion, perinatal exposure, and risk factor not reported or not identified.
[f]Includes hemophilia, blood transfusion, and risk factor not reported or not identified.
Notes: Data include persons with a diagnosis of HIV infection regard less of stage of disease at diagnosis. Data for the year 2015 are preliminary (subject to change) because they are based on only a 6-month reporting delay. Numbers less than 12, and rates based on these numbers, should be interpreted with caution. HIV = human immunodeficiency virus.

SOURCE: "Table 3a. Diagnoses of HIV Infection, by Race/Ethnicity and Selected Characteristics, 2015—United States," in *HIV Surveillance Report, 2015, vol. 27*, U.S. Department of Health and Human Services, Centers for Disease Control and Prevention, November 2016, https://www.cdc.gov/hiv/pdf/library/reports/surveillance/cdc-hiv-surveillance-report-2015-vol-27.pdf (accessed September 6, 2017)

TABLE 6.13

AIDS diagnoses, by race, Hispanic origin, age, and transmission category, 2015

	American Indian/Alaska Native		Asian[a]		Black/African American		Hispanic/Latino[b]		Native Hawaiian/other Pacific Islander		White		Multiple races		Total	
	No.	Rate[c]	No.	Rate[c]	No.	Rate[c]	No.	Rate[c]	No.	Rate[c]	No.	Rate[c]	No.	Rate[c]	No.	Rate[c]
Age at diagnosis (year)																
<13	0	0.0	2	0.1	19	0.3	5	0.0	0	0.0	2	0.0	1	0.0	29	0.1
13–14	0	0.0	0	0.0	8	0.7	1	0.1	0	0.0	0	0.0	0	0.0	9	0.1
15–19	2	1.1	3	0.3	133	4.4	29	0.6	0	0.0	16	0.1	8	1.2	191	0.9
20–24	10	5.0	19	1.5	776	22.8	270	5.6	4	8.5	157	1.3	53	8.8	1,289	5.7
25–29	13	7.1	43	2.9	1,265	40.6	540	11.9	2	3.8	417	3.3	88	19.1	2,368	10.5
30–34	15	9.2	50	3.3	1,152	41.6	619	13.9	3	6.2	489	4.0	66	17.2	2,394	11.0
35–39	12	8.1	39	2.8	987	37.9	593	14.0	4	9.4	504	4.3	70	21.5	2,209	10.8
40–44	9	6.3	57	4.0	964	37.8	515	13.1	1	2.7	565	4.8	76	27.2	2,187	10.8
45–49	10	6.8	39	3.1	1,043	40.3	498	14.2	3	8.6	710	5.4	85	34.2	2,388	11.5
50–54	13	8.0	35	3.1	928	34.2	375	12.3	4	11.5	806	5.4	74	30.6	2,235	10.0
55–59	9	5.9	21	2.0	688	26.9	215	8.8	1	3.3	484	3.2	44	20.1	1,462	6.7
60–64	2	1.6	9	1.0	401	19.5	117	6.4	0	0.0	273	2.0	28	16.3	830	4.4
Over 65	1	0.4	8	0.4	338	8.0	93	2.5	0	0.0	245	0.7	27	7.9	712	1.5
Transmission category[d]																
Male adult or adolescent																
Male-to-male sexual contact	36	—	229	—	3,928	—	2,430	—	15	—	3,096	—	314	—	10,047	—
Injection drug use	8	—	14	—	462	—	247	—	0	—	248	—	39	—	1,018	—
Male-to-male sexual contact and injection drug use	7	—	6	—	206	—	172	—	1	—	319	—	50	—	761	—
Heterosexual contact[e]	7	—	22	—	1,231	—	358	—	3	—	224	—	48	—	1,892	—
Other[f]	0	—	1	—	53	—	25	—	0	—	14	—	4	—	97	—
Subtotal	**57**	**6.1**	**271**	**3.9**	**5,879**	**38.1**	**3,233**	**14.8**	**19**	**8.3**	**3,901**	**4.6**	**455**	**22.2**	**13,815**	**10.5**
Female adult or adolescent																
Injection drug use	11	—	3	—	339	—	121	—	1	—	260	—	49	—	786	—
Heterosexual contact[e]	28	—	47	—	2,423	—	487	—	2	—	496	—	109	—	3,592	—
Other[f]	0	—	2	—	42	—	24	—	0	—	9	—	5	—	82	—
Subtotal	**39**	**4.0**	**52**	**0.7**	**2,804**	**16.2**	**632**	**2.9**	**3**	**1.3**	**765**	**0.9**	**164**	**7.5**	**4,459**	**3.2**
Child (<13 years at diagnosis)																
Perinatal	0	—	2	—	14	—	3	—	0	—	1	—	1	—	21	—
Other[d]	0	—	0	—	5	—	2	—	0	—	1	—	0	—	8	—
Subtotal	**0**	**0.0**	**2**	**0.1**	**19**	**0.3**	**5**	**0.0**	**0**	**0.0**	**2**	**0.0**	**1**	**0.0**	**29**	**0.1**
Region of residence																
Northeast	2	1.6	67	1.8	1,489	23.5	899	11.4	2	9.4	715	1.9	154	17.0	3,328	5.9
Midwest	12	3.0	51	2.4	1,025	14.6	290	5.6	1	3.2	822	1.6	77	6.1	2,278	3.4
South	40	5.1	57	1.4	5,597	24.3	1,602	7.7	2	2.3	2,011	2.9	292	13.5	9,601	7.9
West	42	4.0	150	2.0	591	17.0	1,079	4.8	17	4.1	1,120	2.9	97	4.3	3,096	4.1
Total	**96**	**4.1**	**325**	**1.9**	**8,702**	**21.8**	**3,870**	**6.8**	**22**	**3.9**	**4,668**	**2.4**	**620**	**9.4**	**18,303**	**5.7**

TABLE 6.13

AIDS diagnoses, by race, Hispanic origin, age, and transmission category, 2015 [CONTINUED]

^aIncludes Asian/Pacific Islander legacy cases.
^bHispanics/Latinos can be of any race.
^cRates are per 100,000 population. Rates are not calculated by transmission category because of the lack of denominator data.
^dData have been statistically adjusted to account for missing transmission category.
^eHeterosexual contact with a person known to have, or to be at high risk for, HIV infection.
^fIncludes hemophilia, blood transfusion, perinatal exposure, and risk factor not reported or not identified.
^gIncludes hemophilia, blood transfusion, and risk factor not reported or not identified.
Notes: Data for the year 2015 are preliminary (subject to change) because they are based on only a 6-month reporting delay. Numbers less than 12, and rates based on these numbers, should be interpreted with caution. AIDS = acquired immune deficiency syndrome.

SOURCE: "Table 4a. Stage 3 (AIDS), by Race/Ethnicity and Selected Characteristics, 2015—United States," in *HIV Surveillance Report, 2015,* vol. 27, U.S. Department of Health and Human Services, Centers for Disease Control and Prevention, November 2016, https://www.cdc.gov/hiv/pdf/library/reports/surveillance/cdc-hiv-surveillance-report-2015-vol-27.pdf (accessed September 6, 2017).

TABLE 6.14

Tobacco product use by age, sex, race, and Hispanic origin, 2011 and 2012

[In thousands]

Demographic characteristic	Lifetime (2014)	Lifetime (2015)	Past year (2014)	Past year (2015)	Past month (2014)	Past month (2015)
Total	175,416[b]	171,120	81,141[b]	78,299	66,899[b]	63,959
Age						
12–17	4,591[a]	4,299	3,161[b]	2,877	1,742[b]	1,492
18 or older	170,825[b]	166,821	77,979[a]	75,422	65,157[b]	62,467
18–25	22,290[b]	21,524	16,083[b]	15,301	12,244[b]	11,516
26 or older	148,534[b]	145,297	61,896	60,121	52,913[a]	50,952
Gender						
Male	94,796	93,802	48,527	47,266	39,952[a]	38,451
Female	80,620[b]	77,318	32,614[a]	31,033	26,947[a]	25,509
Hispanic origin and race						
Not Hispanic or Latino	153,315[b]	148,858	70,735[b]	67,951	58,933[b]	56,253
White	126,091[b]	121,895	56,442[b]	53,269	46,927[b]	44,087
Black or African American	17,526	17,192	9,683	9,862	8,425	8,327
American Indian or Alaska Native	1,031	998	616	613	545	531
Native Hawaiian or other Pacific Islander	652[b]	368	365[b]	189	312b	139
Asian	4,960	5,202	2,019	2,209	1,418	1,680
Two or more races	3,054	3,203	1,609	1,810	1,305	1,489
Hispanic or Latino	22,102	22,262	10,406	10,348	7,966	7,706

[a]The difference between this estimate and the 2015 estimate is statistically significant at the 0.05 level. Rounding may make the estimates appear identical.
[b]The difference between this estimate and the 2015 estimate is statistically significant at the 0.01 level. Rounding may make the estimates appear identical.
Note: Tobacco products include cigarettes, smokeless tobacco (i.e., snuff, dip, chewing tobacco, or "snus"), cigars, or pipe tobacco. Tobacco product use in the past year excludes past year pipe tobacco use, but includes past month pipe tobacco use.

SOURCE: "Table 2.21A Tobacco Product Use in Lifetime, Past Year, and Past Month among Persons Aged 12 or Older, by Demographic Characteristics: Numbers in Thousands, 2014 and 2015," in *Results from the 2015 National Survey on Drug Use and Health: Detailed Tables*, U.S. Department of Health and Human Services, Substance Abuse and Mental Health Services Administration, Office of Applied Studies, September 8, 2016, https://pep-c.rti.org/HERO/KB/Documents/NSDUH-DetTabs-2015.pdf (accessed September 6, 2017)

Americans and Alaskan Natives (37.9%), and Native Hawaiians and Pacific Islanders (33.8%). (See Table 6.15.) The rate of binge alcohol use, which is defined as five or more drinks on one occasion in at least one day in the previous month, was lowest among Asian Americans (14%) and Native Hawaiian and Pacific Islanders (17.8%). The rate among non-Hispanic whites (26%) was comparable to that of Hispanics (25.7%), which were both slightly higher than the binge drinking rate among Native Americans and Alaskan Natives (24.1%) and African Americans (23.4%). The rates of heavy alcohol use, which is defined as drinking five or more drinks on each of five or more days in the past 30 days, was also highest among non-Hispanic whites (7.6%), followed by Hispanics (4.8%) and African Americans (4.8%), Native Americans and Alaskan Natives (4.7%), Native Hawaiian and Pacific Islander (3%), and Asian Americans (2.2%).

ILLICIT DRUG USE. According to the CDC, illicit drugs include marijuana/hashish, cocaine (including crack), heroin, hallucinogens, inhalants, and any prescription-type psychotherapeutic drug that is used nonmedically. In 2015 non-Hispanic whites accounted for 17.4 million of 27.1 million (64.2%) of all people who had used illicit drugs during the past month. (See Table 6.16.) According to SAMHSA, in *Results from the 2015 National Survey on Drug Use and Health: Detailed Tables*, however, Native Americans (14.2%) had the highest rate of past month drug use in 2015, followed by non-Hispanic African Americans (12.5%), non-Hispanic whites (10.2%), Native Hawaiian and Pacific Islanders (9.8%), and Hispanics (9.2%). The rate of past month illicit drug use among Asian Americans (4%) was significantly lower than those of other racial and ethnic groups in 2015.

LIFE EXPECTANCY AND DEATH

Life Expectancy

Women tend to live longer than men, and whites are likely to live longer than African Americans. (See Figure 6.9.) According to Kenneth D. Kochanek et al. of the NCHS, in "Deaths: Final Data for 2014" (*National Vital Statistics Reports*, vol. 65, no. 4, June 30, 2016), non-Hispanic African American males born in 2014 had the shortest life expectancy (72 years), whereas Hispanic females had the longest life expectancy (84 years). Non-Hispanic white females had a life expectancy of 81.1 years, non-Hispanic African American females had a life expectancy of 78.1 years, and non-Hispanic white males had a life expectancy of 76.5 years. The life expectancy of all groups at birth had risen since 1970, especially for African Americans. In 2014 African Americans died at a higher rate than whites (1.2 African Americans died for every 1 white death). (See Table 6.17.)

TABLE 6.15

Alcohol use, binge alcohol use, and heavy alcohol use in the past month among persons aged 12 or older, by age, sex, race, and Hispanic origin, 2014 and 2015

[Percentages]

Demographic characteristic	Alcohol use (2014)	Alcohol use (2015)	Binge alcohol use (2014)	Binge alcohol use (2015)	Heavy alcohol use (2014)	Heavy alcohol use (2015)
Total	52.7[a]	51.7	nc	24.9	nc	6.5
Age						
12–17	11.5[b]	9.6	nc	5.8	nc	0.9
18 or older	56.9[a]	56.0	nc	26.9	nc	7.0
18–25	59.6	58.3	nc	39.0	nc	10.9
26 or older	56.5	55.6	nc	24.8	nc	6.4
Gender						
Male	57.3	56.2	30.0	29.6	9.3	8.9
Female	48.4	47.4	nc	20.5	nc	4.2
Hispanic origin and race						
Not Hispanic or Latino	54.3	53.5	nc	24.8	nc	6.8
White	57.7	57.0	nc	26.0	nc	7.6
Black or African American	44.2	43.8	nc	23.4	nc	4.8
American Indian or Alaska Native	42.3	37.9	nc	24.1	nc	4.7
Native Hawaiian or other Pacific Islander	37.9	33.8	nc	17.8	nc	3.0
Asian	38.7	39.7	nc	14.0	nc	2.2
Two or more races	49.5[a]	42.8	nc	22.9	nc	6.8
Hispanic or Latino	44.4	42.4	nc	25.7	nc	4.8

nc = not comparable due to methodological changes.
[a]The difference between this estimate and the 2015 estimate is statistically significant at the 0.05 level. Rounding may make the estimates appear identical.
[b]The difference between this estimate and the 2015 estimate is statistically significant at the 0.01 level. Rounding may make the estimates appear identical.
Note: Binge alcohol use is defined as drinking five or more drinks (for males) or four or more drinks (for females) on the same occasion (i.e., at the same time or within a couple of hours of each other) on at least 1 day in the past 30 days. In 2015, the definition for females changed from five to four drinks. Heavy alcohol use is defined as binge drinking on the same occasion on each of 5 or more days in the past 30 days; all heavy alcohol users are also binge alcohol users.

SOURCE: "Table 2.46B. Alcohol Use, Binge Alcohol Use, and Heavy Alcohol Use in the Past Month among Persons Aged 12 or Older, by Demographic Characteristics: Percentages, 2014 and 2015," in *Results from the 2015 National Survey on Drug Use and Health: Detailed Tables*, U.S. Department of Health and Human Services, Substance Abuse and Mental Health Services Administration, Office of Applied Studies, September 8, 2016, https://pep-c.rti.org/HERO/KB/Documents/NSDUH-DetTabs-2015.pdf (accessed September 6, 2017)

Leading Causes of Death

In 2014 heart disease was the leading cause of death among Americans, with 167 deaths per 100,000 population. (See Table 6.17.) Cancers (malignant neoplasms) were the second-leading cause of death, with 161.2 deaths per 100,000 population, followed by chronic lower respiratory diseases (40.5 deaths per 100,000 population) and accidents (40.5 per 100,000). Cerebrovascular diseases rounded out the top-five leading causes of death that year, with 36.5 deaths per 100,000 population.

In *Health, United States, 2016*, the NCHS notes that in 2015 heart disease was the leading cause of death among non-Hispanic whites and African Americans. That year 540,857 whites died of heart disease, accounting for 23.4% of deaths among whites; 75,249 African Americans (23.5%), and 3,463 Native Americans or Alaskan Natives (18.2%) died of heart disease in 2015. Cancer was the leading cause of death among Hispanics and Asian Americans and Pacific Islanders.

Suicide and homicide were responsible for more deaths among some groups than others. The NCHS reports that in 2015 suicide was the eighth-leading cause of death among Native Americans or Alaskan Natives,

whereas homicide ranked as the seventh-leading cause of death among African Americans.

HOMICIDE. The NCHS indicates in *Health, United States, 2016* that homicides are disproportionately high in the African American population and that the high homicide rate among African Americans is one of the reasons African American men in their 20s and 30s have a higher death rate than men this age in other ethnic and racial groups. In 2015, 8,021 African American males were murdered; overall, African American males had a homicide death rate of 35.4 per 100,000 population that year. The highest rate of death by homicide was among African American men aged 25 to 34 years (81.4 per 100,000 population), followed by African American men aged 15 to 24 years (74.9 per 100,000 population) and African American men aged 35 to 44 years (46.4 per 100,000 population). In comparison, there were 7.3 homicides per 100,000 non-Hispanic white men aged 15 to 24 years, 8 homicides per 100,000 non-Hispanic white men aged 25 to 34 years, and 6.3 homicides per 100,000 non-Hispanic white men aged 35 to 44 years.

According to the NCHS, in 2015 Hispanics, like African Americans, had a higher homicide rate than most

TABLE 6.16

Illicit drug use by age, sex, race, and Hispanic origin, 2015

[In thousands]

Demographic characteristic	Lifetime (2015)	Past year (2015)	Past month (2015)
Total	**130,610**	**47,730**	**27,080**
Age			
12–17	6,297	4,346	2,193
18 or older	124,313	43,384	24,887
18–25	20,083	13,102	7,797
26 or older	104,230	30,281	17,090
Gender			
Male	69,822	26,576	16,164
Female	60,788	21,154	10,915
Hispanic origin and race			
Not Hispanic or Latino	113,700	40,256	23,081
White	91,038	30,534	17,396
Black or African American	15,299	6,625	4,023
American Indian or Alaska Native	779	328	204
Native Hawaiian or other Pacific Islander	348	149	71
Asian	3,544	1,355	584
Two or more races	2,692	1,265	803
Hispanic or Latino	16,910	7,474	3,999

nc = not comparable due to methodological changes.
Note: Illicit drug use includes the misuse of prescription psychotherapeutics or the use of marijuana, cocaine (including crack), heroin, hallucinogens, inhalants, or methamphetamine. Misuse of prescription drugs is defined as use in any way not directed by a doctor, including use without a prescription of one's own medication; use in greater amounts, more often, or longer than told to take a drug; or use in any other way not directed by a doctor. Prescription drugs do not include over-the-counter drugs.

SOURCE: Adapted from "Table 1.28A Illicit Drug Use in Lifetime, Past Year, and Past Month among Persons Aged 12 or Older, by Demographic Characteristics: Numbers in Thousands, 2014 and 2015," in *Results from the 2015 National Survey on Drug Use and Health: Detailed Tables*, U.S. Department of Health and Human Services, Substance Abuse and Mental Health Services Administration, Office of Applied Studies, September 8, 2016, https://pep-c.rti.org/HERO/KB/Documents/NSDUH-DetTabs-2015.pdf (accessed September 6, 2017)

FIGURE 6.9

Life expectancy by race and sex, 1970–2014

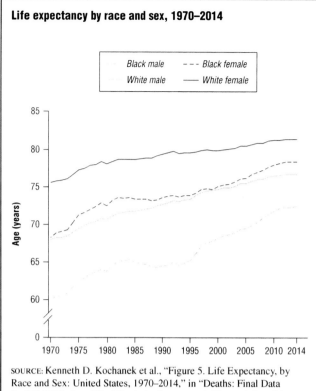

SOURCE: Kenneth D. Kochanek et al., "Figure 5. Life Expectancy, by Race and Sex: United States, 1970–2014," in "Deaths: Final Data for 2014," *National Vital Statistics Reports*, vol. 65, no. 4, June 30, 2016, https://www.cdc.gov/nchs/data/nvsr/nvsr65/nvsr65_04.pdf (accessed September 6, 2017)

other groups, particularly among youth. The homicide rate for Hispanic men aged 15 to 24 years was 16.5 per 100,000 population and for Hispanic men aged 25 to 34 years it was 14.3 per 100,000 population. Even so, between 1990 and 2015 the homicide death rate among all Hispanic men dropped from 27.4 to 7.9 per 100,000 population.

HIV AND AIDS. The difference in the HIV/AIDS death rate among races and ethnic groups is staggering, with a much higher rate among African Americans than any other group of Americans. In 2014, 5,614 African Americans died from AIDS, compared with 3,744 whites, 2,151 Hispanics, 44 Asian Americans, and 41 Native Americans and Alaskan Natives. (See Table 6.18.) African Americans had the highest rate of AIDS deaths, at 14.2 per 100,000 population. In *Health, United States, 2016*, the NCHS reports that the HIV/AIDS death rate for African Americans in 2015 was 7.9 per 100,000 population, compared with 1.8 per 100,000 Hispanics, and 1.1 per 100,000 non-Hispanic whites.

TABLE 6.17

Deaths by causes of death, race, Hispanic origin, and sex, 2013–14

[Crude death rates on an annual basis per 100,000 population; age-adjusted rates per 100,000 U.S. standard population. Rates are based on populations estimated as of July 1 using postcensal estimates. Race categories are consistent with the 1977 Office of Management and Budget (OMB) standards.]

Rank[a]	Cause of death	Number	Percent of total deaths	2014 crude death rate	Age-adjusted death rate			
					2014	Percent change 2013 to 2014	Ratio	
							Male to female	Black[b] to white
—	All causes	2,626,418	100.0	823.7	724.6	−1.0	1.4	1.2
1	Diseases of heart	614,348	23.4	192.7	167.0	−1.6	1.6	1.2
2	Malignant neoplasms	591,700	22.5	185.6	161.2	−1.2	1.4	1.1
3	Chronic lower respiratory diseases	147,101	5.6	46.1	40.5	−3.8	1.2	0.7
4	Accidents (unintentional injuries)	135,928	5.2	42.6	40.5	2.8	2.0	0.8
5	Cerebrovascular diseases	133,103	5.1	41.7	36.5	0.8	1.0	1.4
6	Alzheimer's disease	93,541	3.6	29.3	25.4	8.1	0.7	0.8
7	Diabetes mellitus	76,488	2.9	24.0	20.9	−1.4	1.5	1.9
8	Influenza and pneumonia	55,227	2.1	17.3	15.1	−5.0	1.3	1.1
9	Nephritis, nephrotic syndrome and nephrosis	48,146	1.8	15.1	13.2	0.0	1.5	2.0
10	Intentional self-harm (suicide)	42,826	1.6	13.4	13.0	3.2	3.6	0.4
11	Septicemia	38,940	1.5	12.2	10.7	0.0	1.2	1.8
12	Chronic liver disease and cirrhosis	38,170	1.5	12.0	10.4	2.0	2.0	0.6
13	Essential hypertension and hypertensive renal disease	30,221	1.2	9.5	8.2	−3.5	1.1	2.1
14	Parkinson's disease	26,150	1.0	8.2	7.4	1.4	2.3	0.5
15	Pneumonitis due to solids and liquids	18,792	0.7	5.9	5.1	−1.9	1.9	1.0
—	All other causes	535,737	20.4	168.0	—	—	—	—

— Category not applicable.

[a]Based on number of deaths.

[b]Multiple-race data were reported by 46 states and the District of Columbia in 2014. The multiple-race data for these reporting areas were bridged to the single-race categories of the 1977 OMB standards for comparability with other reporting areas.

SOURCE: Kenneth D. Kochanek et al., "Table B. Number of Deaths, Percentage of Total Deaths, Death Rates, and Age-Adjusted Death Rates for 2014, Percentage Change in Age-Adjusted Death Rates in 2014 from 2013, and Ratio of Age-Adjusted Death Rates by Sex and by Race for the 15 Leading Causes of Death for the Total Population in 2014: United States," in "Deaths: Final Data for 2014," *National Vital Statistics Reports*, vol. 65, no. 4, June 30, 2016, https://www.cdc.gov/nchs/data/nvsr/nvsr65/nvsr65_04.pdf (accessed September 6, 2017)

TABLE 6.18

Deaths of persons with an AIDS diagnosis, by year of death, age, race and Hispanic origin, and transmission category, 2010–14 and cumulative

	2010 No.	2010 Rate[b]	2011 No.	2011 Rate[b]	2012 No.	2012 Rate[b]	2013 No.	2013 Rate[b]	2014 No.	2014 Rate[b]	Cumulative[a] No.
Age at diagnosis (year)											
<13	0	0.0	0	0.0	1	0.0	1	0.0	0	0.0	4,889
13–14	2	0.0	1	0.0	1	0.0	0	0.0	1	0.0	294
15–19	27	0.1	20	0.1	17	0.1	6	0.0	7	0.0	1,307
20–24	147	0.7	149	0.7	131	0.6	124	0.5	113	0.5	9,970
25–29	313	1.5	314	1.5	320	1.5	308	1.4	265	1.2	47,241
30–34	618	3.1	547	2.7	556	2.7	507	2.4	466	2.2	102,168
35–39	996	5.0	890	4.5	779	4.0	691	3.5	678	3.4	128,655
40–44	1,793	8.6	1,539	7.3	1,349	6.4	1,176	5.6	1,052	5.1	123,066
45–49	2,680	11.8	2,466	11.1	2,251	10.4	1,988	9.4	1,724	8.3	97,011
50–54	2,619	11.7	2,618	11.6	2,579	11.4	2,508	11.1	2,361	10.5	67,923
55–59	2,062	10.4	2,182	10.8	2,190	10.5	2,198	10.4	2,220	10.3	43,432
60–64	1,373	8.1	1,401	7.9	1,506	8.4	1,558	8.6	1,668	9.0	26,000
Over 65	1,326	3.3	1,411	3.4	1,541	3.6	1,694	3.8	1,778	3.8	26,553
Race/ethnicity											
American Indian/Alaska Native	58	2.6	48	2.1	40	1.7	50	2.1	41	1.7	1,936
Asian[c]	58	0.4	69	0.5	63	0.4	61	0.4	44	0.3	3,464
Black/African American	6,758	17.8	6,446	16.8	6,265	16.2	5,968	15.2	5,614	14.2	279,958
Hispanic/Latino[d]	2,313	4.6	2,306	4.4	2,108	4.0	2,140	3.9	2,151	3.9	104,222
Native Hawaiian/Other Pacific Islander	6	1.2	9	1.8	6	1.2	8	1.5	5	0.9	366
White	4,069	2.1	3,989	2.0	4,041	2.0	3,791	1.9	3,744	1.9	275,163
Multiple races	694	12.3	671	11.5	698	11.6	741	12.0	734	11.5	13,400
Transmission category[e]											
Male adult or adolescent											
Male-to-male sexual contact	5,316	—	5,235	—	5,156	—	5,075	—	4,944	—	318,968
Injection drug use	2,403	—	2,197	—	2,129	—	2,013	—	1,925	—	132,911
Male-to-male sexual contact and injection drug use	1,151	—	1,106	—	1,085	—	1,055	—	1,030	—	51,951
Heterosexual contact[f]	1,400	—	1,367	—	1,318	—	1,267	—	1,194	—	37,384
Perinatal	26	—	34	—	38	—	32	—	27	—	433
Other[d]	77	—	78	—	68	—	56	—	50	—	8,743
Subtotal	**10,373**	**8.3**	**10,018**	**7.9**	**9,793**	**7.7**	**9,498**	**7.4**	**9,170**	**7.1**	**550,390**

TABLE 6.18

Deaths of persons with an AIDS diagnosis, by year of death, age, race and Hispanic origin, and transmission category, 2010–14 and cumulative [CONTINUED]

	2010 No.	2010 Rate[b]	2011 No.	2011 Rate[b]	2012 No.	2012 Rate[b]	2013 No.	2013 Rate[b]	2014 No.	2014 Rate[b]	Cumulative[a] No.
Female adult or adolescent											
Injection drug use	1,331	—	1,327	—	1,248	—	1,223	—	1,138	—	58,284
Heterosexual contact[f]	2,196	—	2,122	—	2,106	—	1,981	—	1,972	—	60,753
Perinatal	29	—	45	—	44	—	32	—	30	—	549
Other[g]	27	—	26	—	29	—	24	—	22	—	3,643
Subtotal	**3,583**	**2.7**	**3,520**	**2.7**	**3,427**	**2.6**	**3,260**	**2.4**	**3,163**	**2.3**	**123,230**
Child (<13 years at death)											
Perinatal	0	—	0	—	1	—	1	—	0	—	4,437
Other[g]	0	—	0	—	0	—	0	—	0	—	452
Subtotal	**0**	**0.0**	**0**	**0.0**	**1**	**0.0**	**1**	**0.0**	**0**	**0.0**	**4,889**
Region of residence											
Northeast	3,647	6.6	3,489	6.3	3,259	5.8	3,243	5.8	3,027	5.4	210,951
Midwest	1,584	2.4	1,501	2.2	1,482	2.2	1,360	2.0	1,254	1.9	72,180
South	6,702	5.8	6,498	5.6	6,432	5.5	6,176	5.2	6,017	5.0	265,716
West	2,023	2.8	2,050	2.8	2,048	2.8	1,980	2.7	2,035	2.7	129,662
Total	**13,956**	**4.5**	**13,538**	**4.3**	**13,221**	**4.2**	**12,759**	**4.0**	**12,333**	**3.9**	**678,509**

[a]From the beginning of the epidemic through 2014.
[b]Rates are per 100,000 population. Rates are not calculated by transmission category because of the lack of denominator data.
[c]Includes Asian/Pacific Islander legacy cases.
[d]Hispanics/Latinos can be of any race.
[e]Data have been statistically adjusted to account for missing transmission category.
[f]Heterosexual contact with a person known to have, or to be at high risk for, HIV infection.
[g]Includes hemophilia, blood transfusion, and risk factor not reported or not identified.
AIDS = acquired immune deficiency syndrome.
Notes: Deaths of persons with a diagnosis of HIV infection may be due to any cause. Data are based on residence at death. When information on residence at death was not available, state at death (where a person's death occurred) was used. Numbers less than 12, and rates and trends based on these numbers, should be interpreted with caution.

SOURCE: "Table 13a. Deaths of Persons with Diagnosed HIV Infection Ever Classified as Stage 3 (AIDS), by Year of Death and Selected Characteristics, 2010–2014 and Cumulative—United States," in *HIV Surveillance Report, 2015, vol. 27,* U.S. Department of Health and Human Services, Centers for Disease Control and Prevention. November 2016, https://www.cdc.gov/hiv/pdf/library/reports/surveillance/cdc-hiv-surveillance-report-2015-vol-27.pdf (accessed September 6, 2017)

CHAPTER 7
CRIME

VICTIMIZATION OF MINORITIES

Certain groups in U.S. society, including the poor, younger people, males, African Americans, Hispanics, and residents of inner cities, are more likely to be victimized and are more vulnerable to violence than other groups. As is discussed in other chapters of this book, African Americans and Hispanics are more likely to be poor and to be unemployed than are whites. These factors put minorities at an especially high risk of being victimized.

Violent Crimes

Non-Hispanic African Americans are more likely than individuals of other races to be victims of violent crimes. In *Criminal Victimization, 2015* (October 2016, https://www.bjs.gov/content/pub/pdf/cv15.pdf), Jennifer L. Truman and Rachel E. Morgan of the Bureau of Justice Statistics (BJS) report that in 2015, 22.6 per 1,000 non-Hispanic African Americans were victims of a violent crime, compared with 17.4 per 1,000 non-Hispanic whites and 16.8 per 1,000 Hispanics. (See Table 7.1.)

As Table 7.1 shows, non-Hispanic African Americans were also more likely than Hispanics and non-Hispanic whites to be victims of serious violent crimes such as rape or sexual assault, robbery, and aggravated assault in 2015. Non-Hispanic African Americans experienced these crimes at a rate of 8.4 per 1,000 individuals, compared with 7.1 per 1,000 for Hispanics and 6 per 1,000 for non-Hispanic whites.

HOMICIDE. African Americans are also far more likely than people of other races to be victims of homicides. Of 13,455 U.S. homicide victims for whom age, sex, race, and ethnicity were reported to the Federal Bureau of Investigation (FBI) in 2015, more than half (7,039, or 52.3%) were African Americans, and 5,854 (43.5%) were non-Hispanic whites. (See Table 7.2.) That year, nearly one-quarter (1,596, or 22.7%) of the African

American murder victims for whom age was reported were between the ages of 20 and 24 years.

African Americans are also more likely than whites to be homicide offenders. In *Crime in the United States, 2015* (September 2016, https://ucr.fbi.gov/crime-in-the-u.s/2015/crime-in-the-u.s.-2015), the FBI reports offender data for 15,326 murders that took place in 2015. Of these cases in which the race of the offender is known, there were a larger number of African American homicide offenders (5,620) than white homicide offenders (4,636), even though African Americans constitute a much smaller percentage of the overall U.S. population. Most murders are intraracial (of the same race). In 2015, in cases involving a single victim and single offender in which the race of the offender is known, 2,574 of 3,167 (81.3%) white murder victims were murdered by other whites. (See Table 7.3.) That same year, 2,380 of 2,664 (89.3%) African American murder victims were murdered by other African Americans.

Hate Crimes

A hate crime refers to an offense that is perpetrated against a specific race, ethnicity, or other segment of the population, and is driven solely by prejudice toward that particular group. Although the phrase "hate crime" did not enter common usage until the 1980s, hate crimes have existed throughout world history, from the persecution of Christians during the Roman Empire to the mass extermination of Jews by the Nazis during World War II and the mass murder of the Tutsi people by the Hutu in Rwanda in 1994. In the United States hate crimes have targeted specific racial and ethnic communities throughout the nation's history. One of the most notorious perpetrators of hate crimes in the United States has been the Ku Klux Klan, a white supremacist group that first began terrorizing African American communities in the aftermath of the U.S. Civil War (1861–1865). Following the

TABLE 7.1

Rates of violent and serious violent crime, by sex, race, Hispanic origin, and age of victim, 2014 and 2015

Victim demographic characteristic	Violent crime[a]		Serious violent crime[b]	
	2014*	2015	2014*	2015
Total	**20.1**	**18.6**	**7.7**	**6.8**
Sex				
Male	21.1	15.9	8.3	5.4
Female	19.1	21.1	7.0	8.1
Race/Hispanic origin				
White[c]	20.3	17.4	7.0	6.0
Black[c]	22.5	22.6	10.1	8.4
Hispanic	16.2	16.8	8.3	7.1
Other[c, d]	23.0	25.7	7.7	10.4
Age				
12–17	30.1	31.3	8.8	7.8
18–24	26.8	25.1	13.6	10.7
25–34	28.5	21.8	8.6	9.3
35–49	21.6	22.6	8.9	7.8
50–64	17.9	14.2	7.0	5.7
65 or older	3.1	5.2	1.3	1.5
Marital status				
Never married	27.9	26.2	10.7	9.4
Married	12.4	9.9	4.0	3.5
Widowed	8.7	8.5	2.9	2.9
Divorced	30.3	35.3	14.2	13.0
Separated	52.8	39.5	27.7	20.6
Household income[e]				
$9,999 or less	39.7	39.2	18.7	17.7
$10,000–$14,999	36.0	27.7	16.8	12.0
$15,000–$24,999	25.3	25.9	8.4	8.2
$25,000–$34,999	19.7	16.3	8.3	5.5
$35,000–$49,999	19.0	20.5	8.1	7.1
$50,000–$74,999	16.4	16.3	5.4	5.9
$75,000 or more	15.1	12.8	4.7	4.5

*Comparison year.
[a]Includes rape or sexual assault, robbery, aggravated assault, and simple assault. Excludes homicide because the NCVS is based on interviews with victims and therefore cannot measure murder.
[b]In the NCVS, serious violent crime includes rape or sexual assault, robbery, and aggravated assault.
[c]Excludes persons of Hispanic or Latino origin.
[d]Includes American Indian and Alaska Natives; Asian, Native Hawaiian, and other Pacific Islanders; and persons of two or more races.
[e]Household income was imputed for 2014 and 2015.
Note: Victimization rates are per 1,000 persons age 12 or older. NCVS = National Crime Victimization Survey.

SOURCE: Jennifer L. Truman and Rachel E. Morgan, "Table 7. Rate of Violent Victimization, by Victim Demographic Characteristics, 2014 and 2015," in *Criminal Victimizations, 2015*, U.S. Department of Justice, Bureau of Justice Statistics, October 2016, https://www.bjs.gov/content/pub/pdf/cv15.pdf (accessed September 6, 2017)

September 11, 2001, attacks on New York City and the District of Columbia, Muslims, along with people of Middle Eastern or South Asian descent, became the targets of hate crimes, as racially motivated individuals and groups came to associate members of these communities with the activities of terrorist groups such as al-Qaeda.

The Hate Crime Statistics Act of 1990 required the U.S. attorney general to provide the "acquisition and publication of data about crimes that manifest prejudice based on race, religion, homosexuality or heterosexuality, or ethnicity." The Violent Crime and Law Enforcement Act of 1994 amended the Hate Crime Statistics Act to include crimes that are motivated by discrimination against people with physical and/or mental disabilities. For an offense to be considered a hate crime, the law enforcement investigation must reveal sufficient evidence

to lead to the conclusion that the offender's actions were motivated by his or her bias against a certain group. Therefore, data on hate crimes must be considered underreported, as many incidents and offenses that are motivated by bias go uncounted without sufficient evidence concerning this motivation. Although hate crimes can be perpetrated against members of majority groups, most hate crimes are directed at minorities: racial minorities, religious minorities, ethnic minorities, gay and lesbian people, or people with disabilities.

The hate crime data collection program counts one offense for each victim of crimes against people, but only one offense for each distinct crime against property, regardless of the number of victims; therefore, the number of victims is higher than the number of offenses. Of the 6,885 hate-bias offenses reported in 2015, 4,029

TABLE 7.2

Homicide victims by age, sex, race, and ethnicity, 2015

Age	Total	Sex			Race				Ethnicity		
		Male	Female	Unknown	White	Black or African American	Other[a]	Unknown	Hispanic or Latino	Not Hispanic or Latino	Unknown
Total	13,455	10,608	2,818	29	5,854	7,039	366	196	2,028	7,971	2,224
Percent distribution[b]	100.0	78.8	20.9	0.2	43.5	52.3	2.7	1.5	16.6	65.2	18.2
Under 18[c]	1,093	761	329	3	504	544	26	19	193	611	189
Under 22[c]	2,624	2,135	487	2	954	1,598	44	28	488	1,484	443
18 and over[c]	12,228	9,773	2,448	7	5,296	6,451	339	142	1,823	7,305	1,974
Infant (under 1)	168	104	63	1	89	65	8	6	24	104	28
1 to 4	260	153	106	1	130	117	6	7	32	160	58
5 to 8	91	49	42	0	58	30	1	2	12	57	16
9 to 12	56	35	20	1	30	22	3	1	9	30	6
13 to 16	282	218	64	0	110	167	4	1	62	141	49
17 to 19	996	870	126	0	325	647	16	8	191	546	159
20 to 24	2,431	2,102	329	0	764	1,596	45	26	414	1,398	368
25 to 29	2,071	1,733	338	0	717	1,290	48	16	321	1,201	331
30 to 34	1,647	1,340	307	0	650	927	49	21	266	974	254
35 to 39	1,263	1,021	241	1	539	666	45	13	200	728	223
40 to 44	925	701	222	2	467	428	23	7	150	545	158
45 to 49	781	586	194	1	399	330	33	19	118	485	115
50 to 54	737	568	169	0	428	282	17	10	84	468	120
55 to 59	580	425	154	1	363	183	27	7	57	389	102
60 to 64	360	250	109	1	226	114	12	8	36	231	54
65 to 69	235	168	67	0	166	59	6	4	14	168	41
70 to 74	159	93	65	1	113	33	9	4	11	100	33
75 and over	279	118	161	0	226	39	13	1	15	191	48
Unknown	134	74	41	19	54	44	1	35	12	55	61

[a]Includes American Indian or Alaska Native, Asian, and Native Hawaiian or Other Pacific Islander.
[b]Because of rounding, the percentages may not add to 100.0.
[c]Does not include unknown ages.

SOURCE: "Expanded Homicide Data Table 2. Murder Victims by Age, Sex, Race, and Ethnicity 2015," in *Crime in the United States, 2015*, U.S. Department of Justice, Federal Bureau of Investigation, 2016, https://ucr.fbi.gov/crime-in-the-u.s/2015/crime-in-the-u.s.-2015/tables/expanded_homicide_data_table_2_murder_victims_by_age_sex_and_race_2015.xls/output.xls (accessed September 6, 2017)

TABLE 7.3

Race and sex of homicide victims by race and sex of offender, 2015

[Single victim/single offender]

Race/ethnicity of victim	Total	Race of offender				Sex of offender			Ethnicity of offender		
		White	Black or African American	Other*	Unknown	Male	Female	Unknown	Hispanic or Latino	Not Hispanic or Latino	Unknown
White	3,167	2,574	500	49	44	2,817	306	44	633	1,086	1,448
Black or African American	2,664	229	2,380	13	42	2,391	231	42	99	1,135	1,430
Other race[a]	222	60	34	126	2	192	28	2	15	108	99
Unknown race	84	34	20	6	24	49	11	24	4	19	61
Sex of victim											
Male	4,333	1,834	2,299	126	74	3,845	414	74	558	1,682	2,093
Female	1,719	1,029	614	62	14	1,554	151	14	189	647	883
Unknown sex	85	34	21	6	24	50	11	24	4	19	62
Ethnicity of victim											
Hispanic or Latino	757	600	138	9	10	703	44	10	535	180	42
Not Hispanic or Latino	2,360	1,000	1,249	96	15	2,111	234	15	189	2,116	55
Unknown	3,020	1,297	1,547	89	87	2,635	298	87	27	52	2,941

*Includes American Indian or Alaska Native, Asian, and Native Hawaiian or other Pacific Islander.
Note: This table is based on incidents where some information about the offender is known by law enforcement; therefore, when the offender age, sex, race, and ethnicity are all reported as unknown, these data are excluded from the table.

SOURCE: "Expanded Homicide Data Table 6. Murder: Race, Ethnicity, and Sex of Victim by Race, Ethnicity, and Sex of Offender, 2015," in *Crime in the United States, 2015*, U.S. Department of Justice, Federal Bureau of Investigation, 2016, https://ucr.fbi.gov/crime-in-the-u.s/2015/crime-in-the-u.s.2015/tables/expanded_homicide_data_table_6_murder_race_and_sex_of_vicitm_by_race_and_sex_of_offender_2015.xls/output.xls (accessed September 6, 2017)

(58.5%) were motivated by bias against the victim's race, ethnicity, or national origin. (See Table 7.4.) Of these offenses, 2,125 (52.7%) were committed against African Americans, 734 (18.2%) were committed against whites, and 379 (9.4%) were committed against Hispanics. By comparison, as individual groups, Native Americans or Alaskan Natives (137 offenses), Asian Americans (132), Native Hawaiian or Other Pacific Islanders (6), multi-racial individuals (138), and Arabs (47) were targeted in reported hate crimes less than 5% of the time. Of the 5,493 reported hate crime incidents in 2015 for which the offender's race was reported, 2,657 (48.3%) offenders were white and 1,336 (24.3%) were African American. (See Table 7.5.)

Of the hate crime offenses that were perpetrated against African Americans in 2015, 10 were murders, 2 were rapes, 764 were intimidation, 488 were simple assault, and 279 were aggravated assault (an attack intended to produce severe injury, usually involving a weapon). (See

TABLE 7.4

Hate-bias incidents, 2015

Bias motivation	Incidents	Offenses	Victims[a]	Known offenders[b]
Total	**5,850**	**6,885**	**7,173**	**5,493**
Single-bias incidents	**5,818**	**6,837**	**7,121**	**5,475**
Race/ethnicity/ancestry:	**3,310**	**4,029**	**4,216**	**3,196**
Anti-white	613	734	789	681
Anti-black or African American	1,745	2,125	2,201	1,605
Anti-American Indian or Alaska Native	131	137	141	113
Anti-Asian	111	132	136	108
Anti-Native Hawaiian or other Pacific Islander	4	6	6	3
Anti-multiple races, group	113	138	160	83
Anti-Arab	37	47	48	35
Anti-Hispanic or Latino	299	379	392	325
Anti-other race/ethnicity/ancestry	257	331	343	243
Religion:	**1,244**	**1,354**	**1,402**	**809**
Anti-Jewish	664	695	731	387
Anti-Catholic	53	59	60	29
Anti-Protestant	37	47	48	18
Anti-Islamic (Muslim)	257	301	307	228
Anti-other religion	96	104	107	53
Anti-multiple religions, group	51	57	58	30
Anti-Mormon	8	8	8	6
Anti-Jehovah's Witness	1	1	1	0
Anti-Eastern Orthodox (Russian, Greek, other)	48	50	50	36
Anti-other Christian	15	18	18	15
Anti-Buddhist	1	1	1	1
Anti-Hindu	5	5	5	2
Anti-Sikh	6	6	6	4
Anti-atheism/agnosticism/etc.	2	2	2	0
Sexual orientation:	**1,053**	**1,219**	**1,263**	**1,221**
Anti-gay (male)	664	758	786	803
Anti-lesbian	136	168	170	142
Anti-lesbian, gay, bisexual, or transgender (mixed group)	203	235	248	218
Anti-heterosexual	19	23	24	19
Anti-bisexual	31	35	35	39
Disability:	**74**	**88**	**88**	**73**
Anti-physical	43	52	52	40
Anti-mental	31	36	36	33
Gender:	**23**	**29**	**30**	**19**
Anti-male	7	8	8	6
Anti-female	16	21	22	13
Gender identity:	**114**	**118**	**122**	**157**
Anti-transgender	73	75	76	114
Anti-gender non-conforming	41	43	46	43
Multiple-bias incidents[c]	**32**	**48**	**52**	**18**

[a]The term *victim* may refer to a person, business, institution, or society as a whole.
[b]The term *known offender* does not imply that the identity of the suspect is known, but only that an attribute of the suspect has been identified, which distinguishes him/her from an unknown offender.
[c]A *multiple-bias incident* is an incident in which one or more offense types are motivated by two or more biases.

SOURCE: "Table 1. Incidents, Offenses, Victims, and Known Offenders by Bias Motivation, 2015," in *Hate Crime Statistics, 2015*, U.S. Department of Justice, Federal Bureau of Investigation, 2016, https://ucr.fbi.gov/hate-crime/2015/tables-and-data-declarations/1tabledatadecpdf/table_1_incidents_offenses_victims_and_known_offenders_by_bias_motivation_2015.xls/output.xls (accessed September 6, 2017)

TABLE 7.5

Hate crime offenders, by race, ethnicity, and age, 2015

Race/ethnicity/age	Total
Race	**5,493**
White	2,657
Black or African American	1,336
American Indian or Alaska Native	52
Asian	53
Native Hawaiian or other Pacific Islander	4
Group of multiple races[a]	499
Unknown race	892
Ethnicity[b]	**3,421**
Hispanic or Latino	209
Not Hispanic or Latino	882
Group of multiple ethnicities[c]	54
Unknown ethnicity	2,278
Age[b]	**3,331**
Total known offenders 18 and over	2,823
Total known offenders under 18	508

[a]The term *group of multiple races* is used to describe a group of offenders of varying races.
[b]The total number of known offenders by age and the total number of known offenders by ethnicity do not equal the total number of known offenders by race because not all law enforcement agencies report the age and/or ethnicity of the known offender
[c]The term *group of multiple* ethnicities is used to describe a group of offenders of varying ethnicities.
Notes: The term *known offender* does not imply that the identity of the suspect is known, but only that an attribute of the suspect has been identified, which distinguishes him/her from an unknown offender.

SOURCE: "Table 9. Known Offenders: Known Offender's Race, Ethnicity, and Age, 2015," in *Hate Crime Statistics, 2015*, U.S. Department of Justice, Federal Bureau of Investigation, 2016, https://ucr.fbi.gov/hate-crime/2015/tables-and-data-declarations/9tabledatadecpdf/table_9_known_offenders_known_offenders_race_ethnicity_and_age_2015.xls/output.xls (accessed September 6, 2017)

Table 7.6.) Of the offenses that were perpetrated against Hispanics, 116 were intimidation, 98 were simple assault, and 82 were aggravated assault.

The Southern Poverty Law Center (SPLC), a private organization that monitors hate groups and paramilitary organizations nationwide, reports that there were 917 known active hate group chapters in the United States in 2016. (See Figure 7.1.) This figure was down from the all-time high of 1,018 groups in 2011. Still, the 2016 figure was more than double the number of active hate groups known in 1999. These groups included chapters of racist organizations such as the Ku Klux Klan and the Aryan Nation (a particularly violent element of the white supremacist movement), neo-Confederate groups (an alliance of southern heritage organizations that claims allegiance to the antebellum South), and others.

In order to combat hate crimes in the United States, the SPLC developed a law enforcement training program, with the aim of instructing local and state police forces in identifying and neutralizing hate crime groups. At the same time, groups such as the National Crime Prevention Council (2017, http://www.ncpc.org/topics/hate-crime/strategies) have developed educational initiatives designed to increase public awareness of the negative impacts of

racially and ethnically motivated hate crimes on communities. Still, hate crimes remained a persistent problem for U.S. society in 2017.

During the presidential election season of 2016, radical, right-wing, white supremacist groups were galvanized by the Republican nominee, Donald Trump, whose campaign promise to "Make America Great Again" hinged largely on anti-immigrant policy proposals such as building a massive border wall on the U.S.-Mexico border. In "The Year in Hate and Extremism" (February 15, 2017, https://www.splcenter.org/fighting-hate/intelligence-report/2017/year-hate-and-extremism), Mark Potok of the SPLC reports that Trump drew energetic support from white supremacist groups by sanctioning racist ideologies that had long been considered socially unacceptable. Candidate Trump unapologetically characterized Mexican immigrants as drug dealers and rapists, proposed to ban Muslims from entering the United States, and "seemed to encourage violence against black protesters at his rallies, suggesting that he would pay the legal fees of anyone charged as a result." Potok writes, "Trump's run for office electrified the radical right, which saw in him a champion of the idea that America is fundamentally a white man's country."

Potok reports that Trump's election victory in November 2016 was followed by a wave of bias-related incidents of violence, intimidation, and harassment across the country. In the first 34 days following the election, SPLC recorded 1,094 such incidents. Although this surge of incidents eventually subsided, white supremacist groups remained emboldened during the first year of Trump's presidency, asserting their public presence and confronting antiracist opposition at numerous rallies and demonstrations. In August 2017 a rally on the campus of the University of Virginia in Charlottesville descended into a violent street skirmish between the white supremacists and counterprotesters. Although police intervened to disperse the crowd, the day ended in tragedy, when one of the white supremacists drove his car into a crowd of pedestrian counterprotesters, injuring 19 people and killing a 32-year-old woman. In the aftermath of the event, President Trump equivocated on his stance toward the white supremacist groups. In "Trump's Remarks about the Melee in Charlottesville" (ABCNews.com, August 23, 2017), Meghan Keneally and Katherine Faulders report that Trump ultimately "blame[d] both sides of protestors for the conflict, adding that there were 'very fine people' in both the group of white supremacists and white nationalists as well as among the counter-protesters."

Crime at School

Although students are less likely to be victimized at school than they are away from school, any crime at school, especially a violent crime, justifiably horrifies students and the community at large. In *Indicators of*

TABLE 7.6

Hate crimes by bias motivation, 2015

Bias motivation	Total offenses	Murder and nonnegligent manslaughter	Rape[a] (revised definition)	Rape[b] (legacy definition)	Aggravated assault	Simple assault	Intimidation	Other[c]	Robbery	Burglary	Larceny-theft	Motor vehicle theft	Arson	Destruction/ damage/ vandalism	Other[c]	Crimes against society[c]
		Crimes against persons							Crimes against property							
Total	**6,885**	**18**	**12**	**1**	**882**	**1,696**	**1,853**	**20**	**120**	**147**	**255**	**22**	**30**	**1,698**	**66**	**65**
Single-bias incidents	**6,837**	**17**	**12**	**1**	**876**	**1,690**	**1,834**	**20**	**120**	**146**	**253**	**22**	**29**	**1,686**	**66**	**65**
Race/ethnicity/ancestry:	**4,029**	**11**	**4**	**1**	**557**	**967**	**1,258**	**13**	**58**	**81**	**153**	**16**	**14**	**809**	**44**	**43**
Anti-white	734	1	2	1	101	206	165	3	20	25	70	6	3	86	28	17
Anti-black or African American	2,125	10	2	0	279	488	764	3	12	20	27	4	9	489	5	13
Anti-American Indian or Alaska Native	137	0	0	0	8	18	27	1	5	14	28	4	0	22	6	4
Anti-Asian	132	0	0	0	21	32	41	0	2	7	4	2	1	22	0	0
Anti-Native Hawaiian or other Pacific Islander	6	0	0	0	3	1	1	0	0	0	0	0	0	1	0	0
Anti-multiple races, group	138	0	0	0	12	15	34	0	1	3	4	0	0	64	2	3
Anti-Arab	47	0	0	0	2	22	11	0	2	0	0	0	0	10	0	0
Anti-Hispanic or Latino	379	0	0	0	82	98	116	3	15	5	8	0	1	50	1	0
Anti-other race/ethnicity/ancestry	331	0	0	0	49	87	99	3	1	7	12	0	0	65	2	6
Religion:	**1,354**	**4**	**1**	**0**	**68**	**188**	**280**	**1**	**7**	**35**	**60**	**2**	**12**	**678**	**10**	**8**
Anti-Jewish	695	0	0	0	22	78	114	1	1	12	14	0	4	447	2	0
Anti-Catholic	59	0	0	0	1	10	2	0	1	4	5	1	2	30	1	2
Anti-Protestant	47	0	0	0	8	3	4	0	0	2	8	0	1	18	2	1
Anti-Islamic (Muslim)	301	4	0	0	27	64	120	0	4	4	4	0	1	70	0	3
Anti-other religion	104	0	1	0	2	8	28	0	1	6	1	0	3	54	0	0
Anti-multiple religions, group	57	0	0	0	3	7	8	0	0	1	3	0	1	33	0	1
Anti-Mormon	8	0	0	0	0	2	0	0	0	1	3	0	0	1	0	1
Anti-Jehovah's Witness	1	0	0	0	0	0	0	0	0	0	0	0	0	1	0	0
Anti-Eastern Orthodox (Russian, Greek, other)	50	0	0	0	3	10	0	0	0	5	17	1	0	11	3	0
Anti-other Christian	18	0	0	0	1	4	1	0	0	0	3	0	0	7	2	0
Anti-Buddhist	1	0	0	0	0	0	0	0	0	0	0	0	0	1	0	0
Anti-Hindu	5	0	0	0	1	0	0	0	0	0	2	0	0	2	0	0
Anti-Sikh	6	0	0	0	0	2	2	0	0	0	0	0	0	2	0	0
Anti-atheism/agnosticism/etc.	2	0	0	0	0	0	1	0	0	0	0	0	0	1	0	0
Sexual orientation:	**1,219**	**1**	**5**	**0**	**214**	**461**	**253**	**4**	**47**	**22**	**23**	**1**	**3**	**178**	**5**	**2**
Anti-gay (male)	758	1	2	0	140	297	144	2	29	18	8	1	1	112	3	0
Anti-lesbian	168	0	2	0	31	66	38	0	3	3	2	0	0	23	0	0
Anti-lesbian, gay, bisexual, or transgender (mixed group)	235	0	1	0	39	75	58	0	12	1	8	0	2	38	1	0
Anti-heterosexual	23	0	0	0	1	8	5	1	1	0	1	0	0	3	1	2
Anti-bisexual	35	0	0	0	3	15	8	1	2	0	4	0	0	2	0	0
Disability:	**88**	**0**	**0**	**0**	**11**	**27**	**16**	**1**	**2**	**1**	**6**	**1**	**0**	**14**	**4**	**5**
Anti-physical	52	0	0	0	6	17	10	0	2	1	2	1	0	9	0	4
Anti-mental	36	0	0	0	5	10	6	1	0	0	4	0	0	5	4	1
Gender:	**29**	**0**	**1**	**0**	**4**	**11**	**8**	**0**	**0**	**0**	**2**	**1**	**0**	**2**	**0**	**0**
Anti-male	8	0	0	0	0	3	3	0	0	0	2	0	0	0	0	0
Anti-female	21	0	1	0	4	8	5	0	0	0	0	1	0	2	0	0
Gender identity:	**118**	**1**	**1**	**0**	**22**	**36**	**19**	**1**	**6**	**7**	**9**	**1**	**0**	**5**	**3**	**7**
Anti-transgender	75	1	1	0	15	27	15	1	5	1	4	0	0	4	0	1
Anti-gender non-conforming	43	0	0	0	7	9	4	0	1	6	5	1	0	1	3	6
Multiple-bias incidents[d]	**48**	**1**	**0**	**0**	**6**	**6**	**19**	**0**	**0**	**1**	**2**	**0**	**1**	**12**	**0**	**0**

TABLE 7.6

Hate crimes by bias motivation, 2015 [CONTINUED]

[a]The figures shown in the rape (revised definition) column include only those reported by law enforcement agencies that used the revised Uniform Crime Reporting (UCR) definition of rape.
[b]The figures shown in the rape (legacy definition) column include only those reported by law enforcement agencies that used the legacy UCR definition of rape.
[c]Includes additional offenses collected in the National Incident-Based Reporting System.
[d]A *multiple-bias incident* is an incident in which one or more offense types are motivated by two or more biases.

SOURCE: "Table 4. Offenses: Offense Type by Bias Motivation, 2015," in *Hate Crime Statistics, 2015*, U.S. Department of Justice, Federal Bureau of Investigation, 2016, https://ucr.fbi.gov/hate-crime/2015/tables-and-data-declarations/4tabledatadecpdf/table_4_offenses_offense_type_by_bias_motivation_2015.xls/output.xls (accessed September 6, 2017)

FIGURE 7.1

Hate groups in the United States, 1999–2016

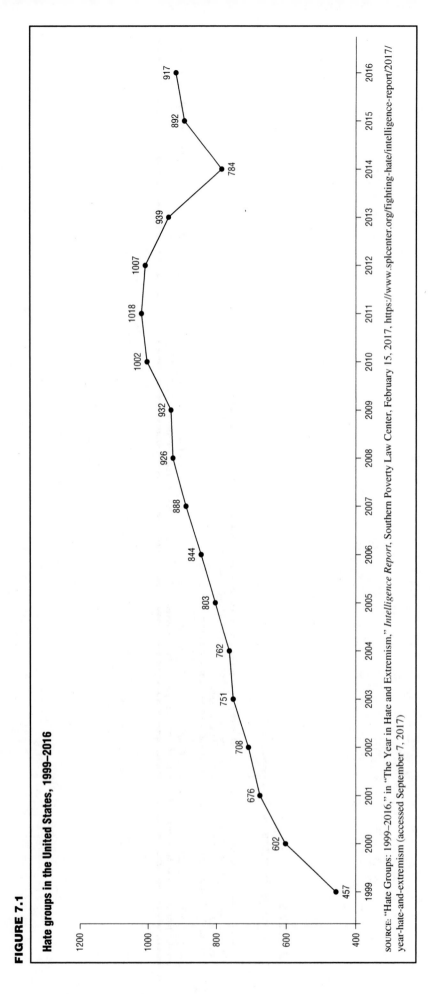

SOURCE: "Hate Groups: 1999–2016," in "The Year in Hate and Extremism," *Intelligence Report*, Southern Poverty Law Center, February 15, 2017, https://www.splcenter.org/fighting-hate/intelligence-report/2017/year-hate-and-extremism (accessed September 7, 2017)

School Crime and Safety: 2017 (May 2017, https://nces.ed.gov/pubs2017/2017064.pdf), Lauren Musu-Gillette et al. state that "any instance of crime or violence at school not only affects the individuals involved, but also may disrupt the educational process and affect bystanders, the school itself, and the surrounding community."

Musu-Gillette et al. find that the rate of crimes per 1,000 students in 2015 was nearly the same among African Americans (29.8 per 1,000) and Hispanics (30 per 1,000). These rates were lower than among white students (34.3 per 1,000). (See Table 7.7.) However, African American and Hispanic students were much more likely than other groups to report that gangs were present at school in 2015. (See Figure 7.2.) Indeed, 17.1% of African American students and 15.3% of Hispanic students reported that gangs were present at school, compared with 7.4% of white students and 4.1% of Asian American students.

Drugs are another serious problem at school, with somewhat higher prevalence among certain minority groups. Pacific Islanders (30.1%) were the most likely to have access to drugs on school property during the previous 12 months, followed by Hispanics (27.2%), multiracial students (24.7%), and African Americans (20.6%). Native Americans and Alaskan Native students (19.8%) and white students (19.8%) reported access to drugs on campus at the same rates; Asian American students (15.3%) were the least likely to report having access to drugs at school. (See Figure 7.3.)

TABLE 7.7

Number of student-reported nonfatal crimes against students aged 12–18 and rate of crimes per 1,000 students at school, by type of crime and selected characteristics, 2015

Location and student characteristic	Number of nonfatal victimizations				Rate of victimization per 1,000 students			
			Violent				Violent	
	Total	Theft	All violent	Serious violent[a]	Total	Theft	All violent	Serious violent[a]
At school[b]								
Total	841,100	309,100	531,900	99,000	32.9	12.1	20.8	3.9
Sex								
Male	407,200	152,200	255,000	62,800	30.9	11.6	19.4	4.8
Female	433,800	157,000	276,900	36,300	34.9	12.6	22.3	2.9
Age								
12–14	501,500	123,800	377,700	61,200	41.3	10.2	31.1	5.0
15–18	339,600	185,300	154,300	37,900!	25.3	13.8	11.5	2.8!
Race/ethnicity[c]								
White	462,900	175,000	287,900	45,900	34.3	13.0	21.3	3.4
Black	107,100	25,400	81,700	15,700!	29.8	7.1	22.7	4.4!
Hispanic	191,800	80,600	111,200	29,000!	30.0	12.6	17.4	4.5!
Other	79,200	28,100	51,100	8,400!	38.2	13.5	24.7	4.1!
Urbanicity[d]								
Urban	272,300	109,100	163,200	26,300!	35.3	14.2	21.2	3.4!
Suburban	499,100	169,000	330,100	67,600	35.9	12.1	23.7	4.9
Rural	69,600	31,000	38,600!	5,200!	17.6	7.8	9.7!	1.3!
Household income[e]								
Less than $15,000	90,000	42,600	47,300	9,400!	36.6	17.3	19.2	3.8!
$15,000–29,999	166,700	44,800	121,900	11,100!	40.3	10.8	29.5	2.7!
$30,000–49,999	150,100	63,200	86,900	18,900!	28.3	11.9	16.4	3.6!
$50,000–74,999	153,600	43,200	110,400	27,100!	36.1	10.1	25.9	6.4!
$75,000 or more	280,600	115,300	165,300	32,500	29.8	12.2	17.5	3.5
Not reported								

!Interpret data with caution. Estimate based on 10 or fewer sample cases, or the coefficient of variation is greater than 50 percent.

[a]Serious violent victimization is also included in all violent victimization.

[b]"At school" includes inside the school building, on school property, and on the way to and from school.

[c]Race categories exclude persons of Hispanic ethnicity. "Other" includes Asians, Pacific Islanders, American Indians/Alaska Natives, and persons of two or more races.

[d]Refers to the Standard Metropolitan Statistical Area (MSA) status of the respondent's household as defined by the U.S. Census Bureau. Categories include "central city of an MSA (urban)," "in MSA but not in central city (suburban)," and "not MSA (rural)."

[e]Income data for 2015 were imputed. Estimates may not be comparable to previous years.

Note: "Serious violent victimization" includes the crimes of rape, sexual assault, robbery, and aggravated assault. "All violent victimization" includes serious violent crimes as well as simple assault. "Theft" includes attempted and completed purse-snatching, completed pickpocketing, and all attempted and completed thefts, with the exception of motor vehicle thefts. Theft does not include robbery, which involves the threat or use of force and is classified as a violent crime. "Total victimization" includes theft and violent crimes. Date in this table are from the National Crime Victimization Survey (NCVS) and are reported in accordance with Bureau of Justice Statistics standards. Detail may not sum to totals because of rounding and missing data on student characteristics. The population size for students ages 12–18 was 25,581,700 in 2015.

SOURCE: Adapted from Lauren Musu-Gillette et al., "Table 2.2. Number of Nonfatal Victimizations against Students Ages 12–18 and Rate of Victimizations per 1,000 Students, by Type of Victimization, Location, and Selected Student Characteristics: 2015," in *Indicators of School Crime and Safety: 2016*, U.S. Department of Education, National Center for Education Statistics and U.S. Department of Justice, Bureau of Justice Statistics, Office of Justice Programs, May 2017, https://nces.ed.gov/pubs2017/2017064.pdf (accessed September 7, 2017)

FIGURE 7.2

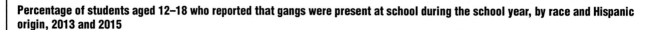

Percentage of students aged 12–18 who reported that gangs were present at school during the school year, by race and Hispanic origin, 2013 and 2015

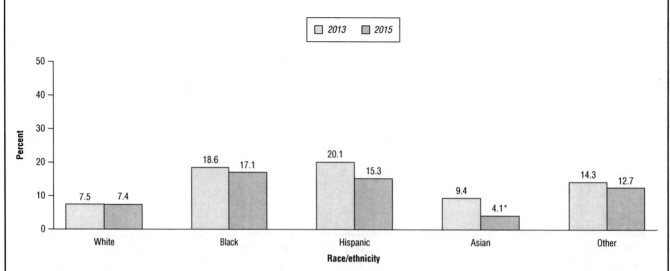

*Interpret data with caution. The coefficient of variation (CV) for this estimate is between 30 and 50 percent.

Note: Race categories exclude persons of Hispanic ethnicity. "Other" includes American Indians/Alaska Natives, Pacific Islanders, and persons of two or more races. All gangs, whether or not they are involved in violent or illegal activity, are included. "At school" includes in the school building, on school property, on a school bus, and going to and from school.

SOURCE: Lauren Musu-Gillette et al., "Figure 8.2. Percentage of Students Ages 12–18 Who Reported That Gangs Were Present at School during the School Year, by Race/Ethnicity: 2013 and 2015," in *Indicators of School Crime and Safety: 2016*, U.S. Department of Education, National Center for Education Statistics and U.S. Department of Justice, Bureau of Justice Statistics, Office of Justice Programs, May 2017, https://nces.ed.gov/pubs2017/2017064.pdf (accessed September 7, 2017)

FIGURE 7.3

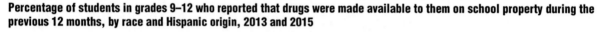

Percentage of students in grades 9–12 who reported that drugs were made available to them on school property during the previous 12 months, by race and Hispanic origin, 2013 and 2015

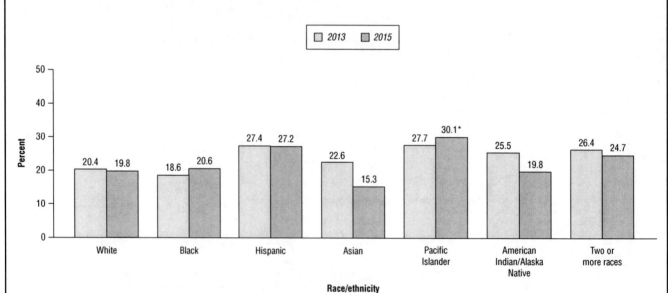

*Interpret data with caution. The coefficient of variation (CV) for this estimate is between 30 and 50 percent.

Note: "On school property" was not defined for survey respondents. Race categories exclude persons of Hispanic ethnicity.

SOURCE: Lauren Musu-Gillette et al., "Figure 9.2. Percentage of Students in Grades 9–12 Who Reported That Illegal Drugs Were Made Available to Them on School Property during the Previous 12 Months, by Race/Ethnicity: 2013 and 2015," in *Indicators of School Crime and Safety: 2016*, U.S. Department of Education, National Center for Education Statistics and U.S. Department of Justice, Bureau of Justice Statistics, Office of Justice Programs, May 2017, https://nces.ed.gov/pubs2017/2017064.pdf (accessed September 7, 2017)

Minority students may also be the target of hate-related words and see hate-related graffiti at school. In 2015 students were asked if someone at school had called them a derogatory word having to do with their race, ethnicity, religion, gender, sexual orientation, or disability and if they had seen any hate-inspired graffiti during the school year. Overall, 7.2% of students reported being the target of hate-related words, including 10.8% of Asian American students, 9.4% of African Americans, 6.5% of Hispanics, and 6.3% of whites. (See Figure 7.4.)

Racial Profiling

Racial profiling refers to the practice of using race or ethnicity to identify suspects who might be violating the law. People who engage in racial profiling rely on certain stereotypes (e.g., an ingrained belief that young African American males are more likely than young white males to be drug dealers) to make assumptions about a certain individual or group. Although racial profiling may occur throughout society, it is most associated with law enforcement. One of the most notable instances of racial profiling concerns New York City's controversial stop-and-frisk procedure, in which police officers acting on any suspicion may temporarily detain and question civilians on the street, often frisking (or searching) them for weapons or contraband. The policy was introduced to the New York Police Department in the early 1990s and was strongly endorsed by mayors Rudolph Giuliani (1946–) and Michael Bloomberg (1942–), who governed the city from 1994 to 2001, and from 2001 to 2013, respectively. Stop-and-frisk policy came under intense scrutiny in the early 21st century, when civil rights advocates began to accuse law enforcement of using racial profiling when engaging in stop-and-frisk actions.

The New York chapter of the American Civil Liberties Union (ACLU) reports in "Stop-and-Frisk Data" (2017, https://www.nyclu.org/en/stop-and-frisk-data) that NYPD stop-and-frisk actions reached their height in 2011, when 685,724 people were detained by law enforcement. Of these individuals, 53% were black, 34% were Hispanic, and 9% were white. Joseph Goldstein writes in "Judge Rejects New York's Stop-and-Frisk Policy" (NYTimes.com, August 12, 2013) that in August 2013 a federal judge ruled that the law "violated the constitutional rights of minorities in the city." The number of NYPD stops and street interrogations declined dramatically following the ruling, with only 12,404 such actions in 2016. Despite the lower frequency, however, there was almost no change in the racial/ethnic proportions of those stopped. In 2016, 52% of individuals stopped by police in New York City were black, 29% were Hispanic, and 10% were white.

In "Ending New York's Stop-and-Frisk Did Not Increase Crime" (April 11, 2016, https://www.brennan center.org/blog/ending-new-yorks-stop-and-frisk-did-not-increase-crime), James Cullen of the Brennan Center for Justice at New York University School of Law finds that crime in New York City did not increase after the NYPD officially discontinued stop-and-frisk policing in January 2014. "Statistically," Cullen concludes, "no relationship between stop-and-frisk and crime seems apparent."

MINORITIES AS OFFENDERS

African Americans (particularly males) commit a higher number of offenses as a proportion of the population than do other groups. Table 7.8 shows murder offenders by age, sex, and race in 2015. During that year 5,620 (36.7%) of 15,326 known murderers were African American. Of the 5,620 known African American murderers, 412 (7.3%) were under the age of 18 years and 1,638 (29.1%) were under the age of 22 years.

In *Homicide Trends in the United States, 1980–2008* (November 2011, https://www.bjs.gov/content/pub/pdf/htus8008.pdf), the most recent study of its kind, Alexia Cooper and Erica L. Smith of the BJS report that the circumstances under which African American and white homicide offenders commit their crimes vary by race. African American offenders are more likely than offenders of other races to commit homicides related to illegal drug activity. Between 1980 and 2008, 65.6% of homicide offenders who had committed their crimes under drug-related circumstances were African American. A high proportion of felony murders (deaths that occur during violent crimes such as burglary, sexual assault, or robbery) between these years were committed by African Americans (59.9%) as well. By contrast, white offenders committed a greater proportion of workplace murders (70.8%), sex-related murders (54.4%), and gang-related murders (53.3%). African American offenders committed the majority of homicides using guns (56.9%), and whites committed the majority of murders using arson (55.6%) and poison (80.6%).

MINORITIES IN PRISONS AND JAILS

In December 2015 there were more non-Hispanic African American males than non-Hispanic white or Hispanic males in state and federal prisons. Out of a total of 1.5 million incarcerated males in the United States, 501,300 were non-Hispanic African American, 446,700 were non-Hispanic white, and 301,500 were Hispanic. Non-Hispanic African American female prisoners (21,700) in 2015, by contrast, did not outnumber their non-Hispanic white counterparts (52,700). (See Table 7.9.)

The rate of incarceration for non-Hispanic African American males greatly exceeds the rates for non-Hispanic white and Hispanic males. In December 2015 the incarceration rate for non-Hispanic African American males was 2,613 inmates per 100,000 U.S. residents in that racial group. (See Table 7.10.) This was nearly six times

FIGURE 7.4

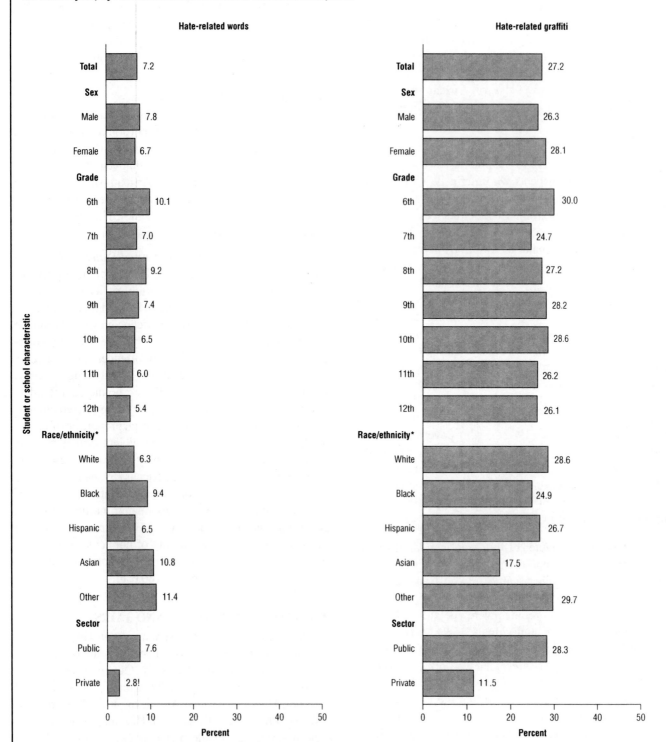

Percentage of students aged 12–18 who reported being targets of hate-related words and seeing hate-related graffiti at school during the school year, by selected student and school characteristics, 2015

!Interpret data with caution. The coefficient of variation (CV) for this estimate is between 30 and 50 percent.
*Race categories exclude persons of Hispanic ethnicity. "Other" includes American Indians/Alaska Natives, Pacific Islanders, and persons of two or more races.
Note: "At school" includes in the school building, on school property, on a school bus, and going to and from school. "Hate-related" refers to derogatory terms used by others in reference to students' personal characteristics.

SOURCE: Lauren Musu-Gillette et al., "Figure 10.1. Percentage of Students Ages 12–18 Who Reported Being the Target of Hate-Related Words and Seeing Hate-Related Graffiti at School during the School Year, by Selected Student and School Characteristics: 2015," in *Indicators of School Crime and Safety: 2016*, U.S. Department of Education, National Center for Education Statistics and U.S. Department of Justice, Bureau of Justice Statistics, Office of Justice Programs, May 2017, https://nces.ed.gov/pubs2017/2017064.pdf (accessed September 7, 2017)

TABLE 7.8

Murder offenders by age, sex, race, and Hispanic origin, 2015

Age	Total	Sex			Race				Ethnicity[a]		
		Male	Female	Unknown	White	Black or African American	Other[b]	Unknown	Hispanic or Latino	Not Hispanic or Latino	Unknown
Total	**15,326**	**9,553**	**1,180**	**4,593**	**4,636**	**5,620**	**283**	**4,787**	**1,312**	**4,598**	**4,408**
Percent distribution[c]	100.0	62.3	7.7	30.0	30.2	36.7	1.8	31.2	12.7	44.6	42.7
Under 18[d]	667	616	51	0	236	412	14	5	104	269	91
Under 22[d]	2,648	2,403	239	6	916	1,638	69	25	404	1,108	322
18 and over[d]	9,456	8,327	1,109	20	4,324	4,755	268	109	1,183	4,125	1,169
Infant (under 1)	0	0	0	0	0	0	0	0	0	0	0
1 to 4	1	1	0	0	0	1	0	0	0	0	0
5 to 8	2	1	1	0	1	1	0	0	0	0	1
9 to 12	9	8	1	0	4	5	0	0	2	2	2
13 to 16	341	320	21	0	119	210	9	3	54	147	44
17 to 19	1,263	1,143	119	1	442	784	28	9	193	527	156
20 to 24	2,448	2,180	262	6	844	1,513	66	25	330	1,030	273
25 to 29	1,814	1,607	204	3	739	997	52	26	214	756	244
30 to 34	1,251	1,082	165	4	610	584	40	17	175	509	173
35 to 39	840	733	107	0	449	368	17	6	104	382	115
40 to 44	594	506	88	0	350	223	17	4	79	269	69
45 to 49	449	384	63	2	251	175	20	3	47	200	56
50 to 54	453	390	60	3	295	128	16	14	46	225	46
55 to 59	278	248	29	1	174	94	9	1	23	148	30
60 to 64	149	136	13	0	103	41	1	4	5	74	23
65 to 69	88	77	11	0	60	27	0	1	7	44	12
70 to 74	52	42	10	0	37	10	4	1	3	32	7
75 and over	91	85	6	0	82	6	3	0	5	49	9
Unknown	5,203	610	20	4,573	76	453	1	4,673	25	204	3,148

[a]Not all agencies provide ethnicity data; therefore, the race and ethnicity totals will not equal.
[b]Includes American Indian or Alaska Native, Asian, and Native Hawaiian or other Pacific Islander.
[c]Because of rounding, the percentages may not add to 100.0.
[d]Does not include unknown ages.

SOURCE: Expanded Homicide Data Table 3. Murder Offenders by Age, Sex, Race, and Ethnicity 2015, in *Crime in the United States, 2015*, U.S. Department of Justice, Federal Bureau of Investigation, 2016, https://ucr.fbi.gov/crime-in-the-u.s/2015/crime-in-the-u.s.-2015/tables/expanded_homicide_data_table_3_murder_offenders_by_age_sex_and_race_2015.xls/output.xls (accessed September 6, 2017)

TABLE 7.9

Percentages of sentenced prisoners under state and federal jurisdiction, by sex, race, Hispanic origin, and age, December 31, 2015

Age group	Total[a]	Male					Female				
		All males[a]	White[b]	Black[b]	Hispanic	Other[b]	All females[a]	White[b]	Black[b]	Hispanic	Other[b]
Total[c]	**100%**	**100%**	**100%**	**100%**	**100%**	**100%**	**100%**	**100%**	**100%**	**100%**	**100%**
18–19	0.8	0.8	0.5	1.2	1.0	1.1	0.5	0.4	0.9	0.6	0.8
20–24	10.5	10.6	7.7	12.5	11.9	12.7	9.2	8.0	11.5	11.2	10.2
25–29	15.6	15.4	13.3	16.3	17.3	16.2	17.8	17.5	17.5	20.1	18.1
30–34	16.5	16.3	15.4	15.9	18.3	17.3	19.0	19.0	17.1	20.7	19.7
35–39	14.6	14.6	13.7	14.5	16.1	15.0	15.2	15.6	13.8	16.2	15.7
40–44	12.1	12.1	12.2	11.8	12.4	12.6	12.5	13.1	12.4	11.7	12.6
45–49	10.3	10.3	11.6	9.9	9.0	9.5	10.5	10.6	11.5	8.9	10.2
50–54	8.6	8.7	10.6	8.4	6.5	7.1	7.9	8.3	8.3	5.6	7.1
55–59	5.4	5.5	7.0	5.2	3.7	4.3	4.1	4.4	4.6	2.8	3.1
60–64	2.8	2.9	3.9	2.5	2.0	2.2	1.8	2.1	1.8	1.1	1.6
65 or older	2.4	2.5	4.1	1.5	1.6	2.0	1.2	1.5	0.9	0.6	0.8
Number of sentenced prisoners[d]	**1,476,847**	**1,371,879**	**446,700**	**501,300**	**301,500**	**122,400**	**104,968**	**52,700**	**21,700**	**17,900**	**12,700**

[a]Includes American Indians and Alaska Natives; Asians, Native Hawaiians, and other Pacific Islanders; and persons of two or more races.
[b]Excludes persons of Hispanic or Latino origin.
[c]Includes persons age 17 or younger.
[d]Race and Hispanic origina totals are rounded to the nearest 100 to accommodate differences in data collection techniques between jurisdictions.
Note: Jurisdiction refers to the legal authority of state or federal correctional officials over a prisoner, regardless of where the prisoner is held. Counts are based on prisoners with sentences of more than 1 year. Federal data include prisoners held in nonsecure, privately operated community corrections facilities and juveniles held in contract facilities. Includes imputed counts for Nevada and Oregon, which did not submit 2015 data to National Prisoner Statistics.

SOURCE: E. Ann Carson and Elizabeth Anderson, "Table 8. Percent of Sentenced Prisoners under the Jurisdiction of State or Federal Correctional Authorities, by Age, Sex, Race, and Hispanic Origin, December 31, 2015," in *Prisoners in 2015*, U.S. Department of Justice, Bureau of Justice Statistics, December 2016, https://www.bjs.gov/content/pub/pdf/p15.pdf (accessed September 7, 2017)

TABLE 7.10

Estimated rate of sentenced prisoners under state and federal jurisdiction, per 100,000 U.S. residents, by sex, race, Hispanic origin, and age, December 31, 2015

Age group	Total[a]	Male					Female				
		All male[a]	White[b]	Black[b]	Hispanic	Other[a, b]	All female[a]	White[b]	Black[b]	Hispanic	Other[a, b]
Total[c]	458	863	457	2,613	1,043	929	64	52	103	63	90
18–19	141	265	90	970	306	332	12	7	29	14	16
20–24	687	1,254	543	3,700	1,443	1,452	89	70	149	85	124
25–29	1,015	1,837	921	5,165	2,165	1,808	167	147	236	166	205
30–34	1,122	2,050	1,101	5,948	2,365	2,085	184	164	255	175	226
35–39	1,047	1,941	1,031	5,802	2,182	1,998	155	140	215	139	195
40–44	896	1,674	939	5,006	1,864	1,736	131	120	199	105	163
45–49	725	1,358	793	4,084	1,508	1,441	104	85	180	89	138
50–54	577	1,098	647	3,331	1,267	1,160	74	59	128	66	104
55–59	365	711	413	2,199	918	781	38	29	69	41	54
60–64	215	428	253	1,300	654	475	19	15	39	21	28
65 or older	74	161	109	440	288	201	5	4	7	7	5
Number of sentenced prisoners[d]	1,476,847	1,371,879	446,700	501,300	301,500	122,400	104,968	52,700	21,700	17,900	12,700

[a]Includes American Indians and Alaska Natives; Asians, Native Hawaiians, and other Pacific Islanders; and persons of two or more races.
[b]Excludes persons of Hispanic or Latino orgin.
[c]Includes persons age 17 or younger.
[d]Race and Hispanic origina totals are rounded to the nearest 100 to accommodate differences in data collection techniques between jurisdictions.
Note: Jurisdiction refers to the legal authority of state or federal correctional officials over a prisoner, regardless of where the prisoner is held. Counts are based on prisoners with sentences of more than 1 year. Federal data include prisoners held in nonsecure, privately operated community corrections facilities and juveniles held in contract facilities. Imprisonment rate is the number of prisoners under state or federal jurisdiction with a sentence of more than 1 year per 100,000 U.S. residents of corresponding sex, age, and race or Hispanic origin. Resident population estimates are from the U.S. Census Bureau for January 2, 2016. Includes imputed counts for Nevada and Oregon, which did not submit 2015 data to National Prisoner Statistics.

SOURCE: E. Ann Carson and Elizabeth Anderson, "Appendix Table A4. Imprisonment Rate of Sentenced Prisoners under the Jurisdiction of State or Federal Correctional Authorities per 100,000 U.S. Residents, by Demographic Characteristics December 31, 2015," in *Prisoners in 2015*, U.S. Department of Justice, Bureau of Justice Statistics, December 2016, https://www.bjs.gov/content/pub/pdf/p15.pdf (accessed September 7, 2017)

the rate of incarceration for non-Hispanic whites, among whom there were 457 inmates for every 100,000 residents in that group during the same period. Among Hispanic men there were 1,043 inmates for every 100,000 residents of that group.

Although non-Hispanic white women (52,700) outnumbered non-Hispanic African American women (21,700) in federal and state prisons in December 2015, non-Hispanic African American women (103 inmates per 100,000 U.S. residents in that group) were incarcerated at nearly twice the rate of non-Hispanic white women (52 per 100,000). (See Table 7.10.) In that year, there were 17,900 Hispanic women in state and federal prisons; they too were incarcerated at a much lower rate (63 per 100,000) than African American women.

In *Created Equal: Racial and Ethnic Disparities in the U.S. Justice System* (March 2009, http://www.nccd global.org/sites/default/files/publication_pdf/created-equal .pdf), a widely cited report from the National Council on Crime and Delinquency, Christopher Hartney and Linh Vuong discuss the overrepresentation of minorities among the ranks of offenders in the criminal justice system. According to Hartney and Vuong, African Americans are 2.5 times more likely than whites to be arrested, and Native Americans and Alaskan Natives are 1.5 times more likely than whites to be arrested.

Discrepancies in incarceration rates were even more pronounced. African Americans were six times more likely than whites to be held in state jails. Native Americans and Alaskan Natives were twice as likely as whites to be imprisoned, and Hispanics were 1.5 times as likely to do jail time as whites. Hartney and Vuong note that factors such as mandatory sentencing guidelines, law enforcement tactics and initiatives, and "get tough on crime" policies have the potential to result in an "inordinate focus on certain geographical areas, socioeconomic classes, or racial and ethnic groups." At the same time, Hartney and Vuong identify several long-term negative effects of criminal records and incarceration on minority groups, including reduced employment opportunities and lower wages, disenfranchisement, higher incidences of family strife, and higher likelihood of physical and mental health problems.

According to the Sentencing Project (2017, http://www.sentencingproject.org/criminal-justice-facts/), an advocacy group dedicated to prison reform, approximately 1 out of every 3 African American men was likely to do prison time in the United States, compared with 1 out of 6 Hispanic men, and 1 out of 17 white men. Similar discrepancies existed within the female population, with 1 out of 18 African American women, 1 out of 45 Hispanic women, and 1 out of 111 white women likely to go to prison. Overall, the Sentencing Project reports that people of color made up 37% of the U.S. population in 2017, but they were 67% of the U.S. prison population.

Discrepancies in arrest and incarceration rates are also found at the level of juvenile crime. In *Racial Disparities in Youth Commitments and Arrests* (April 1, 2016, http://www.sentencingproject.org/wp-content/uploads/2016/04/Racial-Disparities-in-Youth-Commitments-and-Arrests.pdf), Joshua Rovner of the Sentencing Project reports that as of 2013, African American juveniles were 2.3 times as likely to be arrested as white juveniles for all delinquent offenses. Furthermore, African American juveniles were more than four times as likely as white juveniles to be committed to juvenile detention facilities. Meanwhile, Native American juveniles were more than three times as likely to be committed as whites, and Hispanic juveniles were 61% more likely.

Racial Disparities in Sentencing

In 1984 the U.S. Sentencing Commission (USSC) set forth sentencing guidelines in the Sentencing Reform Act of 1984, which was designed to implement uniform sentencing practices that would eliminate disparities based on race. In November 2004 the USSC released *Fifteen Years of Guidelines Sentencing: An Assessment of How Well the Federal Criminal Justice System Is Achieving the Goals of Sentencing Reform* (http://cdn.ca9.uscourts.gov/datastore/library/2013/02/26/Henderson_15Year.pdf), which evaluated the effectiveness of these practices. The USSC concludes that remaining disparity in sentencing is the result of sentencing rules and charging practices that have "institutionalized" disparity. In fact, variables such as mandatory minimums and plea bargaining have had "a greater adverse impact on Black offenders than did the factors taken into account by judges in the discretionary system ... prior to [the] guidelines implementation."

Bill Quigley reports in "18 Examples of Racism in the Criminal Legal System" (HuffingtonPost.com, October 3, 2016) that "African American men were sentenced to 19 percent longer time periods in federal courts across the U.S. than white men convicted of similar crimes in a 4-year study conducted by the U.S. Sentencing Commission." In addition, he reports, federal prosecutors are nearly twice as likely to file charges carrying mandatory minimum sentences for blacks than for whites accused of the same crimes. Among all U.S. prisoners serving life sentences for nonviolent offenses in 2016, Quigley notes, nearly two-thirds (65%) were African American.

Part of this discrepancy can be attributed to drug enforcement policies that target minority communities. For example, federal sentencing guidelines for powder and crack cocaine offenses, which made penalties for crack possession far more severe than for a comparable amount of powder cocaine, had a disproportionate impact on minorities. Quigley notes that studies show that blacks and whites used drugs at roughly the same rates, but blacks are arrested for drugs at a rate more than twice their percentage in the U.S. population, accounting for 29% of all drug arrests. Furthermore, although marijuana use is comparable between black and white communities, blacks are 3.73 times as likely as whites to be arrested for marijuana possession. Citing BJS data, Quigley reports that African Americans and Hispanics accounted for 68% of all state prison inmates serving sentences for drug offenses, whereas whites accounted for 32%.

In order to remedy drug-related sentencing imbalances, President Barack Obama (1961–) signed the Fair Sentencing Act of 2010, which eliminated five-year mandatory minimum sentences for crack cocaine possession, while also reducing the ratio of powder cocaine to crack cocaine used to determine penalties from 100:1 to 18:1. In the ensuing years, additional measures were taken to address the problem of overrepresentation of minorities serving prison time for drug offenses. For example, in April 2014 the USSC voted to significantly reduce sentencing guideline ranges for nonviolent drug crimes and to apply the change retroactively to those already serving prison sentences. In "Changes Lead to Shorter Sentences for 26,000 Drug Defendants" (CBSNews.com, April 14, 2016), CBS News reports that, two years after the USSC decision, 26,000 federal drug offenders had received shorter prison terms, with sentences being cut by an average of two years.

Native Americans in Jail

Todd D. Minton of the BJS reports in *Jails in Indian Country, 2015* (November 10, 2016, https://www.bjs.gov/content/pub/pdf/jic15.pdf) that at midyear 2015, 2,510 inmates were confined in 76 jails, detention centers, and other correctional facilities operated on Native American reservations by tribal authorities or the Bureau of Indian Affairs. The number of inmates in 2015 represented a 5.5% increase over the year before, when 2,380 inmates were serving time in 79 Native American facilities.

Minton reports that most inmates of Native American country jails were male; at midyear 2015, 25% of those being held were female, and 75% were male. About 10% of those being held were juveniles. Of these inmates, roughly one-third (32%) were serving time for violent offenses: 13% for domestic violence, 10% for aggravated or simple assault, 2% for sexual assault or rape, and 6% for other acts of violence.

Parole and Probation

Although African Americans account for the largest proportion of prison and jail inmates, they are outnumbered by whites in the nation's parole system. The parole system grants inmates early release from prison with fewer rights than the general population and under monitored conditions. In 2015 non-Hispanic African Americans accounted for 38% of individuals on parole, compared with 44% who were non-Hispanic white, and 16% who were Hispanic. (See Table 7.11.)

The proportion of non-Hispanic whites on probation, a system in which people who are convicted of a crime are under supervision by a probation officer rather than incarcerated, is disproportionate to their representation in the criminal justice system overall. At year-end 2015, non-Hispanic whites made up 55% of probationers (see Table 7.12), whereas the proportion of non-Hispanic whites among the prison and jail population, at 33%, was significantly lower. By comparison, 30% of probationers at year-end 2015 were non-Hispanic African American, whereas 36.5% of inmates were non-Hispanic African American, and 13% of probationers were Hispanic, whereas 22% of inmates were Hispanic. These numbers suggest that non-Hispanic white offenders were more likely than minority offenders to receive the more lenient sentence of probation.

Minorities on Death Row

Tracy L. Snell of the BJS reports in *Capital Punishment, 2013—Statistical Tables* (December 2014, https://www.bjs.gov/content/pub/pdf/cp13st.pdf) that at year-end 2013, 2,979 state and federal prisoners were incarcerated under the sentence of death. (See Table 7.13.) Non-Hispanic whites (1,663 prisoners) made up 55.8% and non-Hispanic African Americans (1,248) made up 41.9% of all death-row prisoners. Only 2.3% were of other races. Of those sentenced to death row in 2013, 49 (59%) were non-Hispanic white, and 33 (39.8%) were non-Hispanic African American. (See Table 7.13.)

TABLE 7.11

Characteristics of adults on parole, 2005, 2014, and 2015

Characteristic	2005	2014	2015
Sex	**100%**	**100%**	**100%**
Male	88	88	87
Female	12	1	13
Race/Hispanic origin[a]	**100%**	**100%**	**100%**
White	41	43	44
Black/African American	40	39	38
Hispanic/Latino	18	16	16
American Indian/Alaska Native	1	1	1
Asian/Native Hawaiian/other Pacific Islander	1	1	1
Two or more races	0	c	c
Status of supervision	**100%**	**100%**	**100%**
Active	83	84	83
Inactive	4	5	5
Absconder	7	6	6
Supervised out of state	4	4	4
Financial conditions remaining	d	0	0
Other	2	2	3
Maximum sentence to incarceration	**100%**	**100%**	**100%**
Less than 1 year	3	6	6
1 year or more	97	94	94
Most serious offense	**100%**	**100%**	**100%**
Violent	26%	31%	32%
Sex offense	d	7	8
Other violent	d	24	24
Property	24%	22%	21%
Drug	37%	31%	31%
Weapon	d	4%	4%
Other[b]	13%	12%	13%

[a]Excludes persons of Hispanic or Latino origin, unless specified.
[b]Includes public order offenses.
[c]Less than 0.05%.
[d]Not available.
Note: Detail may not sum to total due to rounding. Estimates based on most recent data and may differ from previously published statistics. Characteristics based on parolees with known types of status.

SOURCE: Danielle Kaeble and Thomas P. Bonczar, "Table 6. Characteristics of Adults on Parole, 2005, 2014, and 2015," in *Probation and Parole in the United States, 2015*, U.S. Department of Justice, Bureau of Justice Statistics, December 2016, https://www.bjs.gov/content/pub/pdf/ppus15.pdf (accessed September 7, 2017)

TABLE 7.12

Characteristics of adults on probation, 2005, 2014, and 2015

Characteristic	2005	2014	2015
Sex	**100%**	**100%**	**100%**
Male	77	75	75
Female	23	25	25
Race/Hispanic origin[a]	**100%**	**100%**	**100%**
White	55	54	55
Black/African American	30	30	30
Hispanic/Latino	13	13	13
American Indian/Alaska Native	1	1	1
Asian/Native Hawaiian/other Pacific Islander	1	1	1
Two or more races	b	b	b
Status of supervision	**100%**	**100%**	**100%**
Active	72	73	76
Residential/other treatment program	1	1	1
Financial conditions remaining	c	1	2
Inactive	9	5	4
Absconder	10	8	7
Supervised out of jurisdiction	2	6	2
Warrant status	6	2	5
Other	b	4	4
Type of offense	**100%**	**100%**	**100%**
Felony	50	56	57
Misdemeanor	49	42	41
Other infractions	1	2	2
Most serious offense	**100%**	**100%**	**100%**
Violent	18%	19%	20%
Domestic violence	6	4	4
Sex offense	3	3	4
Other violent offense	10	12	13
Property	23%	28%	28%
Drug	25%	25%	25%
Public order	19%	16%	15%
DWI/DUI	14	14	13
Other traffic offense	5	2	2
Other	14%	11%	12%

[a]Excludes persons of Hispanic or Latino origin, unless specified.
[b]Less than 0.05%.
[c]Not available.
Note: Detail may not sum to total due to rounding. Estimates are based on most recent data and may differ from previously published statistics. Characteristics are based on probationers with a known type of status.

SOURCE: Danielle Kaeble and Thomas P. Bonczar, "Table 4. Characteristics of Adults on Probation, 2005, 2014, and 2015," in *Probation and Parole in the United States, 2015*, U.S. Department of Justice, Bureau of Justice Statistics, December 2016, https://www.bjs.gov/content/pub/pdf/ppus15.pdf (accessed September 7, 2017)

TABLE 7.13

Prisoners under sentence of death, by region, jurisdiction, and race, 2012 and 2013

Region and jurisdiction	Under sentence of death, 12/31/12			Received under sentence of death, 2013			Removed from death row (excluding executions), 2013[a]			Executed, 2013			Under sentence of death, 12/31/13		
	All races[b]	White[c]	Black[c]	All races[b]	White[c]	Black[c]	All races[b]	White[c]	Black[c]	All races[b]	White[c]	Black[c]	All races[b]	White[c]	Black[c]
U.S. total	**3,011**	**1,684**	**1,258**	**83**	**49**	**33**	**76**	**44**	**30**	**39**	**26**	**13**	**2,979**	**1,663**	**1,248**
Federal[d]	56	27	28	2	0	2	2	0	2	0	0	0	56	27	28
State	2,955	1,657	1,230	81	49	31	74	44	28	39	26	13	2,923	1,636	1,220
Northeast	**204**	**87**	**114**	**4**	**2**	**2**	**7**	**2**	**5**	**0**	**0**	**0**	**201**	**87**	**111**
Connecticut	10	4	6	0	0	0	0	0	0	0	0	0	10	4	6
New Hampshire	1	0	1	0	0	0	0	0	0	0	0	0	1	0	1
New York	0	0	0	0	0	0	0	0	0	0	0	0	0	0	0
Pennsylvania	193	83	107	4	2	2	7	2	5	0	0	0	190	83	104
Midwest	**218**	**115**	**99**	**11**	**8**	**3**	**6**	**2**	**3**	**5**	**5**	**0**	**218**	**116**	**99**
Indiana	12	9	3	3	2	1	1	0	1	0	0	0	14	11	3
Kansas	9	6	3	0	0	0	0	0	0	0	0	0	9	6	3
Missouri	45	26	19	3	3	0	1	0	1	2	2	0	45	27	18
Nebraska	11	7	2	0	0	0	0	0	0	0	0	0	11	7	2
Ohio	138	64	72	4	2	2	3	1	0	3	3	0	136	62	73
South Dakota	3	3	0	1	1	0	1	1	0	0	0	0	3	3	0
South	**1,538**	**825**	**693**	**34**	**15**	**18**	**45**	**28**	**16**	**32**	**19**	**13**	**1,495**	**793**	**682**
Alabama	191	98	92	5	1	4	5	3	2	1	1	0	190	95	94
Arkansas	38	15	23	0	0	0	1	1	0	0	0	0	37	15	22
Delaware	16	7	9	1	0	1	0	0	0	0	0	0	17	7	10
Florida	402	252	149	15	10	5	12	11	1	7	5	2	398	246	151
Georgia	89	46	43	0	0	0	6	2	4	1	1	0	82	43	39
Kentucky	34	29	5	0	0	0	1	1	0	0	0	0	33	29	4
Louisiana	85	28	56	0	0	0	1	0	1	0	0	0	84	28	55
Maryland	5	1	4	0	0	0	0	0	0	0	0	0	5	1	4
Mississippi	49	20	28	2	2	0	1	0	1	0	0	0	50	22	27
North Carolina	152	66	79	1	1	0	2	1	1	0	0	0	151	65	79
Oklahoma[e]	56	29	24	1	0	1	3	1	1	6	3	3	48	25	20
South Carolina[f]	49	20	29	0	0	0	4	2	2	0	0	0	45	18	27
Tennessee[e]	79	43	34	0	0	0	4	4	0	0	0	0	75	39	34
Texas	284	166	114	9	2	7	4	4	0	16	8	8	273	156	113
Virginia	9	5	4	0	0	0	1	1	0	1	1	0	7	4	3
West	**995**	**630**	**324**	**32**	**24**	**8**	**16**	**12**	**4**	**2**	**2**	**0**	**1,009**	**640**	**328**
Arizona	125	103	17	4	4	0	5	5	0	2	2	0	122	100	17
California[f]	718	423	263	25	17	8	8	6	2	0	0	0	735	434	269
Colorado	3	0	3	0	0	0	0	0	0	0	0	0	3	0	3
Idaho	12	12	0	0	0	0	0	0	0	0	0	0	12	12	0
Montana	2	2	0	0	0	0	0	0	0	0	0	0	2	2	0
Nevada	80	47	32	2	2	0	1	0	1	0	0	0	81	49	31
New Mexico	2	2	0	0	0	0	0	0	0	0	0	0	2	2	0
Oregon	36	30	4	0	0	0	2	1	1	0	0	0	34	29	3
Utah	8	6	1	0	0	0	0	0	0	0	0	0	8	6	1
Washington	8	4	4	1	1	0	0	0	0	0	0	0	9	5	4
Wyoming	1	1	0	0	0	0	0	0	0	0	0	0	1	1	0

TABLE 7.13

Prisoners under sentence of death, by region, jurisdiction, and race, 2012 and 2013 [CONTINUED]

[a]Includes 25 deaths from natural causes (6 each in Florida and California; 2 each in Alabama and Tennessee; and 1 each in Pennsylvania, Missouri, Ohio, North Carolina, South Carolina, Texas, Arizona, Oregon, and the Federal Bureau of Prisons) and 6 deaths from suicide (2 in Arizona; and 1 each in Ohio, Florida, South Carolina, and California).

[b]Includes American Indians or Alaska Natives; Asians; Native Hawaiians, or other Pacific Islanders; and inmates of Hispanic or Latino origin for whom no other race was identified.

[c]Counts of white and black inmates include persons of Hispanic or Latino origin, which may differ from other tables in this report.

[d]Excludes persons held under Armed Forces jurisdiction with a military death sentence for murder.

[e]One inmate who was previously in the custody of Tennessee is now being reported in Oklahoma where he is under a separate sentence of death.

[f]One inmate who was previously in the custody of South Carolina is now being reported in California where he is under a separate sentence of death.

Note: Counts for yearend 2012 have been revised. Revised counts include 19 inmates who were either reported late to the National Prisoner Statistics program or were not in custody of state correctional authorities on December 31, 2012 (14 in California; 3 in Florida; and 1 each in Pennsylvania and Oregon) and exclude 42 inmates who were relieved of a death sentence before December 31, 2012 (9 each in Pennsylvania and California; 6 each in Georgia and Texas; 4 in Florida; 3 in Tennessee: 2 in Missouri; and 1 each in Ohio, Delaware, and Nevada). Data for December 31, 2012, also include 1 inmate in Pennsylvania who was erroneously reported as being removed from under sentence of death.

SOURCE: Tracy L. Snell, "Table 4. Prisoners under Sentence of Death, by Region, Jurisdiction, and Race, 2012 and 2013," in *Capital Punishment in the United States, 2013—Statistical Tables*, U.S. Department of Justice, Bureau of Justice Statistics, December 2014, https://www.bjs.gov/content/pub/pdf/cp13st.pdf (accessed September 7, 2017)

TABLE 7.14

Executions and other dispositions of inmates sentenced to death, by race and Hispanic origin, 1977–2013

Race/Hispanic origin	Number under sentence of death, 1977–2013[b]	Prisoners executed		Prisoners who received other dispositions[a]	
		Number	Percent of total	Number	Percent of total
Total	8,124	1,359	16.7%	3,786	46.6%
White[c]	3,907	770	19.7	1,843	47.2
Black[c]	3,334	464	13.9	1,635	49.0
Hispanic/Latino	755	111	14.7	255	33.8
All other races[c, d]	128	14	10.9	53	41.4

[a]Includes persons removed from under a sentence of death because of statutes struck down on appeal, sentences or convictions vacated, commutations, or death by other than execution.
[b]Includes 4 persons sentenced to death prior to 1977 who were still under sentence of death on December 31, 2013; 375 persons sentenced to death prior to 1977 whose death sentence was removed between 1977 and December 31, 2013; and 7,745 persons sentenced to death between 1977 and 2013.
[c]Excludes persons of Hispanic or Latino origin.
[d]Includes American Indians, Alaska Natives, Asians, Native Hawaiians, and other Pacific Islanders.
Note: In 1972, the U.S. Supreme Court invalidated capital punishment statutes in several states (*Furman v. Georgia*, 408 U.S. 238 (1972)), effecting a moratorium on executions. Executions resumed in 1977 when the Supreme Court found that revisions to several state statutes had effectively addressed the issues previously held unconstitutional (*Gregg v. Georgia*, 428 U.S. 153 (1976) and its companion cases).

SOURCE: Tracy L. Snell, "Table 12. Executions and Other Dispositions of Inmates Sentenced to Death, by Race and Hispanic Origin, 1977–2013," in *Capital Punishment in the United States, 2013–Statistical Tables*, U.S. Department of Justice, Bureau of Justice Statistics, December 2014, https://www.bjs.gov/content/pub/pdf/cp13st.pdf (accessed September 7, 2017)

Between 1977 and 2013, 8,124 prisoners had been under the sentence of death. (See Table 7.14.) Of those prisoners, 3,907 (48.1%) were non-Hispanic white, 3,334 (41%) were non-Hispanic African American, and 755 (9.3%) were Hispanic. Non-Hispanic white prisoners under the sentence of death were more likely than average (19.7% versus 16.7%) to actually be executed, whereas non-Hispanic African Americans (13.9%) and Hispanics (14.7%) on death row were less likely to be executed.

GANGS

Testifying before the U.S. Senate's Committee on the Judiciary, Steven R. Wiley (April 23, 1997, http://www.hi-ho.ne.jp/taku77/refer/gang.htm) of the FBI explained that law enforcement agencies define a street gang as a "group of people that form an allegiance based on various social needs and engage in acts injurious to public health and safety."

In *2015 National Gang Report* (2016, https://www.fbi.gov/file-repository/national-gang-report-2015.pdf), the National Gang Intelligence Center, an agency of the U.S. Justice Department, notes that gang members generally use a common name, slogan, identifying sign, symbol, tattoo, or other physical marking to identify themselves as part of a gang. Furthermore, most gangs engage in criminal activity, often using violence or intimidation to achieve their criminal objectives. Violent conflicts between different gangs usually arise from disputes over drugs, money, and territory.

Gangs are often (but not always) racially or ethnically based. As a rule, ethnic gangs require that all members belong to a particular race or ethnic group. The National Gang Center reports in "Demographics"

(2017, https://www.nationalgangcenter.gov/Survey-Analysis/Demographics) that in 2011, Hispanics accounted for 46.2% of gang members, whereas African Americans accounted for 35.3%, whites accounted for 11.5%, and other races/ethnicities accounted for 7%.

Erika Harrell of the BJS indicates in "Violence by Gang Members, 1993–2003" (June 2005, https://www.bjs.gov/content/pub/pdf/vgm03.pdf), the most recent BJS publication on this topic as of November 2017, that between 1998 and 2003, 6% of all violent crimes were perpetrated by gang members. The most frightening crime committed by gangs is murder. In *Homicide Trends in the United States, 1980–2008*, Cooper and Smith find that more than half of all gang-related homicides between 1980 and 2008 involved whites. Approximately 56.5% of gang-related homicide victims during this period were white, and 53.3% of offenders were also white. African Americans were the victims of gang-related homicides 40% of the time, and 42.2% of offenders were African American.

The National Gang Center reports in "Measuring the Extent of Gang Problems" (2017, https://www.nationalgangcenter.gov/survey-analysis/measuring-the-extent-of-gang-problems) that gang-related homicides rose from 1,975 in 2007 to 2,363 in 2012, an increase of 19.6% over five years. Nationally, gang-related homicides accounted for about 13% of all homicides annually during this period. In Los Angeles and Chicago, which are commonly referred to as the U.S. "gang capitals," however, gang-related homicides accounted for about half of all homicides annually. The National Gang Center notes that from 2002 to 2012, the number of gang members has averaged around 770,000 nationally. In 2012 there were an estimated 850,000 gang members in the United States.

CHAPTER 8
POLITICAL PARTICIPATION

A truly postethnic America would be one in which the ethno-racial component in identity would loom less large than it now does in politics.

—David A. Hollinger, *Postethnic America: Beyond Multiculturalism* (1995)

David A. Hollinger's words point out the large divide between minority groups and the majority in the political life of the United States. Not only are there racial and ethnic divides in voter registration and voter turnout, but also there are differences in voting by minorities when compared with the majority group. Specifically, minority groups largely cast their support behind Democratic candidates. In addition, only in the last two decades of the 20th century did minority candidates running for office achieve much success. By November 2008, however, an African American candidate had done what was previously considered unthinkable: Barack Obama (1961–), a U.S. senator from Illinois, had been elected the 44th president of the United States.

Perry Bacon Jr. states in "Can Obama Count on the Black Vote?" (Time.com, January 23, 2007) that, in part, Obama's appeal stemmed from "his image as practically a post-racial politician. Not only does he have a mixed-race background, with a white mother from Kansas and a black father from Kenya, but his rhetoric, most notably his 2004 Democratic National Convention speech, emphasizes the importance of Americans moving beyond political, religious, and racial differences." Obama did not rely on racial appeals in the same way that previous African American candidates—notably Jesse Jackson (1941–) in his runs for the Democratic presidential nomination—had done. According to Dan Balz and Jon Cohen, in "Blacks Shift to Obama, Poll Finds" (WashingtonPost.com, February 28, 2007), this emphasis allowed him to appeal to a large portion of the white electorate, and early in the primary season African Americans shifted their support from the front-runner, the U.S. senator Hillary Rodham Clinton (1947–) of New York, to Obama.

Minority voters turned out in record numbers to support Obama's candidacy, leading to his Democratic primary victory and his election in November 2008. Minorities also played a crucial role in reelecting Obama in 2012. William H. Frey reports in "Minority Turnout Determined the 2012 Election" (Brookings Institution, May 10, 2013, https://www.brookings.edu/research/minority-turnout-determined-the-2012-election/) that 87% of African Americans voted for Obama in 2012. That year, African Americans and Hispanics combined accounted for nearly one-fourth (22.8%) of the entire electorate.

Despite Obama's historic presidency, racial tensions remained a prominent aspect of American society, and by the end of his term, many analysts had scaled back their declarations about a postethnic or postracial America. This reality became especially evident during the 2016 presidential campaign, when Republican nominee Donald Trump (1946–) openly appealed to the racial fears of many white Americans, notably on the subject of illegal immigration. In "The 'War on Immigrants': Racist Policies in the Trump Era" (HuffingtonPost.com, August 7, 2017), Alvaro Huerta argues that Trump's pledge to increase law enforcement actions against undocumented immigrants, combined with his campaign slogan "Make America Great Again," embodied an "isolationist and white nativist philosophy, harkening back to the more oppressive periods of U.S. history when racialized groups (e.g., Latinos, African Americans) lacked basic civil rights, privileges and freedoms under the law."

VOTER REGISTRATION

Minority groups traditionally trailed behind whites when it came to registering to vote and actually voting. In 1993 Congress enacted the National Voter Registration Act, which became popularly known as the Motor Voter Act because it included provisions to enable driver's license applicants to simultaneously register to vote.

According to the article "20 Million 'Motor Voters' Increase Rolls" (NYTimes.com, October 16, 1996), less than two years after the law went into effect (in January 1995) approximately 9 million new voters had registered.

The number of minority registered voters in the South increased during the late 20th century due in large part to the passage of the Civil Rights Act of 1964 and the Voting Rights Act of 1965. These laws removed voting restrictions and led to often volatile and dangerous voter registration campaigns that were conducted during the 1960s and 1970s. Before these changes many southern states enforced poll taxes, charging citizens for the right to vote and knowing that many poor African Americans could not afford to pay. Some southern states had so-called grandfather clauses that permitted voting rights only to those whose grandfathers had been eligible to vote. Many elderly African Americans were the grandchildren of slaves who had not been eligible to vote, so these clauses restricted their rights. Furthermore, because they did not have the right to vote, their own children and grandchildren were also prevented from voting under the grandfather clauses. Revising the laws, however, was not enough in itself to effect change and ensure voting rights for African Americans in the South. Removing discriminatory voting restrictions took marches, demonstrations, and the loss of a number of lives.

In November 2016 (a presidential election year) there were 154.5 million non-Hispanic white U.S. citizens eligible to vote in the United States. (See Table 8.1.) Of this number, 114.2 million (73.9%) were registered to vote. That year, 20 million out of 28.8 million eligible African American citizens (69.4%) were registered to vote. By comparison, only 15.3 million of 26.7 million eligible Hispanics (57.3%) and 5.8 million of 10.3 million eligible Asian Americans (56.3%) were registered to vote in November 2016.

On the whole, native citizens are more likely than naturalized citizens to register to vote in the United States. Whereas 71.2% of native-born U.S. citizens were registered to vote in 2016, just 61.7% of naturalized citizens were registered that November. (See Table 8.1.) This discrepancy was most notable among non-Hispanic whites. Whereas nearly three-quarters (74.2%) of native-born non-Hispanic whites were registered to vote in the November 2016 election, just under two-thirds (65.9%) of naturalized non-Hispanic white citizens registered to vote that same year. Native-born African American citizens (69.6%) were also more likely to have registered to vote in 2016 than naturalized African American citizens (66.6%). By contrast, naturalized Asian American (59.3%) and naturalized Hispanic citizens (59.7%) were more likely to have registered to vote in November 2016 than native Asian American (51.5%) and native Hispanic (56.4%) citizens.

VOTER TURNOUT

Registering to vote is one thing, but actually going out to the polls on election day is another. Often people register to vote but fail to exercise their right to vote when the time comes. Whereas 70.3% of the U.S. adult citizen population was registered to vote in the November 2016 election, only 61.4% reported having actually done so. (See Table 8.1.) This discrepancy was largest among Hispanics. Whereas 57.3% of Hispanic adult citizens were registered to vote in 2016, fewer than half (47.6%) reported voting that year. Among African American citizens, 69.4% were registered to vote in 2016, but only 59.4% actually voted. This figure was second only to voter turnout among non-Hispanic whites (65.3%) that year. (See Table 8.1.)

Figure 8.1 traces voting trends by race and Hispanic origin in presidential election years between 1980 and 2016, and Table 8.2 breaks down shifts in voting patterns between the 2012 and 2016 presidential election years. As Table 8.2 shows, voter turnout increased between 2012 and 2016 for all racial and ethnic groups, with the exception of African Americans. Although the number of African Americans who were eligible to vote rose by nearly 1.8 million between 2012 and 2016, the number of African Americans who went to the polls declined by roughly 765,000. By contrast, although the number of eligible non-Hispanic white voters increased by just under 1.6 million between 2012 and 2016, the number of non-Hispanic whites who voted rose by over 2.8 million. Hispanics saw the largest increase in eligible voters between 2012 and 2016, at over 3.3 million. However, voter turnout among Hispanics rose by less than 1.5 million, roughly half the total increase of 2.8 million non-Hispanic white voters between 2012 and 2016.

The decline in voter turnout among African Americans could be attributable to a number of factors. For one, enthusiasm for Obama's candidacy resulted in record voter turnout among minorities in 2008 and 2012, and the absence of an African American candidate in 2016 might have led some African Americans to stay home on election day. At the same time, stricter voting laws likely played a role in lowering voter turnout among minority groups. According to the Brennan Center for Justice at the New York University School of Law, in "New Voting Restrictions in America" (2017, http://www.brennan center.org/new-voting-restrictions-america), between 2010 and 2016, 20 states passed laws that imposed new restrictions on voting, including requirements that individuals present photo identification before voting. Such laws are thought to have a disproportionate effect on minority voters. Zoltan L. Hajnal, Nazita Lajevardi, and Lindsay Nielsen write in "Do Voter Identification Laws Suppress Minority Voting? Yes. We Did the Research" (Washing tonPost.com, February 15, 2017) that the gap in turnout

TABLE 8.1

Reported rates of voting and registration among native and naturalized citizens, by race, Hispanic origin, and region of birth, November 2016

[In thousands]

Nativity status, race and Hispanic origin	Total citizen population	Reported registered Number	Reported registered Percent	Reported not registered Number	Reported not registered Percent	No response to registration[a] Number	No response to registration[a] Percent	Reported voted Number	Reported voted Percent	Reported did not vote Number	Reported did not vote Percent	No response to voting[b] Number	No response to voting[b] Percent
United States													
All races	224,059	157,596	70.3	32,622	14.6	33,841	15.1	137,537	61.4	53,860	24.0	32,662	14.6
White alone	177,865	127,463	71.7	24,822	14.0	25,580	14.4	111,891	62.9	41,356	23.3	24,618	13.8
White non-Hispanic alone	154,450	114,151	73.9	19,210	12.4	21,089	13.7	100,849	65.3	33,310	21.6	20,290	13.1
Black alone	28,808	19,984	69.4	3,732	13.0	5,092	17.7	17,119	59.4	6,674	23.2	5,015	17.4
Asian alone	10,283	5,785	56.3	2,467	24.0	2,032	19.8	5,043	49.0	3,315	32.2	1,926	18.7
Hispanic (of any race)	26,662	15,267	57.3	6,394	24.0	5,001	18.8	12,682	47.6	9,118	34.2	4,862	18.2
White alone or in combination	181,268	129,664	71.5	25,472	14.1	26,133	14.4	113,707	62.7	42,431	23.4	25,130	13.9
Black alone or in combination	30,326	20,935	69.0	4,028	13.3	5,364	17.7	17,875	58.9	7,169	23.6	5,282	17.4
Asian alone or in combination	11,118	6,369	57.3	2,605	23.4	2,143	19.3	5,542	49.9	3,550	31.9	2,025	18.2
Native citizen													
All races	204,212	145,351	71.2	28,134	13.8	30,727	15.0	126,763	62.1	47,782	23.4	29,668	14.5
White alone	167,069	120,760	72.3	22,458	13.4	23,852	14.3	106,047	63.5	38,057	22.8	22,966	13.7
White non-Hispanic alone	149,815	111,095	74.2	18,356	12.3	20,364	13.6	98,255	65.6	31,946	21.3	19,614	13.1
Black alone	26,597	18,512	69.6	3,363	12.6	4,722	17.8	15,756	59.2	6,197	23.3	4,644	17.5
Asian alone	3,976	2,046	51.5	830	20.9	1,100	27.7	1,778	44.7	1,159	29.2	1,039	26.1
Hispanic (of any race)	19,848	11,198	56.4	4,754	24.0	3,896	19.6	9,040	45.5	7,023	35.4	3,784	19.1
White alone or in combination	170,288	122,837	72.1	23,079	13.6	24,372	14.3	107,748	63.3	39,095	23.0	23,445	13.8
Black alone or in combination	28,037	19,428	69.3	3,632	13.0	4,977	17.8	16,477	58.8	6,665	23.8	4,895	17.5
Asian alone or in combination	4,750	2,586	54.4	964	20.3	1,200	25.3	2,238	47.1	1,386	29.2	1,126	23.7
Naturalized citizen													
All races	19,847	12,245	61.7	4,488	22.6	3,115	15.7	10,774	54.3	6,079	30.6	2,995	15.1
White alone	10,796	6,704	62.1	2,365	21.9	1,727	16.0	5,844	54.1	3,300	30.6	1,652	15.3
White non-Hispanic alone	4,635	3,056	65.9	854	18.4	725	15.6	2,594	56.0	1,365	29.4	677	14.6
Black alone	2,210	1,472	66.6	369	16.7	370	16.7	1,363	61.7	477	21.6	370	16.8
Asian alone	6,307	3,738	59.3	1,637	26.0	932	14.8	3,265	51.8	2,156	34.2	887	14.1
Hispanic (of any race)	6,815	4,070	59.7	1,641	24.1	1,105	16.2	3,642	53.4	2,095	30.7	1,078	15.8
White alone or in combination	10,981	6,827	62.2	2,393	21.8	1,761	16.0	5,959	54.3	3,336	30.4	1,686	15.4
Black alone or in combination	2,290	1,507	65.8	396	17.3	387	16.9	1,398	61.1	504	22.0	388	16.9
Asian alone or in combination	6,367	3,783	59.4	1,641	25.8	943	14.8	3,305	51.9	2,164	34.0	898	14.1
Region of birth													
All naturalized citizens	19,847	12,245	61.7	4,488	22.6	3,115	15.7	10,774	54.3	6,079	30.6	2,995	15.1
Europe	2,803	1,879	67.0	490	17.5	434	15.5	1,573	56.1	821	29.3	409	14.6
Asia	7,351	4,335	59.0	1,869	25.4	1,147	15.6	3,782	51.4	2,490	33.9	1,079	14.7
North America	278	230	82.7	23	8.2	25	9.0	207	74.5	42	15.3	28	10.3
Latin America and Mexico	8,305	5,106	61.5	1,862	22.4	1,337	16.1	4,594	55.3	2,398	28.9	1,313	15.8
Africa	980	620	63.3	208	21.2	152	15.5	551	56.2	282	28.8	147	15.0
Other	130	74	57.4	36	28.0	19	14.7	67	51.3	45	34.6	18	14.0

a"No response to registration" includes those who were not asked if they were registered as well as those who responded "don't know" and "refused."
b"No response to voting" includes those who were not asked if they voted as well as those who responded "don't know" and "refused."

SOURCE: "Table 11. Reported Voting and Registration among Native and Naturalized Citizens, by Race, and Region of Origin: November 2016," in *Voting and Registration in the Election of November 2016—Detailed Tables*, U.S. Census Bureau, May 2017, https://www.2.census.gov/programs-surveys/cps/tables/p20/580/table11.xls (accessed September 4, 2017)

FIGURE 8.1

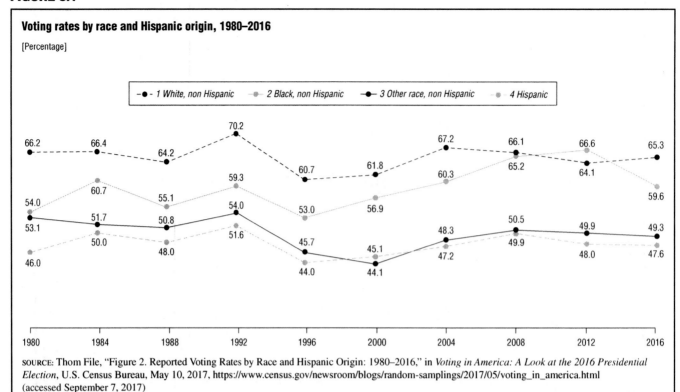

Voting rates by race and Hispanic origin, 1980–2016

[Percentage]

- ● - 1 White, non Hispanic   ● 2 Black, non Hispanic   ● 3 Other race, non Hispanic   ● 4 Hispanic

SOURCE: Thom File, "Figure 2. Reported Voting Rates by Race and Hispanic Origin: 1980–2016," in *Voting in America: A Look at the 2016 Presidential Election*, U.S. Census Bureau, May 10, 2017, https://www.census.gov/newsroom/blogs/random-samplings/2017/05/voting_in_america.html (accessed September 7, 2017)

between non-Hispanic white voters and minority voters has been shown to be significantly wider in states with voter identification laws than in states without such restrictions.

Minority voting patterns also fluctuate considerably among age groups. Figure 8.2 breaks down voting patterns between 2012 and 2016 by race, ethnicity, and age. Over that span, African Americans saw a decline in voter turnout across all age groups. The largest decrease came among African Americans between the ages of 30 and 44 years, whose turnout fell 8.6% between 2012 and 2016. Among African Americans aged 65 years and older, voter turnout fell 6%, the smallest decline for all age groups. Between 2012 and 2016 turnout remained roughly the same among non-Hispanic white voters aged 65 years and older, while rising slightly (0.1%) among non-Hispanic white voters between the ages of 45 and 64 years. Meanwhile, voter turnout among younger non-Hispanic white voters saw larger increases during this span, with the voting rate increasing 1.5% among non-Hispanic white voters between the ages of 30 and 44 years, and 3% among voters aged 18 to 29 years. Hispanic voters saw a decline in turnout for all age groups except 18-to-29-year-olds, among whom the voting rate increased by 1.5% between 2012 and 2016.

Reasons for Not Voting

Age and gender seem to affect one's likelihood to vote. Traditionally, the demographic group between the ages of 18 and 24 years has the lowest percentage of voters. This may partially explain the low voter turnout of Hispanics because they are on average younger than other segments of the U.S. population. According to the U.S. Census Bureau, in *Voting and Registration in the Election of November 2016* (May 12, 2017, https://www.census.gov/data/tables/time-series/demo/voting-and-registration/p20-580.html), only 39.4% of young adults between the ages of 18 and 24 years voted in November 2016. As Americans age, however, they are more likely to vote. The Census Bureau indicates that in November 2016, 49% of the voting-age population between the ages of 25 and 44 years voted, 61.7% of those between the ages of 45 and 64 years voted, and 70.1% of those between the ages of 65 and 74 years voted. Overall, women (58.1%) were more likely than men (53.8%) to have voted in the 2016 election. Among African American voters, this discrepancy was even greater. According to the Census Bureau, 60.4% of African American women voted in the 2016 election, compared with 50.5% of African American men. That year, slightly over one-third of Hispanic women (35.1%) and fewer than one-third of Hispanic men (29.9%) voted.

According to the Census Bureau, the top reason people gave for not voting in the 2016 presidential election was that they did not like the candidates or the campaign issues, a reason that was given by roughly a quarter (24.8%) of registered nonvoters. (See Table 8.3.) Other leading reasons were a lack of interest (15.4%),

TABLE 8.2

[In thousands]

Race and Hispanic-origin	Change in reported voters	Change in citizen voting-age population
All ages		
Total individuals	**4,589**	**8,978**
White non-Hispanic	2,808	1,588
Black non-Hispanic	−765	1,773
Other race non-Hispanic	1,051	2,284
Hispanic	1,494	3,333
18–29 year olds		
Total individuals	**1,081**	**1,267**
White non-Hispanic	695	−301*
Black non-Hispanic	−211*	422
Other race non-Hispanic	196	384
Hispanic	402	761
30–44 year olds		
Total individuals	**177***	**982**
White non-Hispanic	142*	−628*
Black non-Hispanic	−413	292*
Other race non-Hispanic	199*	533
Hispanic	251*	783
44–64 year olds		
Total individuals	**−345***	**905***
White non-Hispanic	−857	−1,314
Black non-Hispanic	−398	374*
Other race non-Hispanic	366	724
Hispanic	544	1,119
65 years and older		
Total individuals	**3,673**	**5,824**
White non-Hispanic	2,828	3,829
Black non-Hispanic	258*	686
Other race non-Hispanic	290	641
Hispanic	298	669

*Indicates that the 2012 and 2016 estimates were not statistically different from each other.

SOURCE: Thom File, "Table 1. Change in Reported Voting Totals, by Age, Race, and Hispanic Orgin: 2012–2016," in *Voting in America: A Look at the 2016 Presidential Election,* U.S. Census Bureau, May 10, 2017, https://www.census.gov/newsroom/blogs/random-samplings/2017/05/voting_in_america.html (accessed September 7, 2017)

being too busy or having a scheduling conflict (14.3%), having an illness or disability (11.7%), and being out of town (7.9%); 3% of registered voters said they forgot to go to the polls in November 2016. Non-Hispanic whites (26%) were the group most likely not to have voted because of a dislike of the candidates or the campaign issues, followed by Hispanics (25.2%), Asian Americans (22.3%), and African Americans (19.6%). Hispanics (16.2%) and Asian Americans (16.2%) were most likely to report not voting in 2016 because they were too busy or had a scheduling conflict, compared with 13.9% of non-Hispanic whites and 13.5% of African Americans who provided the same reason for not going to the polls. African Americans (18.6%) were most likely not to vote in 2016 because they were not interested, followed by Asian Americans (17%), Hispanics (16.5%), and non-Hispanic whites (14.3%). (See Table 8.3.)

AFRICAN AMERICAN POLITICAL PARTICIPATION

Elected Officials

The number of African Americans elected to public offices at all levels of the U.S. government has increased significantly since the 1980s. The largest gain has been in city and county offices, which include county commissioners, city council members, mayors, vice mayors, and aldermen/alderwomen. President Obama became only the fifth African American to serve in the U.S. Senate and only the third since Reconstruction (1865–1877), when he was sworn in as a senator from Illinois on January 4, 2005. He had received international media coverage after delivering a stirring keynote address at the 2004 Democratic National Convention. In November 2008 he won the presidency, becoming the first African American president in U.S. history. Obama subsequently won his reelection bid in November 2012.

Susan Page and Paul Overberg report in "A Changing America: In 2012, Blacks Outvoted Whites" (USAToday.com, May 8, 2013) that two major trends contributed to Obama's reelection. Most significant was his strong support among African American voters, whose turnout percentage (66.2% of all eligible African American voters) exceeded that of non-Hispanic whites (64.1%) for the first time in history. At the same time, a decline in turnout among non-Hispanic white voters ultimately hurt Obama's Republican opponent, Mitt Romney (1947–), as the number of non-Hispanic white voters fell by more than 2 million, despite the fact that the number of eligible non-Hispanic white voters had actually increased by 1 million since 2008. Overall, CNN reports in "President: Full Results" (December 10, 2012, http://www.cnn.com/election/2012/results/race/president#exit-polls) that Obama received 93% of the African American vote and 71% of the Hispanic vote, whereas Romney earned 59% of the non-Hispanic white vote. According to CNN, Obama also received a boost from young voters that year, winning the 18-to-24-year-old demographic by a margin of 60% to 36%.

African Americans and Political Parties

Carroll Doherty et al. of the Pew Research Center write in *The Parties on the Eve of the 2016 Election: Two Coalitions, Moving Further Apart* (September 13, 2016, http://assets.pewresearch.org/wp-content/uploads/sites/5/2016/09/09-13-2016-Party-ID-release-final.pdf) that African Americans are the strongest supporters of the Democratic Party. In 2016 roughly 70% of African Americans who were registered to vote described themselves as Democrats, whereas only 3% identified themselves as Republicans; another 23% of African Americans identified as Independent. Although many Americans shifted toward the Republican Party after the terrorist attacks against the United States on September 11, 2001 (9/11), African Americans did not.

FIGURE 8.2

Percentage changes in reported voting rates by age, race, and ethnicity, 2012–16

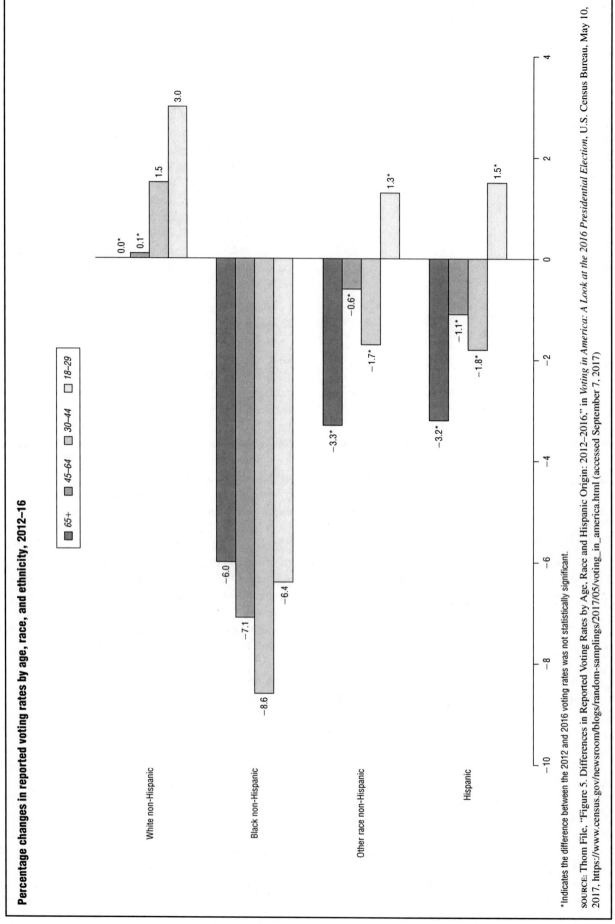

*Indicates the difference between the 2012 and 2016 voting rates was not statistically significant.

SOURCE: Thom File, "Figure 5. Differences in Reported Voting Rates by Age, Race and Hispanic Origin: 2012–2016," in *Voting in America: A Look at the 2016 Presidential Election*, U.S. Census Bureau, May 10, 2017, https://www.census.gov/newsroom/blogs/random-samplings/2017/05/voting_in_america.html (accessed September 7, 2017)

TABLE 8.3

Reasons for not voting, by selected characteristics, November 2016

[In thousands]

Selected characteristics	Total not voting*	Illness or disability	Out of town	Forgot to vote	Not interested	Too busy, conflicting schedule	Transportation problems	Did not like candidates or campaign issues	Registration problems	Bad weather conditions	Inconvenient polling place	Other reason	Don't know or refused
								Percent distribution of reasons for not voting					
Total	**18,933**	**11.7**	**7.9**	**3.0**	**15.4**	**14.3**	**2.6**	**24.8**	**4.4**	**0.0**	**2.1**	**11.1**	**2.7**
Age													
18 to 24 years	3,042	2.7	13.2	4.7	17.3	18.3	1.5	20.6	5.5	—	2.3	10.8	3.1
25 to 44 years	7,246	4.7	7.1	2.4	17.2	19.2	2.0	25.2	6.0	0.0	2.3	11.5	2.6
45 to 64 years	5,420	12.7	7.8	3.4	15.1	12.4	2.5	27.5	2.6	0.1	2.5	10.6	2.9
65 years and over	3,225	33.9	5.1	2.1	10.3	2.8	5.1	23.1	2.9	0.1	1.1	11.5	2.1
Sex													
Male	9,366	8.3	9.9	2.8	16.8	16.0	2.0	25.1	3.9	0.1	2.3	9.8	2.9
Female	9,567	15.0	5.9	3.1	14.0	12.6	3.2	24.4	4.9	0.0	2.0	12.4	2.4
Race and Hispanic origin													
White alone	14,766	12.1	8.1	2.8	14.5	14.4	2.4	25.9	4.5	0.1	2.1	10.6	2.6
White non-Hispanic alone	12,633	12.8	8.3	2.7	14.3	13.9	2.7	26.0	4.4	0.1	2.0	10.2	2.6
Black alone	2,645	11.7	6.7	3.7	18.6	13.5	4.5	19.6	4.0	—	2.6	12.4	2.7
Asian alone	712	6.5	11.0	2.8	17.0	16.2	1.0	22.3	3.3	0.1	0.9	13.8	5.2
Hispanic (of any race)	2,403	7.3	7.6	3.3	16.5	16.2	0.6	25.2	5.4	—	3.2	12.2	2.4
White alone or in combination	15,120	12.0	8.1	2.8	14.6	14.4	2.4	26.0	4.5	0.1	2.1	10.6	2.5
Black alone or in combination	2,824	11.3	6.5	3.5	18.9	13.7	4.3	20.5	3.7	0.1	2.5	12.5	2.6
Asian alone or in combination	798	6.4	11.2	2.5	18.1	15.7	0.9	21.4	2.9	0.1	1.5	14.1	5.3
Educational attainment													
Less than high school graduate	2,214	19.7	3.8	4.4	13.8	10.3	5.7	23.1	3.0	—	1.6	12.9	1.7
High school graduate	6,852	13.4	6.5	3.0	17.4	13.1	2.9	24.0	4.0	0.1	2.3	10.5	2.6
Some college	6,154	8.7	7.8	2.6	15.4	16.7	2.1	26.1	4.5	0.0	1.8	11.6	2.7
Bachelors degree or more	3,712	8.6	13.2	2.8	12.7	14.9	1.0	24.9	5.7	—	2.6	10.4	3.3
Nativity													
Native-born citizen	17,531	11.7	7.6	3.1	15.4	14.2	2.7	25.0	4.4	0.1	2.2	11.1	2.4
Naturalized citizen	1,402	11.0	11.3	1.6	15.3	15.5	0.8	22.3	3.7	—	1.3	11.6	5.5
Duration of residence													
Less than 1 year	3,565	6.6	9.6	3.0	13.7	14.9	2.6	21.6	10.6	0.0	2.1	13.0	2.3
1 to 2 years	2,982	8.1	6.2	3.2	15.5	18.1	3.3	25.6	5.1	—	2.6	9.5	2.7
3 years or longer	12,104	14.2	7.9	3.0	15.8	13.3	2.4	25.7	2.4	0.1	2.0	10.9	2.4
Don't know or refused	282	5.7	5.6	2.5	20.7	10.1	3.2	16.4	4.1	—	1.3	13.1	17.3
Region													
Northeast	3,235	14.3	10.6	2.4	14.3	12.3	2.7	23.6	3.8	0.1	2.2	10.5	3.5
Midwest	4,289	11.4	7.3	2.0	15.6	15.3	3.3	27.8	3.1	—	2.1	10.2	2.0
South	7,870	12.5	7.4	3.1	14.9	15.0	2.9	23.7	4.9	0.1	2.6	11.0	2.0
West	3,540	7.8	7.3	4.5	17.5	13.4	1.0	24.4	5.4	0.0	1.2	13.1	4.2

TABLE 8.3

Reasons for not voting, by selected characteristics, November 2016 [CONTINUED]

[In thousands]

Selected characteristics	Total not voting*	Illness or disability	Out of town	Forgot to vote	Not interested	Too busy, conflicting schedule	Transportation problems	Did not like candidates or campaign issues	Registration problems	Bad weather conditions	Inconvenient polling place	Other reason	Don't know or refused
								Percent distribution of reasons for not voting					
Income													
Total family members	12,583	11.1	8.0	2.9	16.4	15.5	1.7	23.8	4.1	0.1	2.4	11.1	2.9
Less than $10,000	659	15.7	3.1	4.8	20.5	11.3	7.8	21.3	3.9	0.4	3.1	6.9	1.3
$10,000 to $14,999	517	16.9	5.1	1.2	19.5	10.0	8.6	20.6	2.4	—	0.2	13.1	2.4
$15,000 to $19,999	446	18.6	8.1	4.9	13.5	12.1	1.4	16.6	6.6	0.6	5.0	10.3	2.3
$20,000 to $29,999	1,144	16.5	4.8	1.9	14.4	14.6	3.3	26.9	2.5	0.0	2.2	11.6	1.3
$30,000 to $39,999	1,195	13.2	6.3	3.5	15.6	14.9	1.6	22.7	5.6	—	1.8	11.0	3.7
$40,000 to $49,999	910	12.4	6.1	4.0	19.0	16.1	0.2	20.5	4.4	—	2.2	12.7	2.4
$50,000 to $74,999	2,244	8.5	6.4	2.5	14.7	16.9	0.7	25.6	5.3	—	1.4	14.6	3.4
$75,000 to $99,999	1,371	7.2	7.6	2.6	14.9	21.3	1.0	24.9	3.6	—	3.9	10.9	1.8
$100,000 to $149,999	1,435	6.2	12.2	2.4	20.9	14.5	—	24.6	4.2	0.2	2.2	8.7	3.9
$150,000 and over	956	5.6	16.2	4.0	15.4	17.9	0.6	21.3	4.4	—	3.2	8.1	3.4
Income not reported	1,706	13.2	9.3	2.7	15.2	13.6	1.0	25.7	2.3	—	2.8	10.4	3.8

*Only individuals who report not voting but also report being registered are asked the question about reason for not voting.

Note: A dash '—' represents zero or rounds to zero.

SOURCE: "Table 10. Reasons for Not Voting, by Selected Characteristics: November 2016," in *Voting and Registration in the Election of November 2016—Detailed Tables*, U.S. Census Bureau, May 2017, https://www2.census.gov/programs-surveys/cps/tables/p20/580/table10.xls (accessed September 7, 2017)

By November 2008 disillusionment with the administration of Republican President George W. Bush (1946–) and excitement over the candidates in the Democratic primary had drawn more Democratic voters to the polls. The Pew Research Center for the People and the Press notes in "Inside Obama's Sweeping Victory" (November 5, 2008, http://pewresearch.org/pubs/1023/exit-poll-analysis-2008) that although equal numbers of Democrats and Republicans had voted in November 2004, in November 2008 Democrats had the advantage, 39% to 32%. Obama won 60% of those with low or moderate incomes of less than $50,000 per year. He also won 66% of the Hispanic vote, which was 13 percentage points higher than the Democratic candidate had won in November 2004, and 95% of the African American vote, which was 7 percentage points higher than the Democratic candidate won in November 2004. The Pew Research Center reports in *Changing Face of America Helps Assure Obama Victory* (November 7, 2012, http://www.people-press.org/2012/11/07/changing-face-of-america-helps-assure-obama-victory/) that Obama enjoyed a similar turnout advantage en route to his 2012 reelection. That year, Democrats accounted for 38% of voters in November, compared with 32% for the Republicans. In 2016, however, a decline in African American voter turnout likely played a key role in Donald Trump's victory over Democratic nominee Hillary Clinton (1947–). Omri Ben-Shahar notes in "The Non-voters Who Decided the Election: Trump Won Because of Lower Democratic Turnout" (Forbes.com, November 17, 2016) that voter turnout among African Americans fell 11% between 2012 and 2016.

The traditional African American political goals, as presented by the Congressional Black Caucus (CBC; 2017, https://cbc.house.gov/), are to "ensure that African Americans and other marginalized communities in the United States have the opportunity to achieve the American Dream." As of November 2017, there were 49 members of the CBC. Notable members of the CBC included the U.S. representative and civil rights icon John Lewis (1940–; D-GA); the California congresswoman Maxine Waters (1938–), who in November 2017 was the most senior African American woman in the U.S. House of Representatives; and the California congresswoman Barbara Lee (1946–), chair of the CBC and a widely respected leader of the antiwar movement. The CBC encourages and seeks out African American participation in government, especially as elected officials, to correct the ills of the disadvantaged, many of whom are minorities.

As the African American middle class continues to grow, party loyalties may change. Some younger professional African Americans who may not have experienced poverty or the deprivation of the inner cities may be attracted to the Republican Party platform of less government regulation and lower taxes. A vast majority of African Americans embraced the programs of President Lyndon B. Johnson's (1908–1973) Great Society and his War on Poverty during the 1960s. In the 21st century some observers believe that reliance on government has actually disempowered many African Americans and other underprivileged people.

However, movement toward the Republican Party before the 2008 election was slowed by Obama's election in November 2008. In "Strong Confidence in Obama—Country Seen as Less Politically Divided" (January 15, 2009, http://www.people-press.org/2009/01/15/strong-confidence-in-obama-country-seen-as-less-politically-divided/), the Pew Research Center for the People and the Press finds that in 2009 nearly four out of five (79%) African Americans believed that "people like themselves" would gain influence under the Obama administration. This was more than the African Americans who believed they would gain influence under the Bush administration, which took office in January 2001, or under the administration of Democratic President Bill Clinton (1946–), which took office in January 1993. Only 30% of African Americans believed they would gain influence under Bush, and 67% believed they would gain influence under Bill Clinton. The Pew Research Center for the People and the Press finds in "Obama: Weak Job Ratings, but Positive Personal Image" (January 19, 2012, http://www.people-press.org/files/legacy-pdf/1-19-12%20Obama%20Release.pdf) that in 2012, 92% of African Americans maintained their favorable view of Obama. The Pew Research Center reports in *Changing Face of America Helps Assure Obama Victory* that these favorable ratings were reflected in the 2012 presidential election, when 93% of African American voters cast their ballots for Obama.

HISPANIC POLITICAL PARTICIPATION

The Hispanic population in the United States increased dramatically during the late 20th century. Jens Manuel Krogstad reports in "U.S. Hispanic Population Growth Has Leveled Off" (August 3, 2017, http://www.pewresearch.org/fact-tank/2017/08/03/u-s-hispanic-population-growth-has-leveled-off/) that by 2016 there were roughly 57.5 million Hispanics living in the United States. However, Hispanics have not attained political power equal to their proportion of the population. Two characteristics of Hispanic demography help account for this. First, although the Hispanic voting-age population grew during the late 20th and early 21st centuries, Hispanics have a young population, with many in the 18-to-24-year-old category (the age group that is the least likely to vote). In addition, a smaller proportion of Hispanics than of society as a whole are older than age 55 (the age group that is the most likely to vote). The second and perhaps more important characteristic is the issue of U.S. citizenship. As Table 8.1 shows, only 26.7 million of the 57.5 million Hispanics living in the United States were citizens of voting age in 2016. Therefore, 30.8 million (53.6%) Hispanics were either younger than age 18 or were not U.S. citizens and, therefore, could not vote.

Political Participation

Civil rights gains of the 1960s, such as the 24th Amendment eliminating the poll tax, the extension of the Voting Rights Act of 1965 to the Southwest, and the elimination of the English literacy requirement, helped a number of Hispanics attain political office. During the 1970s both major political parties started wooing Hispanic voters and drafting Hispanic candidates. Advocacy groups, such as the Mexican American Legal Defense and Education Fund, the Southwest Voter Registration Education Project, and the Puerto Rican Legal Defense and Education Fund, were formed. All these groups helped develop the political influence of the Hispanic community.

The National Association of Latino Elected and Appointed Officials (NALEO; 2017, http://www.naleo.org) is a research, policy, and education organization that is made up of more than 6,000 Latino elected and appointed officials. The organization's mission is to facilitate the integration of Latino immigrants into U.S. society, to develop leadership abilities among Latino youth, and to support the nation's Latino elected and appointed officials.

In 2004 the NALEO Educational Fund announced that it was collaborating with Univision Communications Inc. in a campaign aimed at mobilizing Hispanic voters throughout the United States. The "Voces del Pueblo" campaign included nonpartisan public service announcements on radio and television as well as voter education forums, phone contact, and targeted mailings. The campaign was an attempt to develop the political influence of the Hispanic community in part by encouraging Hispanics to become citizens. NALEO notes in *2016 Latino Election Handbook* (2016, http://s143989.gridserver.com/downloads/2016/NALEO2016_PresidentialElections_6-20-16-FP.pdf) that the significant rise in naturalized Latinos starting during the first decade of the 21st century translated into an increased political influence at the polls. It argues that Latinos played a crucial role in delivering a number of states to Obama in 2008 that had been won by Bush in 2004 (among them Florida, Colorado, and Virginia).

Hispanics and Political Parties

As a group, Hispanics have been important supporters of the Democratic Party. Like many other Americans in the aftermath of 9/11, many Hispanics began to shift their party affiliation to the Republican Party. Paul Taylor and Richard Fry of the Pew Research Center report in *Hispanics and the 2008 Election: A Swing Vote?* (December 6, 2007, http://pewhispanic.org/files/reports/83.pdf) that although Democrats outnumbered Republicans among Hispanics by more than two to one during the 1990s, after 9/11 Democrats led by a smaller margin. Bush, they note, received an estimated 40% of the Hispanic vote in 2004, a record for a Republican presidential candidate.

Between 2006 and 2007, however, the shift of Hispanic voters to the Republican Party reversed course. Taylor and Fry find that in 2006, 28% of Hispanics said they supported Republicans, and 49% said they supported Democrats. Within a year, only 23% of Hispanics identified as Republicans, and 57% identified as Democrats. According to Taylor and Fry, more Hispanics believed the Democratic Party showed greater concern for Latinos and thought the Democrats were doing a better job on the issue of illegal immigration. In addition, 41% of Hispanics surveyed believed the Bush administration's policies had been harmful to Latinos, whereas only 16% believed these policies had been helpful.

According to Doherty et al., by 2016 Hispanics were far more likely to affiliate themselves with Democrats and Independents than with Republicans. That year, 47% of Hispanics identified as Democrats, and 32% identified as Independents. By contrast, only 16% identified as Republican, down from 20% in 2008. Overall, Hispanics were also far more likely to lean Democratic on a number of key issues. Among Hispanic registered voters in 2016, nearly two-thirds (63%) reported leaning Democratic, compared with approximately a quarter (27%) who reported leaning Republican. These figures represented a shift from 2008, when 59% of Hispanic registered voters leaned Democratic, whereas 31% leaned Republican.

Although more Hispanics align themselves with Democrats than with Republicans, a number of prominent Hispanic political figures have emerged within both parties. Notable Hispanic Democrats have included Bill Richardson (1947–), a former two-term governor of New Mexico who also served as energy secretary under President Clinton; San Antonio, Texas, mayor Julian Castro (1974–), who in 2012 became the first Hispanic American to deliver the keynote speech at the Democratic National Convention; Joaquin Castro (1974–), who represents Texas's 20th district in the House of Representatives and is Julian Castro's twin brother; and Linda Chavez-Thompson (1944–), vice chair of the Democratic National Committee and a former union leader. Prominent Republican Hispanics have included the Cuban American U.S. senator Marco Rubio (1971–; R-FL), the New Mexico governor Susana Martinez (1959–), the Nevada governor Brian Sandoval (1963–), and the Cuban American U.S. senator Ted Cruz (1970–; R-TX).

RACE, ETHNICITY, AND ELECTORAL DISTRICTS

The design of electoral districts can have a tremendous impact on the political power of minorities. Depending on how the lines are drawn, an electoral district might have a large concentration of minorities, enhancing their political power, or minority populations may be split up between many electoral districts, weakening their political influence.

Designing electoral districts to favor one group over another is known as gerrymandering, named after the Massachusetts governor Elbridge Gerry (1744–1814), who became notorious for the salamander-shaped district he approved in 1812. During the first half of the 20th century gerrymandering was widely used as an attempt to prevent African Americans and other minorities from gaining true political representation. Another practice was creating at-large districts, in which the entire population of a large area elected several representatives. The alternative, having several smaller districts each elect only one representative, allowed concentrated populations of minorities to elect their own representatives.

Under the requirements of the Voting Rights Act of 1965, jurisdictions with a history of systematic discrimination (such as a poll tax or literacy test) must create districts with majorities of African Americans or Hispanics, wherever the demographics warrant it. At the same time, they must avoid weakening existing "minority-majority" districts (i.e., districts "in which a majority of the population is a member of a specific minority group"). This law helped eliminate some districts that had been designed to favor whites. At the same time, however, it superseded the traditional criterion of compact districts and made for some oddly defined districts in the name of creating Hispanic- or African American–majority districts.

Computerized Redistricting

Douglas J. Amy notes in *Real Choices/New Voices: How Proportional Representation Elections Could Revitalize American Democracy* (2002) that with computer software, gerrymandering in the 21st century has become highly sophisticated. Redistricters can incorporate information such as party registration, voting patterns, and ethnic makeup from a variety of sources, including census data, property tax records, and old district lines. This information allows them to produce a number of potential scenarios in an instant. Contemporary gerrymandering techniques are called "packing" (concentrating a group of voters in the fewest number of districts), "cracking" (spreading a group of voters across districts), and "kidnapping" (remapping so that two incumbents from the same party are now located in the same district and vying for the same seat). Gerrymandering in the past was essentially self-correcting; by attempting to control as many districts as possible, parties risked losing should a small percentage of voters shift allegiances. Software, however, has become so sophisticated, and politics have become so partisan, that the concept of self-correction is no longer applicable. As a result, few seats in the House of Representatives are now competitive, with incumbents enjoying a locked-in advantage that is almost impossible to overcome.

The article "Political Gerrymandering 2000–2008: 'A Self-Limiting Enterprise'?" (*Harvard Law Review*, vol. 122, March 2009) also argues against the idea that gerrymandering will always be "self-limited." By looking at seven cases of redistricting schemes after the 2000 census, the article finds that the most damaging gerrymandering occurs in areas in which a very strong party is in control and attempts to push its advantage to the limit, and in places where the two political parties collude in gerrymandering in an attempt to keep their own incumbents in office. In particular, "big party gerrymanders at least leave open the possibility of self-correction, but bipartisan gerrymanders make the idea fanciful." Whether voters want a change or not, the bipartisan gerrymanders fix incumbent parties in place for 10 years.

Challenges to Electoral Districting

Redistricting has become a major source of contention between Republicans and Democrats since the 2000 census. One notorious case took place in Texas. The state's lawmakers were unable to agree on new congressional districts because Republicans controlled the state senate and Democrats controlled the state house of representatives. A compromise plan was forced on the parties by a panel of federal judges, essentially leaving the current partisan balance in place. However, after Republicans took control of the state house in 2002, they sought to reopen the redistricting question, breaking an unwritten rule that remapping was to be a matter dealt with once every 10 years to avoid incessant wrangling on the subject. To resist, Democrats in both the state house and senate fled to Oklahoma and New Mexico to prevent the creation of a quorum (the minimum number of representatives needed to conduct business) and thwart the ability of the Republicans to push through their redistricting plan.

Eventually, the Democrats gave in and the congressional districts were redrawn, with the potential that the Republicans would pick up seven seats in the 2004 elections. Staff lawyers in the U.S. Department of Justice approved the plan, although other lawyers for the department had concluded that the redistricting plan undercut minority voting rights. In fact, Republicans won 21 of Texas's 32 seats in the House of Representatives in 2004, up from 15. The U.S. Supreme Court announced in December 2005 that it would consider the constitutionality of the redistricted congressional map. In June 2006 the court ruled that the redistricting violated the rights of some Hispanics, but did not violate the rights of African American voters in the state. Furthermore, it ruled that nothing in the U.S. Constitution barred states from redrawing political lines at any time, and it established no timetable for reviewing the redistricting that had violated the rights of Hispanics.

The state of Texas found itself at the center of another legal battle over redistricting following the 2010 midterm elections. Ari Berman reports in "Federal Court Blocks Discriminatory Texas Redistricting Plan" (Nation.com, August 28, 2012) that the population of Texas grew by 4.3 million between 2000 and 2010, thereby increasing its number of representatives in Congress from 32 to 36 members. However, although minorities accounted for approximately 90% of this population growth, the Republican-led state legislature passed a redistricting map that favored white Republican candidates in three of the four new districts. In December 2011 the U.S. Department of Justice, along with a number of civil rights groups, filed a suit in federal court claiming that the state's redistricting map violated the Voting Rights Act of 1965. Berman reports that in an August 2012 memorandum of opinion, a three-member federal court in the District of Columbia, concurred with the Department of Justice, claiming that the Texas redistricting plan was discriminatory in its intent. Over the next five years, a series of court rulings upheld this opinion, culminating with the decision of a three-judge panel in August 2017, which determined that the redistricting efforts violated both the constitution and the Voting Rights Act of 1965. Josh Gerstein reports in "Supreme Court Blocks Ruling against Texas Redistricting" (Politico.com, September 12, 2017) that the U.S. Supreme Court blocked this ruling a month later, deferring any action on redrawing the districts in question until it has ruled on the state's anticipated appeal. Meanwhile, in October 2017 the Supreme Court heard arguments in another gerrymandering case, *Gill v. Whitford* (No. 16-1161), involving redistricting in Wisconsin following the 2010 Census. A decision in the case was expected in June 2018.

IMPORTANT NAMES
AND ADDRESSES

Alzheimer's Association
225 N. Michigan Ave., 17th Floor
Chicago, IL 60601-7633
(312) 335-8700
FAX: 1-866-699-1246
URL: https://www.alz.org/

American Heart Association
7272 Greenville Ave.
Dallas, TX 75231
1-800-242-8721
URL: http://www.heart.org/HEARTORG/

Bureau of Justice Statistics
810 Seventh St. NW
Washington, DC 20531
(202) 307-0765
E-mail: askbjs@usdoj.gov
URL: https://www.bjs.gov/

**Centers for Disease Control and
Prevention**
1600 Clifton Rd.
Atlanta, GA 30329-4027
1-800-232-4636
URL: https://www.cdc.gov/

Children's Defense Fund
25 E St. NW
Washington, DC 20001
1-800-233-1200
E-mail: cdfinfo@childrensdefense.org
URL: http://www.childrensdefense.org/

Civil Rights Project
8370 Math Sciences, Box 951521
Los Angeles, CA 90095-1521
(310) 267-5562
E-mail: crp@ucla.edu
URL: https://www.civilrightsproject
.ucla.edu/

The College Board
250 Vesey St.
New York, NY 10281
(212) 713-8000
URL: https://www.collegeboard.org/

Congressional Black Caucus Foundation
1720 Massachusetts Ave. NW
Washington, DC 20036
(202) 263-2800
E-mail: info@cbcfinc.org
URL: https://www.cbcfinc.org/

**Congressional Hispanic Caucus
Institute**
1128 16th St. NW
Washington, DC 20036
(202) 543-1771
1-800-EXCEL-DC
FAX: (202) 548-8799
URL: https://chci.org/

**Lawyers' Committee for Civil Rights
under Law**
1401 New York Ave. NW, Ste. 400
Washington, DC 20005
(202) 662-8600
1-888-299-5227
FAX: (202) 783-0857
URL: https://lawyerscommittee.org/

**League of United Latin American
Citizens**
1133 19th St. NW, Ste. 1000
Washington, DC 20036
(202) 833-6130
FAX: (202) 833-6135
URL: http://www.lulac.org/

**National Association for the Advancement
of Colored People**
4805 Mt. Hope Dr.
Baltimore, MD 21215
(410) 580-5777
1-877-NAACP-98
URL: http://www.naacp.org/

**National Association of Latino Elected
and Appointed Officials Educational
Fund**
1122 W. Washington Blvd., Third Floor
Los Angeles, CA 90015

(213) 747-7606
FAX: (213) 747-7664
URL: http://www.naleo.org/

National Black Child Development Institute
8455 Colesville Road, Ste. 910
Silver Spring, MD 20910
(202) 833-2220
1-800-556-2234
E-mail: moreinfo@nbcdi.org
URL: https://www.nbcdi.org/

**National Caucus and Center
on Black Aging**
1220 L St. NW, Ste. 800
Washington, DC 20005
(202) 637-8400
FAX: (202) 347-0895
URL: http://www.ncba-aged.org/

National Hispanic Council on Aging
2201 12th Street NW Ste. 101
Washington, DC 20009
(202) 347-9733
FAX: (202) 347-9735
URL: http://www.nhcoa.org/

National Indian Gaming Association
224 Second St. SE
Washington, DC 20003
(202) 546-7711
E-mail: questions@indiangaming.org
URL: http://www.indiangaming.org/

National Urban League
120 Wall St.
New York, NY 10005
(212) 558-5300
FAX: (212) 344-5332
URL: http://nul.iamempowered.com/

**OCA—Asian Pacific American
Advocates**
1322 18th St. NW
Washington, DC 20036-1803
(202) 223-5500
FAX: (202) 296-0540

E-mail: oca@ocanational.org
URL: https://www.ocanational.org/

Pew Research Hispanic
1615 L St. NW, Ste. 800
Washington, DC 20036
(202) 419-4300
FAX: (202) 419-4349
URL: http://pewhispanic.org/

Poverty and Race Research Action Council
740 15th St. NW, Ste. 300
Washington, DC 20036
(202) 906-8023
E-mail: info@prrac.org
URL: http://www.prrac.org/

The Sentencing Project
1705 DeSales St. NW, Eighth Floor
Washington, DC 20036
(202) 628-0871
FAX: (202) 628-1091
E-mail: staff@sentencingproject.org
URL: http://www.sentencingproject.org/

Southern Poverty Law Center
400 Washington Ave.
Montgomery, AL 36104
(334) 956-8200
1-888-414-7752
URL: https://www.splcenter.org/

U.S. Bureau of Labor Statistics
Postal Square Bldg.
Two Massachusetts Ave. NE
Washington, DC 20212-0001
(202) 691-5200
URL: https://www.bls.gov/

U.S. Census Bureau
4600 Silver Hill Rd.
Washington, DC 20233
1-800-923-8282
URL: https://www.census.gov/

U.S. Department of Education
400 Maryland Ave. SW
Washington, DC 20202

1-800-872-5327
URL: https://www.ed.gov/

U.S. Department of Health and Human Services
200 Independence Ave. SW
Washington, DC 20201
1-877-696-6775
URL: https://www.hhs.gov/

U.S. Department of Labor
200 Constitution Ave. NW
Washington, DC 20210
1-866-487-2365
URL: https://www.dol.gov/

U.S. Equal Employment Opportunity Commission
131 M St. NE
Washington, DC 20507
(202) 663-4900
1-800-669-4000
E-mail: info@eeoc.gov
URL: https://www.eeoc.gov/

RESOURCES

The U.S. Census Bureau collects and distributes the nation's statistics. Demographic data from the bureau include *Profiles of General Demographic Characteristics, Population Projections Program* (projections released periodically), and *American Community Survey* (released annually). Among the census publications that were used in this book were *The Hispanic Population in the United States: 2013* (January 2017) and *Overview of Race and Hispanic Origin: 2010* (Karen R. Humes, Nicholas A. Jones, and Robert R. Ramirez, March 2011).

Each year as part of its *Facts for Features* series the Census Bureau issues reports that offer current estimates of population demographics, educational and income statistics, and other facts related to specific minority groups. Recent publications in this series include "Hispanic Heritage Month 2017" (October 2017) and "American Indian and Alaska Native Heritage Month: November 2017" (October 2017). The bureau releases financial and family statistics in *America's Families and Living Arrangements: 2016* (April 2017), *Income and Poverty in the United States: 2015* (Bernadette D. Proctor, Jessica L. Semega, and Melissa A. Kollar, September 2016), and *Health Insurance Coverage in the United States: 2015* (Jessica C. Barnett and Marina S. Vornovitsky, September 2016). The Census Bureau also compiles statistics on homeownership rates, business data, state and metropolitan population data, and voting data. Publications include *Voting and Registration in the Election of November 2016* (May 2017), *Household and Families: 2010 Census Brief* (April 2012), and *Voting in America: A Look at the 2016 Presidential Election* (Thom File, May 2017).

The U.S. Bureau of Labor Statistics (BLS) provides labor force data. The BLS publishes *Employment and Earnings, Household Data Annual Averages*, and the monthly *Employment Situation Summary*. The *Monthly Labor Review* provides detailed analysis of labor force statistics on a periodic basis. Other job-related sources

are published by the U.S. Equal Employment Opportunity Commission, including *Enforcement and Litigation Statistics* (2016) and *2015 Job Patterns for Minorities and Women in Private Industry* (2015).

A variety of government resources on minority health proved invaluable. The National Center for Health Statistics produces *Health, United States, 2016: With Chartbook on Long-Term Trends in Health* (May 2017) and the monthly *National Vital Statistics Reports*, which provide birth and mortality statistics. The Centers for Disease Control and Prevention publishes the annual *HIV Surveillance Report*. Another helpful source, *America's Children: Key National Indicators of Well-Being, 2017* (July 2017), is published by the Federal Interagency Forum on Child and Family Statistics. The *SEER Cancer Statistics Review, 1975–2014* (Nadia Howlader et al., June 2017), published by the National Cancer Institute, provides invaluable data on cancer.

A number of U.S. Department of Health and Human Services publications were used in this book. The *2016 National Healthcare Quality and Disparities Report* (July 2017) is helpful in examining differences in health care access and utilization among minority populations. *Welfare Indicators and Risk Factors: Fifteenth Report to Congress* (Gilbert Grouse and Suzanne Macartney, 2016) examines the rates of utilization of a variety of social programs. *Results from the 2015 National Survey on Drug Use and Health: Detailed Tables* (September 2016), published by the Substance Abuse and Mental Health Services Administration, provides information on tobacco, alcohol, and illicit drug use.

The U.S. Department of Education's National Center for Education Statistics (NCES) publishes *The Condition of Education 2016* (Grace Kena et al., May 2016). Other NCES reports that proved helpful were *Digest of Education*

Statistics 2015 (Thomas D. Snyder, Cristobal de Brey, and Sally A. Dillow, December 2016), *Indicators of School Crime and Safety: 2016* (Lauren Musu-Gillette et al., May 2017), *Status and Trends in the Education of Racial and Ethnic Groups 2017* (Lauren Musu-Gillette et al., July 2017), *The Children Born in 2001 at Kindergarten Entry: First Findings from the Kindergarten Data Collections of the Early Childhood Longitudinal Study, Birth Cohort* (Kristin Denton Flanagan and Cameron McPhee, October 2009), *Preschool: First Findings from the Preschool Follow-Up of the Early Childhood Longitudinal Study, Birth Cohort* (Jodi Jacobson Chernoff et al., October 2007), and *American Indian and Alaska Native Children: Findings from the Base Year of the Early Childhood Longitudinal Study, Birth Cohort* (Kristin Denton Flanagan and Jen Park, August 2005). The College Board provides useful data in *2016 College-Bound Seniors: Total Group Profile Report* (2016).

The Bureau of Justice Statistics produces *Homicide Trends in the United States, 1980–2008* (Alexia Cooper and Erica L. Smith, November 2011) as well as numerous other reports. Other Bureau of Justice Statistics reports used in this publication include *Capital Punishment, 2013* (Tracy L. Snell, December 2014), *Prisoners in 2015* (E. Ann Carson and Elizabeth Anderson, December 2016), *Probation and Parole in the United States, 2015* (Danielle Kaeble and Thomas P. Bonczar, December 2016), and *Criminal Victimization, 2015* (Jennifer L. Truman and Rachel E. Morgan, October 2016). *Hate Crime Statistics, 2015* (2016) and *Crime in the United States, 2015* (2016) were published by the Federal Bureau of Investigation.

Finally, Gallup, Inc., provides valuable polling information. Gallup publications used in this book include *Americans' Views of Black-White Relations Deteriorate* (Jeffrey M. Jones, August 2015), *Americans' Satisfaction with Way Blacks Treated Tumbles* (Jeffrey M. Jones, August 2015), *More Favor Major Government Role in Assisting Minorities* (Jeffrey M. Jones, September 2016), and *In U.S., 87% Approve of Black-White Marriage, vs. 4% in 1958* (Frank Newport, July 2013).

INDEX

Page references in italics refer to photographs. References with the letter t *following them indicate the presence of a table. The letter* f *indicates a figure. If more than one table or figure appears on a particular page, the exact item number for the table or figure being referenced is provided.*

A

Abercrombie & Fitch, 66

"Abercrombie Fitch Race Discrimination" (Lieff Cabraser Heimann & Bernstein), 66

"About TANF" (Office of Family Assistance), 83

ACA (Affordable Care Act), 92–93

"Academic Expectations as Sources of Stress in Asian Students" (Tan & Yates), 39–41

Access, health care, 88–94

ACLU (American Civil Liberties Union), 133

Acquired immunodeficiency syndrome (AIDS)

death rates for by race/ethnicity, 119

deaths of persons with an AIDS diagnosis, by year of death/age/race/Hispanic origin/transmission category, 121t–122t

diagnoses, among children less than 13 years of age, by race/Hispanic origin, 112t

diagnoses, by race/Hispanic origin/age/transmission category, 115t–116t

diagnosis, persons living with, by race/Hispanic origin, 110t–111t

HIV infection, persons living with diagnosis of, by race/Hispanic origin, 108t–109t

minorities and, 102–107

overview of, 102

ACT scores, 47–48

Ad Council, 54

Adarand Constructors, 73, 75

Adarand Constructors Inc. v. Peña, 75

Addiction, alcohol, 112

"Admissions Studies Find Flaws" (Trounson), 54

"Adult Obesity Facts" (CDC), 112

Advanced placement (AP) courses, 47

AFCARS Report (HHS), 21

AFDC (Aid to Families with Dependent Children), 83

Affirmative action, 53

Affordable Care Act (ACA), 92–93

"Affordable Care Act May Help Close Gap on Health Disparities" (Ross), 93

African Americans

AIDS/HIV and, 103–107

alcohol use by, 112, 117

Alzheimer's disease and, 100

births/fertility rate of, 95–96

cancer and, 98

children, living arrangements of, 19–20

children living in poverty, 82

death, leading causes of, 118–119

on death row, 138, 141

diabetes among, 102

drug use by, 117

in gangs, 141

geographic distribution of, 8

health care, quality of, 88

health insurance, ACA, 93

health insurance coverage among, 90–91

heart disease among, 99–100

household income of, 77–78

in labor force, 57, 63

life expectancy of, 117

low birth weight/infant mortality, 96–97

mental health and, 102

Obama, Barack, support of, 143

obesity among, 112

occupations for, 67, 70

as offenders, 133

overview of, 7–8

on parole/probation, 137–138

political parties and, 147, 151

population, percentage of, 87

prenatal care for, 95

in prisons/jails, 133, 136–137

racial profiling of, 133

retirement and, 79

school crime and, 131

sickle-cell disease in, 107

SNAP benefits, receiving, 85

students/school segregation, 42–43

tobacco use by, 112

treatment of, rates of satisfaction with, 12(f1.2)

treatment of, views on by, 11

unemployment among, 60

as victims of hate crimes, 126–127

as victims of violent crimes, 123

voter turnout, decline in, 144

voting rights, struggle for, 144

whites, perceptions of relations between, 12(f1.1)

"African Immigration" (LOC), 57

Age

AIDS diagnoses by, 115t–116t

birth rates for women aged 10–19 by, 19t

birth rates of unmarried women by, 17t

children living in poverty by, 84t

civilian labor force by, 69t

deaths due to AIDS diagnosis by, 121t–122t

employment status of civilian noninstitutional population by, 65t

employment status of Hispanic population by, 62(t4.2)

employment status of Mexican/Puerto Rican/Cuban populations by, 64t

family, from means-tested assistance programs by, 85t

hate crime offenders by, 127t

health insurance coverage and, 91

health of minorities and, 87

Hispanic origin population by, 5(t1.5)

of Hispanic population, effect on voting, 151

HIV infection, diagnoses of by, 113t–114t

of homicide victims, 123, 125(t7.2)

illicit drug use by, 119t

living arrangements of children/marital status of parents by, 26t

murder offenders by, 135(t7.8)

older Americans, family income sources of by race/Hispanic origin, 79f

population by, 88t

reason for not voting, 146

reported voting totals by, change in, 147t

sentenced prisoners under state/federal jurisdiction, estimated rate of, per 100,000 U.S. residents by, 136t

sentenced prisoners under state/federal jurisdiction, percentages of by, 135(t7.9)

teenagers' birth rates, by age group, 18f

tobacco product use by, 117t

violent/serious violent crime by, 124t

voting patterns among minorities, effects on, 146

voting rates by age, changes in reported, 148f

Agriculture Act (Farm Bill), 86

Aid to Families with Dependent Children (AFDC), 83

AIDS. *See* Acquired immunodeficiency syndrome

Alaska, 11

Albain, Kathy S., 98

Alcohol

alcohol use, binge alcohol use, heavy alcohol use in past month among persons aged 12 or older, by age, sex, race/Hispanic origin, 118t

health consequences of drinking, 112

Aleuts. *See* Native Americans and Alaskan Natives

Alzheimer's Association, 100

Alzheimer's disease, 100

American Civil Liberties Union (ACLU), 133

American Dream Downpayment Assistance Act, 25

American Immigration Council, 39

American Indian and Alaska Native Children: Findings from the Base Year of the Early Childhood Longitudinal Study, Birth Cohort (Flanagan), 43

"American Indian and Alaska Native Heritage Month" (Census Bureau), 11, 63

American Recovery and Reinvestment Act, 85–86

Americans' Views of Black-White Relations Deteriorate (Jones), 11

America's Children: Key National Indicators of Well-Being, 2017 (Federal Interagency Forum on Child and Family Statistics), 81–82

Amy, Douglas J., 153

"Annual Estimates of the Resident Population by Sex, Race Alone or in Combination, and Hispanic Origin for the United States, States, and Counties: April 1, 2010, to July 1, 2016" (Census Bureau), 10, 11

Annual ORR Reports to Congress—1999 (Office of Refugee Resettlement), 10

AP (advanced placement) courses, 47

Arabs, 5

Arizona, 59

"Arrests on Civil Immigration Charges Go Up 38% in the First 100 Days since Trump's Executive Order" (Duara), 60

Artige, Samantha, 93

Aryan Nation, 127

As in 1963, Blacks Still Feel Disadvantaged in Getting Jobs (Jones), 67

The Asian Alone Population in the United States: 2014 (Census Bureau), 78–79

Asian Americans and Pacific Islanders

AIDS/HIV and, 103–107

alcohol use by, 112, 117

births/fertility rate of, 95–96

cancer and, 98

children, living arrangements of, 20

college completion rate of, 48, 51

death, leading causes of, 118–119

diabetes among, 102

drug use by, 117

geographic distribution of, 10

health care, access to, 89

health care, quality of, 88

health insurance and, 90–91, 93

heart disease among, 99–100

household income of, 78–79

immigration, history of, 8–10

jobs and, 71–73

in labor force, 57–58, 63

low birth weight/infant mortality, 96–97

mental health and, 102

obesity among, 112

overview of, 8

performance in school, 29

population, percentage of, 87

prenatal care for, 95

school crime and, 131

students, 39–42

tobacco use by, 112

as victims of hate crimes, 126

Asian Indians, 10

Asian Pacific American Legal Center, 66

Associated General Contractors of Ohio v. Sandra A. Drabik, 75

Associated Press (AP), 59

B

Bachelor's degree, 48, 51–52

Bacon, Perry, Jr., 143

Baker, Bryan, 5

Bakke, Regents of the University of California v., 53

Balz, Dan, 143

Bank of America Corp. v. City of Miami, Florida, 27

Banks, 27–28

Barlett, Donald L., 75

Barnett, Jessica C., 90–91

Barras, Colin, 10–11

Batista, Fulgencio, 7

Baugh, Ryan

on legal immigrants from Asia, numbers of, 10

on legal immigrants from Mexico, numbers of, 6

BBC.com, 60

Benjamin, Emelia J., 99–100

Ben-Shahar, Omri, 151

Berger, Joseph, 7

Berman, Ari, 154

Bias

hate bias incidents, 126t

hate crimes by bias motivation, 128t–129t

as motivation for hate crimes, 124, 126

Binge alcohol use, 117

Birth rates

for teenage mothers, 17–18

for teenagers, by age group, 18f

of unmarried women, by age/race/Hispanic origin, 17t

for women aged 10–19, by age/race/Hispanic origin, 19t

Births

Hispanic origin population by birth status, 5(t1.5)

low birth weight, infant mortality, 96–97

low-birth weight live births, by detailed race/Hispanic origin of mother, 96t

statistics on, 95–96

See also Pregnancy/birth

"Births: Final Data for 2015" (Martin et al.)

on births to single mothers, 16–17

statistics on, 95–96

Black, as term, 3

See also African Americans

Black codes, 57

Black Philosophies of Education (Howard University), 55

Black Psychology (Florida A&M University), 55

Black Social and Political Thought (Howard University), 55

"Blacks Getting Equal Health Care Are Still More Likely to Die from Some Cancers" (Stein), 98

"Blacks Shift to Obama, Poll Finds" (Balz & Cohen), 143

Bloomberg, Michael, 133

BLS (U.S. Bureau of Labor Statistics)

on Asian American professionals, numbers of, 71–73

on unemployment, 60

A Blueprint for Reform: The Reauthorization of the Elementary and Secondary Education Act (Department of Education), 44

Board of Education of Topeka, Kansas, Brown v., 42

Bollinger, Gratz v., 54

Bollinger, Grutter v., 54

Border fence, 59

Boudreau, Catherine, 86

Bracero Program, 58

Brain, Alzheimer's disease and, 100

Breast cancer

incidence/death rates, by race/Hispanic origin, 103f

by race/ethnicity, 98

Brenchley, Cameron, 44–45

Brennan Center for Justice, 144

"Broad Opposition to Guest Worker Program" (AP), 59

Bronchus cancer

incidence/death rates, by race/Hispanic origin, 105f

minorities and, 98

Brooks, Chad, 36

Brown v. Board of Education of Topeka, Kansas, 42

Bureau of Indian Affairs (BIA), 63

Bureau of Justice Statistics, 141

Bush, George W.

disillusionment with administration, 151

guest-worker program of, 59

Hispanic views on, 152

housing for minorities and, 24–25

No Child Left Behind Act and, 44

Business, 73, 75

C

California

affirmative action in, 53–54

Hispanic population of, 6

Native Americans/Alaskan Natives in, 11

California Civil Rights Initiative, 53

Cambodia, 58

"Can Obama Count on the Black Vote?" (Bacon), 143

Cancer

incidence/death rates, colon/rectum cancer, by race/Hispanic origin, 106f

incidence/death rates, female breast cancer, by race/Hispanic origin, 103f

incidence/death rates, lung/bronchus cancer, by race/Hispanic origin, 105f

incidence/death rates, prostate cancer, by race/Hispanic origin, 104f

incidence rates/trends for top 15 cancer sites, by race/Hispanic origin, 99t–100t

as leading cause of death, 118

minorities and, 98

mortality rates/trends for top 15 cancer sites, by race/Hispanic origin, 101t–102t

Capital Punishment, 2013—Statistical Tables (Snell), 138

Capotorti, Francesco, 1

Casinos, tribal, 75

Castro, Fidel, 7

Castro, Joaquin, 152

Castro, Julian, 152

Categories, racial. *See* Classification, racial/ethnic origin

CBC (Congressional Black Caucus), 151

CBPP (Center on Budget and Policy Priorities), 8586

CBS News, 137

Census Bureau. *See* U.S. Census Bureau

"Census: Uninsured Rate Dropped to 8.8 Percent Last Year" (Demko), 93

Center for Research on Education Outcomes, 46–47

Center on Budget and Policy Priorities (CBPP), 8586

Center-based early childhood programs, 32

Centers for Disease Control and Prevention (CDC)

on AIDS, 102–105

on diabetes, 101–102

on illicit drug use, 117

on obesity, 112

on tobacco use, 107

Cerebrovascular diseases, 118

"Changes Lead to Shorter Sentences for 26,000 Drug Defendants" (CBS News), 137

"A Changing America: In 2012, Blacks Outvoted Whites" (Page & Overberg), 147

Changing Face of America Helps Assure Obama Victory (Pew Research Center), 151

Characteristics and Financial Circumstances of TANF Recipients, Fiscal Year (FY) 2016 (Office of Family Assistance), 83

Charter schools, 45–46

Chavez-Thompson, Linda, 152

Chernoff, Jodi Jacobson, 31

Chicago, IL, 141

Child Trends Databank, 95

"Childhood Obesity Facts" (CDC), 112

Children

AIDS diagnoses among children less than 13 years of age, by race/Hispanic origin, 112t

birth rates for women aged 10–19, by age/race/Hispanic origin, 19t

health insurance coverage among, 91

with HIV/AIDS, 104–105

living arrangements of, 19–21

living arrangements of, by race and Hispanic origin, 23f

living arrangements of, marital status of parents, by age/race/Hispanic origin, 26t

living in poverty, 81–82

living in poverty, by age/family structure/race/Hispanic origin, 84t

obesity among, 112

See also Pregnancy/birth

The Children Born in 2001 at Kindergarten Entry: First Findings from the Kindergarten Data Collections of the Early Childhood Longitudinal Study, Birth Cohort (Flanagan & McPhee), 31–32

Chinese, 8

Chinese Exclusion Act, 8

"Chinese Immigration" (Library of Congress), 8

"Chinese Immigration to the United States, 1851–1900" (LOC), 57

Cigarette smoking

minorities and, 112

trends in, 107

CIS (U.S. Citizenship and Immigration Services), 39

Citizens, native/naturalized, 144

Citizenship, Hispanic origin population by, 5(t1.5)

City of Miami, Florida, Bank of America Corp. v., 27

Civil Rights Act

employment protections provided by, 66

minority registered voters, increase of due to, 144

race-based charges filed/resolved under Title VII of, 68t

Civilian population

employed persons by occupation/race/Hispanic origin/sex, 70t–71t

employment status of, by race/sex/age, 61t–62t

labor force, by age/sex/race/ethnicity, 69t

noninstitutional, employment status of by sex/age/race, 65t

Classification, racial/ethnic origin

changing, 2–3

2000 Census, 3–4

2010 Census, 4–5

Clinton, Bill

African Americans' attitude toward, 151

housing for minorities and, 22

tax exemptions for firms in Puerto Rico, 6

Clinton, Hillary Rodham, 143, 151
CNN, 59, 147
*Coalition to Defend Affirmative Action,
Schuette v.*, 54
Cocaine, 137
Cohen, Jon, 143
Cohn, D'Vera, 5
College
historically black colleges/universities,
55
minority attendance in, 48
preparation for, 47
tribal colleges, 55
See also Higher education
College Board, 47–48
Colon cancer, 98, 106*f*
Columbus, Christopher, 11
"Commercial Exploitation of the Third
World" (Howard University), 55
Community Reinvestment Act, 22
Comprehensive Immigration Reform Act,
36
The Condition of Education 2005 (NCES)
on African American/Hispanic children,
preparation for school of, 29
on Asian American children, preparation
for school of, 29
on public school enrollment, 1980s
increase in, 29
The Condition of Education 2016 (Kena et
al.)
on center-based preschool enrollment, 32
on charter schools, 46
on college degrees among minorities, 48,
51–52
on kindergarten enrollment, 32
on public school enrollment, 29
The Condition of Education 2017
(McFarland et al.), 82
Congressional Black Caucus (CBC), 151
Conner, Thaddieus W., 76
"Consideration of Deferred Action for
Childhood Arrivals" (CIS), 39
Contreras, Kate Spilde, 76
Cooper, Alexia
on gang-related homicides, 141
on homicide offenders, 133
Cornell, Stephen, 76
"The Cost of Employee Turnover Due
Solely to Unfairness in the Workplace"
(Level Playing Field Institute), 66
Court cases
Adarand Constructors Inc. v. Peña, 75
*Associated General Contractors of Ohio
v. Sandra A. Drabik*, 75
*Bank of America Corp. v. City of Miami,
Florida*, 27
*Brown v. Board of Education of Topeka,
Kansas*, 42
Fisher v. University of Texas, 54
Gill v. Whitford, 154

Gratz v. Bollinger, 54
Grutter v. Bollinger, 54
Hopwood v. Texas, 53
Loving v. Virginia, 15
*Parents Involved in Community Schools
v. Seattle School District*, 43
*Regents of the University of California v.
Bakke*, 53
Richmond v. J. A. Croson Co., 73
*Schuette v. Coalition to Defend
Affirmative Action*, 54
"Court of Appeals Hands Wells Fargo
Victory over Los Angeles in Fair
Housing Lawsuit" (Lane), 27
Coyote Stories (Salish Kootenai College), 55
Crack, 137
Cracking, electoral district, 153
*Created Equal: Racial and Ethnic
Disparities in the U.S. Justice System*
(Hartney & Vuong), 136
Crime
drugs, students in grades 9–12 who
reported that drugs were made
available to them on school property
during previous 12 months, by race/
Hispanic origin, 132(*f*7.3)
executions/other dispositions of inmates
sentenced to death, by race/Hispanic
origin, 141*t*
gang, students aged 12–18 who reported
that gangs were present at school,
132(*f*7.2)
gangs, 141
hate bias incidents, 126*t*
hate crime offenders, by race/ethnicity,
age, 127*t*
hate crimes, 123–124, 126–127
hate crimes, by bias motivation,
128*t*–129*t*
hate crimes, students aged 12–18 who
reported being targets of hate-related
words/seeing hate-related graffiti at
school during school year, 134*f*
hate groups in U.S., 130*f*
homicide victims, by age, sex, race/
ethnicity, 125(*t*7.2)
homicide victims, race/sex of, by race/
sex of offender, 125(*t*7.3)
illegal immigrants with criminal records,
60
murder offenders by age, sex, race/
Hispanic origin, 135(*t*7.8)
offenders, minorities as, 133
parole, characteristics of adults on,
138(*t*7.11)
prisoners under sentence of death, by
region/jurisdiction/race, 139*t*–140*t*
prisons/jails, 133, 136–138, 141
probation, characteristics of adults on,
138(*t*7.12)
racial profiling, 133
at school, 127, 131, 133

sentenced prisoners under state/federal
jurisdiction, estimated rate of, per
100,000 U.S. residents, by sex/race/
Hispanic origin/age, 136*t*
sentenced prisoners under state/federal
jurisdiction, percentages of, by sex/
race/Hispanic origin/age, 135(*t*7.9)
student-reported nonfatal crimes against
students aged 12–18/rate of crimes per
1,000 students at school, by type of
crime, 131*t*
violent crimes, 123
violent/serious violent crime, by sex/
race/Hispanic origin/age of victim,
124*t*
Crime in the United States, 2015 (FBI), 123
Criminal Victimization, 2015 (Truman &
Morgan), 123
Crouse, Gilbert, 83, 85
Cruz, Ted, 152
Cuban Americans
employment opportunities for, 71
population, employment status of by sex/
age, 64*t*
population, overview of, 7
Cubans in the United States (Pew Hispanic
Center), 7
Cullen, James, 133
Cumberland Environmental Resources
Company, 59
*Current Population Survey, March and
Annual Social and Economic
Supplements* (Census Bureau)
on divorce, numbers of, 16
on marriages, numbers of, 15

D

DACA (Deferred Action for Childhood
Arrivals), 39
Daniels, Charles, 66
"Data & Statistics" (CDC), 107
"Data on Race and Ethnicity: Revising the
Federal Standard" (Wallman), 2
DBE (Disadvantaged Business Enterprise)
program, 73
De Brey, Cristobal
on African American/Hispanic high
school graduation rates, 42
on black colleges/universities,
enrollment numbers in, 55
on college preparatory work in high
school, 47
on graduate degrees earned by
minorities, 52
on higher education enrollment among
minorities, 48
on Hispanic students, educational
attainment of, 43
on math/science scores, 4th/8th graders,
36
on reading scores, 4th/8th graders, 32–33
on school segregation, 43

Death row
    prisoners on, 138, 141
    prisoners under sentence of death, by
        region, jurisdiction, race, 139t–140t
Deaths
    by causes of death, race/Hispanic origin,
        sex, 120t
    from diabetes, 101
    from heart disease, 100
    incidence/death rates, colon/rectum
        cancer, by race/Hispanic origin, 106f
    incidence/death rates, female breast
        cancer, by race/Hispanic origin, 103f
    incidence/death rates, lung/bronchus
        cancer, by race/Hispanic origin, 105f
    incidence/death rates, prostate cancer, by
        race/Hispanic origin, 104f
    infant mortality rates, 96–97
    leading causes of death, 118–119
    of persons with an AIDS diagnosis, by
        year of death/age/race/Hispanic origin/
        transmission category, 121t–122t
    spouse, death of, 16
    from tobacco use, 107
"Deaths: Final Data for 2014" (Kochanek
    et al.), 117
Deferred Action for Childhood Arrivals
    (DACA), 39
"Definition of a Disadvantaged Business
    Enterprise" (DOT), 73
Demko, Paul, 93
Democratic Party
    African American support of, 147
    electoral districting and, 153
    Hispanic support of, 151, 152
    Obama, Barack, election of and, 151
"Demographics" (National Gang Center),
    141
Deportation, 60
Development, Relief, and Education for
    Alien Minors (DREAM) Act, 36
DeVos, Betsy, 45
Diabetes
    overview of, 100–101
    prevalence among adults aged 20/older,
        by diagnosis status, race/ethnicity, 107f
    by race/ethnicity, 101–102
Digest of Education Statistics 2015 (Snyder,
    de Brey, & Dillow)
    on African American/Hispanic high
        school graduation rates, 42
    on black colleges/universities,
        enrollment numbers in, 55
    on college preparatory work in high
        school, 47
    on graduate degrees earned by
        minorities, 52
    on higher education enrollment among
        minorities, 48
    on Hispanic students, educational
        attainment of, 43

    on math/science scores, 4th/8th graders,
        36
    on reading scores, 4th/8th graders, 32–33
    on school segregation, 43
Dillow, Sally A.
    on African American/Hispanic high
        school graduation rates, 42
    on black colleges/universities,
        enrollment numbers in, 55
    on college preparatory work in high
        school, 47
    on graduate degrees earned by
        minorities, 52
    on higher education enrollment among
        minorities, 48
    on Hispanic students, educational
        attainment of, 43
    on math/science scores, 4th/8th graders,
        36
    on reading scores, 4th/8th graders, 32–33
    on school segregation, 43
Disadvantaged Business Enterprise (DBE)
    program, 73
"Discrimination at Work Growing Subtle"
    (Ostrov), 66
Discriminatory employment practices
    economic opportunities, views of, 67
    Equal Employment Opportunity
        Commission, 66–67
    overview of, 66
Diseases
    AIDS, 102–107
    AIDS diagnoses, among children less
        than 13 years of age, by race/Hispanic
        origin, 112t
    AIDS diagnoses, by race/Hispanic
        origin/age/transmission category,
        115t–116t
    AIDS diagnosis, persons living with, by
        race/Hispanic origin, 110t–111t
    Alzheimer's disease, 100
    cancer, 98
    cancer incidence rates/trends for top 15
        cancer sites, by race/Hispanic origin,
        99t–100t
    cancer mortality rates/trends for top 15
        cancer sites, by race/Hispanic origin,
        101t–102t
    death, leading causes of, 118119
    diabetes, 100–102
    diabetes prevalence among adults aged
        20/older, by diagnosis status/race/
        ethnicity, 107f
    heart disease/stroke, 98–100
    HIV infection, diagnoses of, by race/
        Hispanic origin/age/transmission
        category, 113t–114t
    HIV infection, persons living with
        diagnosis of, by race/Hispanic origin,
        108t–109t
    incidence/death rates, colon and rectum
        cancer, by race/Hispanic origin, 106f

    incidence/death rates, female breast
        cancer, by race/Hispanic origin, 103f
    incidence/death rates, lung and bronchus
        cancer, by race/Hispanic origin, 105f
    incidence/death rates, prostate cancer, by
        race/Hispanic origin, 104f
    mental health, minorities and, 102
    sickle-cell disease in African Americans,
        107
Divorce, 16
"Do Voter Identification Laws Suppress
    Minority Voting? Yes. We Did the
    Research" (Hajnal, Lajevardi, &
    Nielsen), 144, 146
Doctor visits
    health care visits to doctor offices,
        emergency departments, home visits
        within past 12 months, by race,
        Hispanic origin, poverty level, 94t–95t
    by minorities, 93
Doherty, Carroll
    on African American political party
        affiliations, 147
    on Hispanic political party affiliations,
        152
DOJ (U.S. Department of Justice), 153–154
DOT (U.S. Department of Transportation),
    73
"The Dream Act, DACA, and Other
    Policies Designed to Protect Dreamers"
    (American Immigration Council), 39
Dreamers, 36, 39
Dropping out
    among African Americans, 42
    of college, 48
    among Native Americans, 43
    of school, results of, 36, 39
Drug abuse
    alcohol, 112, 117
    illicit drug use, 117
Drugs
    homicide offenders and, 133
    illicit drug use, 117
    illicit drug use by age/sex/race/Hispanic
        origin, 119t
    racial disparities in sentencing and, 137
    at school, 131
    students in grades 9–12 who reported
        that drugs were made available to
        them on school property during
        previous 12 months, by race/Hispanic
        origin, 132(f7.3)
Duara, Nigel, 60

E

Early Childhood Longitudinal Study, Birth
    Cohort (NCES)
    on Native American education, 43
    on preschoolers' readiness for school,
        29, 31
East Harlem, 7

Economic opportunities, 67

Economic Policy Institute, 59

EdChoice, 45

Education

    bachelor's degree or higher, 25- to 29-year-olds with, by race/Hispanic origin, 44*f*

    dropout rates, 16/24-year-olds, by race/Hispanic origin/nativity, 42*f*

    enrollment rates, 18- to 24-year-olds in degree-granting institutions, by type of institution/sex/race/Hispanic origin of student, 50*t*

    full-time faculty at degree-granting institutions, by academic rank/sex/race/ethnicity, 52*f*

    high school dropouts, 16/24-year-olds who were, by sex/race/Hispanic origin, 41*t*

    high school students earning AP/IB credits, percentage of by academic subject/race/ethnicity, 48*f*

    higher education, 47–48, 51–55

    kindergarten/elementary/secondary, 32–33, 36, 39

    mathematics scores, 4th/8th-grade students, by race/Hispanic origin/jurisdiction/urban school district, 37*t*–38*t*

    mathematics scores, 12th-grade, by race/Hispanic origin/highest mathematics level attained, 39*f*

    minority students in school, 39–43

    overview of, 29

    preprimary, 32

    preschool enrollment, by race/ethnicity/attendance status, 33(*f*3.2)

    public elementary/high school students, number/percentage distribution of by race/ethnicity, 30*t*

    public high school freshman graduation rates, by race/Hispanic origin, 43*f*

    public school students in prekindergarten–12th grade, number of by region/race/ethnicity, 31*f*

    public school students in prekindergarten–12th grade, percentage distribution of by race/Hispanic origin, 33(*f*3.3)

    public school system, reforming, 44–47

    reading scores of 4th/8th-grade students, by race/Hispanic origin/jurisdiction/urban school district, 34*t*–35*t*

    risk factors in, 29, 31–32

    SAT scores of college-bound seniors, by race/Hispanic origin, 49*t*

    science scale scores by sex/grade/race/Hispanic origin, 40*t*

    status dropout rates, 16/24-year-olds, by race/Hispanic origin, 41*f*

    traditional public/charter schools, percentage of by racial/ethnic concentration, 46*f*

undergraduate enrollment distribution, by institutional level/race/ethnicity, 51*f*

"Education Department Awards More than $2.7 Million to 12 Colleges to Strengthen Minority Participation in STEM-Related Fields" (Department of Education), 52–53

EEOC. *See* U.S. Equal Employment Opportunity Commission

"18 Examples of Racism in the Criminal Legal System" (Quigley), 137

1860 census, 7

El Nasser, Haya, 3–4

El Salvador, 58

Elauf, Samantha, 66

ELC (Eligibility in the Local Context), 54

Electoral districts, 152–153

"Elementary & Secondary Education: ESEA Flexibility" (Department of Education), 44–45

Elementary school. *See* School

Eligibility in the Local Context (ELC), 54

"Eligibility in the Local Context" (University of California), 54

Emancipation Proclamation, 7, 57

Emergency departments, 94*t*–95*t*

Employment

    practices, discriminatory, 66–67

    by race/ethnicity, 63–65

    See also Labor force

The Employment Situation—August 2017 (BLS), 60

"Ending New York's Stop-and-Frisk Did Not Increase Crime" (Cullen), 133

English, college preparatory courses for, 47

Eskimos. *See* Native Americans and Alaskan Natives

Estimates of the Unauthorized Immigrant Population Residing in the United States: January 2012 (Baker & Rytina), 5

Ethnic classifications, 2–5

Evaluating Components of International Migration: Legal Migrants (Perry et al.), 58

"Every Student Succeeds Act" (Department of Education), 45

Every Student Succeeds Act (ESSA), 45

Evich, Helena Bottemiller, 86

Extreme poverty, 80

F

"Facts about Sickle Cell Disease" (CDC), 107

Facts on U.S. Latinos, 2015 (Flores, López, & Radford), 87

Fair Sentencing Act, 137

Families

    birth rates for teenagers, by age group, 18*f*

    birth rates for women aged 10–19, by age/race/Hispanic origin, 19*t*

births/birth rates to unmarried women, by age/race/Hispanic origin, 17*t*

Census Bureau definition of, 18

children's living arrangements, by race/Hispanic origin, 23*f*

family groups, types of, by race/Hispanic origin, 22(*t*2.5)

family life/living arrangements, overview of, 15

health characteristics of mother/infant at birth, by Hispanic origin of mother, 21*t*

health characteristics of mother/infant at birth, by race, 20*t*

Hispanic origin households, by household type, 22(*t*2.6)

homeownership among, 21–25, 27–28

homeownership rates by race/Hispanic origin of householder, 27*t*

living arrangements of children/marital status of parents, by age/race/Hispanic origin, 26*t*

marital status among, 15–16

means-tested assistance, female-headed families receiving, 85

minority, structure of, 18–21

multigenerational households, by race/Hispanic origin, 24*t*

one-parent households, by race/sex, 23*t*

in poverty, 81*t*–82*t*

pregnancy among, 16–18

same-sex couples, by differences in race/Hispanic origin/age, 25*t*

whites/African Americans, approval of marriages between, 16*f*

Fan, Weihua, 39–41

Fannie Mae (Federal National Mortgage Association)

    housing for minorities and, 23–24

    mortgage program for low-income borrowers, 28

Farm Bill, 86

Farmworker Justice, 59

Faulders, Katherine, 127

Fears, Darryl, 59

Federal Bureau of Investigation (FBI), 123

"Federal Court Blocks Discriminatory Texas Redistricting Plan" (Berman), 154

Federal Equal Opportunity Recruitment Program (FEORP), Fiscal Year 2014 (U.S. Office of Personnel Management), 73

Federal government. *See* Government, federal; United States

Federal Home Loan Mortgage Corporation (Freddie Mac)

    housing for minorities and, 23–24

    subprime mortgage crisis and, 27

Federal Housing Finance Agency, 27

Federal Interagency Forum on Child and Family Statistics, 81–82

"Federal Judge Blocks Trump's Third Travel Ban" (Zapotosky), 60

Federal National Mortgage Association (Fannie Mae)

    housing for minorities and, 23–24

    subprime mortgage crisis and, 27

Felsenthal, Mark, 93

Female-headed families, 85

Females

    breast cancer among, 98

    deaths from heart disease, 100

    HIV/AIDS transmission, 106–107

    incidence/death rates, female breast cancer, by race/Hispanic origin, 103f

    life expectancy of, 117

    minorities in prisons/jails, 133, 136–137

    See also Gender; Mothers

Fence, border, 59

Fertility rate, Hispanics, 87

Fifteen Years of Guidelines Sentencing: An Assessment of How Well the Federal Criminal Justice System Is Achieving the Goals of Sentencing Reform (USSC), 137

15th Amendment, 7

Findings from the First-Grade Rounds of the Early Childhood Longitudinal Study, Kindergarten Class of 2010–11 (Mulligan et al.), 31–32

Findings from the Third-Grade Round of the Early Childhood Longitudinal Study, Kindergarten Class of 2010–11 (Mulligan et al.), 31–32

Finegold, Kenneth, 93

"First Americans May Have Been Neanderthals 130,000 Years Ago" (Barras), 10–11

Fisher, Abigail, 54

Fisher v. University of Texas, 54

Flanagan, Kristin Denton

    on early reading scale scores of kindergarten students, 31–32

    on educational risk factors among Native Americans, 43

Fletcher, Michael A., 59

Flores, Antonio, 87

Flores, Stella M., 54

Florida

    Opportunity Scholarship voucher system, 45

    stand-your-ground gun law of, 11

Florida A&M University, 55

Floyd, Ife, 85–86

Food Stamp Act, 83

Foreign languages, college preparatory courses for, 47

Foster care, 20–21

14th Amendment

    African Americans and, 7

    ratification of, 57

Foutz, Julia, 93

"Frank to Recommend Replacing Fannie Mae, Freddie Mac" (Kopecki & Vekshin), 27

Freddie Mac (Federal Home Loan Mortgage Corporation)

    housing for minorities and, 23–24

    subprime mortgage crisis and, 27

Frey, William H., 143

Friedman, Milton, 45

From Colonia to Community: The History of Puerto Ricans in New York City (Sánchez Korrol), 6–7

Fry, Richard, 36, 152

Frye, Joanna R., 55

Fund for Advancement of Minorities through Education (Pittsburgh, PA), 54–55

G

"Gambling Expansion Advocates Ignore the Facts about Tribal Gaming" (Williams), 93

"Gaming Revenue Tight in 2008" (Stutz), 76

Gangs

    overview of, 141

    students aged 12–18 who reported that gangs were present at school, 132(f7.2)

GAO. *See* U.S. Government Accountability Office

Gee, Emily, 93

Gender

    alcohol use, binge alcohol use, heavy alcohol use in past month among persons aged 12 or older by, 118t

    cancer incidence rates and, 98

    civilian labor force by, 69t

    deaths by causes of death by, 120t

    deaths from heart disease by, 100

    diabetes and, 101–102

    employed Hispanic workers by, 72t

    employed persons by, 70t–71t

    employment status of civilian noninstitutional population by, 65t

    employment status of civilian population by, 61t–62t

    employment status of Hispanic population by, 62(t4.2)

    employment status of Mexican/Puerto Rican/Cuban populations by, 64t

    full-time faculty at degree-granting institutions by, 52f

    high school dropouts, 16/24-year-olds who were, 41t

    Hispanic origin population by, 5(t1.5)

    HIV/AIDS transmission and, 105–107

    homicide rates and, 118

    homicide victims by, 125(t7.2)

    illicit drug use by, 119t

    life expectancy and, 117, 119f

    minorities in prisons/jails by, 133, 136–137

    murder offenders by, 135(t7.8)

    occupational employment in private industry by, 74t

    population by, 88t

    reason for not voting, 146

    science scale scores by, 40t

    sentenced prisoners under state/federal jurisdiction, estimated rate of, per 100,000 U.S. residents by, 136t

    sentenced prisoners under state/federal jurisdiction, percentages of by, 135(t7.9)

    tobacco product use by, 117t

    violent/serious violent crime, by sex/race/Hispanic origin/age of victim, 124t

Genetics, sickle-cell disease and, 107

Gentlemen's Agreement, 58

Geographic distribution

    of Asian Americans and Pacific Islanders, 10

    of Hispanics in U.S., 6

    of Native Americans and Alaskan Natives, 11

Gerry, Elbridge, 153

Gerrymandering, 153

Gerstein, Josh, 154

Get tough policy, 58–59

Gibson, Campbell, 9–10

Gill v. Whitford, 154

Giuliani, Rudolph, 133

Glasser, Ruth, 6–7

Glink, Ilyce R., 27

Goldstein, Joseph, 133

Government, federal

    minority employment in, 73

    poverty, programs of addressing, 82–85

    See also United States

Graduate school, 52–53

Gratz v. Bollinger, 54

Great Recession

    poverty thresholds, effect on, 79

    tribal casinos and, 76

    unemployment and, 60

Great Society, 151

The Green Book (U.S. House of Representatives Committee on Ways and Means), 83

Grutter v. Bollinger, 54

Guatemala, 58

Guest-worker programs, 59

Guidelines, poverty, 80t

H

H-2B program, 59

Hajnal, Zoltan L., 144, 146

Harrell, Erika, 141

Hartney, Christopher, 136

Harvard Law Review, 153

Hate Crime Statistics Act, 124

Hate crimes

    by bias motivation, 128t–129t

    hate bias incidents, 126t

hate crime offenders, by race/ethnicity/ age, 127t

hate groups in U.S., 130f

history of, 123–124

by race/ethnicity, 126–127

at school, 133

students aged 12–18 who reported being targets of hate-related words/seeing hate-related graffiti at school during school year, 134f

Hate groups, 127

Health

AIDS diagnoses, among children less than 13 years of age, by race/Hispanic origin, 112t

AIDS diagnoses, by race, Hispanic origin, age, transmission category, 115t–116t

AIDS diagnosis, persons living with, by race/Hispanic origin, 110t–111t

alcohol use, binge alcohol use, heavy alcohol use in past month among persons aged 12 or older, by age/sex/ race/Hispanic origin, 118t

behaviors that threaten, 107, 112, 117

cancer incidence rates/trends for top 15 cancer sites, by race/Hispanic origin, 99t–100t

cancer mortality rates/trends for top 15 cancer sites, by race/Hispanic origin, 101t–102t

deaths by causes of death/race/Hispanic origin/sex, 120t

deaths of persons with AIDS diagnosis, by year of death/age/race/Hispanic origin/transmission category, 121t–122t

diabetes prevalence among adults aged 20/older, by diagnosis status/race/ ethnicity, 107f

diseases, 98–107

health care, 87–94

health care, proportion of minority groups that experienced better, same, or poorer access to, compared with reference group, 89(f6.2)

health care, proportion of minority groups that experienced better, same, or poorer quality of, compared with reference group, 89(f6.1)

health care visits to doctor offices, emergency departments, home visits within past 12 months, by race/ Hispanic origin/poverty level, 94t–95t

health insurance coverage, of noninstitutionalized Medicare beneficiaries 65 years of age/over, by type of coverage/race/Hispanic origin, 92t

health insurance coverage, people without, 90f

HIV infection, diagnoses of, by race/ Hispanic origin/age/transmission category, 113t–114t

HIV infection, persons living with diagnosis of, by race/Hispanic origin, 108t–109t

illicit drug use by age/sex/race/Hispanic origin, 119t

incidence/death rates, colon and rectum cancer, by race/Hispanic origin, 106f

incidence/death rates, female breast cancer, by race/Hispanic origin, 103f

incidence/death rates, lung and bronchus cancer, by race/Hispanic origin, 105f

incidence/death rates, prostate cancer, by race/Hispanic origin, 104f

infant, neonatal, postneonatal mortality rates, by detailed race/Hispanic origin of mother, 97t

life expectancy, by race/sex, 119f

life expectancy/death, 117–119

low-birth-weight live births, by detailed race/Hispanic origin of mother, 96t

Medicaid coverage among persons under 65 years of age, by race/Hispanic origin, 91t

mother/infant at birth, characteristics of by Hispanic origin of mother, 21t

mother/infant at birth, characteristics of by race, 20t

overview of, 87

population by sex/age/race/Hispanic origin, 88t

pregnancy and, 18

pregnancy/birth, 94–97

tobacco product use by age/sex/race/ Hispanic origin, 117t

Health, behaviors that threaten

alcohol use, binge alcohol use, heavy alcohol use in past month among persons aged 12 or older, by age/sex/ race/Hispanic origin, 118t

cigarette smoking, 107, 112

drug abuse, 112, 117

illicit drug use by age/sex/race/Hispanic origin, 119t

obesity/poor nutrition, 112

tobacco product use by age/sex/race/ Hispanic origin, 117t

Health care

access to care, 88–94

health insurance coverage of noninstitutionalized Medicare beneficiaries 65 years of age/over, by type of coverage/race/Hispanic origin, 92t

health insurance coverage, people without, 90f

Medicaid coverage among persons under 65 years of age, by race/Hispanic origin, 91t

mental health care, access to, 102

proportion of minority groups that experienced better, same, or poorer access to, compared with reference group, 89(f6.2)

proportion of minority groups that experienced better, same, or poorer quality of, compared with reference group, 89(f6.1)

quality of care, 87–88

visits to doctor offices, emergency departments, home visits within past 12 months, by race/Hispanic origin/ poverty level, 94t–95t

Health insurance

Affordable Care Act, 92–93

health insurance coverage of noninstitutionalized Medicare beneficiaries 65 years of age/over, by type of coverage/race/Hispanic origin, 92t

health insurance coverage, people without, 90f

lack of, 90–91

Medicaid coverage among persons under 65 years of age, by race/Hispanic origin, 91t

Health Insurance Coverage and the Affordable Care Act, 2010–2016 (Demko, Uberoi, & Gee), 93

Health, United States, 2016: With Chartbook on Long-Term Trends in Health (NCHS)

on deaths from heart disease, 100

leading causes of death, 118119

on low birth weight, 96

Heart disease, 118

"Heart Disease and Stroke Statistics— 2017 Update" (Benjamin et al.), 99–100

Heart disease/stroke

deaths from, 100

high blood pressure, 99–100

incidence of, 98–99

Heterosexual contact, HIV/AIDS transmission via, 106–107

HHS. *See* U.S. Department of Health and Human Services

High blood pressure, 99–100

High school

college preparation in, 47

dropouts, 16/24-year-olds who were, by sex/race/Hispanic origin, 41t

dropout rates, 16/24-year-olds, by race/ Hispanic origin/nativity, 42f

public high school freshman graduation rates, by race/Hispanic origin, 43f

SAT scores of college-bound seniors, by race/Hispanic origin, 49t

SAT/ACT scores, 47–48

status dropout rates, 16/24-year-olds, by race/Hispanic origin, 41f

students earning AP/IB credits, percentage of by academic subject/ race/ethnicity, 48f

See also School, crime at

The Higher Dropout Rate of Foreign-Born Teens: The Role of Schooling Abroad (Fry), 36

Higher education
  affirmative action in, 53–54
  bachelor's degree, earning, 48, 51–52
  bachelor's degree or higher, 25- to 29-year-olds with, by race/Hispanic origin, 44f
  black colleges/universities, 55
  college preparation, 47
  enrollment rates, 18- to 24-year-olds in degree-granting institutions, by type of institution/sex/race/Hispanic origin of student, 50t
  full-time faculty at degree-granting institutions, by academic rank/sex/race/ethnicity, 52f
  graduate school, 52–53
  minority college attendance, 48
  minority education advocacy, 54–55
  SAT scores of college-bound seniors, by race/Hispanic origin, 49t
  SAT/ACT scores, 47–48
  tribal colleges, 55
  undergraduate enrollment distribution, by institutional level/race/ethnicity, 51f

Hill, Paul T., 46

Hirschfeld, Julie, 39

"Hispanic Heritage Month 2017" (Census Bureau), 6

The Hispanic Population in the United States: 2013 (Census Bureau), 77, 79–80

Hispanics
  AIDS/HIV and, 103–107
  alcohol use by, 112, 117
  Alzheimer's disease and, 100
  birth rates for women aged 10–19, 19t
  birth rates of unmarried women, 17t
  births/fertility rate of, 95–96
  cancer and, 98
  children, living arrangements of, 20
  children living in poverty, 81–82
  college completion rate of, 51
  Cuban Americans, 7
  death, leading causes of, 118–119
  on death row, 141
  diabetes among, 102
  drug use by, 117
  educational attainment, increase of, 43
  employed, by sex/occupation/class of workers/full or part-time status/ethnic group, 72t
  employment status of, by race/sex/age, 62(t4.2)
  employment status of Mexican/Puerto Rican/Cuban populations, by sex/age, 64t
  in gangs, 141
  geographic distribution of, 6
  health care, access to, 88–91
  health care, quality of, 88

health insurance, ACA, 93
health insurance coverage among, 90–91
health of, 87
health of mother/infant at birth, characteristics of by Hispanic origin of mother, 21t
heart disease among, 99–100
Hispanic origin households, by household type, 22(t2.6)
Hispanic origin population, by birth status, 5(t1.4)
Hispanic origin population, by citizenship/birth status/age/sex, 5(t1.5)
Hispanic origin population, by type, 6t
homeownership rates by Hispanic origin of householder, 27t
household income of, 77
jobs and, 71
in labor force, 63
in labor force, historical perspective, 58–59
life expectancy of, 117
living arrangements of children/marital status of parents, by Hispanic origin, 26t
low birth weight/infant mortality, 96–97
mental health and, 102
Mexican Americans, 6
obesity among, 112
origins of, 5–6
overview of, 5
political participation of, 151–152
preference for Latino, 2–3
prenatal care for, 95
in prisons/jails, 133, 136–137
on probation, 138
public school, enrollment in by, 29
Puerto Ricans, 6–7
racial profiling of, 133
retirement and, 79
school crime and, 131
school dropout rates of, 36
SNAP benefits, receiving, 85
subgroups, poverty among, 79–80
tobacco use by, 112
as victims of hate crimes, 126–127
as victims of violent crimes, 123
voting patterns of, 146
workforce projections for 2024, 67

Hispanics and the 2008 Election: A Swing Vote? (Taylor & Fry), 152

Hispanics of Cuban Origin in the United States, 2013 (López), 7

Hispanics of Puerto Rican Origin in the United States, 2013 (López & Patten), 7

Historical Census Statistics on Population Totals by Race, 1790 to 1990, and by Hispanic Origin, 1970 to 1990, for the United States, Regions, Divisions, and States (Gibson & Jung), 9–10

Historical Marriage Tables (Census Bureau), 78

"Historically Black Colleges and Universities" (NCES), 55

"History of the DOT DBE Program" (DOT), 73

HIV. *See* Human immunodeficiency virus

"HIV among Pregnant Women, Infants, and Children" (CDC), 104–105

HIV Surveillance Report, 2015 (CDC), 102–103

Holding NCLB Accountable: Achieving Accountability, Equity, and School Reform (Sunderman), 44

Hollinger, David A., 143

"Homeland Security Chief Cancels Costly Virtual Border Fence" (CNN.com), 59

Homeownership
  overview of, 21–22
  rates of, by race/Hispanic origin of householder, 27t
  subprime mortgage crisis and, 22–25, 27–28

Homicide
  by gangs, 141
  offenders, by age/sex/race/Hispanic origin, 135(t7.8)
  offenders, by race/ethnicity, 133
  rates of by race/ethnicity, 118–119
  victims, by age/sex/race/ethnicity, 125(t7.2)
  victims, race/sex of, by race/sex of offender, 125(t7.3)
  victims of, 123

Homicide Trends in the United States, 1980–2008 (Cooper & Smith)
  on gang-related homicides, 141
  on homicides, circumstances of, 133

Homosexual contact, HIV/AIDS transmission via, 106

Hopes, Fears, and Reality: A Balanced Look at American Charter Schools in 2005 (Lake & Hill), 46

Hopkinson, Jenny, 86

Hopwood v. Texas, 53

Horn, Catherine L., 54

"House Approves Farm Bill, Ending a 2-Year Impasse" (Nixon), 86

"Household and Families: 2010 Census Brief" (Census Bureau), 15

Households
  Hispanic origin households, by household type, 22(t2.6)
  income, median household/per capita income, 78t
  income among minorities, 77
  married-couple, income of, 77
  married-couple families, 18
  multigenerational, 18
  multigenerational, by race/Hispanic origin, 24t
  one-parent, by race/sex, 23t
  same-sex, 19
  single-parent, 18

Howard University, 55
Howlader, Nadia, 98
HUD (U.S. Department of Housing and Urban Development), 22–23
Huerta, Alvaro, 143
Human immunodeficiency virus (HIV)
  death rates for by race/ethnicity, 119
  HIV infection, diagnoses of, by race, Hispanic origin, age, transmission category, 113t–114t
  HIV infection, persons living with diagnosis of, by race/Hispanic origin, 108t–109t
  transmission of, 102

I

ICE. *See* U.S. Immigration and Customs Enforcement
Illegal immigration
  Hispanic political position and, 153
  overview of, 58–60
  unauthorized immigrants living in U.S., numbers of, 5
  See also Unauthorized immigrants
Immigration, 2016 presidential election and, 60
Immigration Act, 10
Immigration Reform and Control Act, 58
Immune system, 102
"Impact of Census' Race Data Debated" (Kasindorf & El Nasser), 3–4
"The Impact of Gaming on the Indian Nations in New Mexico" (Conner & Taggart), 76
In U.S., 87% Approve of Black-White Marriage, vs. 4% in 1958 (Newport), 15
Incarceration rates, 136–137
  See also Prisons/jails
Income
  family, from means-tested assistance programs, by race/Hispanic origin/age, 85t
  household, married-couple, 77
  household, statistics on, 77
  median household/per capita income, 78t
  among minorities, 77–79
  older Americans, family income sources of, by race/Hispanic origin, 79f
  poverty thresholds, people with income below specified ratios of their, 83t
  quality of health care and, 88
  retirement, minorities and, 79
"The Income and Health Effects of Tribal Casino Gaming on American Indians" (Wolfe), 94
Income, Poverty, and Health Insurance Coverage in the United States: 2015 (Barnett & Vornovitsky), 90–91
Income-to-poverty ratios, 80
"Indian Gaming and Tribal Revenue Allocation Plans: A Case of 'Play to Pay'" (Conner & Taggart), 76

Indian Gaming Regulatory Act, 75
Indian Health Service, 93–94
Indicators of School Crime and Safety: 2017 (Musu-Gillette et al.), 127, 131
Industry, occupational employment in by race/ethnicity/sex/industry, 74t
Infant mortality
  infant/neonatal/postneonatal mortality rates, by detailed race/Hispanic origin of mother, 97t
  rates, trends in, 96–97
Infants, health at birth, 20t
"Inside Obama's Sweeping Victory" (Pew Research Center for the People and the Press), 151
Insulin, 100–102
Intellectual Entrepreneurship Program (University of Texas), 53
International Baccalaureate (IB) program, 47

J

J. A. Croson Co., Richmond v., 73
Jablon, Robert, 27
Jackson, Jesse, 143
Jails. *See* Prisons/jails
Jails in Indian Country, 2015 (Minton), 137
Japanese, 8
"Japanese Immigration" (Library of Congress)
  on Japanese immigrants, 58
  on Japanese internment in WWII, 8–9
Jefferson County, Meredith v., 43
Jobs. *See* Employment; Labor force
Johnson, Lyndon B., 151
Jones, Jeffrey M.
  on employment discrimination, 67
  on treatment of African Americans, 11
"Judge Rejects New York's Stop-and-Frisk Policy" (Goldstein), 133
Jung, Kay, 9–10
"Justices Take Up Race as a Factor in College Entry" (Liptak), 54
Juvenile crime, 137

K

Kaposi's sarcoma, 102
Kasindorf, Martin, 3–4
Kena, Grace
  on center-based preschool enrollment, 32
  on charter schools, 46
  on college degrees among minorities, 48, 51–52
  on kindergarten enrollment, 32
  on public school enrollment, 29
Keneally, Meghan, 127
Kenyon.edu, 8
Kewal-Ramani, Angelina
  on preschool programs, effects of, 32
  on school dropouts, unemployment rates of, 36

Kidnapping, electoral district, 153
Kindergarten, 32
Klein, Alyson, 45
Kochanek, Kenneth D., 117
Kopecki, Dawn, 27
Korean War, 10
Koreans, 10
Krogstad, Jens Manuel, 151
Ku Klux Klan
  hate crimes by, 123–124
  hate groups in U.S., 127

L

"LA Sues Wells Fargo, Citigroup over Foreclosures" (Jablon), 27
"Labor Department Reverses Bush Administration Changes to Guestworker Program" (Farmworker Justice), 59
"Labor Dept. Issues New Rules for Guest Workers" (Preston), 59
Labor force
  African Americans, 57
  Asian Americans, 57–58
  business, minorities in, 73, 75
  Civil Rights Act, race-based charges filed/resolved under Title VII of, 68t
  civilian labor force, by age/sex/race/ethnicity, 69t
  definition of, 60
  employed Hispanic workers by sex/occupation/class of workers/full- or part-time status/detailed ethnic group, 72t
  employed persons by occupation/race/Hispanic origin/sex, 70t–71t
  employment practices, discriminatory, 66–67
  employment status of civilian noninstitutional population, by sex/age/race, 65t
  employment status of civilian population, by race/sex/age, 61t–62t
  employment status of Hispanic population, by sex/age, 62(t4.2)
  employment status of Mexican/Puerto Rican/Cuban populations, by sex/age, 64t
  federal government, minorities and, 73
  Hispanics in, 58–59
  minorities in, historical perspective, 57
  occupational employment in private industry, by race/ethnicity/sex/industry, 74t
  occupations, 67, 70–73
  participation in/unemployment, 60–65
  tribal casinos, 75–76
  workforce projections, 2024, 67
Lajevardi, Nazita, 144, 146
Lake, Robin J., 46
Lam, Andrew, 39–40

"Lands of Opportunity: Social and Economic Effects of Tribal Gaming on Localities" (Marks & Contreras), 76

Lane, Ben, 27

Laos, refugees from, 58

"Last of Refugees from Cuba in '94 Flight Now Enter U.S." (Navarro), 7

"Late or No Prenatal Care" (Child Trends Databank), 95

Latin America, 5

Latinos, 5–7

See also Hispanics

Law enforcement, racial profiling by, 133

Laws

interracial marriage, prohibiting, 15

state immigration, 59

Lee, Barbara, 151

Legislation and international treaties

Agriculture Act (Farm Bill), 86

American Dream Downpayment Assistance Act, 25

American Recovery and Reinvestment Act, 85–86

California Civil Rights Initiative, 53

Chinese Exclusion Act, 8

Civil Rights Act, 66, 68*t*, 143

Community Reinvestment Act, 22

Comprehensive Immigration Reform Act, 36

Development, Relief, and Education for Alien Minors (DREAM) Act, 36

Every Student Succeeds Act, 45

Fair Sentencing Act, 137

Food Stamp Act, 83

Gentlemen's Agreement, 58

Hate Crime Statistics Act, 124

Immigration Act, 10

Immigration Reform and Control Act, 58

Indian Gaming Regulatory Act, 75

Motor Voter Act, 143

National Voter Registration Act, 143

No Child Left Behind Act, 44–47

Personal Responsibility and Work Opportunity Reconciliation Act, 82–83

Sentencing Reform Act, 137

stand-your-ground gun law (Florida), 11

Surface Transportation Act, 73

Surface Transportation and Uniform Relocation Assistance Act, 75

Violent Crime and Law Enforcement Act, 124

Voting Rights Act, 144, 152, 153, 154

Level Playing Field Institute, 66

Lewis, John, 151

Library of Congress (LOC)

on African Americans, migration north of, 57

on Chinese immigrants, 8, 57

on Japanese immigrants, 8–9, 58

on Mexican immigrants, 58

Lieff Cabraser Heimann & Bernstein LLP, 66

Life expectancy

overview of, 117

by race/sex, 119*f*

Light, Joe, 28

Lincoln, Abraham, 7, 57

Linton, Ralph, 1

Liptak, Adam

"Justices Take Up Race as a Factor in College Entry," 54

"Muslim Woman Denied Job over Head Scarf Wins in Supreme Court," 66

"Supreme Court Upholds Affirmative Action Program at University of Texas," 54

Living arrangements

of children, 19–21

of children, by race/Hispanic origin, 23*f*

of children/marital status of parents, by age/race/Hispanic origin, 26*t*

family, overview of, 15

See also Families

"Living Arrangements of Black Children under 18 Years Old: 1960 to 2005" (Census Bureau), 20

LOC. *See* Library of Congress

Lockheed Martin, 66

"Lockheed Martin to Pay $2.5 Million to Settle Racial Harassment Lawsuit" (EEOC), 66

López, Gustavo

on Cuban Americans, 7

on health of Hispanics, 87

Los Angeles, CA, gang-related homicides in, 141

Loving v. Virginia, 15

Low birth weight

infant mortality and, 96–97

low-birth weight live births, by detailed race/Hispanic origin of mother, 96*t*

Low income, definition of, 80

Lum, Lydia, 53

Lung cancer

incidence/death rates, lung and bronchus cancer, by race/Hispanic origin, 105*f*

minorities and, 98

M

Macartney, Suzanne, 83, 85

"Make America Great Again" campaign slogan, 127

Males

deaths from heart disease, 100

HIV/AIDS transmission, 105–106

life expectancy of, 117

minorities in prisons/jails, 133, 136–137

prostate cancer, 98

See also Gender

Male-to-male sexual contact, HIV/AIDS transmission via, 106

Mandatory minimums, 137

"Mariel Boatlift" (Pike), 7

Marijuana, racial disparities in sentencing and, 137

Marriage

death of a spouse, 16

divorce, 16

interracial/interethnic marriage, 15

marital status, families, 15

never married, 16

same-sex couples, by differences in race/Hispanic origin/age, 25*t*

between whites/African Americans, approval of, 16*f*

Married-couple families

household income of, 77

overview of, 18

Martin, Joyce A.

on births/fertility rates, 95–96

"Births: Final Data for 2015," 16–17

Martin, Trayvon, 11

Martinez, Susana, 152

Mason, Jeff, 93

Mathematics

college preparatory courses for, participants in, 47

performance in school, 36

scores, 4th/8th-grade students, by race/Hispanic origin/jurisdiction/urban school district, 37*t*–38*t*

scores, 12th-grade, by race/Hispanic origin/highest mathematics level attained, 39*f*

McFarland, Joel, 82

McKenzie, Bill, 53

McKinley, James C., Jr., 53

McPhee, Cameron, 31–32

Means-Tested Assistance Programs, 83, 85

"Measuring the Extent of Gang Problems" (National Gang Center), 141

Median income, 77

Medicaid

ACA and, 93

coverage among persons under 65 years of age, by race/Hispanic origin, 91*t*

minorities with health insurance coverage through, 91

Medical profession, African Americans in, 67

Medicare, 92*t*

Medigap plan, 91

Men. *See* Gender; Males

Mental health, 102

"Mental Health and African Americans" (Office of Minority Health), 102

"Mental Health and American Indians/Alaskan Natives" (Office of Minority Health), 102

"Mental Health and Asian Americans" (Office of Minority Health), 102
"Mental Health and Hispanics" (Office of Minority Health), 102
Meredith v. Jefferson County, 43
Mexican American Legal Defense and Education Fund, 66, 152
Mexican Americans
    employment opportunities for, 71
    employment status of, by sex/age, 64*t*
    population, employment status of, by sex/age, 64*t*
    population, overview of, 6
Mexican-American War, 58
Migration Policy Institute, 60
Minorities
    African Americans, 7–8
    African Americans, rates of satisfaction with treatment of, 12(*f*1.2)
    Asian Americans, 8–10
    education advocacy for, 54–55
    health of, overview of, 87
    Hispanic origin population, by birth status, 5(*t*1.4)
    Hispanic origin population, by citizenship/birth status/age/sex, 5(*t*1.5)
    Hispanic origin population, by type, 6*t*
    Hispanics/Latinos, 5–7
    income among, 77–79
    in labor force, 57
    mental health and, 102
    minority students, 39–42
    national percentage of, increasing, 2
    Native Americans/Alaskan Natives, 10–11
    as offenders, 133
    overview of, 1
    population by race/Hispanic origin, 2*t*
    population by race/state, 9*t*
    population estimates by race/Hispanic origin, 3*t*
    population size, projected change in, by race/Hispanic origin, 4*t*
    poverty status among, 79–80
    in prisons/jails, 133, 136–138, 141
    public school, enrollment in by, 29
    races, perceptions of relations between by racial group, 13*t*
    racial/ethnic classifications, changing, 2–5
    retirement among, 79
    U.S. government role in improving lives of minorities, preference for by race, 13*f*
    as victims, 123–124, 126–127, 131, 133
    whites, relations with, 11
    whites/African Americans, perceptions of relations between, 12(*f*1.1)
    See also Race/ethnicity
Minority Business Development Agency, 73
Minority Rights: International Standards and Guidance for Implementation (UN), 1

"Minority Rolls Cut by Hopwood" (Lum), 53
"Minority Turnout Determined the 2012 Election" (Frey), 143
Minton, Todd D., 137
Mitchell, Tazra, 86
Money. *See* Income
Morales, Dan, 53
Morgan, Rachel E., 123
Mortality rates
    for cancer, 98
    cancer mortality rates/trends for top 15 cancer sites, by race/Hispanic origin, 101*t*–102*t*
    incidence/death rates, colon and rectum cancer, by race/Hispanic origin, 106*f*
    incidence/death rates, female breast cancer, by race/Hispanic origin, 103*f*
    incidence/death rates, lung and bronchus cancer, by race/Hispanic origin, 105*f*
    incidence/death rates, prostate cancer, by race/Hispanic origin, 104*f*
    infant mortality rates, 96–97
    infant/neonatal/postneonatal, by detailed race/Hispanic origin of mother, 97*t*
Mortgages, home. *See* Subprime mortgage crisis
"Most Behaviors Preceding Major Causes of Preventable Death Have Begun by Young Adulthood" (National Institutes of Health), 107
Mothers
    births/fertility, 95–96
    health at birth, characteristics of by race, 20*t*
    infant, neonatal, postneonatal mortality rates, by race/Hispanic origin of mother, 97*t*
    low birth weight, infant mortality, 96–97
    low-birth weight live births, by race/Hispanic origin of mother, 96*t*
    pregnancy, health and, 18
    prenatal care, 94–95
    teenage, 17–18
    transmission of HIV/AIDS, 104–105
    unwed, 16–17
Motor Voter Act, 143
Mulligan, Gail M., 31–32
Multigenerational households
    overview of, 18
    by race/Hispanic origin, 24*t*
Murder. *See* Homicide
"Muslim Woman Denied Job over Head Scarf Wins in Supreme Court" (Liptak), 66
Muslims, 124
Musu-Gillette, Lauren
    on AP/IB courses, students who earned credit in, 47
    on college completion rates among minorities, 51
    on crime at school, 131

N

Napolitano, Janet, 39
National Assessment of Educational Progress (NAEP)
    math/science proficiency, measuring of by, 36
    reading/math proficiency, measuring of by, 32
National Association for the Advancement of Colored People, Legal Defense and Educational Fund, 66
National Association of Latino Elected and Appointed Officials (NALEO), 152
National Center for Education Statistics (NCES)
    on black colleges/universities, 55
    on preschoolers' readiness for school, 29, 31
National Center for Health Statistics (NCHS)
    on death, leading causes of, 118–119
    on deaths from heart disease, 100
    on heart disease, 98–99
    on low birth weight, 96
    on prenatal care, 95
National Charter School Study 2013 (Center for Research on Education Outcomes), 46–47
National Conference of State Legislatures, 45
National Crime Prevention Council, 127
National Diabetes Statistics Report, 2017 (CDC), 101–102
National Education Association, 45
National Gang Center, 141
National Gang Intelligence Center, 141
National Health Service Corps, 93
National Indian Gaming Commission
    on casino gambling revenues, 65
    on Native American tribes, numbers engaged in gaming, 75
National Institutes of Health, 107
"National Minority Mental Health Awareness Month" (Office of Minority Health), 102
National School Lunch Program, 82
National Voter Registration Act, 143
Native Americans and Alaskan Natives
    AIDS/HIV and, 103–107
    alcohol use by, 112, 117
    births/fertility rate of, 95–96
    cancer and, 98
    death, leading causes of, 118–119
    diabetes among, 101–102
    educational attainment of, 43
    geographic distribution of, 11
    health care, access to, 89
    health care, quality of, 88
    heart disease among, 99–100
    Indian Health Service, 93–94
    jobs and, 73

in labor force, 63–65
low birth weight/infant mortality, 96–97
Medicaid coverage among, 91
mental health and, 102
overview of, 10–11
prenatal care for, 95
in prisons/jails, 136, 137
school crime and, 131
tobacco use by, 112
as victims of hate crimes, 126
Native Hawaiians and Pacific Islanders. *See* Asian Americans and Pacific Islanders
Navarro, Mireya, 7
NCES. *See* National Center for Education Statistics
NCHS. *See* National Center for Health Statistics
NCLB. *See* No Child Left Behind Act
Nearly Half of Blacks Treated Unfairly "in Last 30 Days" (Norman), 67
Nelson, Christine A., 55
Neo-Confederate groups, 127
"New Evidence Puts Man in North America 50,000 Years Ago" (ScienceDaily.com), 10
"New Voting Restrictions in America" (Brennan Center for Justice), 144
New York City, New York, 7, 133
New York Police Department (NYPD), 133
Newport, Frank, 15
Nicotine, 107
Nielsen, Lindsay, 144, 146
Nixon, Richard M., 73
Nixon, Ron, 86
No Child Left Behind (NCLB) Act
    charter schools, 45–47
    overview of, 44–47
    vouchers, school, 45
"The Non-voters Who Decided the Election: Trump Won Because of Lower Democratic Turnout" (Ben-Shahar), 151
Norman, Jim, 67
"North by South: The African American Great Migration" (kenyon.edu), 8
Nursing, African Americans in, 67
Nutrition, 112
NYTimes.com, 143

O

Obama, Barack
    American Recovery and Reinvestment Act, 85–86
    District of Columbia voucher program, 45
    DREAM Act, support of, 36, 39
    election of, 143, 151
    Fair Sentencing Act, 137
    government service history of, 147
    guest-worker program, revision of by, 59
    public schools, reformation of by, 44–45

"Obama: Weak Job Ratings, but Positive Personal Image" (Pew Research Center for the People and the Press), 151
"Obamacare Enrollment Exceeds Seven Million Target Despite Setback" (Mason & Felsenthal), 93
Obesity, 112
Occupations
    African Americans, jobs and, 67, 70
    Asian Americans, jobs and, 71–73
    employed Hispanic workers by, 72*t*
    employed persons by, 70*t*–71*t*
    Hispanics, jobs and, 71
    Native Americans/Alaskan Natives, jobs and, 73
    occupational employment in private industry, by race/ethnicity/sex/industry, 74*t*
O'Connor, Sandra Day, 73
Offenders
    hate crime offenders, by race/ethnicity/age, 127*t*
    homicide victims, race/sex of, by race/sex of offender, 125(*t*7.3)
    minorities as, 133
    murder offenders by age/sex/race/Hispanic origin, 135(*t*7.8)
    by race/ethnicity, 123
Office of Family Assistance, 83
Office of Management and Budget
    racial categories identified by, 2
    2000 census, race recategorization of, 3–4
Office of Minority Business Enterprise, 73
Office of Minority Health
    ACA and, 93
    on mental health, 102
Office of Refugee Resettlement, 10
O'Rourke, Sheila, 53
Ostrov, Barbara Feder, 66
Overall Number of Unauthorized Immigrants Holds Steady (Passel & Cohn), 5
Overberg, Paul, 147

P

Pacific Islanders. *See* Asian Americans and Pacific Islanders
Packing, electoral district, 153
Page, Susan, 147
"Parental Involvement in Predicting School Motivation: Similar and Differential Effects across Ethnic Groups" (Fan, Williams, & Wolters), 39–41
Parents Involved in Community Schools v. Seattle School District, 43
Park, Jen, 43
Parole
    characteristics of adults on, 138(*t*7.11)
    minorities on, 137–138

The Parties on the Eve of the 2016 Election: Two Coalitions, Moving Further Apart (Doherty et al.)
    on African American political party affiliations, 147
    on Hispanic political party affiliations, 152
Passel, Jeffrey S., 5
Patten, Eileen, 7
Pavetti, Ladonna, 85–86
Peña, Adarand Constructors Inc. v., 75
Peña Nieto, Enrique, 60
Pepsi Beverages, 66
"Pepsi to Pay $3.13 Million and Made Major Policy Changes to Resolve EEOC Finding of Nationwide Hiring Discrimination against African Americans" (EEOC), 66
Percent Plans in College Admissions: A Comparative Analysis of Three States' Experiences (Horn & Flores), 54
Perry, Marc, 58
Personal Responsibility and Work Opportunity Reconciliation Act, 82–83
Pew Hispanic Center, 7
Pew Research Center
    on Obama, Barack, election victory of, 151
    on unauthorized immigrants living in U.S., numbers of, 5
Philippines, 10
Pike, John, 7
Plea bargaining, 137
Pneumocystis carinii pneumonia, 102
"The Political Economy of American Indian Gaming" (Cornell), 76
"Political Gerrymandering 2000–2008: 'A Self-Limiting Enterprise'?" (*Harvard Law Review*), 153
Political participation
    African American, 147, 151
    electoral districts, race/ethnicity and, 152–154
    Hispanic, 151–152
    overview of, 143
    public office, African Americans elected to, number of, 147
    reasons for not voting, 149*t*–150*t*
    reported voting totals by age/race/ethnicity, change in, 147*t*
    voter registration, 143–144
    voter turnout, 144, 146–147
    voting rates by age/race/ethnicity, changes in reported, 148*f*
    voting rates by race/Hispanic origin, 146*f*
    voting/registration among native/naturalized citizens, by race/Hispanic origin/region of birth, 145*t*
Poll taxes
    southern state, 144
    24th Amendment to eliminate, 152

Population
    African Americans, 7–8
    Hispanic origin population, by birth status, 5(t1.4)
    Hispanic origin population, by citizenship/birth status/age/sex, 5(t1.5)
    Hispanic origin population, by type, 6t
    Hispanic population in U.S., 5, 6
    minorities populations in U.S., 2
    Native Americans/Alaskan Natives, 11
    population by race/Hispanic origin, 2000/2010, 2t
    population estimates by race/Hispanic origin, 2015, 3t
    population size, projected change in, by race/Hispanic origin, 4t
    in poverty, 81t–82t
    by race/state, 9t
    by sex, age, race/Hispanic origin, 88t
Population Reference Bureau, 4
Postethnic America: Beyond Multiculturalism (Hollinger), 143
Potok, Mark, 127
Poverty
    in charter schools, 46
    children living in, 81–82, 84t
    family income from means-tested assistance programs, by race/Hispanic origin/age, 85t
    government programs addressing, 82–85
    guidelines for, 80t
    health care, access to, 89
    levels of, 80
    Medicaid coverage and, 91
    among minorities, status of, 79–80
    number in poverty/poverty rates, 80f
    people/families in, 81t–82t
    people with income below specified ratios of their poverty thresholds, 83t
    TANF/SNAP/SSI, numbers receiving assistance from, 86t
Pregnancy/birth
    births and fertility, 95–96
    births to Hispanic women, 87
    infant, neonatal, postneonatal mortality rates, by race/Hispanic origin of mother, 97t
    low birth weight, infant mortality, 96–97
    low-birth weight live births, by detailed race/Hispanic origin of mother, 96t
    prenatal care, 94–95
    teenage mothers, 17–18
    unwed mothers, 16–17
Prejudice, 123
    See also Hate crimes
Prenatal care, 94–95
Preprimary education, 32
Preschool enrollment, by race/ethnicity/attendance status, 33(f3.2)

Preschool: First Findings from the Preschool Follow-Up of the Early Childhood Longitudinal Study, Birth Cohort (Chernoff et al.), 31
"President: Full Results" (CNN), 147
"President Trump's Budget Cuts TANF Despite Stated Goal to Reduce Poverty, Boost Work" (Mitchell), 86
Preston, Julia, 59
Prisons/jails
    death row, minorities on, 138, 141
    minorities in, 133, 136–137
    Native Americans in, 137
    parole, characteristics of adults on, 138(t7.11)
    parole/probation, 137–138
    prisoners under sentence of death, by region, jurisdiction, race, 139t–140t
    probation, characteristics of adults on, 138(t7.12)
    sentenced prisoners under state/federal jurisdiction, estimated rate of, per 100,000 U.S. residents, by sex, race, Hispanic origin, age, 136t
    sentenced prisoners under state/federal jurisdiction, percentages of, by sex, race, Hispanic origin, age, 135(t7.9)
    sentencing, racial disparities in, 137
Probation
    characteristics of adults on, 138(t7.12)
    minorities on, 137–138
"The Problem of Minority Groups" (Wirth), 1
Prostate cancer
    incidence/death rates, by race/Hispanic origin, 104f
    minorities and, 98
Public acceptance, 15
Public schools, 32
    See also School
Puerto Rican Legal Defense and Education Fund, 152
"A Puerto Rican Rebirth in El Barrio; After Exodus, Gentrification Changes Face of East Harlem" (Berger), 7
Puerto Ricans
    employment opportunities for, 71
    U.S. population of, 6–7

Q

Quality Education for Minorities, 54
Quigley, Bill, 137

R

Race/ethnicity
    AIDS diagnoses, among children less than 13 years of age by, 112t
    AIDS diagnoses, by race/Hispanic origin/age/transmission category, 115t–116t

AIDS diagnosis, persons living with, by race/Hispanic origin, 110t–111t
    alcohol use, binge alcohol use, heavy alcohol use in past month among persons aged 12 or older by, 118t
    bachelor's degree or higher, 25- to 29-year-olds with, 44f
    birth rates for women aged 10–19 by, 19t
    birth rates of unmarried women by, 17t
    cancer and, 98
    cancer incidence rates/trends for top 15 cancer sites by, 99t–100t
    cancer mortality rates/trends for top 15 cancer sites by, 101t–102t
    children living in poverty by, 84t
    Civil Rights Act, race-based charges filed/resolved under Title VII of, 68t
    civilian labor force by, 69t
    colon/rectum cancer, incidence/death rates by, 106f
    death, leading causes of, 118–119
    deaths by causes of death by, 120t
    deaths of persons with AIDS diagnosis, by year of death/age/race/Hispanic origin/transmission category, 121t–122t
    diabetes and, 101–102
    diabetes prevalence among adults aged 20/older, by diagnosis status, race/ethnicity, 107f
    dropout rates, 16/24-year-olds by, 42f
    drug abuse by, 112, 117
    drugs, students in grades 9–12 who reported that drugs were made available to them on school property during previous 12 months, by race/Hispanic origin, 132(f7.3)
    employed persons by, 70t–71t
    employment status of civilian noninstitutional population by, 65t
    employment status of civilian population by, 61t–62t
    enrollment rates, 18- to 24-year-olds in degree-granting institutions, by type of institution, 50t
    family groups, types of by, 22(t2.5)
    family income from means-tested assistance programs by, 85t
    female breast cancer, incidence/death rates by, 103f
    full-time faculty at degree-granting institutions by, 52f
    gangs and, 141
    government role in improving lives of minorities, preference for by, 13f
    hate crime offenders by, 127t
    health insurance coverage of noninstitutionalized Medicare beneficiaries 65 years of age/over, by type of coverage/race/Hispanic origin, 92t
    heart disease/stroke and, 98–100

high school dropouts by, 41*t*

high school students earning AP/IB credits, percentage of by, 48*f*

HIV infection, diagnoses of by, 113*t*–114*t*

HIV infection, persons living with diagnosis of by, 108*t*–109*t*

homeownership rates by, 27*t*

homicide victims by, 125(*t*7.2), 125(*t*7.3)

illicit drug use by, 119*t*

infant, neonatal, postneonatal mortality rates, by race/Hispanic origin of mother, 97*t*

life expectancy by, 117, 119*f*

living arrangements of children/marital status of parents by, 26*t*

low-birth-weight live births, by race/ Hispanic origin of mother, 96*t*

lung/bronchus cancer, incidence/death rates by, 105*f*

mathematics scores, 12th-grade, by, 39*f*

mathematics scores of 4th/8th-grade students by, 37*t*–38*t*

Medicaid coverage among persons under 65 years of age by, 91*t*

mental health and, 102

murder offenders by, 135(*t*7.8)

obesity/poor nutrition by, 112

occupational employment in private industry by, 74*t*

offenders, minorities as, 133

older Americans, family income sources of by, 79*f*

population by, 2*t*

population by sex/age/race/Hispanic origin, 88*t*

population estimates by, 2015, 3*t*

population of by state, 9*t*

population size, projected change in, 4*t*

preschool enrollment, by, 33(*f*3.2)

prisons/jails, minorities in, 133, 136–138, 141

prostate cancer, incidence/death rates by, 104*f*

public elementary/high school students, number/percentage distribution of by, 30*t*

public high school freshman graduation rates by, 43*f*

public school students in prekindergarten–12th grade, number of by, 31*f*

public school students in prekindergarten–12th grade, percentage distribution of by, 33(*f*3.3)

reading scores of 4th/8th-grade students by, 34*t*–35*t*

SAT scores of college-bound seniors by, 49*t*

school, crime at by, 131

science scale scores by, 40*t*

sentenced prisoners under state/federal jurisdiction, by sex/race/Hispanic origin/age, 135(*t*7.9)

sentenced prisoners under state/federal jurisdiction, estimated rate of, per 100,000 U.S. residents, by sex/race/ Hispanic origin/age, 136*t*

status dropout rates, 16/24-year-olds by, 41*f*

tobacco use by, 112, 117*t*

traditional public/charter schools, percentage of by racial concentration, 46*f*

undergraduate enrollment distribution, by institutional level, 51*f*

victimization of minorities, 123–124, 126–127, 131, 133

violent/serious violent crime by, 124*t*

voting among native/naturalized citizens by, 145*t*

voting rates by, 146*f*

voting rates by, changes in reported, 148*f*

voting totals by, change in reported, 147*t*

Races, relations between, 13*t*

Racial classifications
   changing, 2–5
   Office of Management and Budget, racial categories identified by, 2

Racial disparities, in sentencing, 137

Racial Disparities in Youth Commitments and Arrests (Rovner), 137

Racial diversity, school, 42

Racial profiling, 133

Racism. *See* Hate crimes

Radford, Jynnah, 87

Reading
   performance in school, 32–33, 36
   scores of 4th/8th-grade students, by race/ Hispanic origin/jurisdiction/urban school district, 34*t*–35*t*

Real Choices/New Voices: How Proportional Representation Elections Could Revitalize American Democracy (Amy), 153

"Real Estate Matters: Is the Housing Crisis Over? Maybe Not for Minorities" (Glink & Tamkin), 27

Rectum cancer, 98

Red blood cells, 107

Redistricting, computerized, 153

Regents of the University of California v. Bakke, 53

Registration, voter
   among native/naturalized citizens, by race/Hispanic origin/region of birth, 145*t*
   overview of, 143

Republican Party
   African American support of, 147, 151
   electoral districting and, 153
   Hispanic support of, 152

Respiratory diseases, 118

Results from the 2015 National Survey on Drug Use and Health: Detailed Tables (SAMHSA), 112

Retirement, 79

Richardson, Bill, 152

Richmond v. J. A. Croson Co., 73

Risk factors, education, 29, 31–32

Robinson-Avila, Kevin, 93

Roosevelt, Franklin D., 8

Roosevelt, Theodore, 58

Ross, Janell, 93

Rovner, Joshua, 137

Rubio, Marco, 152

Rytina, Nancy, 5

S

Salish Kootenai College, 55

Salish Kootenai College 2016–2017 Catalog (Salish Kootenai College), 55

Same-sex couples, 25*t*

Same-sex households, 19

SAMHSA (Substance Abuse and Mental Health Services Administration), 112

Sánchez Korrol, Virginia E., 6–7

Sandoval, Brian, 152

Sandra A. Drabik, Associated General Contractors of Ohio v., 75

SAT scores
   of college-bound seniors, by race and Hispanic origin, 49*t*
   by race/ethnicity, 47–48

"SAT Scores and Asian American Academic Achievements" (Lam), 39–40

Savage, David G., 27–28

SBA (U.S. Small Business Administration), 75

Schmid, Julie, 66

School
   dropping out, results of, 36, 39
   kindergarten/elementary/secondary, 32–33, 36
   National School Lunch Program, 82
   preprimary, 32
   preschool enrollment, by race/ethnicity/ attendance status, 33(*f*3.2)
   public elementary/high school students, number/percentage distribution of by race/ethnicity, 30*t*
   public school students, prekindergarten–12th grade, number of by region/race/ethnicity, 31*f*
   public school students, prekindergarten–12th grade, percentage distribution of by race/ Hispanic origin, 33(*f*3.3)
   public system, reforming, 44–47
   segregation of, 42–43
   traditional public/charter schools, percentage of by racial/ethnic concentration, 46*f*
   vouchers, 45
   See also Higher education

School, crime at
drugs, students in grades 9–12 who reported that drugs were made available to them on school property during previous 12 months, by race/Hispanic origin, 132(*f*7.3)
drugs at school, 131
gang, students aged 12–18 who reported that gangs were present at school, 132(*f*7.2)
hate crimes, 133
hate crimes, students aged 12–18 who reported being targets of hate-related words/seeing hate-related graffiti at school during school year, 134*f*
impact of, 127, 131
rates of, 131
student-reported nonfatal crimes against students aged 12–18/rate of crimes per 1,000 students at school, by type of crime, 131*t*
"School Vouchers" (National Conference of State Legislatures), 45
Schott, Liz, 85–86
Schuette v. Coalition to Defend Affirmative Action, 54
Science
college preparatory courses for, participants in, 47
performance in school, 36
scale scores, 40*t*
The Science of Man in the World Crisis (Linton), 1
Science, technology, engineering, and mathematics (STEM)
African Americans/Hispanics in, 36
courses of study, 54
fields of study, 53
ScienceDaily.com, 10
SDB (Small and Disadvantaged Business) Set-Aside Program, 75
Seattle School District, Parents Involved in Community Schools v., 43
Secondary school. *See* School
Secure Border Initiative: Technology Deployment Delays Persist and the Impact of Border Fencing Has Not Been Assessed (GAO), 59
SEER Cancer Statistics Review, 1975–2014 (Howlader et al.), 98
Sentencing Project, 136–137
Sentencing Reform Act, 137
September 11, 2001, terrorist attacks, 124
Set-aside programs
government contracts for minority businesses and, 73
Supreme Court rulings on, 75
Shear, Michael D., 39
Sickle-cell disease, 107
Single-parent households, 18

Slavery
enslaved Africans arrival in North America, 57
slave population, 1860 census on, 7
Small and Disadvantaged Business (SDB) Set-Aside Program, 75
"Small Disadvantaged Businesses" (Small Business Administration), 75
Smith, Dylan, 59
Smith, Erica L.
on gang-related homicides, 141
on homicide offenders, 133
SNAP. *See* Supplemental Nutrition Assistance Program
Snell, Tracy L., 138
Snyder, Thomas D.
on African American/Hispanic high school graduation rates, 42
on black colleges/universities, enrollment numbers in, 55
on college preparatory work in high school, numbers participating in, 47
on graduate degrees earned among minorities, 52
on higher education enrollment among minorities, 48
on Hispanic students, educational attainment of, 43
on math/science scores, 4th/8th graders, 36
on reading scores, 4th/8th graders, 32–33
on school segregation, 43
Social Security: A Key Retirement Income Source for Older Minorities (Waid), 79
Sociology of the Black Experience (Florida A&M University), 55
Southeast Asia Resource Action Center, 58
Southeast Asian Americans at a Glance: Statistics on Southeast Asians Adapted from the American Community Survey (Southeast Asia Resource Action Center), 58
Southern Poverty Law Center (SPLC), 127
Southwest Voter Registration Education Project, 152
Stand-your-ground law, 11
States
immigration laws of, 59
population of by race, 9*t*
Statistical information
African Americans, rates of satisfaction with treatment of, 12(*f*1.2)
AIDS diagnoses, among children less than 13 years of age, by race/Hispanic origin, 112*t*
AIDS diagnoses, by race/Hispanic origin/age/transmission category, 115*t*–116*t*
AIDS diagnosis, persons living with, by race/Hispanic origin, 110*t*–111*t*
alcohol use, binge alcohol use, heavy alcohol use in past month among

persons aged 12 or older, by age/sex/race/Hispanic origin, 118*t*
bachelor's degree or higher, 25- to 29-year-olds with, by race/Hispanic origin, 44*f*
birth rates for teenagers, by age group, 18*f*
birth rates for women aged 10–19, by age/race/Hispanic origin, 19*t*
births/birth rates to unmarried women, by age/race/Hispanic origin, 17*t*
cancer incidence rates/trends for top 15 cancer sites, by race/Hispanic origin, 99*t*–100*t*
cancer mortality rates/trends for top 15 cancer sites, by race/Hispanic origin, 101*t*–102*t*
children living in poverty, by age/family structure/race/Hispanic origin, 84*t*
children's living arrangements, by race/Hispanic origin, 23*f*
Civil Rights Act, race-based charges filed/resolved under Title VII of, 68*t*
civilian labor force, by age/sex/race/ethnicity, 69*t*
deaths by causes of death, by race/Hispanic origin/sex, 120*t*
deaths of persons with AIDS diagnosis, by year of death/age/race/Hispanic origin/transmission category, 121*t*–122*t*
diabetes prevalence among adults aged 20/older, by diagnosis status/race/ethnicity, 107*f*
dropout rates, 16/24-year-olds, by race/Hispanic origin/nativity, 42*f*
drugs, students in grades 9–12 who reported that drugs were made available to them on school property during previous 12 months, by race/Hispanic origin, 132(*f*7.3)
employed Hispanic workers by sex/occupation/class of workers/full- or part-time status/detailed ethnic group, 72*t*
employed persons by occupation/race/Hispanic origin/sex, 70*t*–71*t*
employment status of civilian noninstitutional population, by sex/age/race, 65*t*
employment status of civilian population, by race/sex/age, 61*t*–62*t*
employment status of Hispanic population, by sex/age, 62(*t*4.2)
employment status of Mexican/Puerto Rican/Cuban populations, by sex/age, 64*t*
enrollment rates, 18- to 24-year-olds in degree-granting institutions, by type of institution/sex/race/Hispanic origin of student, 50*t*
executions/other dispositions of inmates sentenced to death, by race/Hispanic origin, 141*t*

family groups, types of by race/Hispanic origin, 22(t2.5)

family income from means-tested assistance programs, by race/Hispanic origin/age, 85t

full-time faculty at degree-granting institutions, by academic rank/sex/race/ethnicity, 52f

gangs, students aged 12–18 who reported that gangs were present at school, 132(f7.2)

hate bias incidents, 126t

hate crime offenders, by race/ethnicity, age, 127t

hate crimes, by bias motivation, 128t–129t

hate crimes, students aged 12–18 who reported being targets of hate-related words/seeing hate-related graffiti at school during school year, 134f

health care, proportion of minority groups that experienced better, same, or poorer access to, compared with reference group, 89(f6.2)

health care, proportion of minority groups that experienced better, same, or poorer quality of, compared with reference group, 89(f6.1)

health care visits to doctor offices, emergency departments, home visits within past 12 months, by race/Hispanic origin/poverty level, 94t–95t

health characteristics of mother/infant at birth, by Hispanic origin of mother, 21t

health characteristics of mother/infant at birth, by race, 20t

health insurance coverage, of noninstitutionalized Medicare beneficiaries 65 years of age/over, by type of coverage/race/Hispanic origin, 92t

health insurance coverage, people without, 90f

high school dropouts, 16/24-year-olds who were, by sex/race/Hispanic origin, 41t

high school students earning AP/IB credits, percentage of by academic subject/race/ethnicity, 48f

Hispanic origin households, by household type, 22(t2.6)

Hispanic origin population, by birth status, 5(t1.4)

Hispanic origin population, by citizenship/birth status/age/sex, 5(t1.5)

Hispanic origin population by type, 6t

HIV infection, diagnoses of, by race, Hispanic origin, age, transmission category, 113t–114t

HIV infection, persons living with diagnosis of, by race/Hispanic origin, 108t–109t

homeownership rates by race/Hispanic origin of householder, 27t

homicide victims, by age, sex, race/ethnicity, 125(t7.2)

homicide victims, race/sex of, by race/sex of offender, 125(t7.3)

illicit drug use by age, sex, race/Hispanic origin, 119t

incidence/death rates, colon/rectum cancer, by race/Hispanic origin, 106f

incidence/death rates, female breast cancer, by race/Hispanic origin, 103f

incidence/death rates, lung/bronchus cancer, by race/Hispanic origin, 105f

incidence/death rates, prostate cancer, by race/Hispanic origin, 104f

income, median household/per capita income, 78t

infant, neonatal, postneonatal mortality rates, by detailed race/Hispanic origin of mother, 97t

life expectancy by race/sex, 119f

living arrangements of children/marital status of parents, by age/race/Hispanic origin, 26t

low-birth-weight live births, by detailed race/Hispanic origin of mother, 96t

mathematics scores, 4th/8th-grade students, by race/Hispanic origin/jurisdiction/urban school district, 37t–38t

mathematics scores, 12th-grade, by race/Hispanic origin/highest mathematics level attained, 39f

Medicaid coverage among persons under 65 years of age, by race/Hispanic origin, 91t

multigenerational households, by race/Hispanic origin, 24t

murder offenders by age, sex, race/Hispanic origin, 135(t7.8)

occupational employment in private industry, by race/ethnicity/sex/industry, 74t

older Americans, family income sources of by race/Hispanic origin, 79f

one-parent households, by race/sex, 23t

parole, characteristics of adults on, 138(t7.11)

people with income below specified ratios of their poverty thresholds, 83t

population by race/Hispanic origin, 2t

population by race/state, 9t

population by sex/age/race/Hispanic origin, 88t

population estimates, 2015, by race/Hispanic origin, 3t

population size, project changed in, by race/Hispanic origin, 4t

poverty, number in/poverty rates, 80f

poverty, people/families in, 81t–82t

preschool enrollment, by race/ethnicity/attendance status, 33(f3.2)

prisoners under sentence of death, by region/jurisdiction/race, 139t–140t

probation, characteristics of adults on, 138(t7.12)

public elementary/high school students, number/percentage distribution of by race/ethnicity, 30t

public high school freshman graduation rates, by race/Hispanic origin, 43f

public school students in prekindergarten–12th grade, number of by region/race/ethnicity, 31f

public school students in prekindergarten–12th grade, percentage distribution of by race/Hispanic origin, 33(f3.3)

races, perceptions of relations between by racial group, 13t

reading scores of 4th/8th-grade students, by race/Hispanic origin/jurisdiction/urban school district, 34t–35t

same-sex couples, by differences in race/Hispanic origin/age, 25t

SAT scores of college-bound seniors, by race/Hispanic origin, 49t

science scale scores by sex/grade/race/Hispanic origin, 40t

sentenced prisoners under state/federal jurisdiction, estimated rate of, per 100,000 U.S. residents, by sex/race/Hispanic origin/age, 136t

sentenced prisoners under state/federal jurisdiction, percentages of, by sex/race/Hispanic origin/age, 135(t7.9)

status dropout rates, 16/24-year-olds, by race/Hispanic origin, 41f

student-reported nonfatal crimes against students aged 12–18/rate of crimes per 1,000 students at school, by type of crime, 131t

TANF/SNAP/SSI, numbers receiving assistance from, 86t

tobacco product use by age/sex/race/Hispanic origin, 117t

traditional public/charter schools, percentage of by racial/ethnic concentration, 46f

undergraduate enrollment distribution, by institutional level/race/ethnicity, 51f

U.S. government role in improving lives of minorities, preference for by race, 13f

violent/serious violent crime, by sex/race/Hispanic origin/age of victim, 124t

voting, reasons for not, 149t–150t

voting, reported voting totals by age/race/ethnicity, change in, 147t

voting rates by age/race/ethnicity, changes in reported, 148f

voting rates by race/Hispanic origin, 146f

voting/registration among native/naturalized citizens, by race/Hispanic origin/region of birth, 145t whites/African Americans, approval of marriages between, 16f

whites/African Americans, perceptions of relations between, 12(f1.1)

Status and Trends in the Education of Racial and Ethnic Groups (Musu-Gillette et al.), 47, 51

Status and Trends in the Education of Racial and Ethnic Minorities (Kewal-Ramani et al.)

on preschool programs, effects of, 32

on school dropouts, unemployment rates of, 36

Steele, James B., 75

Stein, Rob, 98

STEM (science, technology, engineering, and mathematics)

African Americans/Hispanics in, 36

courses of study, 54

fields of study, 53

"Stop-and-Frisk Data" (New York chapter of ACLU), 133

Stop-and-frisk policy, 133

"Strategies for Achieving Faculty Diversity at the University of California in a Post–Proposition 209 Legal Climate" (O'Rourke), 53

"Strong Confidence in Obama—Country Seen as Less Politically Divided" (Pew Research Center for the People and the Press), 151

Students

African American, 42–43

Asian American, 39–42

foreign-born, dropout rates of, 36

mathematics scores of 4th/8th-grade, by race/Hispanic origin/jurisdiction/urban school district, 37t–38t

minority, 39–43

reading scores of 4th/8th-grade, by race/Hispanic origin/jurisdiction/urban school district, 34t–35t

See also School; School, crime at

Study on the Rights of Persons Belonging to Ethnic, Religious and Linguistic Minorities (Capotorti), 1

Stutz, Howard, 76

Subprime mortgage crisis, 22–25, 27–28

Substance Abuse and Mental Health Services Administration (SAMHSA), 112

Suicide, 118

"Suit Points to Guest Worker Program Flaws" (Preston), 59

Sunderman, Gail L., 44

Supplemental Nutrition Assistance Program (SNAP)

budget reduction of, 86

description of, 83

numbers receiving assistance, 86t

Supplemental Security Income Program

description of, 83

numbers receiving assistance, 86t

Supporting Minority Education (Ad Council), 54

"Supreme Court Blocks Ruling against Texas Redistricting" (Gerstein), 154

"Supreme Court Clears the Way for Cities, Including L.A., to Sue Banks over Foreclosure Crisis" (Savage), 27–28

"Supreme Court Strikes Down Most SB1070 Provisions" (Smith), 59

"Supreme Court Upholds Affirmative Action Program at University of Texas" (Liptak), 54

"Supreme Court Upholds Affordable Care Act, a Boon to Minority Health in the U.S." (Ross), 93

Surface Transportation Act, 73

Surface Transportation and Uniform Relocation Assistance Act, 75

Sy, Stephanie, 5

T

Tables of Summary Health Statistics (NCHS), 98–99

Taggart, William A., 76

Tamkin, Samuel J., 27

Tan, Joyce Beiyu, 39–41

TANF. *See* Temporary Assistance for Needy Families

TANF Contingency Fund, 86

TANF Reaching Few Poor Families (Floyd, Pavetti, & Schott), 85–86

Taylor, Paul, 152

Teenagers

birth rates for teenagers, by age group, 18f

birth rates of, by age group, 18f

Temporary Assistance for Needy Families (TANF)

criticism of, 85–86

description of, 83

numbers receiving assistance, 86t

Trump, Donald, budget cuts by, 86

"Temporary Worker Program Is Explained" (Fears & Fletcher), 59

Terrorism, 124

Test scores, preschool/elementary school children, 31–32

Texas

affirmative action in, 53–54

electoral districting in, 153–154

Texas, Hopwood v., 53

"Texas Vote Curbs a College Admission Guarantee Meant to Bolster Diversity" (McKinley), 53

13th Amendment, 57

Tobacco

cigarette smoking, 107, 112

tobacco product use by age, sex, race/Hispanic origin, 117t

"Tobacco Valley: Puerto Rican Farm Workers in Connecticut" (Glasser), 6–7

"Topic A: Obama's Compromise on D.C.'s School Vouchers Program" (WashingtonPost.com), 45

Transmission

AIDS diagnoses, by race/Hispanic origin/age/transmission category, 115t–116t

deaths of persons with an AIDS diagnosis, by year of death/age/race/Hispanic origin/transmission category, 121t–122t

HIV infection, diagnoses of, by race/Hispanic origin/age/transmission category, 113t–114t

of HIV/AIDS, 102, 104–107

Travel bans, 60

"Trends in the Prevalence of Tobacco Use" (CDC), 107

Tribal casinos

global economic recession and, 76

self-regulation of, 75–76

Tribal College and University Funding: Tribal Sovereignty at the Intersection of Federal, State, and Local Funding (Nelson & Frye), 55

Tribal colleges, 55

"Tribes Hit the Jackpot" (Robinson-Avila), 93

Trounson, Rebecca, 54

Truman, Jennifer L., 123

Trump, Donald

ACA, attempts to repeal, 93

DACA, ending of, 39

election victory of, reasons for, 151

ESSA Act, weakening, 45

presidential election, immigration and, 60

racial campaign tactics of, 143

TANF, weakening of, 86

white supremacist groups and, 127

"Trump Education Dept. Releases New ESSA Guidelines" (Klein), 45

"Trump Moves to End DACA and Calls on Congress to Act" (Shear & Hirschfeld), 39

"Trump's Budget Takes Aim at SNAP, Crop Insurance" (Evich, Boudreau, & Hopkinson), 86

"Trump's Education Secretary Supports School Vouchers—but Studies Suggest They Don't Help Students" (Weller), 45

"Trump's Promises before and after the Election" (BBC.com), 60

"Trump's Remarks about the Melee in Charlottesville" (Keneally & Faulders), 127

Turnout, voter

overview of, 144

voting, reasons for not, 146

"20 Million 'Motor Voters' Increase Rolls" (NYTimes.com), 143

24th Amendment, 152

2000 Census, 3–4

2010 Census, 4–5

"2010 Census Offends Some Americans with Handling of Race" (Sy), 5

"The 2010 Census Questionnaire: Seven Questions for Everyone" (Population Reference Bureau), 4

2013 American Indian Population and Labor Force Report (BIA), 63

2015 American Community Survey (Census Bureau), 2

2015 National Gang Report (National Gang Intelligence Center), 141

2016 College-Bound Seniors: Total Group Profile Report (College Board), 47–48

"2016 Indian Gaming Revenues Increased 4.4%" (National Indian Gaming Commission)
  on casino gambling revenues, 65
  on Native American tribes, numbers engaged in gaming, 75

2016 Latino Election Handbook (NALEO), 152

2016 National Healthcare Quality and Disparities Report (HHS)
  on access to health care, 88–89
  on health care, quality of, 87–88
  on health insurance, 90

2016 presidential election, 60

2017 Alzheimer's Disease Facts and Figures (Alzheimer's Association), 100

U

Uberoi, Namrata, 93

Ubri, Petry, 93

UN (United Nations), 1

Unauthorized immigrants, 5
  See also Illegal immigration

Undocumented workers, 58–59

Unemployment
  of African Americans, 63
  of Asian Americans, 63
  definition of, 60
  of Hispanics, 63
  minorities and, 63–65
  overview of, 60–61

United Nations (UN), 1

United States
  Chinese Exclusion Act, 8
  government, minority employment by, 73
  government role in improving lives of minorities, preference for by race, 13*f*
  hate groups in, 127, 130*f*
  Hispanic population of, 6
  minorities, growing population of, 2
  minorities in federal government, 73
  poverty, programs addressing, 82–85

University of California, 54

University of Michigan, 54

University of Texas, Austin, 53

University of Texas, Fisher v., 54

University of Texas (UT) School of Law, 53

University of Virginia, 127

Univision Communications Inc., 152

U.S. Blacks Less Satisfied with Way Blacks Are Treated (Jones), 11

U.S. Bureau of Labor Statistics (BLS)
  on Asian American professionals, numbers of, 71–73
  on unemployment, 60

U.S. Census Bureau
  on African American children, living arrangements of, 20
  on African Americans, number of, 8
  on Asian Americans, geographical distribution of, 10
  on Asian Americans, university degrees earned by, 78–79
  on divorce, numbers of, 16
  1860 census, 7
  on family, definition of, 18
  on Hispanic household income, 77
  on Hispanic population, 6
  on Hispanic subgroups, poverty of, 79–80
  on households with death of spouse, numbers of, 16
  on interracial/interethnic marriage, numbers of, 15
  on marriage among African Americans, 78
  on marriages, numbers of, 15
  on Mexican American population, 6
  on Native Americans/Alaskan Natives, 11, 63
  on population, minorities and, 2
  poverty thresholds of, 79
  2000 census, race categories of, 3–4
  2010 census, race categories of, 4–5
  on voting patterns, effects of age/sex on, 146

U.S. Citizenship and Immigration Services (CIS), 39

U.S. Constitution, 7

U.S. Department of Education
  on Elementary and Secondary Education Act flexibility, 44–45
  "Every Student Succeeds Act," 45
  on higher education for minorities, program supporting, 52–53
  on monies for STEM-related studies for minorities, 52–53
  on public school reform, 44

U.S. Department of Health and Human Services (HHS)
  on access to health care, 88–89
  on children in foster care, 21
  on health care, quality of, 87–88
  on health insurance, 90

U.S. Department of Homeland Security (DHS)
  border fence and, 59
  on unauthorized immigrants living in U.S., 5

U.S. Department of Housing and Urban Development (HUD), 22–23

U.S. Department of Justice (DOJ), 153–154

U.S. Department of Labor, 59

U.S. Department of Transportation (DOT), 73

U.S. Equal Employment Opportunity Commission (EEOC)
  complaint settlement provisions of, 66–67
  employment discrimination lawsuits filed by, 66
  Native Americans/Alaskan Natives, data on, 73

U.S. Government Accountability Office (GAO), 59

"U.S. Hispanic Population Growth Has Leveled Off" (Krogstad), 151

U.S. House of Representatives Committee on Ways and Means, 83

U.S. Immigration and Customs Enforcement (ICE), 60

U.S. Lawful Permanent Residents: 2015 (Baugh & Witsman), 6

U.S. Office of Personnel Management, 73

U.S. Sentencing Commission (USSC), 137

U.S. Small Business Administration (SBA), 75

U.S. Supreme Court
  ACA ruling, 93
  affirmative action, rulings on, 54
  DBEs, rulings on, 73
  set-aside programs, rulings on, 75
  Texas, electoral redistricting, findings on, 153

"UT's Intellectual Entrepreneurship Program Is Trying to Expand Minority Graduate School Enrollment" (McKenzie), 53

V

Vekshin, Alison, 27

Victims
  of crime at school, 127, 131, 133
  of hate crimes, 123–124, 126–127
  homicide victims, by age/sex/race/ethnicity, 125(*t*7.2)
  homicide victims, race/sex of, by race/sex of offender, 125(*t*7.3)
  of racial profiling, 133
  of violent crimes, 123
  violent/serious violent crime, by sex/race/Hispanic origin/age of victim, 124*t*

Vietnam, 58

"Violence by Gang Members, 1993–2003" (Harrell), 141

Violent crime
  homicide victims, by age/sex/race/ethnicity, 125(*t*7.2)
  homicide victims, race/sex of, by race/sex of offender, 125(*t*7.3)
  murder offenders by age/sex/race/Hispanic origin, 135(*t*7.8)
  victims of, 123
  violent/serious violent crime, by sex/race/Hispanic origin/age of victim, 124*t*

Violent Crime and Law Enforcement Act, 124

Virginia, Loving v., 15

"Voces del Pueblo" campaign, 152

Vornovitsky, Marina S., 90–91

Voter registration, 143–144

Voter turnout
  overview of, 144, 146
  reasons for not voting, 146–147

Voting
  of African Americans, patterns of, 151
  of Hispanics, patterns of, 151
  among native/naturalized citizens, by race/Hispanic origin/region of birth, 145*t*
  rates by age/race/ethnicity, changes in reported, 148*f*
  rates by race/Hispanic origin, 146*f*
  reasons for not, 149*t*–150*t*
  rights, African Americans' struggle for, 144
  voter registration/turnout of minorities, 143
  voting totals by age/race/ethnicity, change in reported, 147*t*

Voting and Registration in the Election of November 2016 (Census Bureau), 146

Voting Rights Act
  electoral districting, 153
  Hispanic gains in political offices and, 152
  minority registered voters in South, increase of due to, 144
  Texas, violations of, 154

"Vouchers" (National Education Association), 45

Vouchers, school, 45

Vuong, Linh, 136

W

Waid, Mikki, 79

Wallman, Katherine K., 2

"The 'War on Immigrants': Racist Policies in the Trump Era" (Huerta), 143

WashingtonPost.com, 45

Waters, Maxine, 151

"We Can't Wait: 10 States Approved for NCLB Flexibility" (Brenchley), 44–45

Weight, 112
  See also Low birth weight

Weisman, Jonathan, 59

Welfare, 82

Welfare Indicators and Risk Factors: Fifteenth Report to Congress (Crouse & Macartney), 83, 85

Weller, Chris, 45

"What Is at Stake for Health and Health Care Disparities under ACA Repeal?" (Artige, Ubri, & Foutz), 93

"Wheel of Misfortune" (Barlett & Steele), 75

White supremacists, 127

Whites
  African Americans, perceptions of relations between, 12(*f*1.1)
  alcohol use by, 112, 117
  Alzheimer's disease and, 100
  births/fertility rate of, 95–96
  cancer and, 98
  death, leading causes of, 118–119
  on death row, 138, 141
  diabetes among, 102
  doctor visits by, 93
  drug use by, 117
  in gangs, 141
  health care, access to, 88–89
  health care, quality of, 88
  health insurance coverage among, 90–91
  health of, 87
  heart disease among, 99–100
  as homicide offenders, 133
  life expectancy of, 117
  low birth weight/infant mortality, 96–97
  mental health and, 102
  minority groups, relations with, 11
  obesity among, 112
  prenatal care for, 95
  in prisons/jails, 133, 136–137
  on probation, 138
  racial profiling and, 133
  school crime and, 131
  SNAP benefits, receiving, 85
  tobacco use by, 112
  as victims of hate crimes, 126
  as victims of violent crimes, 123

Whitford, Gill v., 154

Wiley, Steven R., 141

Williams, Cathy M., 39–41

Williams, Herman, Jr., 93

Wilson, Pete, 53

Wirth, Louis, 1

Wisconsin, 154

"With Senate Vote, Congress Passes Border Fence Bill" (Weisman), 59

Witsman, Katherine, 6, 10

Wolfe, Barbara, 93–94

Wolters, Christopher A., 39–41

Women. *See* Females; Gender; Mothers

"Women and Minorities Underrepresented in STEM Jobs" (Brooks), 36

Workforce. *See* Labor force

Y

Yates, Shirley, 39–41

"The Year in Hate and Extremism" (Potok), 127

Youth Risk Behavior Survey, 107

Z

Zapotosky, Matt, 60

Zimmerman, George, 11

CPSIA information can be obtained
at www.ICGtesting.com
Printed in the USA
FFOW04n1915130518
46624902-48683FF